'Nicholas O'Shaughnessy has come up with an incisive and intriguing way of looking at the Third Reich through its fiendishly effective brand marketing. The methods of Joseph Goebbels' sinister genius at PR is laid bare superbly, and this book is replete with fascinating and important lessons for the present day.'

Professor Andrew Roberts, *Author*, The Storm of War

'"Only first class business and that in a first class way" was a motto of David Ogilvy. But what if the product and clients were loathsome? Like a barrister's advocacy the power of brilliant marketing can serve a false and perverse master. Never has this been truer than in the case of the Third Reich. Nicholas O'Shaughnessy's extraordinary book shows how it set out to be a well-managed brand and previewed many of the techniques of modern marketing communications in a sedulously first class way.'

Miles Young, *Non-Executive Chairman, Ogilvy and Mather Worldwide*

'This is an accomplished, rare, interdisciplinary text. It provides an historical overview of how one of the most heinous regimes in history used prototype marketing and propaganda to gain and retain power. It's a must-read both for those who would wish to govern us and those who are governed alike.'

Professor Paul Baines, *Cranfield University, UK*

'Professor O'Shaughnessy has found an innovative new way of examining the Third Reich, by looking closely at how it was sold and marketed.'

Giles MacDonogh, *Writer and Historian*

'Nicholas O'Shaughnessy's elegant and detailed historical scholarship has previously drawn our attention to unsettling traces of brand marketing strategy behind the calamitous rise of Adolf Hitler and the Nazis. In *Marketing the Third Reich* O'Shaughnessy emboldens his thesis to show that the Nazis were ineluctably masters of marketing. He challenges conventional wisdom in both political history and in marketing scholarship by arguing that both are swayed by the nebulous yet compelling techniques of mass persuasion. In our propagandistic era of tumultuous political populism, this penetrating work is alarmingly resonant.'

Professor Chris Hackley, *Royal Holloway University of London, UK*

MARKETING THE THIRD REICH

In this fascinating volume, Nicholas O'Shaughnessy elucidates the phenomenon of the Nazi propaganda machine via the perspective of consumer marketing, conceptualising the Reich as a product campaign. Building on his acclaimed *Selling Hitler* (2016), he uses marketing scholarship to show how propaganda and political marketing existed not merely as an instrument of government in Nazi Germany, but as the very medium of government itself.

Marketing the Third Reich explores the insidious connection between a mass culture and a political movement, and how the cultures of consumption and politics influence and infect each other – consumerised politics and politicised consumption. Ultimately its concern is with the 'engineering of consent' – the troubling matter of how public opinion can be manufactured, and governments elected, via sophisticated methodologies of persuasion developed in the consumer economy. Nazism functioned as a brand, packaging almost everything with persuasive purpose.

Revealing obvious parallels between Adolf Hitler's use of the living theatre of politics, and our present public–political dramaturgy, between Nazi lies and our post-truth, the book raises the chilling question: was Hitler ahead of his time? This radical, original, in-depth study will be an invaluable resource for all scholars of marketing history, political marketing, propaganda and history.

Nicholas O'Shaughnessy is Professor of Communication at Queen Mary University of London, UK and latterly director of their Marketing and Communications Group; Visiting Professor in the Department of War Studies at King's College London, and a Quondam Fellow of Hughes Hall Cambridge. He has written and edited numerous books on commercial and political persuasion, including *Politics and Propaganda*; *Weapons of Mass Seduction* and most recently *Selling Hitler: Propaganda and the Nazi Brand*.

ROUTLEDGE STUDIES IN FASCISM AND THE FAR RIGHT

Series editors:
Nigel Copsey, *Teesside University*, and Graham Macklin, *Teesside University*

This new book series focuses upon fascist, far right and right-wing politics primarily within a historical context but also drawing on insights from other disciplinary perspectives. Its scope also includes radical-right populism, cultural manifestations of the far right and points of convergence and exchange with the mainstream and traditional right.

Titles include:

Marketing the Third Reich
Persuasion, Packaging and Propaganda
Nicholas O'Shaughnessy

Russia and the Western Far Right
Tango Noir
Anton Shekhovtsov

Understanding Racist Activism
Theory, Methods and Research
Kathleen M. Blee

Corporatism and Fascism
The Corporatist Wave in Europe
Edited by António Costa Pinto

Anti-Fascism in Britain
(Second Edition)
Nigel Copsey

Right-Wing Terrorism in the 21st Century
The 'National Socialist Underground' and the History of Terror from the Far-Right in Germany
Daniel Koehler

MARKETING THE THIRD REICH

Persuasion, Packaging and Propaganda

Nicholas O'Shaughnessy

LONDON AND NEW YORK

First published 2018
by Routledge
2 Park Square, Milton Park, Abingdon, Oxon OX14 4RN

and by Routledge
711 Third Avenue, New York, NY 10017

Routledge is an imprint of the Taylor & Francis Group, an informa business

© 2018 Nicholas O'Shaughnessy

The right of Nicholas O'Shaughnessy to be identified as author of this work has been asserted by him in accordance with sections 77 and 78 of the Copyright, Designs and Patents Act 1988.

All rights reserved. No part of this book may be reprinted or reproduced or utilised in any form or by any electronic, mechanical, or other means, now known or hereafter invented, including photocopying and recording, or in any information storage or retrieval system, without permission in writing from the publishers.

Trademark notice: Product or corporate names may be trademarks or registered trademarks, and are used only for identification and explanation without intent to infringe.

British Library Cataloguing in Publication Data
A catalogue record for this book is available from the British Library

Library of Congress Cataloging in Publication Data
A catalog record for this book has been requested

ISBN: 978-1-138-06056-2 (hbk)
ISBN: 978-1-138-06058-6 (pbk)
ISBN: 978-1-315-16300-0 (ebk)

Typeset in Bembo
by Taylor & Francis Books
Printed and bound by CPI Group (UK) Ltd, Croydon, CR0 4YY

CONTENTS

List of figures ix
Preface xi

Introduction 1

PART I
Advocacy: The Nazi brand and its protagonists 13

1 Was there a Nazi brand? 15
2 Political marketing managers of the Reich: A chaos theory of government 26

PART II
Operational: Implementing the Nazi brand 57

3 Promotion: Political marketing communication: the ministry of illusion 59
4 Product, Adolf Hitler: The ersatz kaiser 105
5 Packaging of the Reich: The politics of consumption and the consumption of politics 136
6 Place: political marketing channels: The entrepreneurship of the public space 194

PART III
Legacy: The implications of the Nazi brand   **253**

7 Hitler our contemporary: Brand heritage: the Reich as a power brand   255

8 Was Adolf Hitler ahead of his time? A review of comparative self-presentation   264

Epilogue: the Führer and the Donald: The ghost of a resemblance?   277

Index   *282*

FIGURES

3.1	German mother	73
3.2	Womens labour service	74
3.3	Nazi women voters pre-1933 poster	75
4.1	Ja! Referendum poster	122
4.2	Ja! Referendum poster	123
4.3	Hitler Youth wartime poster	127
4.4	Motivational speaker pre-1933 poster	128
4.5	Hitler floating head pre-1933 poster	129
5.1	Labour service poster	139
5.2	Storm trooper poster pre-1933	140
5.3	SA Mann poster	144
5.4	SA Mann Brand film poster	153
5.5	Wounded storm trooper pre-1933 poster	154
5.6	Work and fight wartime poster	155
5.7	Saar referendum poster	156
5.8	Volkswagen advertisement	169
6.1	German People's Receiver	199
6.2	SS Netherlands recruiting poster	202
6.3	Farmer with scythe pre-1933 poster	218
6.4	Adolf Hitler is Victory wartime poster	219
6.5	Hitler wounded pre-1933 poster	220
6.6	Hitler frontline soldier pre-1933 poster	221
6.7	Hitler with sealed lips pre-1933 poster	222
6.8	The Marshal and the Corporal March 1933 poster	223
6.9	Hitler Youth SS wartime recruiting poster	225

6.10 Winter Aid poster (1) — 226
6.11 Winter Aid poster (2) — 227
6.12 Coal Thief wartime poster — 228
6.13 Blacksmith: home and front wartime poster — 229
6.14 Nazi workman pre-1933 poster — 230
6.15 Anti-Semite pre-1933 election poster — 231
6.16 Anti-Semite wartime poster — 232
6.17 *The Eternal Jew* 1940 poster — 233
6.18 The 'Genetically Ill' poster — 234

PREFACE

This journey to the Third Reich was not propelled by an original interest in Nazism per se, but rather by its status as the ultimate, because the biggest and most historically significant, political marketing and propaganda campaign in history. The genesis of this work lies with my much earlier studies (starting with *The Phenomenon of Political Marketing*, Macmillan, 1990): but this primary concentration on political marketing evolved into a more general engagement with propaganda (for example *Politics and Propaganda: Weapons of Mass Seduction*, University of Michigan, University of Manchester Press, 2004). The common focus is the migration of techniques from the consumer economy to the political economy. Specifically, this particular book is a further evolution of a recent work, *Selling Hitler: Propaganda and the Nazi Brand* (Hurst, July 2016). Both books try to re-balance discourse towards a greater awareness of the role of propaganda and marketing in pursuing and retaining power. Their argument is that, uniquely in history, propaganda and marketing were the operational ethos of a regime, the core of its idea, and not just another instrument of management and control.

Symbolism, myth and rhetoric were the analytical structure of that predecessor volume, for these constitute a universal framework via which the complexity of propaganda is captured. Those elements reinforce each other: it would for example be difficult to have a myth (or a story with a didactic frame) unless it were also projected through the effective choice of words and phraseology (rhetoric). It is impossible to imagine Nazism without its symbols, myths and rhetorics, it would in fact be something else: it would not be Nazism. And it seems to have worked: this does, indeed, help explain the success of the Nazi Party in colonising the hearts and minds of many Germans.

In this second volume, both propaganda and marketing are discussed with the primary emphasis on marketing: that there is a close conceptual relationship between the two domains is an underlying assumption of this work. So this new book invokes the formative notions of consumer marketing: the Reich is here conceptualised as a product campaign in the conventional sense. It seeks to illuminate the phenomenon of persuasion via the secondary perspective of marketing and the classic marketing categories of branding, packaging etc. (such a framework is not designed to exclude traditional nostrums on propaganda, but rather to supplement them).

The argument is that consumerism was for the Nazis a political appeal; but it was also a source of method. Their posters resembled advertisements for products or for films. Their slogans, typography, the very professionalism and stylisation of their public performance activities, resonated with a people habituated to consumption. Nor is it surprising that a political creed which arose out of a commercially defined environment, namely the industrial power of early twentieth-century Germany, should actually mimic the features of the society which gave it birth. For example there was no question that Nazism functioned as a brand with a series of brand logos: the extent of brand control is significant, using the legal protection of patent for instance. Political systems and ideologies therefore, including Nazism, express the society they were incubated in both in their content (ideology) and in their communication (political marketing).

And yet today there is for obvious reasons a renewed interest in propaganda in an era where the boundary between reality and fiction seems to dissolve, when we speak of a 'post-truth' society; and where notions of objectivity have themselves been challenged by the postmodernists with their claim that there are no facts, only interpretations. Suddenly therefore the world of the Third Reich seems less strange as it recedes in time. A world of disinformation and organised deceitfulness reminds us of something and illuminates a curiously familiar landscape. And it is this propensity to tell (in the words of Sir Harold Nicholson) 'dynamic lies' that establishes the relationship between Nazi propaganda then, and our experience today. This is why indeed I have devoted much space to explaining the present through the prism of the Third Reich, something which would discomfort conventional scholars. But Hitler is quite simply a major idea and a symbol across a large stratum of our contemporary discourse: he is, unfortunately, a contemporary present as well as a historic past.

In conclusion I would like to thank those who have encouraged me during the writing of both works: my parents, John and Marjorie, and my brother Andrew; and my cousin Mary, a linguist who carefully read the volumes for errors; my editor Daniel Hunt of Oriel College Oxford; Professor Paul Baines of Cranfield University who scrutinised the manuscript; and Jacqueline Curthoys of Routledge who gave me such support. And, more generally, thanks to the Department of War Studies at King's College London, whose generous hospitality has been a delightful experience.

It would be appropriate to end this beginning with a warning, as judicious as it is ancient, about the destructive powers of persuasion, and, specifically, the menace of rhetoric:

So also the tongue is a small member, yet it boasts of great exploits. How great a forest is set ablaze by a small fire! And the tongue is a fire. The tongue is placed among our members as a world of iniquity; it stains the whole body, sets on fire the cycle of nature, and is itself set on fire by hell. For every species of beast and bird, of reptile and sea creature, can be tamed and has been tamed by the human species, but no one can tame the tongue – a restless evil, full of deadly poison. With it we bless the Lord and Father, and with it we curse those who are made in the likeness of God. From the same mouth come blessing and cursing. My brothers and sisters, this ought not to be so. Does a spring pour forth from the same opening both fresh and brackish water? James 3:5–11 (RSV)

Nicholas O'Shaughnessy
London, April 2017

INTRODUCTION

After contemplating the former century one might indeed be tempted to concur with the misanthrope Jonathan Swift's observation on humanity in *Gulliver's Travels*: 'I cannot but conclude that the Bulk of your Natives, to be the most pernicious Race of little odious Vermin that Nature ever suffered to crawl upon the Surface of the Earth.'[1] Yet, as Germans recovered from the Hitler regime, as they looked back into the afterglow of a brutal orgy, they could never call themselves victims: except in one sense. They were the targets of the most vigorous, lucid and sophisticated public relations campaign ever conjured in all of history, and one which both anticipated and surpassed the public opinion sorcery of the twenty-first century.

Persuasion was integrated with the entire political narrative of the Nazi era from its first beginnings in 1920 right up to the end of the Second World War. The key ideas were reductivist, that is to say the sacrifice of complexity to coherence, and the formula for its achievement was the arousal of emotion: yet the art of the demagogue, the regressiveness of the appeal, was packaged using the latest promotion and marketing techniques, for as Paxton reminds us, the peculiar contradiction of Fascism is that it both embraces and excoriates modernity: regressive ideas, progressive techniques, a paradox.[2] I have noted that 'there was the influence of Americanisation, for the Reich played with and structurally incorporated its antithesis. It was a series of contradictions – progressive and reactionary, modern and anti-modern, American and anti-American.'[3]

The argument is that propaganda and political marketing existed not merely as an instrument of government, as with other regimes, but the very medium through which government governed. Ultimately the concern is with the 'engineering of consent' – the troubling matter of how public opinion can be manufactured, and governments elected, via sophisticated methodologies of persuasion developed in the consumer economy. So this book outlines the connection between a mass culture and a political movement; and argues that the culture of consumption influences, even contaminates, politics – and that the two spheres affect each other, a consumerised politics and a politicised consumption. The aim is both historical and contemporary: to explain the past by surfacing the role of organised persuasion, but also seeking to illuminate the perplexing present by reference to the same idea. This broader perspective would accord persuasion the status of history's core dynamic, which stands in contrast to prevailing scholastic trends which generally ascribe to persuasion a subsidiary role, if indeed it is acknowledged at all.

This book is the second volume of a study of persuasion in the Third Reich, and follows on from *Selling Hitler: Propaganda and the Nazi Brand*.[4] The two perspectives invoked, political marketing and propaganda, are independent and interdependent; therefore the phenomenon of persuasion under the Third Reich should be scrutinised through these two conceptual structures.

Political marketing

I therefore offer two related analytical structures for telling the story and teasing out the ulterior meaning of Adolf Hitler's persuasion campaigns. Both are necessary to capture its essence, but this new volume is the first book to treat the Third Reich as a marketing exercise among other things. In fact, persuasion in the Third Reich is certainly complex; but it was *inter alia* a marketing campaign. One key justification for using the term 'marketing' as well as propaganda is that Goebbels, history's most notorious propagandist, craved invisibility for his craft and saw in entertainment the ultimate propaganda vehicle: propaganda the more powerful because the more concealed, persuasion by stealth. (Hence the focus on cinema, along with radio, the only German media channel that he fully controlled.)

Political marketing is a well-established sub-discipline of marketing, and, more peripherally, political science. The validity of political marketing as a secondary subject within the disciplinary embrace of political science is accepted by the Political Science Association of United Kingdom.[5] And a substantial body of literature on political marketing has been published over the last thirty years such as our *Theory and Concepts in Political Marketing*, or the three-volume (key readings in) *Political Marketing*.[6] This literature is no uncritical celebration and finds certain conceptual limitations in the idea of political marketing, which in some ways is a metaphor for what actually happens as well as a descriptor.

Political marketing as a commercially derived discipline represents essentially a transfer from consumption, and this gives it a different tone to propaganda, and different tools. Firstly, it is at least in theory based on opinion research (which indeed the Nazis did). So political marketing like consumer marketing rests on some notion of 'consumer' sovereignty, that value is derived from the consumers, and this conceptualisation is different from competitor notions of people as citizens, as in political science, or Marxist ones of the suppressed proletariat. Secondly, marketing also tends to exploit the full range of human emotions and, while it can, for example, resort to fear appeals, in general its evoked set is broader than propagandists would seek – emotions for example such as aspiration. Moreover, marketing gives much more focus to the management of process, to the operationalisation of a campaign. In general marketing theory conceives the disaggregating of some total group so that appeals can be refined (segmentation).

There is perhaps a tendency to dismiss the language, concepts and frameworks of marketing as 'mere' jargon. But one must not confuse the ostensible superficiality of marketing communications (or indeed the worst excesses of modern consumer society) with the art and science and psychology that seek to explain their manipulative power.

While one (secondary) aim of the book is to establish the status of marketing persuasion as historical actor, some will recoil from the idea. And the language of marketing does indeed seem to trivialise. But the Third Reich worked because it was *inter alia* a consumption experience. Beyond this there is a further and perhaps instinctive reaction to the language of consumption, or what I liken to (Chapter 1) the language of the fragrance emporium, evoking something as monstrous as Nazism with its signature of industrialised mass murder of the racially excluded. Only an advanced civilisation could have killed that many people that quickly. But the language of consumption was a central feature of that society and, indeed, it assisted the demonisation of Jews, which made the Holocaust possible. An obvious point of comparison is the way the Holocaust was prepared for via a persuasion campaign, everything from the three anti-Semite movies of 1941 to the radicalisation of anti-Semitic rhetoric in the press and the posters.

And propaganda

But marketing is a much newer field than propaganda (a word derived from the Counter-Reformation), which had existed since ancient times in one form or another. In terms of business disciplines, what is taught in business schools for example, propaganda would be more closely associated with public relations than with marketing (and indeed marketing texts and courses usually ignore public relations). However, the categories of propaganda and political marketing are neither rigid nor mutually exclusive; for example, both propaganda and marketing project a utopian vista and sell it as an idea of perfection and the perfectible: *There is probably no essentialist meaning to the term propaganda or clear way to distinguish it from other forms of dynamic persuasion, except via its practice as revealed over time.*

What then is the (latent) distinction between political marketing and propaganda? Propaganda is a version of political persuasion and a term which long predates political marketing since it represents a form of pre-commercial influence – that is to say, it revolves around speeches and auditoria, powerful rhetoric, resonant symbols and compelling mythologies.[7] The currency of propaganda is emotion (as indeed is the case with marketing and political marketing). However, the range of emotions mobilised is quite narrow. They tend to be the emotions that relate to our survival, such as fear and the mobilisation of threat; the propagandist conjures an existential threat to our future. This distinguishes it, tentatively at least, from marketing. Historically it has proved to be a vehicle for promoting and sustaining war and promulgating ideology; such elements are not inherent in the definition of propaganda but they are manifest in its practice. Propaganda works because it simplifies with broad, vivid brushstrokes; its offer is to explain and make intelligible. But it promotes a coherence theory of truth at the expense of complexity and banishes nuance.

Thus while both marketing and propaganda seek to manipulate emotion, propaganda functions primarily as a form of political agitation and is associated with fomenting discord, even hysteria. Propagandists recognise that grievance can be talked into people even when objectively these grievances are imaginary: a minority psychosis can be created as well as inherited; there are, in other words, manufactured grievances as well as real ones. While propaganda has often been represented as embodying a kind of hypodermic or stimulus-response model of persuasion, the truth is more interesting. It is and remains primarily a co-production where the target is in effect invited to share a fantasy which both producer and consumer know to be false. Propaganda is not necessarily deceitful but, in practice, is associated with 'post-truth' manoeuvrings; advocacy without rules or limits. The ambitions of the marketer are more modest, or less ruthless: the propagandist is inclined to believe that the end, or apocalyptic end, justifies the means. And the means is the creation of pseudo-reality: propaganda techniques are used to construct a semi-fictive world as distinct from a pack of lies (which can be easily exposed). I have argued that *Through the building blocks of symbolism the propagandist constructs an imaginary world that is neither true nor false but a pseudo-reality energised by the emotion of fear and both defined and constricted by ideology/beliefs.*[8]

Propaganda in contrast to marketing and political marketing is also much more inclined to conceive the target as an undifferentiated mass, to be accessed by all media, and uses every channel conceivable – and that would even include (in the case of the Third Reich) things like rumour or graffiti or horoscopes. While marketing resembles 'tell and sell', propaganda is didactic; for we begin with the ideology and then project it onto people rather than gauging their wants and needs. The target is browbeaten, as well as seduced, via hyperbole and polemic. Indeed, violence can also be a form of propaganda as well as an alternative to it. Violence and propaganda are forms of persuasion and in this and other senses war is a subset of propaganda rather than the other way round. War is organised violence, but the function of that organised violence is to persuade. Ultimately it is impossible to hold down a people forever, and the apparatus of coercion will someday collapse, eventually if not immediately. Therefore, war and violence and terror have limitations as forms of persuasion. This is why they so rarely exist on their own but normally operate in conjunction with other and non-physical forms of persuasion, specifically propaganda which often reveals itself as psychological warfare.

Questions and reservations

Is the term 'political marketing' an anachronism? Political marketing is a framework entirely alien to historians and they have never used it. They would object to the term 'marketing' being applied to historical phenomena: propaganda is an acceptable term in historical discourse but marketing is not. To say propaganda was significant in the Third Reich is not controversial (how significant is another matter and historians disagree), but to invoke marketing and indeed even to represent marketing and propaganda as a linked conceptual entity, two sides of the same coin, has never been attempted before and is, very definitely, controversial. It may even seem that this imposed structure is an anachronism and does not represent ideas and frameworks that were understood at the time or employed politically: that the concepts and structures of marketing date from later.

While it is defensible to impose on the past an interpretive structure which explains phenomena and relationships not necessarily obvious at the time, the language and practice of marketing was in fact well understood (as we discuss in this book). Under the auspices of Wilhelm Vershofen, the Society for Consumer Research promoted a rigorous scientific approach to the investigation of consumption, and other gurus included the organisation and marketing theorist Johann Plenge.[9] Since the general, if not universal, German opinion about the First World War was that they had been defeated by the superior British and American propaganda, post-World War I the persuasion industries enjoyed a new prestige. Germany, at this time, had a mature advertising industry which included the study of the psychology of advertising and experimental, analytic approaches via pioneers like Hugo Munsterberg, and the teaching of advertising for example at the University of Cologne. American agencies opened branches in major German cities. The 1929 World Advertising Conference was in Berlin. Indeed, G. Stark had written in *Modern Political Propaganda* that propagandists should 'study advertising methods and see how we can use them'.[10] It is recognisably in fact our world.

The example of branding will suffice, for the art and science of branding was already well understood. Thinkers on branding included branding expert Hans Domizlaff. In fact a rich German literature has introduced the notion of Hitler and Nazism as 'political trademarks' starting with S. Behrenbeck.[11] Nazism was a brand and functioned as such with the swastika icon and a series of secondary logos such as the SS rune. Brand building, brand design, super-brands and sub-brands were all part of the Third Reich ecology of political marketing. Thus, in *Selling Hitler* we described Klemperer's conception of the SS symbol as a masterpiece of condensed meaning evoking the initials SS, a Nordic rune, the sign of an electricity substation, the symbol of lightning, all suggested by the same logo. These things are neither random nor accidental. In fact, the Nazi state sought protection of its iconic properties against brand infringement via patents (Law for the Protection of National Symbols, 19 May 1933). Brand excellence was catalysed in the political sphere – to the envy of contemporary German business.

Why was Hitler exceptional? Hitler was historically unique. There is no risk of overstating Hitler's centrality to the propaganda script: in essence, he wrote it. The obvious comparison remains with that other totalitarian state, the USSR. Germany was a much better educated country than Russia and therefore needed greater recourse to propaganda rather than coercion; the regime of Stalin relied more largely on coercion (as in the battle of Stalingrad itself, where behind advancing Russian troops were the NKDV (Soviet secret police) men with pistols drawn).[12] Joseph Stalin had caused the deaths of millions by 1 September 1939 in the terror and the purges and the collectivisation of Ukraine – 'the death of one man is a tragedy, the deaths of a million men are a statistic'. After 1 September 1939 so did Hitler, starting with the invasion of Poland which involved a decapitation strategy on the governing and professional elites. But the years 1933–39 are a different story and represent the primacy of persuasion not coercion.

Another obvious comparison is Italy. And, indeed, Mussolini was in many ways the originator of symbols and rituals plagiarised by Hitler, promulgating a secular nationalist religion via spectacle and public theatre.[13] But there is no contradiction here – in Italy there were alternative foci of loyalty spiritual and secular, the Roman Catholic Church and the monarchy. Italy did not have a Babelsberg – or a Goebbels. One can also point to the extraordinary scale of the Reich propaganda organisation compared to other countries. It was no mere function of government, but its ethos. Hitler and Goebbels did not, *ab initio*, intentionally and systematically launch Nazism and Hitler into a globally recognised brand: they were opportunists, making up the script as they went along. To what extent, then, was Hitler's pursuit of propaganda-driven strategy self-initiated, or merely orchestrated or borrowed from elsewhere? Both propositions are true: the methods were borrowed but the stylisation was his and his party's, as was the particular insight that a regime could universalise and methodologise its propaganda.

The neglect of ideology? In this volume we have tended to treat the 'product' as Hitler himself although it was also the party, the ideology and more generally the notion of retrieved German greatness. But the ideology, defined by ethno-nationalism and increasingly by apocalyptic anti-Semitism, was also fluid (views on modern art for example took some years to crystallise). The one constant fixture of the ideology was the Führer principle. And the other was the anti-Semitism. But this work focuses less on the specific consequence of the ideology, that is the Holocaust; anti-Semitism and political violence are not central to the text. This is because they are discussed at length in the preceding volume, in the chapters on rhetoric and mythology. Anti-Semitism relates more to the propagandistic than the political marketing elements, which focus primarily on the entertainment, theatrical and idealistic parts of the persuasion programme.

Hitler our contemporary? Representations in popular culture The book, rather unusually, discusses the after-life of Nazism, its representation in popular culture.[14] But the point is not to celebrate the forms of kitsch and melodrama generated by the mass media navigation of the Third Reich, or its imagistic legacy in popular cultural areas as diverse as fashion and science fiction. Rather it is simply to demonstrate the power of the original idiom and the marketing and propaganda – that no regime in history can possibly rival the Reich's efficiency in depositing its idealised self-image on human consciousness forever. Indeed, media remain transfixed with everything to do with Adolf Hitler and his regime, everything from the alleged attempts to create so-called Nazi cattle, the breeding plans to revive the ancient Auroch under the Heck brothers,[15] to the Führer's taste in domestic interior design.[16]

A note on language The author would argue that the aim of this – or any – book is never finality or closure, but to forge an argument sufficient to make a case, since a book is rarely more than an episode in a conversation in which there is seldom an endpoint. And language is the vehicle of argument. The historian A.J.P. Taylor supposedly once opined that the historian should 'write with dry biscuits' – but manifestly he did not. The style appropriate to the task of history – dispassionate, analytical – is more difficult to deploy in relation to the Third Reich since the scale of the phenomena under discussion, which includes the causation and conduct of the entire Second World War, as well as the genocide of the Jews and other peoples, cannot be invoked via dry biscuits even if you tried.

Argument is all we have The objective is not to give a final answer, but merely to take an argument forward. One cannot of course obtain 'proof' in history with the certainty of science, only advance an argument which often can be neither proved nor disproved. A strong argument is simply that – in fact a limited amount in history can sustain the juridical maxim of 'beyond reasonable doubt' or even the scientific one of 'best hypothesis'. The history of the period 1919 to 1945 and beyond, which is the subject of this book and its predecessor, could not be written if one did not hazard generalisations – for example, that of the claim to historical uniqueness of Hitler and his persuasion/propaganda regime. But without generalities one is confined to local statements about particular instances, to restrict history to the firmly demonstrable and, therefore, to the parochial and the micro-spheric. And this is a denial of permission to abstract from the particular to the general as a sense-making device.

A note on literature Over many years a slim body of literature has appeared on the theme of Nazi propaganda such as Robert Herzstein's *The War That Hitler Won* (1979), but relative to its scale and significance there are surprisingly few general treatments (such as Susan Bacharach and Steven Luckert's *State of Deception: The Power of Nazi Propaganda*; or David Welch's *The Third Reich: Politics and Propaganda*; or Randall Bytwerk's *Bending Spines: The Propagandas of Nazi Germany and the German Democratic Republic*).[17] Rarely do scholars hazard such a comprehensive overview study. More usually the focus is on a specific medium such as cinema, as with the work of Erica Carter or Antje Ascheid, or on specific actors such as Goebbels.[18] Propaganda's impact is hard to determine; it is difficult, too, to find a language with which to discuss a theme so curiously elusive. Moreover, the topic too easily lends itself to popular picture book treatments which pre-empt serious analysis, given the visually ravishing material. Certainly, though, the more mainstream literature has come to recognise Hitler's rhetorical skill, that famous demagogic craft (indeed, he came to define the idea of a demagogue), forging resonant phrases round an edifice of lies, for example Volker Ullrich's *Hitler: Ascent 1889–1939*.[19]

Over the length of the two volumes, I consulted some six hundred original sources. Particularly valuable was a capacious online library, the Calvin College German Propaganda Archive, curated by the propaganda scholar Professor Randall Bytwerk. This extraordinary resource has been described by one academic expert on Nazi propaganda, Aristotle Kallis, as 'a real gem'; no scholar working in this field could avoid exploiting it or fail to recognise its indispensability.[20] Many hundreds of documents dating from the Nazi era are contained therein – propaganda manuals, training programmes, internal reports, journal pieces from the in-house magazines of Nazi institutions, speeches, posters, theoretic articles, reflective discussions, empirical reports, practitioner bulletins etc. There is simply nothing like it.

But this work also owes a particular debt to two seminal works on German media and consumption. Corey Ross's *Media and the Making of Modern Germany* is splendidly researched and an invaluable resource for information on the scale and sophistication of the consumer economy (see also Wiesen's *Creating the Nazi Marketplace*; and Shelley Baranowski's *Strength through Joy: Consumerism and Mass Tourism in the Third Reich*).[21] And secondly there is Rentschler's *Ministry of Illusion*, a particularly informative, original and insightful analysis of the film industry whose core premise – that the Reich seduced rather than scared – is a key explanation for the success of Hitler's regime.[22]

A note on *Selling Hitler: Propaganda and the Nazi Brand*

In the previous volume, *Selling Hitler: Propaganda and the Nazi Brand*, I explained the rise of Hitler and the National Socialist German Workers' Party via their unique grasp of propaganda, and sought to understand exactly why propaganda was so important to them.[23] Here was the story of a regime which believed that ideology alone would be redundant unless it were vigorously promulgated. I explored the enigma of Third Reich propaganda through the trinity of Myth, Symbolism and Rhetoric as the conceptual framework. *Selling Hitler* presented propaganda as a way of seeing but equally a way of not seeing. The reality sabotaged the illusion: propagandists, like advertisers, over-promise and under-deliver. They offer a utopia. But propaganda, a source of strength, was in many ways also a source of Nazism's demise: a graduation from hubris to nemesis in the sense in which Greek tragedians understood. But a part of their nemesis was that they believed their own self-created myths, their own well-told stories.

Symbolism, Myth, Rhetoric 'Selling Hitler' argues that Nazism was based on a conspiracy theory and the myth underlying the theory, that of Jewish malice, ubiquity and nihilism; and beneath the myth there was the metaphor, that of infection. Then there was the rhetoric, which was a utilitarian function to be judged by results, and much of it was banal, seeking not so much to inspire as to saturate and browbeat. These verbal strategies were invasive, the attempt to control the German mind through changing the nature of its public vocabulary, and beyond this, to re-mould human thought by altering the language through which we think. And then there were the symbols, a harvest of symbols: the day, and daily living, was bounded by them, there was no escape; life in the Third Reich was a travelogue through a mighty landscape rich with symbolic structures.

Towards a Nazi theory of persuasion In *Selling Hitler* we suggest that the choice of an instrument – like propaganda – and its effective use is governed by what ideas (theories) we have about the utility of that instrument and the ways in which it can be most effectively deployed. That the propaganda of the Nazis has a 'house style', a familiar texture and tone, is derivative from the actual theorising they did and the sources of pedagogy to which they had turned. These theories were famously expressed in the sixth chapter of *Mein Kampf*, the chapter on propaganda, and this was a script from which the Nazis neither deviated nor transcended.[24] This was the final word on how propaganda could be made to work. For example, the exclusive stress on simplicity and repetition, though by no means a comprehensive formula even then, was adhered to rigidly by the Nazi propaganda cadre and their principal director, Dr Goebbels.

Rather more generally *Selling Hitler* locates the origins of the Nazi ideological-rhetorical system deep within the ethno-nationalist polemical tradition of German nineteenth-century public culture. Any propaganda is based on some kind of theory of persuasion derived from somewhere. What were their historical models, the revolutionaries and messiahs from which they sought inspiration? These included practitioners like Lenin or Karl Lueger, Mayor of Vienna, but also sundry theoreticians and particularly the ideas of Gustave Le Bon in the nineteenth century (and also what they absorbed, or thought they observed, from British practice in World War I).

These were indeed reductivist ideas and a general group view was that propaganda is an instrument and therefore must be instrumentalist. But at the same time *Selling Hitler* argues that the Nazis embedded and embodied it in mass media culture; the clever ways they had of retelling the same message, and the scale of the organisation necessary to deliver, thus takes the discussion well beyond the elemental ideas of simplicity and repetition. Thus, it would be an error to present their propaganda theory as endorsing saturation rather than sophistication. Moreover Goebbels saw explicit propaganda – any propaganda that was perceived as such – as failure.

Historians' debates 'Selling Hitler' also briefly reviewed the historiography of the Nazi era and its debates – specifically about Reserve Police Battalion 101: for the battalion participated in the mass murder of Jews even though its members were middle-aged reservists and they were, unusually, given the choice as to whether to participate or not. Nearly all of them did. For Christopher Browning this represented the unquestioning habit of innate obedience to authority; Daniel Goldhagen went much further than Browning however with his claim that their willingness to do so represented an inherent and inherited anti-Semitism.[25] We also recalled the other major debate in late twentieth-century German historiography which was the division between the leftist or 'Sonderweg' view that argued for the unique moral outrage of German Fascism as distinct from Fascist Italy, versus an essentially conservative view which saw Nazism as a variant of totalitarianism like Communism.

To some extent these views are not irreconcilable and represent a false opposition, since both sets of propositions can, in fact, be true. Propaganda, in other words, would be the hidden hand, encouraging the unquestioning obedience to authority (manifest in the Reserve Police Battalion) and similarly fomenting the formerly latent anti-Semitism which seized control. And the Reich was never entirely totalitarian either – the totalitarianism was imposed, directed and lubricated by powerful propaganda and in this way was very distinct from Stalinist horrors which were enacted under peacetime as well as wartime conditions. Genocide and mass murder were a feature of Stalinism throughout its tenure.

Why propaganda won and lost the war We recount in *Selling Hitler* that during the Second World War, starting with the propaganda event with which it began, the manufactured attack on the radio station at Gleiwitz, Nazi Germany used propaganda as a subsidiary (but still vastly important) form of warfare to reinforce the conviction of its own people from soldier to the factory worker. But the secondary aim was to use propaganda as psychological artillery to demoralise the enemy, in a mirror image of what they believed the British had done to them in the First World War. The volume argued that propaganda, like the military success, did communicate an idea of German invincibility which was actually far from the truth, and helped ensure a Germany that was, generally, loyal to its Führer until nearly the end. Though one must never neglect the role of coercion, this solidarity was also the achievement of many years of comprehensive and insistent propaganda. And there was versatility, a change in tempo as events developed, the propaganda response to the growing shadows of defeat after Stalingrad. Under the tutelage of its mephistophelian orchestrator, Dr Joseph Goebbels, a range of mediums were now integrated within the propaganda assault, everything from 'miracle weapons' technology to the use of astrology.

Conclusion Nobody is born a terrorist: nobody is born a Nazi. They are made such by persuasion and polemic, in this case the entire cultural world saturated with propaganda such that there was no part of society from which it was absent, not even the churches. The mind had no oasis of apoliticality in which to bathe; or breathe. *Selling Hitler* suggested that even the dark side of the regime, the depraved events inflicted on world consciousness in the 1930s, were part of this propaganda thrust even though prima facie the motivation would seem to be exclusively ideological. At the same time, there were other events (as well as the diplomatic triumphs) which would easily fit into a more traditional construction of propaganda – the great exhibitions, the Olympic Games: all of this, a theatre of regime symbolism, vivid and alive. Moreover, the communications regime was never exclusionary. Germans possessed casual access to international media for a very long time and they were eager to have this, creating a society which has been rightly described as being based on a split consciousness. That was deliberate.

Notes

1 Jonathan Swift, *Gulliver's Travels*, London: Penguin, 2010.
2 Robert O. Paxton, *The Anatomy of Fascism*, London: Allen Lane, 2004.
3 Nicholas J. O'Shaughnessy, *Selling Hitler: Propaganda and the Nazi Brand*, London: Hurst, 2016.
4 Ibid.
5 The PSA includes a political marketing section within its annual conference.

6 Robert Ormrod, Stephan Henneberg and J. O'Shaughnessy, *Political Marketing: Theory and Concepts*, London: Sage, 2013; Paul Baines (Key Readings In) *Political Marketing*, three volumes, London: Sage, 2010.
7 The definitions and theories on propaganda are explored in Nicholas J. O'Shaughnessy, *Politics and Propaganda: Weapons of Mass Seduction*, London: Manchester University Press, 2004; and (Key Readings In) *Propaganda* (with Paul Baines); four volumes, London: Sage, 2012.
8 Nicholas J. O'Shaughnessy, 'Putin, Xi And Hitler? Propaganda and the Paternity of Pseudo-democracy' *Defence Strategic Communication: The Official Journal of the NATO Strategic Communications Centre for Excellence*, vol. 2 (2017).
9 S. Jonathan Wiesen, *Creating the Nazi Marketplace*, Cambridge: Cambridge University Press, 2011.
10 G. Stark, *Modern Political Propaganda*, Munich: Verlag Frz Eher Nachf, 1930, Calvin College German Propaganda Archive.
11 Sabine Behrenbeck, 'Der Führer', in G. Diesner and R. Gries, *Political Propaganda in Deutschland: Zut Geschichte der politischen Massenbeeinflussung in 20 Jahrhundert*, Berlin: Wissenschaftliche Buchgesellschaft, 1996.
12 Anthony Beevor, *Stalingrad*, London: Penguin Books, 1999.
13 Emilio Gentile, *The Sacralization of Politics in Fascist Italy*, Cambridge, MA: Harvard University Press, 1996.
14 This has been done comprehensively in Gavriel D. Rosenfeld, *Hi Hitler! How the Nazi Past is Being Normalised in Contemporary Culture*, London: Cambridge University Press, 2015.
15 Andrew Meaghan, *Modern Farmer*, 8 January 2015.
16 Despina Stratigakos, *Hitler at Home*, Connecticut: Yale University Press, 2015.
17 Robert Edwin Herzstein, *The War that Hitler Won*, London: Hamish Hamilton, 1979; Susan Bacharach and Steven Luckert, *State of Deception: The Power of Nazi Propaganda*, London: W.W. Norton & Co., 2009; David Welch, *Propaganda and the German Cinema, 1933–1945*, London: I.B. Tauris, 2007; Randall Bytwerk, *Bending Spines: The Propagandas of Nazi Germany and the German Democratic Republic*, East Lansing: Michigan State University Press, 2004.
18 See Erica Carter, *Dietrich's Ghosts: The Sublime and the Beautiful in Third Reich Film*, London, BFI, 2007; Antje Ascheid, *Hitler's Heroines: Stardom and Womanhood in Nazi Cinema*, New York: Temples University Press, 2003; Peter Longerich, *Goebbels: A Biography*, London: Random House, 2015.
19 Volker Ullrich, *Hitler: Volume 1 Ascent 1889–1939*, Berlin: Kopf, 2013.
20 Aristotle A. Kallis, *Nazi Propaganda and the Second World War*, Basingstoke: Palgrave Macmillan, 2005.
21 Corey Ross, *Media and the Making of Modern Germany*, Oxford: Oxford University Press, 2008 (also see Pamela E. Swett, *Selling Under the Swastika: Advertising and Commercial Culture in Nazi Germany*, New York: Stanford University Press, 2014); Wiesen, *Creating the Nazi Marketplace*; Shelley Baranowski, *Strength through Joy: Consumerism and Mass Tourism in the Third Reich*, London: Cambridge University Press, 2004.
22 Erik Rentschler, *The Ministry of Illusion*, Cambridge, MA: Harvard University Press, 1996.
23 O'Shaughnessy, *Selling Hitler*.
24 Adolf Hitler, *Mein Kampf*, Munich: Eher Verlag, 1925.
25 Christopher Browning, *Ordinary Men: Reserve Police Battalion 101 and the Final Solution in Poland*, London: Harper Collins, 1992; Daniel Goldhagen, *Hitler's Willing Executioners: Ordinary Germans and the Holocaust*, New York: Alfred A. Knopf, 1996.

PART I
Advocacy
The Nazi brand and its protagonists

1

WAS THERE A NAZI BRAND?

> *All advertising, whether in the field of business or politics, achieves success through the continuity and sustained uniformity of its application.*
>
> – *Adolf Hitler*

Nazism intuitively understood the concept of a cohesive iconic system whose function was to remind citizens every moment of the day of the omnipotence and omnipresence of the regime, the Nazi state. Its logo, the swastika, was quite simply everywhere (and plagiarised; many other groups were using the swastika as their symbol after the end of the First World War, including the German Racial Defence and Defiance League).[1] The Nazis sought to create a total public persona articulated via symbolic props, everything from Hitler's moustache to the SS rune and the Iron Cross. Imagistic coherence, harmony and control were the consequence of a structure that calibrated and organised the serial invention of imagery as no regime has ever done before in history; the icon system of the Third Reich was possessed of a unique clarity, a coordinated process that organised mental thought.

The success of Nazi branding rested also on its management of the trinity of rhetoric, symbolism and mythology. It was the dexterity with which these elements were coerced and shaped that gives to Nazi branding its hinterland of vivid phrases and mythology, elements which their logo system condensed and summarised. Their underlying synergy fed the constant evocation of a utopian or even paradisal state, not unlike that of consumer marketing. Indeed, the contemporary German branding authority Hans Domizlaff had argued that the aim of the propagandist was to develop a brand personality 'whose entire aura generated a sense of trust and well-being'.[2] Domizlaff's (Le Bon-derived) view of the mass public was as inferior in reasoning to the private self, irrational, desperately craving 'the simplification of abstract ideas via symbols and stereotypes', and susceptible to 'the primitive sensory organs'.[3]

Motifs included eagles, as in the gigantic eagle motif designed for Nuremberg by Speer. Eagles appeared everywhere, on insignia, and at rallies, on posters. There were also the oak leaves and the image of the oak whose symbolism is self-explanatory: thus the leader of the British team at the 1936 Berlin Olympics, the oarsman Jack Beresford, was given an oak tree sapling by Hitler which he then planted in the grounds of his old school.[4] Hence to a great extent the Third Reich was formula-driven, facilitating the creation of consistent symbol structures, a unity of symbolism and message – as Klemperer remarks, 'the splendour of the banners, parades, garlands, fanfares, choruses, the all-embracing framework of speeches, these all remained constant features – undoubtedly modelled on the example of Mussolini.'[5] And party occasions had a highly prescriptive element. For example, at memorial events party officials spoke and there then followed the comrade hymn 'Ich Hatt' Einen Kameraden' and verses from the epic 'Edda', then elegiac poems and finally the Old Netherlands Hymn of Prayer.[6] The Nazis had a house style.

Moreover, with a sharp eye to the economics of the process, party events were often self-financing through the sale of regime tat.[7] The symbolism of pins, badges, mothers' crosses constituted a cacophony of usable imagery and self-decoration. Nazi propaganda was immensely artefactual, the masses of insignia of the myriad groupings, the many medals (e.g. for the injured of the First World War);[8] and then the Knight's Cross with its ultimate amplification, the Oak Leaves and Diamonds. There were symbols such as the ceremonial daggers which all branches and functionaries of the Nazi world received, a kind of celebration of anticipatory violence, given also to the ten-year-old boy 'Pimpfe' on joining:[9] this micro-symbolism appealed to personal vanity. The aesthetic of the Nazi brand rested also on the symbolism and mythology of the hyper-heroic. It was a world of visual superlatives, a blending of the romantic and neo-classic traditions to produce a new reality very different from either. It was a militaristic quintessence foregrounded against symbols of a classic world of cultural patrimony and a folk world of political and genetic ancestry. It was also morbid, a brand adrift among the dead as well as anchored among the living: fixated, and summoning their vanished ghosts with the drumbeat and the marching feet. For example, the brand symbol set of the magazine *Art in the Third Reich* is a stylised Greek in hoplite armour, gold against a cream background; torch and swastika are wreathed in leaves and surmounted by a formula eagle.

Was there a Nazi brand?

What, then, is a brand? A brand is a stylised public signature into which an organisation has packed, through its public performance, ideas, associations and feelings; indeed, advertising itself has been described as 'pouring meaning into the brand'. Management of the brand is a core competence of the organisation today since standard product performance is now assumed: often all organisations possess in order to differentiate themselves is the chicanery and make-believe of branding. Did the Nazi Party function as a brand? If it did, and to the extent that it did, how far was this a contributory factor both to its success in gaining power and its success in retaining it? Nazism functioned as a brand in many senses as we have seen: it was of course an entirely coherent brand logo and secondary logo system. What they offered was a brand identification paradigm whose elements have defined both the way they are remembered and the mythology surrounding that memory.

One commentator, one of Germany's top advertisers, observed that Nazism had not only 'proven its effectiveness in the sphere of political advertising', but was 'propagated better than any factory or firm's symbol ever was'.[10] A new generation of thinkers, a kind of branding intelligentsia, had offered theoretical support. Domizlaff's essay of June 1930 had extended his ideas of brand philosophy into the realm of politics. He argued that 'a people can never maintain long-term enthusiasm about an abstract idea such as the state commonwealth if the idea is not objectified by symbols perceptible to the senses'; Johann Plenge, meanwhile, celebrated the power of symbols since they can condense complex meanings – they enable 'the entire meaning to emerge within the inner experience of the observer'.[11] The swastika itself was compressed meaning: an example of this brand resonance is cited by the historian Alistair Horne in his book on the Algerian war, *A Savage War of Peace*.[12] The independence fighters, the FLN, purchased swastika-branded Luger pistols from Czechoslovakia, even though these pistols were made post-war and by a (Communist) society which had been the victim of the Nazis. Such was the authority of the swastika as a highly marketable military brand.

Impact is related to the elements of superordinate design, a completeness of imagistic system. Arnold (1992) argues that:

> Party appropriation of prehistoric data was evident in the use of Indo-European and Germanic design symbols in Nazi uniforms and regalia. The double lightning bolt, a symbol of Hitler's SS organisation, was adapted from a Germanic rune. The swastika is an Indo-European sun symbol which appears in ceramic designs as early as the Neolithic in Western Europe and continues well into early mediaeval times.[13]

Domizlaff had stressed that symbolic communication must be underpinned by what he called a uniformity of style. Hence, as Ross points out, 'then as now, one of the keys to effective branding lay in consistency and uniformity, for only by propagating the same symbol for a long period of time is it possible to achieve a high degree of recognisability'.[14] As Hitler himself wrote: 'all advertising, whether in the field of business or politics, achieves success through the continuity and sustained uniformity of its application'.[15] Beyond these integrated logo systems there was a broader stylistic convergence in the Nazi aesthetic which reinforced brand building, everything from the architecture of Speer or the design of the People's Car to, even, state-approved hairstyles for girls (the 'Gretchen' locks) or the familial resemblance of the various uniforms; the giganticism of the statuary; the monumentalism and regressiveness of the arts. All this, however, might be described as the superficial manifestations of deep structure. A deliberation of design marks everything in the Third Reich, for example the smart cut of uniforms helped foster a collective identity. British battledress, by contrast, a kind of ugly green-brown boiler suit, more fitting to a plumber than a legionnaire, flatters the vanity of the wearer far less, as with the images of the surrender of Major General Fortune and his 51st Highland Division to General Rommel at St-Valéry-en-Caux, on 12 June 1940:[16] the contrast between the two generals, victor and vanquished, is striking.

The visual was underpinned by the ideological, and the visuality expressed the idea. There was a process: 'this blatant reliance on mass effects, employed to cover up basic weaknesses, this medley of pagan, ritual and music-hall elements anticipated the era of mass hypnosis'.[17] The NSDAP, National Socialist German Workers' Party (Nazi), synthesised nationalism and socialism; it was a tortuous, even contradictory, piece of ideological prestidigitation. It needed mystification, ritual and mumbo-jumbo to conceal the illogic of its intellectual essence; that is to say, branding serviced an important political as well as persuasive function – it served to disguise the intellectual vacuity of the product and the internal contradictions of the ideological melange.

Brand language Beyond these, the regime was more than (visual) brand; it was a serial (verbal) branding exercise with especially resonant names chosen for military contexts and events – Sea-Lion, Wolf's Lair, Eagle's Nest, Wehrmacht and so on. And there were the well-known slogans, shop-worn mantras which at one time must have seemed refreshing – 'Children, Church, Kitchen', 'Ein Volk, Ein Reich, Ein Führer'. Such phrases come trippingly off the tongue, yet these are not mere slogans but an integral part of the Nazi brand in the same way that a corporate logo often encapsulates the slogan or strapline as part of its total perceptual construct. The party had even actually changed its name (February 1920) and was accorded the acronym 'Nazi' by its opponents.[18] All brands retain a sort of demotic poetry, as a brand has little without slogans, without a language and even a commercial eloquence to celebrate it. These words help shape our perceptions of brands and give them resonance, they direct and broaden their meaning; they open up the cognitive territory of the brand. The Nazis were also ahead of their time in inventing the concept of city branding, so that Nuremberg was the 'City of Rallies', and Munich was the 'Capital of the Movement'.[19] Everything therefore, every place name, was rigorously invested with Nazi meaning. Nothing existed independent of the ideology that had a historical essence or a non-political presence.

Seldom has anyone sought to describe Nazism as a brand or attribute its extraordinary tenacity to that idea. While branding is only a partial explanation of the Nazis' success, it is a necessary one and without it our understanding of the Third Reich is conceptually impoverished. Was Nazism a brand, then? To many, the question would seem to be anachronistic, the (retrospective) imposition of a modern understanding which was not shared by contemporaries. It would also seem an appalling trivialisation, for understandable reasons. For to apply to the unleashed forces of master-race nihilism the vocabulary of the perfume counter would appear not just irrelevant, but even offensive. Yet that is precisely the point: the vocabulary of marketing and advertising really do help elucidate at least part of the reason for Nazism's ability to persuade because Nazis themselves understood the cultural drift of the society in which they had matured, and its world of powerful posters, cheap magazines, sentimental movies and cultural ephemera. Even if they had not grasped these essentials, the First World War had been a protracted tutorial in modern techniques of mass persuasion and incendiary polemic, particularly for Hitler – a tutorial administered by the victorious Allies, Britain and America.

Brand management

Meetings formula

A brand whose symbol systems were random and heterogeneous would not be a brand. A brand has to possess consistency: standardised imagery precipitates cognitive reinforcement, and has the happy consequence of creating a professionalism of tone as well, a surrogate indicator of competence. So the process becomes formulaic. Nor indeed could a totalitarian system sell itself via an anarchic imagery since the very uniformity of brand decoration is itself freighted with political meaning. The formula for meetings stressed its imagistic side: pleated curtains, the giant eagle mounted over the swastika, greenery, steps, podium, bust of Hitler; the same public temple was continuously erected throughout Germany every night with the same building blocks of imagery and symbols.[20] No minor detail was ignored, for example the podium itself should have no decorations at all, not even the swastika. And the dignity of the Nazi brand symbols should be zealously protected; care must be taken with a display of the swastika: 'symbols of battle are not decorative wall paintings'.[21]

Then there was the party's fear of kitsch. If the unenthusiastic folk comrade was one source of menace, the hyper-zealous comrade was another. The regime struggled to protect the integrity of the brand from the over-enthusiastic devotion of its followers: excesses of kitsch discouraged and latterly suppressed included a swastika-branded lady's fan. Sheet music of the Horst Wessel song designed to be sung in barbershop quartet style was permitted, however.[22] The party feared the maudlin excesses of romantic patriotism – 'these events can easily turn into slimy nationalism or songfests'.[23] Officials demanded that examples of kitsch should be sent to the local party office. The Nazis had an out-and-out terror of kitsch, partly of course because of the German public's fondness for it, but also because the effusive popular outpourings of love for the Führer often took the form of the vulgar, the demented and the imbecilic, such as the butcher who sculpted a relief of Hitler out of lard.[24] Nazi slogans and emblems were exploited by manufacturers, especially the swastika which could be found on common objects from shoehorns to butter patties; this span out of control, including swastika-shaped loaves of bread.[25] Hence the Nazis jealously sought to defend their symbols, many of which were derivative from Hitler and were conceived as brands from the very beginning.[26] The Nazi brand now became a patent seeking protection from contamination with only officially approved images for sale or display, and even constraints on the word Führer which was now tightly controlled via a range of speech conventions.[27] Thus the 'Law for the Protection of National Symbols' (19 May 1933). This law subsequently had to be updated to prevent swastikas and Hitler's image being purloined for advertising, so that exclusivity became important alongside recognisability and consistency. Party symbols were effectively copyright – 'the party might borrow as much as it wanted from the advertising industry, even arranging cabinet level meetings with the American public relations guru Ivy Lee, but commercial businesses were strictly prohibited from using Nazi brands'.[28]

A brand, to function as a brand, has to be actively managed since the essence of a brand is consistency of symbol system. Images of Hitler, for example, were borrowed from Hoffmann's photo-bank, and this limited supply preserved a high level of consistency and recognition, two of the essential components of branding method; thus one textless poster (sixteen identical Hoffmann images of Hitler) 'led to enhanced brand recognition, based as it was on the principle of spatial repetition, whose effectiveness was highly prized by advertisers'.[29] A brand must also be intact, clean, undamaged, as otherwise the received impression is one of amateur neglect. Thus the detailed policy instructions contained in *A Propaganda Primer*.

> Despite the temporary nature of the decorations, one should always avoid bad taste and carelessness. Artificial greenery is not an option. There will usually be electric lighting. In such cases, gold garlands and oak leaves may be used. Pictures and busts of the Führer must be of the appropriate sizes. Using real greenery is encouraged. Take care in securing appropriate tree branches and flowers. Before cutting branches from trees, contact the forester or the local farming leader. Since the meeting hall will be used often, it is advisable to secure decorations that can be used repeatedly. This is particularly true of party symbols, flags, wreaths, white and red cloth, etc. Party symbols, if at all possible, should be handmade. The speaker's platform should be decorated in a way that does not obstruct the decorations on the wall behind it. A handmade podium is recommended, with a carved wooden eagle, since this will be used repeatedly. The seating layout must correspond to the hall. (Remove restaurant tables, etc!) Keeping an open centre aisle is essential when there is to be an entrance march with flags. In larger halls, pleated cloth wall hangings with folds leading to a central point are much more effective than flat cloth hangings, particularly with proper illumination. The use of three-dimensional swastikas, party symbols, etc., is to be preferred over two-dimensional ones. Remember that everything must fit the given hall. Securing artistically trained assistance is recommended. The drawings provided give suggestions for a variety of conditions. They show what is possible. Using them as a starting point, each propagandist will be able to find the proper solution.[30]

This was a 'professional' organisation.

Since symbols were so important in the construction of Nazi identity, they had to be cherished. They had to offer a burnished, uncluttered look, using national symbols in a manner concordant with the law for the protection of national symbols: these had to be positioned in the right places in a dignified way.[31] Those holding party meetings in restaurants and other public places were instructed to ensure that all signs of normal use were removed; the tatty, dirty or torn would always negate the orchestration, the high polish that the party wanted. For example, banners functioned both as advertising and decoration. So instructions mandated that they must be properly hung, observed, conserved and stored, and they had to be furled properly after use.[32] It is quite clear that the local hacks and cronies infuriated the party with their inertia and inattention to detail. The brand is an administered construct. A decentralised brand would cease to function as a brand. The Nazis understood this. Consistency underpinned delivery of message and delivery of the impression of insistent and universal power. But there was an inherent conflict in that there were local contexts, local conditions; and an imagistic dictatorship that excised provincial initiative was hardly likely to motivate party workers. So there was tension. But the argument for centralisation inevitably won, as it was guarantor of a unitary image.

Implementation No party was ever organised on this scale.[33] There was a vision and then the implementation of that vision: 'from the beginning, they operated a political system which relied on the meticulous organisation of appearances, careful simulation, constant stimulation and the sophisticated stage management of huge public spectacles'[34] (other scholarly authorities also stress that the theatrical effects were actually achieved via a rigorous and comprehensive organisation).[35] Hitler wanted a mass movement and dismissed the mystical, unworldly folkish movement which had preceded him and anticipated him.[36] Poor implementation can destroy great strategy, and the strength of Nazi propaganda lay not in its creativity but in the operationalisation of its creative concepts. But the feedback loop – that is, finding out what worked – represented a form of organisational learning and the distillation of best practice; these are modern clichés and the argot of modern management but nevertheless they represented a mechanism for distributing successful methodologies via manuals, training courses, and journals such as *Will and Way* or *SS Black Corps*. There was in other words a managerialist pedagogy in circulation, advice about how to achieve that corporate tone, that Nazi signature. Then there was the role of declamatory public rhetoric (speakers were paid via the size of the crowd they could attract; a limited number of the best were accorded the honour of being Reich Speaker). Nazis organised such meetings with a fine degree of precision and attention to detail; for example, one of the instructions for Nazi events was that 'a flag entrance should occur only when there is a large number of flags'.[37] The over-determining effect of their finely crafted propaganda on their posthumous brand image is clear, for no regime in history ever gave successor generations such a vision of itself or made itself a permanent object of public obsession for evermore. Flower arranging and other such banalities are a minor but curiously important subset of the genre of Nazi marketing management. It is, however, unclear how far the Reich drew from the existing reservoir of marketing professionals, that there was, in other words, a direct conduit of information and method from professional marketing to the political sphere. But there are interesting examples such as Gustav Ucicky, an ex-advertising man and one of the most aggressive propagandists of the Third Reich (he made the film *Homecoming* in 1941).[38] The scale of the orchestration and media management made all Germany seem a huge soundstage, the production of 'Hitler' as a vast film.

These pedestrian matters of ritual and organisation are tedious to recount. They are also absolutely essential, as otherwise all that remains is inchoate noise. Sufficient posters had to be printed, and the display sites organised. The halls had to be booked. Contemporary marketing thinkers had also been stressing organisation, as with Johann Plenge's blending of psychological perspectives with organisational methods, which helped make him the most influential propaganda thinker of Weimar Germany.[39] And thus 'just as the American agencies prioritise the scientific market survey over the "clever idea", so too did the Nazi leadership emphasise planning and deliberation over spontaneous strokes of genius. A hallmark of rationalised publicity was the "targeting" of specific groups on their own terms.'[40] This emphasis on the management underpinning the brand cannot be overstressed: without it the effects would have been random, impulsive and lacking in the core symmetry of design so memorable in the generated imagery. But by doing this they created a kind of brand insistence: the Nazi public product had universally the same (or similar) look and feel, the same packaging. Moreover, it created an illicit inference of efficiency; if the packaging was so good, so impressive, so therefore was the regime, an intuitive connection though not a logical one.

Brand imagery: signs and symbols

The early electoral struggles resolved into a war of brand logos. Everyone was doing it: 'the political struggle became reduced to what the Social Democrats called – without the slightest hint of criticism – a war of symbols'.[41] The consequent clash of icons, uniforms and banners was the main arena in what Ross also describes as this 'war of symbols' that defined Weimar's public culture, particularly during the era of crisis post-1929, as for example with the five-pointed star and party greeting of the Red Front with its raised fist.[42] There was the forging of the Iron Front, a liberal–left alliance. Thus in the elections of July 1932 the Social Democrats promulgated the clenched fist greeting and the slogan 'Freedom', and to counter the swastika and hammer and sickle they offered the three parallel arrows of the Front devised by Serge Chakotin.[43] This signified a visible thrust towards psycho-technical election tactics; yet one journal asked how they could create such a symbol 'without prior psychoanalytical examination', and complained that the symbol was a trigger for 'unconsciously negative thoughts'.[44] For example, the arrows point downwards, suggesting 'things are going downhill', and another similarly sophisticated critique asserted that the symbol must become familiar over time before acceptance is gained.[45]

Choice of symbol is the core of the branding process. Symbols which are tentative or confused fail to ignite public curiosity, and they can neither sustain the idea of the brand, its aspirational self, nor build its heritage. It was Nazism's triumph, and the world's tragedy, that their understanding of brand building and brand stylisation was so complete, that the images sought and realised were so endlessly capable of reproduction and a conduit of mass stimulus. This was no accident but a result of careful planning and experiment and the recognition that without them the organisation would be just another cacophony of militant noise. Finding the 'right' symbols, whereby meaning can be communicated most effectively, that is to say finding symbols that are both parsimonious and resonant, is an important part of any propaganda task. In times of revolutionary change it is the core of that task. Hitler's avid pursuit of the best symbol structure was therefore no frivolity but a key part of his mission, and the brand signage system was his personal choice. He had an instinctual appreciation of the core role of symbolism in arousing and structuring human consciousness:

> he spent many hours hunting through old art magazines and the heraldic department of the Munich State Library to find a model for the Eagles to be used on the official rubber stamp of the party. His first circular letter as chairman was largely concerned with party symbolism, which he prescribed in loving detail. He instructed the heads of local groups 'to energetically promote the wearing of the party badge; the members are to be continually reminded to go about everywhere and at all times with the party emblem'.[46]

Ingenuity went into the creation of Nazi brand signifiers. One consequence was a coherence and completeness of brand and symbol system which lent to the Nazi regime its extraordinary sensations of omnipotence, omnicompetence and omnipresence. Rutherford has argued that 'the visual ground-base was in the ubiquitous swastika flag':[47]

> Every detail was the product of premeditation. There was for example the thought given to the proportion in relationship of each colour: the dominant areas of red, the white carefully picked to accent both the red and the black. There was the thickness of the arms of the swastika in itself and the angle at which it was displayed. If the arms were too thin, the image conveyed was one of timidity; if too thick, of dumpy inertia. Equally, it was placed aslant instead of on a strictly horizontal and vertical plane, thus imparting to it a sense of relentless forward motion.[48]

As we have already seen, like much else the swastika was not a symbol invented by the Nazis; Hitler was stylist not conceptualiser, his skill lay in orchestration not creation. The swastika had long functioned as a symbol of the German right (for example, a photograph from March 1919, a few months after the end of the First World War, reveals many demonstrators wearing swastikas even though the Nazi Party did not apparently exist; they dress incoherently, mixing folk dress with ordinary coats and military tunics).[49] Yet the interest was not merely instrumental but was an end in itself. Hitler was the enraptured ornamentalist of the Third Reich, its costumier and its stage manager. The brand imagery was his devising. Thus he

> made a point of military correctness in ranks and uniforms, and in general stressed all formalities: the setting of scenes, the decorative details, the increasingly solemn ceremonies of dedicating flags, reviews, and parades, all the way up to the mass spectacles of the party rallies, where he directed great blocks of human beings against mighty stone backdrops and revelled in the exercise of his demi talents as actor and architect.[50]

For Hitler's competence lay in taking someone else's idea and giving it focus and form: 'none of the basic ideas originated with him. His genius lay in knowing which symbols to choose and how to present them in an arresting way.'[51] The swastika itself was as we have seen a case in point: 'He therefore raised it to the status of a party emblem and made it obligatory. Later he would do the same with the standards, which he took over from Italian Fascism and conferred upon the storm troops.'[52]

Conclusions

Products once had a semi-commodified aspect, but by the twentieth century a product was not merely a set of functions performed but also meanings celebrated (branding did not originate in fact with companies but with customers, who used the warehouse marks and identification symbols as a basis of choice and quality discrimination). The Nazis seized this new corporate language, branding, with alacrity: the 'proliferation of symbols, stereotypes, and imagery that accompanied the shift to "mass politics"'.[53] This party brand identification system rested on symbols which were tangible, heritable and universal, everything from the swastika to the rune. The purpose, and the effect, was to create a penumbra of mysticism around the National Socialist idea. No regime ever succeeded in creating a branding system like the Nazis; the symbol system is inseparable from the idea, the ideology. Without this they would have lacked memorability now, and durability then; without the baleful necromancy of brand/symbolisation they might have amounted to less.

Notes

1 Richard Evans, *The Coming of the Third Reich*, London: Penguin, 2005.
2 Ross, *Media*.
3 Ibid.
4 Michael De la Noy, *Bedford School: A History 1552–2002*, Bedford: Bedford School, 1999.
5 Victor Klemperer, *The Language of the Third Reich*, London: Athlone Press, 2000.
6 Jay Baird, *To Die for Germany: Heroes in the Nazi Pantheon*, Bloomington: Indiana University Press, 1992.

7 W.S. Allen, *The Nazi Seizure of Power*, New York: Franklin Watts Inc., 1984.
8 Richard Grunberger, *A Social History of the Third Reich*, London: Penguin, 1991.
9 Ibid.
10 Ross, *Media*.
11 Ibid.
12 Alistair Horne, *A Savage War of Peace: Algeria 1954–1962*, London: Pan Books, 2002.
13 Bettina Arnold, 'The Past as Propaganda: How Hitler's Archaeologists Distorted European Prehistory to Justify Racist and Territorial Goals', *Archaeology*, July/August 1992: 30–37.
14 Ross, *Media*.
15 Ibid.
16 www.ww2today.com
17 Joachim Fest, *Hitler*, London: Penguin, 2002.
18 Evans, *Third Reich*.
19 Ward Rutherford, *Hitler's Propaganda Machine*, London: Bison Publishing, 1978.
20 Franz D. Huber, *A Propaganda Primer*, Wels: Leitner and Co., 1942, Calvin College German Propaganda Archive.
21 Ibid.
22 Rutherford, *Hitler's Propaganda*.
23 Stark, *Modern Political Propaganda*.
24 Ross, *Media*.
25 Ibid.
26 Ibid.
27 Ibid.
28 Ibid.
29 Ibid.
30 Huber, *Propaganda Primer*.
31 Ibid.
32 Ibid.
33 Karl Dietrich Bracher, *The German Dictatorship*, New York: Holt, Rinehart and Winston, 1970.
34 Robert S. Wistrich, *Weekend in Munich*, London: Pavilion Books Ltd, 1995.
35 Z.A.B. Zeman, *Nazi Propaganda*, New York: Oxford University Press, 1994.
36 Bracher, *German Dictatorship*.
37 Huber, *Propaganda Primer*.
38 Hilmar Hoffmann, *The Triumph of Propaganda*, Oxford: Berghahn Books, 1996.
39 Ross, *Media*.
40 Ibid.
41 Evans, *Third Reich*.
42 Ross, *Media*.
43 Evans, *Third Reich*.
44 Ross, *Media*.
45 Ibid.
46 Fest, *Hitler*.
47 Rutherford, *Hitler's Propaganda*.
48 Ibid.
49 See Laurence Rees, *The Nazis: A Warning from History*, London: BBC Books, 1997.
50 Fest, *Hitler*.
51 Frederic Spotts, *Hitler and the Power of Aesthetics*, New York: Overlook Press, 2004.
52 Fest, *Hitler*.
53 Ross, *Media*.

2

POLITICAL MARKETING MANAGERS OF THE REICH

A chaos theory of government

> ... and here too we see the elite of the Thousand Year Reich as a set of flatulent clowns, swayed by purely random influences. Even Mussolini was embarrassed, but then Mussolini had, after all, like Goebbels, a Latin mind; he could never be at home among those cavorting Nibelungs.
>
> – Hugh Trevor-Roper

> Cultural life, as ever, is of intense interest to him. I told him about the new Kolberg film, and described to him a few of the scenes, which moved the Führer almost to the point of tears. He asked me to release the film as quickly as possible, and described it after my summary as a successful battle in the political issues for war ... It is already daylight when I say goodbye to the Führer.
>
> – Goebbels, Diaries, 2 December 1944

Part 1: Hitler and his henchmen

Introduction

The emphasis the Nazis placed on organisation arose from their analysis of the reasons behind the success of the Bolsheviks. In 1928 Goebbels declared that the racialist had the better idea in 1918, but the Marxist triumphed, because they were better organised; Bolshevism was a competitor brand which represented a superior methodology and an inferior ideology, or so Goebbels appears to have believed.[1] Organisation was key to the effectiveness of Nazi propaganda. The party structure represented the enthronement of absolute subordination as the meta-organisational principle – the character of the party was military not just militant.[2] In Lord Bullock's words: 'A reciprocal interaction was thus established between terror, propaganda and organisation, with Stalin in the

1930s relying more on the first, Hitler on the second, and both putting equal stress on the third.'[3] Despite significant differences between the two regimes, there was consequently a clear parallel in terms of the social control mechanisms and practices they used (i.e. 'coercive persuasion').

Hitler as auteur Nazi propaganda had a supreme director, Dr Goebbels, and a supreme star, Hitler himself. Yet the relation between the two of them was often that of propaganda conceptualiser and propaganda subcontractor. Hitler reviewed and critiqued films and speeches and cuts were made at his suggestion: he was not merely a theorist on propaganda. It remains a fascinating truth that the essentials of the Nazi symbol system, as well as the idea of locating the regime within an ideology of propaganda, were defined by Hitler himself – such as his design sketches for the People's Car (later as the VW Beetle a favoured symbol of the 1960s counter-culture), which anticipated its final refinement under the tutelage of Ferdinand Porsche. While, as Fest says, the suggestion that the younger Hitler designed advertising posters is probably fiction, it is nevertheless a credible fiction. Hitler subsequently became a student of propaganda as well as its ultimate practitioner.[4]

Management – structure

Organisational structure In *Behemoth* (1942) Franz Neumann reminds us that the Reich was not totalitarian in the sense of a 'monolithic, authoritarian system inspired by a unified policy'.[5] In fact there were four autonomous groups which pursued their own claims: party, army, bureaucracy and industry: above them all, the Leader.[6] Hitler conceived his organisation as a hierarchy of dictators, so that party officials had 'unconditional authority and freedom of action downward, but … unlimited responsibility upward'.[7] Scholars speak of 'the polycratic confusion of Nazi Germany'.[8] Here then was not one hierarchical power structure but a series of competing structures, all of which were involved in numerous activities, and particularly in propaganda. These power hierarchies did not exist to obey orders but to compete with each other in interpreting the vaguely enunciated will of Hitler – a kind of creative political entrepreneurship – and to steal more power from each other.

Alongside the formal set, or power hierarchies, were the individual paladins of the Reich who had official positions in a number of these hierarchies and interests and power bases in perhaps all of them. And then there were the Gauleiters. But beyond this there was also the SS; no mere police force, it can best be described as a state within a state, a shadow state with interests in everything and constantly expanding via the award of general officer commissions to all persons of status/ influence in the Reich. The structure of Nazi Germany cannot therefore be expressed by a business text-type organisational flow chart or by a matrix. It can be described merely as an ecology, a complex and ever fluctuating congeries of powers, paladins and bureaucracies: 'The result, made worse by Hitler's own unpredictable interventions, has been variously described as "authoritarian anarchy", "permanent improvisation", "administrative chaos". However described, this polycratic state, with competing centres of power, was very different from the outside world's picture of a monolithic, totalitarian state run with typical German efficiency.'[9] All of this relates to Hitler's belief in Social Darwinism, that is to say a brutal competition between his underlings for power via the interpretation of his obscure will. Indeed, one aim was not management but the avoidance of management from the centre, to create, in other words, a self-organising system, for example the self-regulatory methodology of the Reich Chambers (pseudo-professional bodies representing areas like the arts or journalism which controlled their conscripted memberships via powers such as expulsion etc.) which avoided the necessity for central micromanagement.[10]

Power in Nazi Germany: the dual state One view of Nazi administration is of an illogical mess of confused networks without a coherent structure or focus, while also recognising the deliberateness of this anti-design, that the bizarre pattern was not a default one. The dual, or binary, state with its complex weave, its horizontal and vertical patterns, its myriad party and state governments and jurisdictions, precipitated the condition, and the culture, of permanent crisis. Other scholarly authorities have seen this as a kind of 'neo-feudalism' resting on medieval notions of loyalty that supply a social and administrative bond throughout. Thus rationale, of a kind, is given to ostensible confusion.[11] Kershaw speaks of a phrase, 'working towards the Führer', which is both descriptive – that is how the system worked – and prescriptive: that is how one accumulated authority in Nazi Germany.[12] The idea of 'working towards the Führer' conceptualises initiative as arising not from leader to led but from subordinate individuals and agencies seeking his favour. So there was a rise of 'political laboratories' via which 'prominent members of the charismatic community work towards fulfilling their impression of their leader's will'.[13] Hitler thus emerged as a supreme mediator between the competitive forces within his system, supervising a culture of creative conflict.[14] Hence, for example, Goebbels recorded needing to use the Nazi Party to raise a matter since the leadership had to remain silent on certain things for political reasons.[15]

Propaganda leadership contested

Neither party nor state had a monopoly of propaganda, as both were retailers of it. The great problem was competing state and party authority – Goebbels 'correctly diagnosed his leader's unwillingness to resolve the party–state dualism'; this is because it suited Hitler's purposes not to do so, and hence 'radio, press, film, culture, all became individual battlegrounds'.[16] History has given Goebbels an exaggerated, post-war image of omnipotence. He was of course particularly important in film and radio and he sought control of all newsreels (the newsreel companies were combined under the D.W. label in 1940).[17] He had other roles such as inspector general for war damage, and began (1933) by securing unprecedented power (Hitler's 13 March decree), but after 1933 his power base was constantly challenged and sometimes eroded.[18] Satrap authority in the Reich was liquid, it ebbed and flowed. Orders to the press, for example, could come from Dietrich as well as from Goebbels, and sometimes those orders were contradictory. On one occasion in 1940, for instance, each had ordered the press to carry a different lead story: 'Hitler once locked them together in a railway car with instructions not to leave until they had made peace.'[19] In another incident, Goebbels ordered press coverage of his own speech, and Dietrich countermanded it by saying the focus must be on Hitler.[20] The power territory of Goebbels and Dietrich continuously changed so that no assertion about them and their territorial sovereignty is immutable. Dietrich was administratively junior to Goebbels but he was also a Reichsleiter, complicating the question of authority even further (i.e. his was the paradox of a non-subordinate subordinate, and Dietrich saw Hitler far more often than Goebbels. His interpretations were also more optimistic, reflecting Hitler's optimism).[21]

The paladins of the Reich and their conflictual authorities Understanding the organisation of propaganda is not just a matter of the structure of power but also who held it, and for how long. The Third Reich was a series of interwoven political biographies.[22] The key individuals were Goebbels, Dietrich, Ley, Rosenberg, Ribbentrop, Max Amann, Bouhler: these were all (apart from Ribbentrop) carriers of the title and function of Reichsleiter, that is to say titular members of the Reich's most senior leadership cadre; the lines of responsibility and authorities were overlapping.[23] The Reich effectively had a binary management structure. Thus there was Ribbentrop's own-label foreign propaganda (from 1937), while control over literary censorship belonged to Philip Bouhler. There was also Max Amann, the president of the press section of the Reich Chamber of Culture (RKK) (whose brief was business and administration but who had licence to intrude on issues of content).[24] Hale speaks of the 'standing feuds' within the leadership over control of the press – that is to say, Dietrich controlled editors and journalists, and Amann controlled publishing; Amann fought the moves of other paladins/leaders to invade his territory and he enjoyed unique influence over Hitler.[25] Other interests included Ley of the Labour Front who aspired to control labour's 'enlightenment' and therefore stressed propaganda, for example the Labour Front published a journal aimed at organisers of meetings.[26] And then there was Rosenberg, the editor of the party newspaper *Völkischer Beobachter* until 1938, and his organisation published *Art in the Third Reich*, the upscale art magazine.[27] But responsibility for foreign radio propaganda was in fact divided between the Propaganda Ministry of Goebbels and the Foreign Ministry of Ribbentrop.[28]

Propaganda was simply one of the most important territorial symbols, and weapons, in the inter-ministerial squabbles for turf within the Third Reich. But no one satrap's propaganda empire was ever inviolate. Goebbels had control over film but even his radio imperium was subject to challenge. By the end of 1939 he was forced to 'defend his grip over radio' for the first time against the Foreign Ministry.[29] Possessing a propaganda operation was a status symbol and an insignia of authority in the culture of the Third Reich: everybody wanted one. Hence the regional leaders also joined in this elite competition for propaganda control, pushing to dominate the newspapers within their Gau, to undermine or supervene the work of the national party propaganda office and seeking to drive content in a more thoroughly Nazified direction.[30] During the war there were new incursions into the realm of propaganda from Himmler, the interior minister, Speer, who was in charge of armaments and labour conscription, and Rosenberg, the minister for the occupied eastern territories, while Bormann, the head of the Chancellery, 'came to dominate the party apparatus'.[31] Then there was the Armed Forces High Command, the OKW (Oberkommando der Wehrmacht), which elevated its press officer and office to the status of a division of the Wehrmacht, controlled by the chief of staff.[32] Nothing perhaps could better illustrate the prestige of propaganda in the Third Reich than the fact that even the army – which, like all armies, was used to the idea of the application of coercive force as their supreme task – could have elevated propaganda to a top priority and military function. Propaganda was the breath of the regime. Hence most of the paladins had a propaganda operation of some significance.

A chaos theory of government: some case studies

Art policy Art policy is a representative prism through which to view the management of the Reich; Hitler was always the final arbiter, but here, as everywhere, policy evolved competitively among the rival paladins as each sought to promote their perspective as the dominant orthodoxy – for example, over the status of modern art which also of course meant its status as propaganda. As a hyper-nationalist Goebbels was reluctant to inhibit creativity because he wanted Germany to succeed here as elsewhere. Thus he 'consented to serve on the committee for the March 1934 show of Italian futurist art', and he repeatedly articulated the phrase 'we guarantee freedom in art'.[33] For example, he approved of Emil Nolde and even telegrammed Edvard Munch on the occasion of the latter's seventieth birthday.[34] Goebbels's rival in arts policy was the mystical-regressive Rosenberg with his espousal of the folkish dogmas, a nineteenth-century fetish for 'radical traditionalism'. Hitler, not unusually, was at first a study in ambivalence, dismissing the folkish programme as 'Teutonic nonsense' in 1934, but also attacking 'stuttering Cubists', and then modern art generally at Nuremberg in 1935.[35] Hitler resolved the issue in typical form by licensing Rosenberg and also commissioning him with a new journal, *Art in the Third Reich*: now there would be a rival private-party arts enterprise to Goebbels's public-state one.[36]

Poland Hitler's approach to art policy is relevant because it is typical, a paradigm of the creative/destructive anarchy he superintended, and also a case study in the navigation of ideology and the definition of what it actually was. Ideological rectitude would thus arise from below, an outcome of the struggles between the paladins. One cited example is the dispute between Gauleiters Forster and Greiser over the interpretation of Hitler's mandate in Poland.

Albert Forster of West Prussia was a committed Nazi (and later sentenced to death), but he had a very pliable attitude to racial classification and joked that if he had looked like Heinrich Himmler 'he wouldn't talk about race so much'.[37] Forster 'did not enforce tedious individual classification of the population. He decided to reclassify some Poles as Germans en masse, without detailed examination. After all, hadn't Hitler said that in the pursuit of Germanising Poland he would "ask no questions about their methods".'[38] Thus in the case of one town about eighty per cent of people signed the Germanisation list. But an adjacent area to Forster's, the Wartheland, was headed by the literalist Arthur Greiser, the hardest of the hard men, and he 'took care to implement seriously the detailed criteria the Nazis used to determine which of the Poles could be Germanised and which could not. This policy was one of ruthless, uncompromising racial segregation.'[39]

Von Kleist on the Eastern Front This approach, the licensing of different and even antithetical versions of the mandate, even applied to military affairs. There was, for example, the curious case of the eastern policies of Field Marshal Ewald von Kleist (as discussed by Mitcham):

> ironically, some of the successes to which Kleist owed his promotion were due to his ignoring Hitler's instructions concerning the treatment of the peoples who previously had lived under Communist domination. In September 1942, Kleist had remarked: 'these vast spaces depress me. And these vast hordes of people! We're lost if we don't win them over.'[40]

And win them over he did — by the thousands. With great foresight, he appointed two former military attachés from the Moscow embassy to his staff (Niedermayer and Koestring). Niedermayer had been a professor of geopolitics, and 'was an outspoken critic of the Nazi policy of treating the non-German peoples of the Soviet Union as subhumans'.[41] These two men gave Kleist expert advice on the various ethnicities under their control: 'as a result of these policies, 825,000 men were recruited to fight Stalin's regime ... Ingush Azerbaijanis, Kalmucks, Uzbeks, and especially Cossacks ...'[42] The protests of senior Nazi plenipotentiaries against these humane policies were simply ignored: 'Kleist had even ordered his subordinates to make sure that the "voluntary" labour recruitment programmes in his area were actually voluntary!' Success was rewarded, even if it meant contradicting most of the operational policies, and the ideology, of the Nazi state: Kleist 'went so far as to summon SS, Gestapo and "Police" officials to his headquarters and categorically tell them to their face that he would tolerate no excesses in his zone of command'.[43]

Goebbels of course appreciated the propaganda values of this even if he was deaf to the humanitarian ones: 'Kleist's humane policy was so successful that it even elicited half-hearted praise from Joseph Goebbels, the Nazi minister of propaganda. Had Kleist's ideas been implemented throughout the east, they very conceivably could have changed the course of the war.'[44] And indeed, Goebbels's brief was public communication not political policy, something he seems to have had no influence over. If this had not been the case, then the history of the Reich might have been very different. For example, he was appalled by the atrocities in eastern Europe and the reservoirs of hatred they excavated, as indeed was Speer. Perhaps he was beginning to understand that even war is a branch of the advertising industry and he saw the insanity: 'one cannot characterise these eastern peoples, who owe their liberation at our hands, as beasts, barbarians, etc. and then expect them to show interest in a German victory'.[45] Goebbels heard of complaints about bullying of the Czechs which he described as bad propaganda and sought to redress the balance. His frustration was that action and message were out of sync, and he also criticised the tactics of the Nazi extremists and 'the senseless arrests carried out by the SS' (November 1940), a fascinating insight into the collision of propaganda values with Nazi brutality.[46] Speer records how Goebbels and Göring opposed the war and how 'we' regarded them as the degenerate peace party. Goebbels was horrified by the Ukraine barbarities, such as the deliberate blowing up of a church in Kiev to destroy Ukrainian national pride:

> Goebbels told the story with displeasure; he was horrified by the brutal course being pursued in occupied sectors of the Soviet Union. In fact, the Ukraine at that time was still so peaceable that I could drive through the extensive forests without an escort. Half a year later, thanks to the twisted policy of the eastern commissioners, the whole area was infested with partisans.[47]

Hitler's personal supervision

Adolf Hitler was a media mogul, not because of its instrumental value alone but because he loved it as truly and fondly as any one of the great Hollywood magnates of the 1930s. Media was a passion and an instrument of authority, but it was also much more than that: it was a mode of being and a totalising framework for governance. Nazism would be inconceivable without this: but 'it', the media product, could only become what it was because of the direct and personal control Hitler exercised, the inscription of his personal signature. He scrutinised, orchestrated and even managed its imagery. Micromanaged even – Hitler or Hess had the final say on the major posters and pieces of literature, at least in the early days.[48] Nothing, films, newsreels, speeches, the design of uniforms, were beneath the radar screen of his rhetorical and visual awareness. He was the leader of the Reich and its supreme editor and stage manager; for example, his ordering press and radio to help the Italians in December 1940 ('We must do something to buck them up again');[49] or his approval of Goebbels's action against rumour-mongers;[50] or Goebbels's delight when 'the Führer was particularly pleased with my article against Churchill' (again this suggests Hitler's fitful personal involvement in trivial detail).[51] Sometimes Hitler intervened directly, seizing the controls of the propaganda machine and driving it himself, imposing some initiative unilaterally and without the assent of his subcontractors. For example, on 29 June 1941 'the notorious twelve triumphant "special announcements"' were his direct initiative, announcing the breakthrough on the Eastern Front, 'a stratagem masterminded and executed by Hitler and his Press Chief, Otto Dietrich to the annoyance of Goebbels'.[52] It is impossible to imagine Churchill, Roosevelt, or even the dictators of other totalitarian states, managing the regime's media/news product to such a personal degree. In addition to ordaining the government's global press line on a daily basis, Hitler also viewed the weekly newsreels in advance to check them. Goebbels had also done this, reviewing each reel twice, once with sound and once without.[53] But it was Hitler who had the final verdict:

> since the beginning of the war, the weekly newsreel copy was edited in Berlin and sent to the Hitler headquarters by Monday for approval. The established routine was that a private screening for Hitler was taking place on Monday evening that offered him the opportunity to make changes; these ... had to be communicated back to the editing offices and be implemented immediately. [Hitler ceased to do this by early 1944.][54]

And Hitler could disagree with Goebbels, as is clear from one of Goebbels's diary entries from 1941: 'the Führer wants more polemical material in the script. I would rather have the pictures speak for themselves and have the script explain only what the audience would not otherwise understand. I consider this to be more effective, because then the viewer does not see the art in it.'[55] But some historians argue that 'More than any other exponent of propaganda, Hitler had an extremely sensitive awareness of the tolerance level of the mass of the population – of whom he was at one and the same time both contemptuous and distrustful.'[56] On another occasion Goebbels's account of the latest Request Concert (the popular radio programme) 'pleases him visibly'.[57] So the media product received Hitler's close personal scrutiny, his plaudits and his rebuke. Sometimes he liked the latest newsreel: 'all in all, he is so nice to me that I set to working with a renewed love'.[58] Or again 'put together the weekly newsreel. Turned out very well again. I asked the Führer's verdict on one thorny point. Now it is ready.'[59] Or again: 'watch the newsreel with the Führer, who is very pleased with it. The shots of London burning make a particularly profound impression on him'.[60] And Hitler was active in setting standards, including new guidelines on newsreels. Goebbels even recorded one meeting where the Führer was dissatisfied with the weekly newsreel, and Goebbels replied that simply not enough was going on to make them stimulating.[61] The Führer's finger was continually on the pulse: thus the weekly newsreel would be observed and commented upon, or a decision would be taken to re-edit on his instructions. Similarly, after just surviving an assassination attempt, he was preoccupied with how it should be presented in the public domain. Thus Hitler was no mere grandee reviewer but an active protagonist in the media production. Goebbels, for example, ordered the press to attack a *Times* article, adding that he would supply 'some withering arguments myself' and that 'the Führer too, makes some very effective points'.[62] Or he records 'Hitler's satisfaction with my work and his suggestions'.[63] Hitler's media activism was directed against enemy as well as home media. Goebbels read out George Bernard Shaw's 'subversive' article which he imagined to be representative of a section of British opinion. Hitler's gratification was recorded, and also his observations on the article.[64] On another occasion 'the Führer was particularly pleased with my article against Churchill'.[65] Goebbels describes Hitler laughing at anecdotes about characters in the British Ministry of Information, adding 'these gentlemen are totally inferior to us. As they will soon learn.'[66] It seems astonishing that Hitler would even bother to be interested in such puny actors in a global struggle. And he was the fount of approval and the source of affirmation to whom Goebbels continually turned for support and indeed affection. All media actions were judged against the template of his approbation; thus Goebbels speaks of Hitler's agreement with him that Germans must not be led to believe that there will be a quick English defeat.[67] Hitler, then, intervened directly in the media war: Goebbels, for example, recorded that the 'Poland film' had to be 're-edited yet again at the Führer's wish'.[68]

Hitler might also even edit colleagues' speeches. Speer gives an illuminating example of this:

> when we were co-ordinating our texts, the propaganda minister advised me to shorten my speech, since his would take an hour. 'If you don't stay considerably under half-an-hour, the audience will lose interest'. As usual, we sent both speeches to Hitler in manuscript, with a note to the effect that mine was going to be condensed by a third. Hitler ordered me to come to Obersalzberg. While I was sitting by, he read the drafts Bormann handed to him. With what seemed to me eagerness, he ruthlessly cut Goebbels's speech by half within a few minutes. 'Here, Bormann, inform the Doctor and tell him that I think Speer's speech excellent.'[69]

Thus he was, or became, also the supreme micromanager of major regime speeches: 'in 1939 Hitler ordered the texts of speeches that dealt with the Nazi world view be approved in advance by Rudolf Hess; after Hess flew to England, Hitler personally approved such speeches'.[70] On another occasion Goebbels addressed German cultural workers in Prague, and afterwards 'the Führer changes only a few details from the press release of the speech'.[71] So Hitler could even intervene to the extent of altering a press release of his own minister of propaganda. Indeed, who was the real minister of propaganda? And Hitler's media focus was not of course confined to Germany or Germany's British enemies as the Nazi media product in the occupied territories also concerned him: Goebbels, for example, observed that Hitler was not so satisfied with the work of Germany's propaganda man in Norway.[72]

Hitler, Dietrich and the media control process

The Ministry of Propaganda was licensed to assume control of all press functions soon after the assumption of power, and the press bureau of the Reich government became a division of that ministry.[73] Yet this did not translate directly into enhanced authority for Goebbels, for it was Dietrich who became Reich press chief and later state secretary in the Propaganda Ministry.[74] The central role in shaping the press narrative was in fact Adolf Hitler's. Dietrich would submit a digest of the global press and news to Hitler on an almost daily basis and Hitler ordained the response of the German media and propaganda machine; Dietrich and his colleagues 'then transformed Hitler's suggestions into daily and weekly press directives'.[75] And this is critical to our understanding of how propaganda worked in the Third Reich, so that to emphasise Dietrich is also to assert the centrality of Hitler himself in the production of the daily public narrative; recognition of this 'thus reinserts Hitler into the day-to-day construction of the story the Nazi regime told Germans and the world on a daily and weekly basis'.[76] Hence a new thesis would place Hitler at the centre of propaganda in the Third Reich rather than the delegator of that task to a cadre of subcontractors, and conceive him in fact as *the* propaganda director – not Goebbels, or anyone else. Hitler 'had the last word, and he frequently delayed the issue of the W.B. (Wehrmacht Report) until he had made some typical linguistic changes'.[77] Only then would the reports appear, via Dietrich, in the evening newspapers and afternoon radio bulletins.

Goebbels's ministerial conference The importance of the Dietrich Reich Press Office lay in creating a coherent narrative of events. In fact there were two daily conferences on news content, the press conference run by Otto Dietrich and the ministers' conference run by Goebbels one hour before: and so the Propaganda Ministry offered two daily platforms wherein the party line would be given.[78] It is easy to confuse the two, but great significance is attached to their being separate events. Goebbels aspired of course to gain control over this later Dietrich press conference. The rivalry between Goebbels and Dietrich became so intense that Hitler intervened – a Führer order on 23 August 1942 required Goebbels to issue press directives only via Dietrich, and Dietrich and his team were now the only ones who could give the midday daily press conference.[79]

On-message Consistency and coherence were created throughout the realm, impressing foreign observers with an ostensible unity and identity of national purpose, and this approach assured that all the German media were 'on-message': there was never any vagueness or ambiguity in the Reich unless it was intended.[80] There were also intimate briefings concerned with interpretations and special manoeuvres, for example that the colonial question could be dropped.[81] About two hundred journalists would attend these daily Propaganda Ministry conferences, which laid out the party line rigorously (e.g. praise Greta Garbo, denigrate Thomas Mann);[82] detailed instructions were issued about what stories were relevant, on language and on presentation (including the size of headlines). There was, for example, a prohibition on showing pictures of bibulous officials framed by the ranks of wine bottles at public functions – or burning synagogues.[83] Directives concerned tone as well as content, orchestrating not only the stories but also the literary and presentational aspects: it has been suggested that there were as many as 75,000 such directives during the life of the Reich.[84]

Content of directives The press directives were the hidden strings of the puppeteers. They were the way political information was issued, coordinated and controlled in Nazi Germany but they had to be kept secret, otherwise the propaganda edifice on which the regime was constructed would have been publicly exposed. But the directives were capable of subtlety; the crudeness of the Nazis, of Nazism as a political creed, must not obscure the fact that Nazi propaganda was manipulative and capable of guile, even on occasion nuance. And the party liked spice, commending, in the early years, the use of scandal-mongering and sensationalism as a draw.[85]

Part 2: Goebbels

Goebbels seeks control

Hitler and Goebbels Goebbels was the ill-used mistress of the Reich, devoted to her lover, but insufficiently loved. Yet his relation to Hitler was more apprentice to sorcerer than the other way around. Goebbels could act as ably and effectively as he did because of the ethos and parameters set by the master; if propaganda was to be the core methodology of governing, then much else followed as a logical consequence. It was clearly enjoyable work for Goebbels, but he saw micromanagement as a bulwark against drift and mediocrity, the only way via which a fresh and exciting propaganda product could be produced daily without falling victim to institutionalised sclerosis and ponderously formulaic management.

Goebbels was not of course the first propaganda head of the Nazi Party, as Hitler had originally been appointed to that role before becoming leader. Himmler was in charge of propaganda in the Munich headquarters until his promotion to head of the SS.[86] Goebbels was the sous-chef, the under-manager, the greatest power in the Nazi propaganda industry, but he was not all-powerful and rarely achieved the dominion popularly attributed to him (for example, even Martin Bormann had a significant role).[87] His ministry exercised varying degrees of authority, given it soon after Hitler became chancellor, including over radio, film, theatre, foreign press and news and so forth as well as such things as fairs and exhibitions and festivals.[88] He was a missionary, the zealot for communicating the idea of communicating. His frustrations with the military, and with their non-comprehension of the propagandist's perspective (the Propaganda Companies were his conception), often overwhelm his diaries. And his fights were also of course with the party and its dull-witted propagandist sensibility – for example, his complaints about funeral orations by party officials deaf to the emotional resonances. And Goebbels was also the ideologue: film and newsreel had to conform to his political strictures; under the Reich Film Law the producer had to prevent 'topics from being treated that run counter to the spirit of the age'.[89]

And Goebbels's speeches possessed intellectual content, a logically flawless rationale would lead to an inexorable conclusion; his advocacy was 'typically brilliant, decked out with half-truths, deliberate misinterpretations and statistics without foundation or quoted source'.[90] Goebbels was the sophist of the Reich, coining new words or re-defining old ones: 'freedom' for example now meant the liberty of Germany to do exactly as it wished, unconstrained. He was a skilled casuist, an oratorical portraitist of the terrors of Sovietism, of its mass murders, the epics of starvation, and linked them to the domestic menace; the inference was that Germany had to be ruthless to survive.[91] There was a content, but also a tone, fair-seeming and balanced. Goebbels nevertheless had aggressive foreign adversaries in the Allied media. Thus he observed that press leaks (about old regulations on the eating of dog meat) had been turned by the Americans into a sensational famine story. The Reich minister was peevish – 'trivialities are turned into world-wide sensations'.[92] This demonstrates the problem in the control of any information super-highway: trivia can leak and be turned by malign interpretation and rumour into horror stories.

The satraps of the Reich were bureaucratic imperialists and each coveted the domain of the other. Dietrich had ambitions over radio, Goebbels's domain, and tenaciously defended his viceroyalty over the news policy. Yet Goebbels successfully excluded other ministries from authority over the radio and this was the consequence of Hitler's direct intervention: radio and regional radio was his, and his ministry's, exclusionary monopoly.[93] Goebbels sought 'a unitary propaganda mission across all media', but he was often frustrated, and coherence and unity of mission were only possible in the final years.[94] It was then that he emerged as the omnipotent director of popular myth, the imagined Goebbels of public fiction became the real one. He defends, strikes pre-emptively or re-claims, making late war incursions into the press, re-gaining control over news agencies: 'the Goebbels network was the only propaganda institution that kept functioning literally until the end, adapting in the face of mounting adversity and keeping propaganda noise loud and clear through well-managed channels'.[95] He had come full circle. Goebbels originally became propaganda director of Berlin in 1926, where he built a comprehensive structure including the scandal-fomenting *Der Angriff*. He blended the functions of a Reich leader in charge of propaganda (a party position) with that of Minister for Public Enlightenment and Propaganda (a state position) and of Gauleiter and defence commissar for Berlin. Thus he held propaganda roles in both party and state. Subsequently he was exclusively responsible for only two areas, radio and film, but not magazines, newspapers, books, public meetings and ceremonies, foreign propaganda, and theatre; in these he has to share power with others,[96] and therefore to deploy many sources of influence, coercion, persuasion, cajolery. Goebbels had to compete, and he encountered institutional resistance. Hence speaking about the usages of air force propaganda he records: 'a few reactionary officers continued to have doubts about whether Luftwaffe officers should speak to the public'.[97]

Structure of the Propaganda Ministry In the view of one wartime commentator 'he is and will remain an indispensable tool of the regime that, more than ever before, has to rely on the manipulation of the masses. The undisputed mastery of this art makes him next to Himmler, Göring, Bormann and Speer the best-known figure among the paladins of Hitler'.[98] Goebbels's ministry resembled both a kind of pseudo-Napoleonic directoire, with a monsieur le ministre who issues orders, but also a propaganda warehouse, buying in and sending out the propaganda merchandise: 'the Goebbels network actually resembled a weak administrative centre for a spate of semi-independent, uncoordinated and often contradictory propaganda initiatives generated elsewhere'; in this, it simply replicated Nazi administrative culture.[99] The ministry operated a market-driven funding formula via the receipt of radio licences, that is to say the ministry was 'almost self-supporting', a consequence of the People's Receiver.[100] There were seventeen divisions to Goebbels's (RMVP) Propaganda Ministry, which employed more than 1,900 people by the war, and the regional propaganda under-offices accounted for another 1,400 people.[101] He was also head of the RKK (Reich Chamber of Culture) which organised the speaker system, leaflet distribution and the production of reports.[102]

Goebbels the supreme manipulator: internal/external morale Goebbels believed he could manage the temperature of public sentiment. A less sedulous, less subtle mind would have merely celebrated Germany's titanic military achievements in its epic year of 1940. Instead, he was perceptive enough to recognise that final victory might not be easy. Expectations had to be managed, and optimism dampened; toughness was needed to intrude on the public mood at such an epic moment, but Goebbels knew the cost of inaction. And he could also manipulate internal party feeling simply by giving out false information to keep the local party officials happy. For example, the party's lust for anti-Bolshevik films was not shared by a more tentative public, a clear case of the limitations of selling the ethos of Nazism in a popular context, so the films were much discussed but seldom commissioned (a mere two in fact).[103]

Morale was hence a key concern of Goebbels, both as Gauleiter of Berlin and as minister of enlightenment and propaganda – that is, the management of public emotion. He sought to avoid creating a climate of euphoria since he felt that the inevitable counter-reaction would be so much the worse: 'Goebbels frequently issued warnings about false hopes and illusions; records his fear of reducing German credibility by incorrect reports of air victories.'[104] He needed to convince the nation that this was going to be a long war; thus, on 3 November 1940 he recorded the sinking of ships and the reports of great pessimism emanating from London, which he refused to publicise so as to avoid engendering false optimism among German people.[105] And so he made an important point about avoiding the impression that defeating England and France is 'child's play'; in other words, striking a balancing act between defeatism and false optimism.[106] And on 18 December 1939 he claimed that he had concealed SD (Security Service) reports of defeatism in Paris and London because this would have undermined the resolve of Germans, and there must be no premature self-satisfaction.[107] The observations of, and constant attempts to manipulate, public sentiment were sometimes counter-intuitive. For example, the churches were an intense source of irritation, but the regime restrained itself: 'the soldier must have something to cling to'.[108]

Goebbels and film

Goebbels thought authentic film art must transcend the everyday and be 'intensified life'.[109] He stressed the importance of variation, of repeating the same things in different forms. The Nazi state 'became a grand aesthetic construction in which "the political itself is instituted and constituted (and regularly re-grounds itself) in and as a work of art"'.[110] Thus 'as early as 1934, the minister decreed that after the intense emotional experience represented by the Nuremberg party rally, the radio should emphasise light music for several weeks'.[111] And he observed the propaganda of others with the practised eye of the connoisseur, for example *All Quiet on the Western Front* was a very clever propaganda vehicle but 'at the time we had to sabotage it'.[112]

Goebbels was the supreme producer of the German cinema of the Third Reich, of moving imagery, choosing scenes and actors and directors, even inserting his own language into the scripts. Every film was shown at his home prior to being launched and he determined their political content and had a veto over their aesthetic.[113] And in this role he was invulnerable, as no jealous fellow paladin managed to trespass on this 'Ministry of Illusion'. Thus in a diary entry on 24 October 1939 he speaks of 'further problems with the Jew film', but adds 'synagogue shots extraordinarily powerful'.[114] The aim, according to him, was to create 'a propaganda masterpiece'. And then more is noted, 'he is reworking the script yet again', and on 18 December 1939 even further changes on the 'Jew film' are referenced by him; the 'Jew film' was clearly a demanding cause.[115] Goebbels describes another film as 'not quite politically watertight. I shall have it re-edited and a few scenes re-shot'.[116] In November 1940 he observed that the Bismarck film was now 'politically watertight',[117] whereas the Rothschild film needed more ideological work – thus on 10 August 1940 he had recorded revising the Rothschild film (presumably to make it more anti-British).[118] On another occasion an afternoon was spent censoring photographs and articles – again, the detail. Then he records further checking of newsreels and laying down guidelines for the text. He also noted his decision to have two full film shows every month for the Hitler Youth to 'cement the political direction'.[119] Goebbels also banned the film *Titanic* (1943) because it had the potential to lead the audience to pity the British victims.[120]

The military epics: Kolberg and The Great King Goebbels interfered repeatedly in, and protracted the production of, *Kolberg*. His great planned epic was to be the swansong of the Third Reich. It was structured via the central role of the bürgermeister, Nettelbeck; a love interest/family subplot; and the proto-feminist interest (the plea of the female lead, Söderbaum, for a more dynamic commander, and not to a male king but to a female queen).[121] A framing device book-ended the film. Goebbels revised the major speeches,[122] and the lines of his Total War oration (1943) were reflected in the speech calling for a fight to the finish which Nettelbeck makes on his knees to Gneisenau[123] ('The people rise, the storm erupts' ends the Sportpalast oration of 18 February 1943, and is a slightly modified line from a well-known poem).[124] The aim of the film according to Goebbels was to show the power of people united: the message was to follow a younger revolutionary leadership and accept subordination to a visionary commander, as do the aldermen of Kolberg after debate; another theme was that 'dying in war, whatever the outcome, is a blessing'.[125] There are contemporary resonances such as the wearing of caps (not introduced until 1813) and the revolutionary anthem sung by massed troops, its melody and the sound of marching feet.[126] Goebbels expected that the film would reflect future war conditions and that it would inspire blitzed areas and anticipate the military and political landscape that was to come. Thus on 7 May 1943 he commented in his diaries 'this film will above all offer a powerful lesson in areas subject to air raids', and on 5 June 1943 'I put such great hope for our inner peace of mind in this *Kolberg* film'; and on 1 December 1944 'it offers an answer to all the questions that currently preoccupy the German people'.[127] And on 5 June 1943 he had confided 'who knows in what position we will find ourselves. We must therefore have a film ready to encourage and support the toughness of civilian resistance ... I predict that the *Kolberg* film, if properly done as I envision, will do us great service in the coming winter.'[128] Goebbels's diaries illuminate how life imitated art. It is Kolberg, March 1945, and Hitler replaces an allegedly passive commander with a younger officer. But the city was now nearly eighty per cent destroyed, and finally it surrendered in mid-March. Goebbels had removed media accounts about Kolberg and said he would ensure this evacuation was not mentioned in the High Command report: 'in view of the severe psychological repercussions on the *Kolberg* film we could do without that for the moment'.[129] Culbert asks:

> is this not an unusual purpose for a policy of civilian sacrifice? A town must not surrender to the enemy, no matter what the cost, because it will undermine the propaganda message of a recently released feature film. It is hard to see why the military commander of Kolberg had to be replaced in March 1945 by a 'younger officer', unless Goebbels could not bear the thought of surrender when his new film showed that victory could be achieved against hopeless odds. Dying to maintain the integrity of a feature film's propaganda message is an unusual definition of patriotism.[130]

Goebbels felt that no film could live up to his mythical creation: 'he delayed the premiere of the film, sending it back for reworking and only reluctantly authorising its release'.[131] The re-shooting had continued until as late as July 1944 and on 23 December 1944 Goebbels recorded his disapproval that the imagery had been coarsened: 'Goebbels was more concerned that the dramaturgy of *Kolberg* be right than it find civilian release in time to make sense as a propaganda vehicle, an ironic comment about the practicality of one who considered himself to be a consummate propagandist.'[132] He wanted to moderate the scenes of obliteration since they would demoralise the public and ordered the director to cut some of the fighting and shelling.[133] Then there was the earlier *Great King* (1942), and here as elsewhere Goebbels ordered scenes to be rewritten, and this was typical: for him this film was an opportunity to excoriate the senior military, their conservatism, their faithless defeatism (the theme of *Kolberg* as well).[134] But in *The Great King* the masses are also implicated in the collective failure to accept greatness in a leader and to have faith. 'With this film we can make politics too': his remark is a good definition of celluloid propaganda.[135] However, he did not necessarily permit a propaganda vehicle to stand alone and could take an integrative approach, as here, where he requested newsreel images of Hitler solitary at headquarters as part of the cinema programme.[136] Goebbels also directed that the press should not relate the film to Germany's present state or to Hitler, but audiences nevertheless got the message.[137]

Hitler's intervention in film Hitler took an intense personal interest in film production:

> cultural life, as ever, is of intense interest to him. I told him about the new *Kolberg* film, and described to him a few of the scenes, which moved the Führer almost to the point of tears. He asked me to release the film as quickly as possible, and described it after my summary as a successful battle in the political issues for war ... It is already daylight when I say goodbye to the Führer.[138]

Hence it was not only Goebbels who intervened; Hitler also, and for the same reasons, did it because he could, and he saw it as important to the continuity of his regime. Hitler might even choose an actor (Otto Gebühr, who had always played Frederick). The senior military recognised that they were the intended targets of *The Great King*, mollified only by Field Marshal Keitel's intervention. Goebbels commented:

> I came to know of the hard fight which has broken out in the Führer HQ over the Frederick the Great film. In the end the Führer resolved the matter ... He asked me to place a copy of the film at his disposal. He intends sending it with an accompanying letter to the Duce ...[139]

Yet it is difficult to imagine, at any time in modern history, a military general staff quarrelling with a government over the content of an entertainment film, and especially a history film, and for the matter to be resolved at the level of the head of state. This could only have happened in Nazi Germany, and for reasons unique to it, namely that propaganda was no mere tool but an entire philosophy of governing.

Hitler then could intervene directly in conception, execution and evolution, both helping to create media texts and organise their content. For example, on 10 July 1941 an order went from Führer headquarters to RMVP: 'the Führer wants shots of Russian cruelty towards German prisoners to be incorporated in the newsreel so that Germans know exactly what the enemy is like. He specifically requests that such atrocities should include genitals being cut off and the placing of hand grenades in the trousers of prisoners'; the SD reports testified to the success of media portrayals of Communist savagery.[140] By 1942 Goebbels judged the time ripe for *The Dismissal*, the story of Bismarck's demise and a jeremiad against bureaucracy, but the question of its release was complicated by the continuity of the Soviet war and the party's demands – Rosenberg, for example, expressed concern that audiences would be reminded of the Kaiser's complicity in the First World War.[141] Goebbels went to Hitler, who then subcontracted the viewing and the decision to Bormann.[142] Again we observe the senior leadership cadre of a belligerent imperial nation actually debating the merits of a film.

Goebbels also possessed an enthusiasm for surveying the material assets of enemy propaganda, and plagiarising them; *Life Goes On* was already in production by war's end. Goebbels wanted a Nazi epic, one that might capture the essence of that sugared Hollywood confection, *Mrs Miniver* (1942). The scene, late-war Berlin, with a 'miracle weapons' aeroplane manufacturer. Goebbels intended this as a companion volume to *Kolberg*, and he screened *Miniver* a number of times to demonstrate how endurance should be portrayed; scenes were being filmed in Lüneberg one day before the British overwhelmed the area.[143]

Goebbels's fight with British media

The Nazis were capable in equal measure of ruthless and outright fraud alongside sanctimonious assertion of the honour and rectitude of their ways. And they were restless, opportunistic. Thus in the 1930s the BBC often used material directly from the wireless services; Goebbels noticed, and on one occasion managed to get his text broadcast as straight BBC news.[144] So the Nazis were great manipulators, and skilful ones, since this is how they understood their task, not as the provision of information, or even mere persuasion, but the actual creation/management of opinion. In other words there is no objective reality, and in understanding this they were ahead of their time. They really did believe they could create their own truth.

Goebbels's public struggle was with the British media. He believed in omnipresent, personal supervision as the guarantor of effective results, in immediate, fierce response; and incontinent polemic precipitated claim and counter-claim in a kind of international debate, the non-belligerent world as spectator, a curious farrago of charge and counter-charge. His analysis of the British press was detailed. In November 1940 he complained that 'the British press in general has recovered its arrogance and cockiness, doubtless on orders from above. But it will soon go sour.'[145] Goebbels's outrage at the British media foams from every page: 'London has, of course, become correspondingly insolent. The London press is puffed up with arrogance.'[146] This captures the essence of Goebbels, his attitude to the British media, fury at its assertiveness and the conviction that it is all about to collapse. Thus the English press is still playing it 'obdurate and cocky'.[147] All of these resentments are personified in the character of Churchill himself. So on 23 October 1939 he wrote in his diaries about Churchill's response to German allegations in the 'ship affair': 'this enrages me so much that I immediately set to dictating a radio speech in reply, which summarises the entire case against him in the most biting form. It is a huge success, comes pouring out like water from a spring.'[148] The speech was transmitted in all the world's languages, according to Goebbels –

'now I am working stubbornly to bring about this man's downfall. He is the cause of this war, and of its prolongation.' Hence on 14 November 1939 he delivered another riposte to Churchill, more evidence of Goebbels's obsession with him;[149] and personally attacked the British minister of war, Leslie Hoare-Belisha (who was Jewish).[150]

'Spin' is the affixing of a public interpretation on to fluid events, the assertive shaping of the inchoate matter of conflicting and ambivalent signals; and in all of this the Nazis were past-masters. Affairs have loose texture and even a deviant interpretation can persuade if forcefully articulated. Goebbels was the first of the spin doctors. He jumped on enemy assertions in a forceful effort to expose their alleged untruths and devious libels against the Reich. The embarrassments of war could be stifled. Hess, for example, could be 'positioned' as mentally unwell or as a deluded idealist deceived as to the real nature of the vicious British.[151] And this news market was not just domestic, but global, as even in the war there were many neutrals to impress, including Turks, Swiss, Swedes and South Americans, where opinion mattered to the Nazis. William Joyce rivalled the BBC for listeners. And censorship was always aggressive, for example when before the war (1938) the great fighter Max Schmeling was broken by the American Joe Lewis, the Germans cut the live link and subsequently refused to show the match.[152]

Part of this art of manipulation was a sharp opportunism and finely tuned tactical awareness; thus, when an 'English diplomat', Sir Robert Vansittart, broadcast a jeremiad which was not merely a 'savage attack' on the German regime but on the German race (Vansittart's notorious 1940 'Black Record'), Goebbels was ready: 'I intend to play this card at the next opportunity. I also bring it to the Führer's attention.'[153] Similarly with an article by David Lloyd George (who had once visited the Führer at the Berghof); his 'positive article' was subtly promulgated by Goebbels: 'I ordered it to be published without too much fuss, however, so as not to compromise LG.'[154] So Goebbels zealously scrutinised his enemy and its media product for targets of opportunity; a leader in *The Times*, for example, could propel him into a little paroxysm of rage, and riposte would be swift in coming. What is perhaps extraordinary is why it mattered to Goebbels so much. So the propaganda war underpinned the hard war with both sides sweeping deep inside each other's territories.[155] To Goebbels, the verbal fight with England which paralleled the physical fight was bitterly personal, a compound of his fury at purblind English arrogance, underpinned in his opinion by their myopia: they utterly failed to see the objective truth of their situation.

So he personalised the struggle. Hence on 13 October 1939 he recorded in his diaries further descriptions of the conflict between the German and London presses and London's 'bare-faced denial', this time on the 'issue' of mustard gas to the Poles. Goebbels attacked what he called the 'Ministry of Lies': 'from now on we shan't let the English get away with anything'. He discussed English 'lies' against Germany, 'a nonsensical barrage of lies'.[156] He was even aware of English ministerial speeches: 'Morrison babbles about a future in Europe under English leadership. We go straight for the throat on this issue. Our polemical stock is back at a high level.' Again then this international rhetorical exchange, what English ministers were saying in their speeches actually mattered to the Nazis. This alacrity in pursuit arose out of his own ideology of propaganda; Goebbels genuinely saw it as an important part of the war and a military weapon of considerable status. And this process of attack and riposte was a constant rhythm between London and Berlin, for instance 'we give him a suitable answer, and straight away'; that is, a moral, or amoral, equivalence, and 'we intend, in old National Socialist style, not to operate defensively but offensively. The English will be amazed.'[157] By the logic of the same belief, enemy propaganda was an important weapon of the enemy. Everything in the rhetorical arsenal – denial, assertion, fibs, false equivalences – was enlisted by Goebbels, but the key premise was agility: no statement of the enemy could go unchallenged. It is perhaps unclear who exactly he was trying to impress, however: the dwindling audience of neutral nations perhaps, but primarily the population of the Axis, including the illicit radio listeners, in order to reassure them of the rectitude of their cause.

Culture nation Goebbels was in thrall to the idea of Germany as the 'culture nation' and it followed that among the tasks of pan-European hegemony would be the spreading of German high culture. Powerfully, but indirectly, this was propaganda. He discusses, for example, Norway and the German cultural campaigns and their positive impact which he intends to take further, or the importance of 'our musical prestige in Prague'.[158] He was also intimately involved in trivial details such as the work of Viennese theatre. Culture was also a weapon of internal propaganda within Germany, for example his discussion of 'the position of the theatre in Baden',[159] or concern for raising the pension of a musician.[160] The suffering artists received special favours, allegedly a contrast to the philistinism of the English. Goebbels's Reich music train visited many desolate places.[161]

Despite its propaganda achievements in the First World War, the bombast and the imagery and the atrocity polemics, Britain seemed to have entered a lethe of forgetfulness. Perhaps the propagandistic thrust had been too publicly vilified in retrospectives on the First World War. The Nazis had learned; the English had unlearned. Nicholas Cull has evoked the sluggishness of the British propaganda effort in the early Second World War period: thus, the Berlin machine was sharper than London in supplying news to the American media, and the imagery was vivid: 'the blitzkrieg on Poland was infinitely more photogenic than scenes of Frenchmen filing into bunkers along the Maginot line, and German photographs soon outnumbered Allied pictures by a ratio of four to one'.[162] The Germans were the first with data on Allied shipping sinkings and 'their figures gained acceptance by default and quickly became a serious deterrent to US approval of aid to Britain. Despite American suspicion of German news, both the *New York Times* and the Foreign Office soon conceded that Hitler was winning the propaganda war in the United States.'[163] And the Germans were dominating war photography, so that the Ministry of Information had to issue all official British pictures directly to the American photographic agencies. But the service departments were not offering hard news, especially the Admiralty:

victories were as badly presented as defeats. The American press had difficulty covering the sinking of the *Graf Spee* and the pursuit of that ship's service vessel, the *Altmark*. Even though the *Altmark* incident unfolded like a *Boy's Own* story – with a boarding party from *HMS Cossack* leaping onto the Nazi prison ship and shouting to their imprisoned comrades 'the Navy's here!' – the Admiralty still refused to blow its own horn.[164]

And thus Lord Lothian, the ambassador to Washington, urged a policy of openness in order to challenge German claims and that full information given to American journalists was 'the best counterpropaganda'.[165] Sir Dick White (later head of MI5 and then of MI6) agreed, pointing out that 'confidence cannot live in a twilight of scepticism'.[166]

Goebbels, morale and opinion research

Dr Goebbels struggled, often furiously, against the dulled sensitivities of the elephantine bureaucracies of the Third Reich, a zealot not for the rights of humans but for humans seeing rightly – that is, faith in the rectitude of Führer and regime. Thus Goebbels's diaries record his protest to the High Command about problems with the field post.[167] Then there was the evacuation of children from Berlin, where he complained about the sabotaging of his order (that the process should be carried out without compulsion); the morale problems of child evacuation continue to vex him.[168] And surgical tactics could be adopted by Goebbels to restore morale in bombed areas, such as the propaganda office in Kiel organising army bands and theatre to revive confidence.[169]

Morale and opinion research The later war problem was the obverse of the earlier, once overweening elation, now despair. And Goebbels always knew (even within the information restrictions of a totalitarian society) about the state of morale because he sponsored opinion research of an early kind. For one thing, he could even do it himself by visiting bombed areas and sensing the atmosphere as a way of bypassing official channels to garner intelligence.[170] Goebbels was also aware of the importance of public context in opinion research – things had to be seen in public to be judged, not just studied in reports, thus he attended a Hitler Youth Festival and adds 'one must see films in public now and then, since otherwise one becomes too one-sided in one's judgments'.[171] The decline in civilian morale was registered in SS and RPL (the Nazi Party Propaganda Department) reports, and the old sensitivity to language was now taxed with new demands; but Goebbels eschewed mention of death in slogans, preferring ones like 'For Freedom and Life'.[172] Midwar presented a new set of creativity challenges. The informed knew Germany was losing but for the uninitiated, however, the mass, there had to be hope. Clever new ways had to be found to maintain the momentum of the propaganda and, while displaying candour, to carry conviction of final triumph. The tone had to change: radio had to be less polemical, according to its head, with more human interest. And propaganda had to legitimate a more remote Führer (*The Great King*).[173] One source of intelligence was the letters radio itself received, which served as raw material he could analyse: 'I study a heap of letters to the radio which provide a good cross-section of German public opinion.'[174]

Goebbels's diaries evidence close observation of public opinion (i.e. political meteorology), and, in the public space, his secret listeners were everywhere. Another aspect of opinion research involved gauging audience response to the Nazi media products and calibrating their effectiveness: 'the Nazis dictated how films were to be publicised and discussed, painstakingly watching over audience response, monitoring applause and laughter in the cinema, listening to and worrying about word of mouth on the street'.[175] Nor was opinion research restricted to the domestic arena; he needed information about the effectiveness of propaganda externally, for example studying what he called 'a fat report about my propaganda abroad' (i.e. close scrutiny of the overseas).[176] Nor of course was he convinced by the official reports. For example, he recorded his suspicion of SD reports on morale because he regarded them as increasingly unreliable and composed of vague non-verifiable statements.[177]

Class envy Goebbels well understood the power of class envy and how its exploitation could be a source of control. Hence in his diaries he recorded that 'in the press conference, I attacked those so-called officers who make themselves comfortable in commandeered cars and so arouse much resentment'.[178] At his home the Reich minister ostentatiously closed public rooms and removed electric bulbs.[179] Much later, the great Total War speech vastly augmented his authority, and his eloquent advocacy of austerity resonated even within a regime that had used consumerism as an important tool of popularity. Goebbels then closed Berlin's finest restaurants and extravagances (but not without a fight), and the public applauded.[180] Speer commented:

> Göring, to be sure, promptly interposed his bulk to protect his favourite restaurant, Horcher's. But when subsequently some demonstrators (set on by Goebbels) appeared at the restaurant and smashed the windows, Göring yielded. The result was a serious rift between him and Goebbels.[181]

So the paladins of the Reich could even use the mob in their relationships with each other. But Goebbels's agents had relayed to him the details of popular disenchantment, for example the desire that luxuries be prohibited, but also the willingness to suffer: 'in fact, significant restrictions were a necessity if only to revive popular confidence in the leadership'.[182] Typically, Goebbels invited public input into ideas for operationalising Total War and the response was enormous.[183] Giving was encouraged, and advertisements for luxuries were banned in cinemas: 'but the official response was symbolic: the displacement of beauty salons into other neighbourhoods etc'.[184] Goebbels sought to become even a kind of vox populi or articulated public consciousness, an expression of the national sentiment.

Micromanage the media content Goebbels was Nazi Germany's aspirational media supremo, promulgator of the product and observer of its impact both at home and abroad. For example, he described a propaganda broadcast about the returning U-boat that sunk the great British battleship HMS *Royal Oak* at Scapa Flow in October 1939 and registered his approval.[185] Again, the minute observation. He was constantly checking news or reviewing text, for example he described studying 'scripts for propaganda films, and reports on morale in France and England';[186] or working 'long hours on films and the newsreel'.[187] Goebbels was also the universal media critic. Part of this micromanagement of the media product was aesthetic and not just political; he excoriated the awkward, the unprofessional and the mundane: 'newsreel ready. Incidental music wrong. Will be reworked.'[188] Goebbels envisioned a film that 'edified as it entertained, that diverted attention while directing desire, incorporating political values in well-crafted popular packages'.[189] Thus he dismissed *In the Name of the People* as 'a bad crime film immediately recognisable as official in its inspiration'.[190]

Dull media

The ideal Nazi integrated standardised beliefs and pre-packaged role models; the Nazis felt 'they were operating the control panel of the human psyche'.[191] But their propaganda faced a problem. In the first place, the attempt to place a society under a constant velocity of stimulus does of itself raise this issue of mental exhaustion. How can the stimulus be sustained? Can we risk periods of lower intensity? The aim was to represent old ideas in new ways by innovative format, but it was a creativity of form not message. The restricted ideological sources of messaging, the difficulty of disguising the reality of coercion and the brutal hubris of conquest-seeking made for a constrained imaginative space. And this continuously obsessed Goebbels: a coerced creative cadre cannot engage with experiment or take artistic risk, because, to work, creativity must ask questions, and that is what totalitarianism explicitly forbids. Goebbels saw the mediocrity of so much Nazi propaganda, and his diaries report agonies of frustration at being confronted with the nonentity products of terrified minds. And yet, when he did encourage editors to become more irreverent, one journalist took him at his word and ended up in prison. And this was the nub of the problem.

All big bureaucracies find originality difficult to sustain because with size comes process, and, therefore, rules: formula replaces inspiration, and the imaginative individual is lost amid the vastness of hierarchy, inertia, institutionalised conservatism and bureaucratic fiat. Add to this the terrors of a state which was not just totalitarian but, selectively and secretively, murderous, and the magnitude of the problems against which Goebbels railed becomes apparent. Authority was sustained through a state terror unrestrained by the law, religion, tradition or individual shame. For theirs was a revolutionary state and they had the amorality of the true revolutionary: therefore why bother, why take creative risk in a totalitarian order, a state closely monitored by depraved policemen? Process could atrophy as it did in the USSR after the Zhdanov decrees in 1946, and much of Nazi propaganda was also moribund; Germany could never rival Hollywood or ever hope to do so. Goebbels's biggest problem was the contradiction implicit in the context; creativity is best succoured by freedom, yet trivial hackwork, tedious hyperbole and vacuous superlatives characterised the Nazi media product. Goebbels used to become infuriated. Thus he recorded that the newspapers were too dull, and discussed the importance of freedom for individual creative work 'otherwise we shall choke slowly on bureaucracy'.[192] He found the latest propaganda films too didactic and 'this schoolmarmish business makes me sick'.[193] He noted that he actually banned poor propaganda and became preoccupied with the quality of films; he considered removing a 'bad army propaganda film'.[194] Living in the New Jerusalem does not seem to have stimulated exertion, sublime or otherwise, from the artistic cadres. On the one hand Goebbels exhorted originality, yet on the other he pushed censorship and periodic threats, the one effectively undermining the other. There was eventually a ban on art criticism since Goebbels decided that this was a Jewish phenomenon.

A huge problem for the Reich thus lay in sustaining the euphoric tone with which it was first created. There had been the film problem – 'insufficient ticket sales, widespread public dissatisfaction, declining export revenues, and an overall sense of crisis, which by 1937 reached alarming proportions'.[195] And freedom of creativity was further limited by the needs of wartime censorship. Goebbels was an evangelist for evangelism, a self-styled scourge of mediocrity. He attacked the propaganda of the High Command on the grounds that it 'comes straight out of the filing cabinet. Real bureaucrats! But I simply forbid such idiocies.'[196] He also described the German press as dull-witted, stating 'we must have no lax habits here'.[197] Then there was the poster war, something which as ever he had an opinion on, hence he excoriated the 'psychologically inept' insensitivity of a poster about air defence, which he managed to stop.[198] The people working in the offices of the Reich Propaganda Leadership, Goebbels claimed, were really mediocre (this was distinct from the Ministry of Propaganda).[199] He complained about an 'idiotic' production from the Bavaria Studios.[200] He also recorded concern about the Propaganda Companies and the stifling effect of irrelevant military drills.[201] Then there was the German Foreign Office's 'stupid, intellectual propaganda against France', again demonstrating his underlying theory of propaganda, that meaning should be unambiguous.[202] Thus in November 1939 he stated 'I urge a more primitive approach in our entire propaganda.'[203] This surfaces the essence of the Nazi view, that successful propaganda is simple though not simple-minded and must avoid the miasma of mind: 'Intellectualism is the worst enemy of propaganda. I am constantly reaffirming this.'[204]

He also recorded his antagonism to censorship, claiming that the regime was suppressing too much news.[205] He had already announced a relaxation of restrictions on the press, 'and we must spread our wings a little';[206] again, this constant tension between the need to control and the need to stimulate. And he adds 'I take measures to mitigate the crazy excesses being perpetrated by our censors', and further 'things that are common knowledge all over the world are being treated as state secrets'.[207] And for Goebbels, humour in the Reich, or rather its absence, was no laughing matter and he discussed the importance of humour in media output, 'we are taking everything so dreadfully seriously'.[208] He felt it made no sense to enforce an authoritarian dogmatism, to 'proselytise from morning to night', but 'arousing the masses, that is something we know a thing or two about'. Satire, for example, should have 'room to manoeuvre', and a particular concern was that the venerable periodical *Simplicissimus* was being checked and censored by too many different authorities: 'I put a stop to it.'[209] There really were of course some comedy films produced in Nazi Germany, such as *Hot Wine Punch* (1944).[210]

Goebbels and the spinning of Stalingrad

Stalingrad, and the concomitant loss of confidence by the German military that the war could be won, was the ultimate challenge to Goebbels. Germans, initially nervous about the war, had begun to warm to it. Hence the horror of the winter of 1941–2 and later of Stalingrad at the end of 1942 when 330,000 German soldiers were surrounded.

Stalingrad had always been primarily a propaganda struggle for the city of Stalin's name, a battle over a symbol. After all, the city could have been merely bypassed and bombed to smithereens. Beevor claims that 'altogether, the Axis must have lost over half a million men', and the cost was also material, as for example with the loss of nearly 500 transport planes during the airlift.[211] Perception management went beyond the mere control of information and priming of public sentiment, for newsreels now suggested Germany had almost won at Stalingrad, the supreme command bulletins saying that these were 'mopping up operations'.[212] According to *Das Reich* (mid-October) 'a symbol smoulders in endless fields of ruins. A mighty power has received the decisive blow.'[213] Triumphalist newsreels fed into glowing civilian morale reports. Sixth Army headquarters announced on 26 September that 'the battle flag of the Reich flies over the Stalingrad party building'.[214] Goebbels as usual warned against this. But he 'had limited control over the press' and complained that 'I feel absolutely not guilty of this obvious fizzle. I have always encouraged greater frankness in news.'[215] Concerned about excess optimism, he ordered editors to focus on the toughness of the battle and his mood on Stalingrad vacillated. On 19 October he ordered recipients of the Knight's Cross to return for press interviews.[216] He wanted to remind people of the magnitude of the achievements so far; since the city still had not fallen, signs were erected showing the distance to Stalingrad. And names, Red October, Red Barricade and such like, were excised from reports lest German Communists be encouraged.[217] SD reports for December noted public disquiet, but even Goebbels was not really aware of the imminence of the end. His propaganda machine was as ever without shame, and German soldiers at Stalingrad listened to the radio announcing 'This is Stalingrad' followed by a choir singing 'Silent Night'; some went along with this charade, others were furious.[218]

Then, the Sixth Army facing imminent extinction, the official silence rarely punctuated by mention of the city, newsreels sought refreshment elsewhere, such as North Africa, the Atlantic, as well of course as Nazi ceremonial: they could for example legitimately show Soviet forces being driven back on other fronts.[219] The author of this media strategy was Adolf Hitler, it was he who 'approved the final draft of each day's OKW communiqué' and he who 'consistently removed any mention of Stalingrad'.[220] Goebbels proclaimed this to be a German Christmas, suggesting austere duty and, perhaps, to prepare for the fall, and ordered that 'the German press must prepare appropriate coverage of the victorious outcome of this great battle in Stalin's city'.[221] He told his ministerial conference the end was near so that what he meant by victory in this context was purely symbolic.[222] Only on 16 January had the OKW communiqué admitted that the army was surrounded, and then it began to use ominous language like 'eternal honour' and 'valiant and sacrificial struggle'.[223] Funeral music played over the radio for several days, thus was the announcement of the death of the Sixth Army at Stalingrad made obliquely and even with dignity.[224] Hence on 16 January the army was fighting a 'heroically courageous defensive struggle'.[225] Then suddenly the Reich press chief spoke of 'heroic sacrifice' – without prior warning. The Sixth Army was itself a manufactory of propaganda, thus its headquarters message to Hitler on 29 January: 'the swastika flag still flies over Stalingrad. May our struggle be an example to present and future generations never to surrender in hopeless situations so that Germany will be victorious in the end.'[226] But 'Hitler was not, of course, concerned with saving lives, he was interested only in creating potent myths.'[227] Goebbels carefully crafted the public obituary of the Sixth Army with an 'appropriately heroic form. I work out all the details with the Führer personally, who fully approves my proposals.'[228] He instructed newspapers on how they were to project the defeat, for example the press was ordered to use the word Bolshevik, not Russian:[229] 'the whole of German propaganda must create a myth out of the heroism of Stalingrad which is to become one of the most treasured possessions in German history'. The army communiqué had to be phrased so as to 'move hearts for centuries to come', to rank with Caesar and Frederick the Great.[230] Then on 3 February 1943, accompanying the opening bars of Beethoven's Fifth, came the Special Announcement:[231] 'True to its oath of allegiance, the Sixth Army under the exemplary leadership of Field Marshal Paulus has been annihilated by the overwhelming superiority of enemy numbers ... The sacrifice of the Sixth Army was not in vain ... They died so that Germany might live.'[232]

But nothing was said about surrender.[233]

Then there followed three days of national mourning with the closure of entertainment facilities; all the stations played solemn music, but no flags were flown at half-mast.[234] The regime denied there were any survivors, but Soviet international radio was claiming 91,000 prisoners and their postcards were now reaching Germany, offering in the government's view 'an access door to Germany for Bolshevik propaganda'.[235] On the Saturday every cinema and theatre closed its doors. The daily press directive gave a universal rhetorical template – the days of mourning to honour the brave sons, fought to the last bullet and so forth, 'broken the back of the Bolshevik assault on Eastern front', heroic battle, heroic epic, stirring event, outshines every feat of heroism known to history, sublime example of heroism, self-sacrificing dedication, blaze forth like a sacred flame, eternal heroism.[236] All this was supposed to 'assure the nation of the victory it is now more fanatically than ever resolved to win', thus via verbal sophistry real defeat became mythic victory.[237] The press really did report along these lines – they said that Stalingrad became a necessary sacrifice that held Bolshevik forces down while the front was strengthened elsewhere.[238] The Nazis often did this, they provided not merely rhetoric but rationale, one that seemed tightly logical in the absence of superior information; and the focus of the propaganda then proceeded to neglect the Eastern Front as the Reich's defeated legions staggered back. The rhetoric now seized instead on the perversity of Allied grand strategy, the folly of the West's dalliance with the Bolshevik entity and the inevitability of its surrender of Europe in the event of a German defeat.[239]

Conclusions

The Hitler regime, with the sovereignty of propaganda as its core organising principle, offers us insights which go beyond the mere events of Europe in the years before and during the Second World War, for they tell us much about the ability of humanity to be persuaded, our symbol mindedness, the binary cognitive universe we apparently inhabit. The propaganda directors of the Reich really did understand the apoliticality of people, they recognised quickly, if not initially, the fact that for the masses politics is always boring. Their task was to make it both less boring, through direct propaganda, and also to talk about it in an entirely fresh and different way through indirect propaganda, the medium of entertainment. Nazism was garbed in the symbolism of the previous and the familiar, recent traditions perhaps but traditions none the less; historical romanticism and stirring musicals and smart productions are vistas of normalcy, they created an aura of contemporaneity that connected Germany to the rest of the advanced world, particularly America.

The focus was not, however, on selling the party but on selling Hitler. An attempt to sell the party would have been unintelligible without the life-giving aura of Hitler's personality, for bereft of him it would have been a moribund idea. He animated it with his persona, he made it real and he transcended it; for he made loyalty intimate, not something given to an abstraction, and a corrupt one, like a political party, but loyalty to himself personally. The core of the propaganda remains the act of a great and mesmeric actor, a rhetorician, the grand dramaturgy that blended script and physical performance; all else was mere support act and stage prop designed to sustain the performance, and anything that detracted from it was edited out. He was the precise human personification of an imprecise credo and he was the credo, it was inseparable from him.

Notes

1 Joseph Goebbels, 'Knowledge and Propaganda', 1928 (9 January); 'Erkenntnis und Propaganda', *Signale der neuen Zeit. 25 ausgewählte Reden von Dr. Joseph Goebbels* (Munich: Zentralverlag der NSDAP, 1934), pp. 28–52.

2 Bracher, *German Dictatorship*.
3 Alan Bullock, *Hitler and Stalin: Parallel Lives*, London: Fontana Press, 1993.
4 Fest, *Hitler*.
5 David Welch, *Propaganda and the German Cinema, 1933–1945*, London: I.B. Tauris, 2007.
6 Ibid.
7 Ibid.
8 Bytwerk, *Bending Spines*.
9 Bullock, *Hitler and Stalin*.
10 Ross, *Media*.
11 Kallis, *Nazi Propaganda*.
12 Bytwerk, *Bending Spines*.
13 Kallis, *Nazi Propaganda*.
14 Ibid.
15 Joseph Goebbels, 2 November 1940 in Fred Taylor (ed.), *The Goebbels Diaries 1939–1940*, London: Sphere Books, 1983.
16 Kallis, *Nazi Propaganda*.
17 Hoffmann, *Triumph*.
18 Kallis, *Nazi Propaganda*.
19 Bytwerk, *Bending Spines*.
20 Ibid.
21 Ibid.
22 Jonathan Petropoulos, *Art As Politics In The Third Reich*, Chapel Hill, NC: University of North Carolina Press, 1996.
23 Bytwerk, *Bending Spines*.
24 Ibid.
25 Oren Hale, *The Captive Press in the Third Reich*, Princeton: Princeton University Press, 1964.
26 Bytwerk, *Bending Spines*.
27 Jeffrey Herf, *The Jewish Enemy: Nazi Propaganda During World War II And The Holocaust*, Cambridge, MA: The Belknap Press, 2006.
28 Nigel Farndale, *Haw-Haw: The Tragedy of William and Margaret Joyce*, London: Pan Books, 2006.
29 Kallis, *Nazi Propaganda*.
30 Ibid.
31 Ibid.
32 Ibid.
33 Petropoulos, *Art*.
34 Ibid.
35 Ibid.
36 Ibid.
37 Rees, *Warning*.
38 Ibid.
39 Ibid.
40 S.W. Mitcham, 'Kleist', in Corelli Barnett (ed.), *Hitler's Generals*, London: Weidenfeld and Nicholson, 1989.
41 Ibid.
42 Ibid.
43 Ibid.
44 Ibid.
45 Robert Edwin Herzstein, *The War that Hitler Won*, London: Hamish Hamilton, 1979.
46 *Goebbels Diaries*, 7 November 1940.
47 Albert Speer, *Inside The Third Reich: Memoirs by Albert Speer*, London: Macmillan, 1970.
48 Bracher, *German Dictatorship*.
49 *Goebbels Diaries*, 13 December 1940.

50 *Goebbels Diaries*, 12 October 1939.
51 *Goebbels Diaries*, 15 October 1939.
52 Kallis, *Nazi Propaganda*.
53 Bytwerk, *Bending Spines*.
54 Kallis, *Nazi Propaganda*.
55 Bytwerk, *Bending Spines*.
56 Ian Kershaw, *The Hitler Myth*, Oxford: Oxford University Press, 1987.
57 *Goebbels Diaries*, 4 December 1940.
58 *Goebbels Diaries*, 15 October 1940.
59 *Goebbels Diaries*, 10 October 1939.
60 *Goebbels Diaries*, 4 December 1940.
61 *Goebbels Diaries*, 10 December 1939.
62 *Goebbels Diaries*, 3 February 1940.
63 *Goebbels Diaries*, 1 November 1940.
64 *Goebbels Diaries*, 17 October 1939.
65 *Goebbels Diaries*, 15 October 1939.
66 *Goebbels Diaries*, 18 December 1939.
67 *Goebbels Diaries*, 4 December 1940.
68 *Goebbels Diaries*, 13 December 1940.
69 Speer, *Memoirs*.
70 Bytwerk, *Bending Spines*.
71 *Goebbels Diaries*, 6 November 1940.
72 *Goebbels Diaries*, 15 November 1940.
73 Hale, *Captive Press*.
74 Ibid.
75 Jeffrey Herf, *Nazi Propaganda for the Arab World*, New Haven: Yale University Press, 2009.
76 Ibid.
77 Herzstein, *War*.
78 Herf, *Arab World*.
79 Ibid.
80 Rutherford, *Hitler's Propaganda*.
81 Herzstein, *War*.
82 Michael Burleigh, *The Third Reich: A New History*, London: Pan Books, 2001.
83 Ibid.
84 Herf, *Arab World*.
85 Stark, *Modern Political Propaganda*.
86 Bracher, *German Dictatorship*.
87 Herzstein, *War*.
88 Hale, *Captive Press*.
89 Hoffmann, *Triumph*.
90 Rutherford, *Hitler's Propaganda*.
91 Ibid.
92 *Goebbels Diaries*, 17 November 1940.
93 Ross, *Media*.
94 Kallis, *Nazi Propaganda*.
95 Ibid.
96 Bytwerk, *Bending Spines*.
97 *Goebbels Diaries*, 1 November 1940.
98 Franz Neumann, *The Structure and Practice of National Socialism 1933–44*, New York: Harper and Row, 1966.
99 Kallis, *Nazi Propaganda*.
100 Bytwerk, *Bending Spines*.
101 Ibid.
102 Ibid.

103 Welch, *Propaganda*.
104 Anthony Pratkanis and Elliot Aaronson, *Age of Propaganda: The Everyday Use and Abuse of Persuasion*, New York: Henry Holt, 2001.
105 *Goebbels Diaries*, 3 November 1940.
106 *Goebbels Diaries*, 8 November 1939.
107 *Goebbels Diaries*, 18 December 1939.
108 *Goebbels Diaries*, 17 January 1940.
109 Rentschler, *Ministry*.
110 Ibid., citing Lacoue-Labarthe.
111 Herzstein, *War*.
112 *Goebbels Diaries*, 29 May 1939.
113 Herzstein, *War*.
114 *Goebbels Diaries*, 24 October 1939.
115 *Goebbels Diaries*, 18 December 1939.
116 *Goebbels Diaries*, 27 January 1939.
117 *Goebbels Diaries*, 4 November 1940.
118 *Goebbels Diaries*, 10 August 1940.
119 Hoffmann, *Triumph*.
120 Welch, *Propaganda*.
121 Peter Paret, 'Kolberg As Historical Film And Historical Document' in John Whiteclay Chambers and David Culbert (ed.) *World War II Film and History*, New York: Oxford University Press, 1996.
122 David Culbert, 'Kolberg: The Goebbels Diaries and Poland's Kolobrzeg Today', in John Whiteclay Chambers and David Culbert (ed.) *World War II Film and History*, New York: Oxford University Press, 1996.
123 Hoffmann, *Triumph*.
124 Culbert, 'Kolberg'.
125 Paret, 'Kolberg'.
126 Ibid.
127 *Goebbels Diaries*, 7 May 1943, 5 June 1943 and 1 December 1944 in Culbert, 'Kolberg'.
128 *Goebbels Diaries*, 5 June 1943 in Culbert, 'Kolberg'.
129 Cited in Culbert, 'Kolberg'.
130 Culbert, 'Kolberg'.
131 Baird, *Die for Germany*.
132 Culbert, 'Kolberg'.
133 Paret, 'Kolberg'.
134 Welch, *Propaganda*.
135 Ibid.
136 Ibid.
137 Ibid.
138 *Goebbels Diaries*, 2 December 1944.
139 Welch, *Propaganda*.
140 Ibid.
141 Ibid.
142 Ibid.
143 Culbert, 'Kolberg'.
144 J. W. West, *Truth Betrayed*, London: Duckworth, 1987.
145 *Goebbels Diaries*, 7 November 1940.
146 *Goebbels Diaries*, 21 October 1939.
147 *Goebbels Diaries*, 2 October 1940.
148 *Goebbels Diaries*, 23 October 1939.
149 *Goebbels Diaries*, 14 November 1939.
150 *Goebbels Diaries*, 15 October 1939.
151 Herzstein, *War*.

152 Giles MacDonogh, *A Good German: Adam von Trott zu Solz*, London and New York: Quartet Books, 1989.
153 *Goebbels Diaries*, 1 February 1940.
154 *Goebbels Diaries*, 15 October 1939.
155 *Goebbels Diaries*, 12 October 1939.
156 *Goebbels Diaries*, 13 October 1939.
157 *Goebbels Diaries*, 7 October 1940.
158 *Goebbels Diaries*, 9 January 1940.
159 *Goebbels Diaries*, 13 December 1939.
160 *Goebbels Diaries*, 28 October 1940.
161 Herzstein, *War*.
162 Nicholas J. Cull, *Selling War: The British Propaganda Campaign Against American "Neutrality" in World War II*, New York: Oxford University Press, 1995.
163 Ibid.
164 Ibid.
165 Ibid.
166 Ibid.
167 *Goebbels Diaries*, 25 October 1939.
168 *Goebbels Diaries*, 1 October 1940.
169 Herzstein, *War*.
170 Ibid.
171 *Goebbels Diaries*, 6 November 1939.
172 Herzstein, *War*.
173 Kershaw, *Hitler Myth*.
174 *Goebbels Diaries*, 9 October 1939.
175 Rentschler, *Ministry*.
176 *Goebbels Diaries*, 19 January 1939.
177 *Goebbels Diaries*, 8 November 1939.
178 *Goebbels Diaries*, 15 October 1939.
179 Speer, *Memoirs*.
180 Ibid.
181 Ibid.
182 Ibid.
183 Herzstein, *War*.
184 Ibid.
185 *Goebbels Diaries*, 15 October 1939.
186 *Goebbels Diaries*, 14 November 1939.
187 *Goebbels Diaries*, 13 December 1939.
188 *Goebbels Diaries*, 25 January 1940.
189 Rentschler, *Ministry*.
190 *Goebbels Diaries*, 24 January 1939.
191 Hoffmann, *Triumph*.
192 *Goebbels Diaries*, 13 October 13 1939.
193 *Goebbels Diaries*, 5 November 1939.
194 *Goebbels Diaries*, 16 November 1939.
195 Rentschler, *Ministry*.
196 *Goebbels Diaries*, 29 October 1940.
197 *Goebbels Diaries*, 3 December 1939.
198 *Goebbels Diaries*, 21 November 1940.
199 Ibid.
200 *Goebbels Diaries*, 15 December 1940.
201 *Goebbels Diaries*, 13 December 1939.
202 *Goebbels Diaries*, 18 November 1939.
203 Ibid.
204 *Goebbels Diaries*, 15 December 1940.

205 *Goebbels Diaries*, 12 November 1940.
206 *Goebbels Diaries*, 5 December 1939.
207 *Goebbels Diaries*, 16 December 1939.
208 *Goebbels Diaries*, 15 November 1940.
209 *Goebbels Diaries*, 7 December 1940.
210 Hoffmann, *Triumph*.
211 Beevor, *Stalingrad*.
212 Bytwerk, *Bending Spines*.
213 Ibid.
214 Beevor, *Stalingrad*.
215 Bytwerk, *Bending Spines*.
216 Beevor, *Stalingrad*.
217 Ibid.
218 Ibid.
219 Bytwerk, *Bending Spines*.
220 Ibid.
221 Beevor, *Stalingrad*.
222 Ibid.
223 Bytwerk, *Bending Spines*.
224 Kershaw, *Hitler Myth*.
225 Bytwerk, *Bending Spines*.
226 Beevor, *Stalingrad*.
227 Ibid.
228 Bytwerk, *Bending Spines*.
229 Beevor, *Stalingrad*.
230 Ibid.
231 Kershaw, *Hitler Myth*.
232 Beevor, *Stalingrad*.
233 Kershaw, *Hitler Myth*.
234 Beevor, *Stalingrad*.
235 Ibid.
236 Bytwerk, *Bending Spines*.
237 Ibid.
238 Ibid.
239 Sebastien Saur, 'The Soviet Union in *Signal*', *Histoire de Guerre*, 38 (2003).

PART II
Operational
Implementing the Nazi brand

3

PROMOTION

Political marketing communication: the ministry of illusion

> *But there was one theater of the war where Americans were still not big enough, sure enough or smart enough to challenge Axis superiority – the theater of political warfare or propaganda ...*
> – Life, 22 March 1943

> *The Admiralty is even worse. We complain that there are no photographs of the sinking of the Bismarck. Tripp says that the official photographer was in the Suffolk and that the Suffolk was too far away. We say, but why didn't one of our reconnaissance machines fly over the ship and take photographs? He replies: well you see, you must see, well upon my word, well after all, an Englishman would not like to take snapshots of a fine vessel sinking. Is he right? I felt abashed when he said it. I think he is right.*
> – Sir Harold Nicholson, Diaries

Part 1: Marketing method

The Nazis were not leaning against an open door but were confronting the same problems that proselytisers had faced throughout human history as enthusiastic evangelists amid a disinterested mass. Those soaring truths that the Nazi had understood and internalised had to be communicated. At this period of time the marketing concept had not self-liberated from the sales era but nevertheless we can see the emergent outline of the 'marketing mix'. Marketing communications (advertising, public relations, selling) are the articulative, public-image-regenerating function of the product market campaign; and the Nazis were in fact intuitively (if not entirely consciously) using target marketing techniques such as direct mail, as well as concepts like relationship marketing and segmentation, and the methodologies of market research. The analogy was with commerce:

> It was widely agreed that the huge expansion of commercial markets and the political public required new forms of communication to replace the personal

bonds of smaller traditional communities. Just as commercial 'propaganda' enabled producers to communicate with the mass, anonymous market of consumers, so did political 'propaganda' become indispensable with the emergence of a mass electorate.[1]

Neumann claimed that 'the superiority of National Socialist over Democratic propaganda lies in the complete transformation of culture into saleable commodities'.[2] And another authority observed:

> The simplicity and primitiveness of National Socialist ideas and programmes, theses and revolutionary recipes, visions and power ideas that might have repelled the unbiased bystander were helped along by the mastery of slogans and a vast propaganda effort skilled in the appeal to mass emotions and in the use of varied and unscrupulous means.[3]

Yet strategy is not discernible in much that the Nazis did, since in everything, including ideology, foreign policy and law, they appeared to have made the script up as they went along. Marketing and communications existed as an ad hoc arrangement independent of any strategic plan. In general, the era of struggle had great influence on the methodology of Nazi propaganda. As with many revolutionary movements, they relied on the methods of the street fight: poster, polemic, rhetorical riposte. These methods continued to be used in government, and against their domestic and global enemies. As tacticians they were cunning and quick-witted but they lacked strategic depth; they employed the subterfuge of a revolutionary organisation with a clandestine past and judged tools purely by utility rather than ethics. The Nazis were originally influenced by the tactics of the Italian Fascists. However, they

> made much more determined and successful use of modern means of mass communication through the unrivalled combination of force and persuasion, terror and propaganda, pseudo-legal measures and deception and violence. The National Socialists pitted the technique of the fait accompli of quick, propagandistically inflated sham successes against the effectiveness of institutional and traditional safeguards.[4]

Methodology

The Nazis combined a dreamlike vision with pragmatics, the aim being to proselytise an evangelical formula, printed and circulated, with occasional latitude for interpretation and licensed heterogeneity. Regular monthly circulars supplied local groups with guidelines, lists of available speakers with topics, whole catalogues of leaflets and pamphlets for a variety of specific needs, slide shows and films: all these were to be ordered directly from the national headquarters in Munich, with payment in advance.[5] And there was always a fund of good, homespun advice, for example that it was important to manage expectations – followers were ordered to avoid calling a slide show a 'film'. Micro-detail was a facet of their work. Thus advice to the Nazi Party members on saliva emission must be one of the more curious managerial directives of all European political history: they thought stickers should be small enough so the person applying them will have enough saliva. They should be brief (few, but vivid words). The layout should be good, with no white space at the edges where graffiti can be written. Each party member should carry such stickers with him. One can apply them quickly and inconspicuously.[6]

The purpose of stickers 'is to be a constant reminder to the indifferent and gradually unsettle them', since '"many drops wear away stone" … Incessantly, repeatedly, people must see our stickers!' (once more, the belief in repeated exposure effects – an article of faith).[7] So the focus was always on the operational detail, on application, such as the need for a special group skilled in hanging posters.[8] They tell us, for example, that propaganda must be attached in ways that make it difficult to remove (but also to avoid the illegality of random application). And they note what works, such as using glass and display windows as a base, or multiple stickers – 'identical stickers next to each other make a good effect'.[9] The Nazis of course already had a working model of how a regime could obtain and sustain a powerful propaganda base. It was the Communist model and it was one with which the Nazis were very familiar; they learned eagerly from their rivals, whether the British in the trenches or the Communists in the streets. From the Bolsheviks they absorbed the importance of discipline and implementation, of careful organisation and gimmickry, the manufacture of slogans and so on, and of the choreography of crowds. They also borrowed specific methods – hence they stressed the so-called 'neighbourhood newspaper', which was imitating the Communists.[10] And there was the factory newspaper, designed for a specific factory (we are reminded that such newspapers are monitored by the central office).[11] They were omnivorous, pillaging multiple early century cultural sources for their ideas on political evangelism and the management of public theatre, from Lenin to Busby Berkeley. Yet the Nazis were not the first highly organised post-war ultranationalist party, and there were examples to learn from. Thus German Racial Defence and Defiance had claimed some 200,000 members which it had inherited from the Fatherland Party and 'it ran a sophisticated propaganda machine, churning out millions of leaflets and putting on mass meetings where the public numbered thousands rather than the hundreds which Drexler's organisation was able to attract'.[12]

The Nazi propagandist was a trained propagandist and necessarily so; it was not a job for inspired amateurs since it was the sacramental essence of the regime, the way messiah and message were enabled. There was no obvious reservoir of trained propagandists to turn to so they had to create them, and the numbers of personnel involved in propaganda both full and part time were immense. The Nazis organised continuous voter and recruitment drives and established speaker schools for 'primitive yet forceful propaganda speakers' where 'the trainees memorise standardised texts and rehearsed answers in front of a mirror – techniques more in keeping with acting than politics'; such training was also achieved through correspondence courses.[13] Specialist schools offering a methodology of proselytisation had graduated 6,000 speakers by the end of 1932.[14] Incentive systems were market mechanisms that rewarded via numbers, they were 'simple, self-correcting, self-reinforcing. Future tactics were adjusted accordingly and could be constantly fine-tuned by this feedback system. Thus the Nazis' incessant campaigning may be primarily explained by the interlink between mass meetings and financing methods.'[15] The range of materials and the self-financing via sales (e.g. buttons) made for a culture of persuasion that was both flexible, devolved and, to a degree, marketised; local leaders could select combinations suited to local needs.[16] Moreover, the party was ordered to be inclusive. The Nazis understood that community organisations and recreational clubs and affiliated groups, such as war veterans, contained many who could not be addressed directly in Nazi terms or brought over to active Nazi participation. The great events and meetings were consequently positioned as community foci so that other associations were mobilised, like the German Colonial League.[17] The aim was to permeate all of Germany with the party's idea and to absorb civic organisations of every kind. Nazism as an evangelical creed knew no boundaries; as long as there remained a single individual to be converted its activities would never cease. Everything was to be cajoled into the Nazi bailiwick: 'if we make other organisations part of propaganda campaigns, we give them a National Socialist character'.[18]

Distribution According to Stark, party newspapers needed to be distributed widely if they were to be effective, including at railway stations. Reading rooms were to be provided with copies of the paper, and seemingly minor acts were important for success, such as 'accidentally' leaving propaganda material at the station, the barber's or the doctor's surgery.[19] Stark stressed the effectiveness of party members in normal clothing distributing brochures at busy corners: here is a softening of the Nazi image (again the elements of technique, hiding the rip-roaring fanaticism). Old marketing nostrums were applied to the political sphere, for example the importance of the free brochure (people love something when it is free). But literature was only to be distributed in cases where it would be read immediately and they consequently recommended train stations (those getting on the train but not coming off, and long-distance trains) or in the morning at factory gates (but not at the end of the shift). They also recommended giving such material to people waiting in unemployment offices. In short, 'anywhere where time must be killed and people will read anything'. And small leaflets could be left in shops. Stark thought the best success came through systematic distribution of 'advertising material' from door to door and advises 'this should be done only on Sunday mornings so that people can read them at their leisure with their morning coffee … Get every citizen a brochure on Sunday morning!'[20]

Content A leaflet 'should contain a brief, easily understandable idea' and 'the most important phrases should be in bold or larger type'. They warned against 'tiny text, bad organisation and boring material'. They also suggested that the same message should be conveyed through varying forms, for example identical slogans, some with caricatures, and the flyers in various colours. They were constantly testing what was working and what was not. They were innovators who tried new things out in order to observe their effectiveness – for example claiming that the street-distributed flyer had now lost its impactfulness and was soon thrown away.[21]

Parsimony Parsimony was another characteristic of their early operation – 'but we are a financially weak party', and this candid point was made by others. In 1927 they complained that 'because of the fear and cowardliness of German businessmen, they also get few German advertisements'.[22] Each local group, according to Stark, should train the propaganda wardens, and this shows how the propaganda effort penetrated the microsphere, the block and the street.[23] Each party member was instructed to help in disseminating the Nazi message; it was a duty incumbent on all, for example in distributing house-to-house propaganda. A propaganda warden who was unable to get the funds was unsuitable for the role. And Nazi holidays/festivals were to be conducted without incurring major costs: 'ideally, propaganda pays for itself', that is to say, again, that it operates through a process of marketisation. Propaganda activities were self-sustained also by the sale of books and literature and newspapers.[24]

Sales force motivation

The Nazi Party was intensively organised at local levels with a concomitant propaganda presence. Fourteen regional districts were fed by 30,000 local groups, all of which engaged in propaganda via 14,000 propaganda functionaries; activity at the local level could be intense, for example the sixty-two meetings in Breslau on a single day in March 1939.[25] The block warden was the parish agency for distributing propaganda, offering leaflets, pamphlets, tickets to party meetings and so forth.

Time and again the tragedy of the apathetic and disinterested folk comrade emerges. The Nazis have to sweat in their electioneering. The folk consciousness was slothful and unwilling; people did not appreciate the epic era in which they lived, or the historic, histrionic answer which Adolf Hitler gave to all their questions and fears.[26] According to these activists, the masses were difficult both to motivate and inspire due to their languor and inertia: 'it is particularly effective if it can dominate the streets during an election. Unfortunately, one has to work hard to persuade supporters to do this. The only place we succeeded in doing really well in the streets was in Hanover, and that took constant effort'.[27] An interesting remark: it was not easy to get people to display the swastika, here in 1932, in Germany! Not only the masses, but also the party members were beginning to yawn. A *Propaganda Primer* by Franz J. Huber complained that leaflets were simply given out with their message left unexplained.[28] After the assumption of power, party members were becoming too grand, 'leaders and block wardens often resist such tasks, saying that they are not message boys. Their feelings are understandable, given the general level of overwork, but it is not acceptable.' Those distributing leaflets were once persecuted, but the new era of struggle was against comfort and indifference, 'to-day and in the future, the propagandist has job after job to do'. And selling race consciousness effectively was also apparently difficult. Racist ideas are not an election bestseller but, 'even if they unfortunately were often neglected in election propaganda', they remained 'the highest thinking of the People's Movement'.[29]

Hitler had envisaged a massive party numbering ten per cent of the population and this had almost been reached in 1939 when membership went beyond five million; membership of the Hitler Youth became compulsory from 1936.[30] In both Russia and Germany it was the party which organised, both indirectly through associated groups and directly through party networks of 'primary organisation'.[31] But the party was also a voluntary organisation. Membership was optional, and members had to be motivated, for example to applaud visiting speakers and sustain the party's standards. The party had a truly monumental and ponderous sense of its own dignity and it was terrified that this would be jeopardised by supine folk comrades. Latent popular enthusiasm had already been dissipated at the very dawn of the regime: in the autumn of 1932 'the only sure way that Northeim's Nazis could get the townspeople to a meeting was to make it an "evening of entertainment"'.[32] In other words, 'pure political propaganda had lost its pulling power for the average Nazi voter. Popular apathy and exhaustion had replaced curiosity and enthusiasm, the financial bubble had burst, and the party, denied the external focus provided by the expectation of imminent victory, had begun to attack itself. Nazi hyperactivism also exacted a toll from the leaders on the local level; they were burned out in a hurry ... The whole thing was like a death-or-glory cavalry charge ....'.[33] Nazi Germany had begun to find Nazism, *inter alia*, boring.

Marketing output

The ministry's 'product' can be quantified, which, while no measure of effectiveness, at least establishes the supreme importance which the Nazi state granted propaganda. It was costly because it was a major industry, a roaring torrent of reports, bulletins, journals such as *Will and Way* which discussed techniques. And this industry was tenacious. Klemperer records that Nazi material was published almost to the last day: *Das Reich* still appeared when Berlin was surrounded.[34]

Peace The Nazis cite a number of genres of propaganda – the written, the spoken, but also cultural gatherings, and a further typology they articulated was propaganda through mass marches: 'all that needs to be said is that good discipline is the best propaganda'.[35] They seemed ubiquitous, and that was part of their skill – for example 1,300 meetings in Saxony just before the state elections in June 1929.[36] In 1930 the party held some 34,000 meetings, considerably more than any of its rivals; in the early days the Nazis held about three rallies a month in the town of Northeim.[37] But there was overkill with an excess of meetings and of compulsion: over the course of one winter alone, party members had to attend an event every three days and schedules were prepared eight months in advance.[38] Yet not everything in the Reich was duty. If the meetings and parades could be described as business, then the films and radios were a form of pleasure. And the party never stinted on quantity. For example, there was the advent of the aggressively promoted People's Receiver, with production beginning in May 1933. It was one of the least expensive receivers in Europe and a double first from the regime – an extra communication channel and a gift of social policy, a happy confluence of markets and politics, constituting half of radio sales in 1933 and two-thirds in 1934.[39] The price was then reduced and a mini-version offered; the People's Receiver had accounted for perhaps 2.5 million new sets by 1937.[40]

Then there was the production line of brief propaganda films – 140 in 1935 alone.[41] The regional film offices sponsored shows for 48,000 villages. There were 120,000 such screenings in 1935, with twenty-one million visitors.[42] Thus the system was not a fixed structure either, as it went where the people were and motorised film units invaded remote towns and communities. In wartime these were a significant adjunct to the propaganda state and some 1,000 film vehicles offered nearly a quarter of a million village screenings in 1940 alone, reaching an audience of fifteen million.[43] In the autumn of 1939 UFA (*Universum Film-Aktien Gesellschaft*: German motion-picture production company) more than quadrupled the number of its newsreel copies, thus ensuring they remained up to date, and in May 1940 the length of newsreels was doubled to forty minutes.[44] And newly commissioned newsreel theatres offered up to ten hour-long shows per day.[45] There were no scruples either about Sabbath violation, with popular Sunday performances of Nazi films like *Victory in the West*.[46] Yet in one area productivity was calculatedly reduced; film production and film companies were rationalised and the new approach was to make fewer and better films, a privileging of quality over quantity, a 'strategic decision to prioritise big budget blockbusters' with output almost halving between 1939 and 1942.[47]

War This industrialisation of communication, this determination to deafen the cognitive environment with polemic, thus reached its apogee at the beginning of the Second World War. By the winter of 1941, the RPL had distributed two million brochures, seven million placards and more than sixty million magazines, as well as sixty-seven million leaflets.[48] The illustrated weeklies reached around nine million readers during the war.[49] The party had a total of nearly 10,000 speakers.[50] Propaganda then was a major wartime industry and an accompaniment to everything the Reich did; it was an integrated part of its daily act. The NSDAP claimed 30,000 slideshows and 200,000 public meetings over the war's first year.[51] Then there was the poster campaign, whose domain was incendiary polemic but also teaching people how to live civically in a newly constrained environment, one that was alive with danger. Thus such posters 'might appear in editions of 300,000 (Take Cover From Flak), 650,000 (Flag Is Victory) and even one million (Down With Germany's Enemies). By the end of 1940, 700,000 photos of Hitler had been produced and distributed; 23,000 colour posters were produced to accompany the film *The Eternal Jew*'.[52]

And propaganda was an ancillary of conquest. The arrival of German armies in North Africa was inevitably accompanied by a vigorous propaganda thrust to win new friends for Germany. As usual the propaganda manufactory went into hyperbolic overdrive. Rommel asked for 'immediate implementation of active propaganda in Egypt': 700,000 leaflets were ready in response, and this was not a one-off process as there were further instalments and consignments.[53] Herf estimates that up to four million Arabic-language leaflets were distributed either by plane or soldiers and agents. Germany claimed to broadcast in Arabic to Iraq, Egypt, Syria, Palestine, Transjordan, Saudi Arabia, Yemen, Aden, the Gulf Emirates, Morocco, Algeria and Tunisia, with slogans like 'Egypt for the Egyptians'.[54] Radio Berliner made five shortwave Arabic programmes every day.[55]

Goebbels's bureau: range and limits Goebbels's Propaganda Ministry and its parallel organisation within the Nazi Party itself, the RPL, became an obese bureaucracy, a behemoth of sections and departments manufacturing the entire imaginable range of public communication: everything from sport to state festivals to exhibitions about the Jews to communications with Germans living abroad.[56] His employee numbers grew voraciously, from 350 in 1933 to over 1,900 by 1941.[57] And Goebbels's power of ministry lay also in prohibition. In November 1933, 1,500 publishers were banned and (self-) censorship became universal. His Reich Press Chamber exercised power via, for example, publication licences and the blacklisting of journalists.[58] Its *raison d'être* was non-objectivity.

Localism versus centralisation Propaganda imagery and message became centralised since the benefits of coherence and consistency outweighed those of parochial individualism. This in turn made for brand insistence and clarity. It ensured unity of theme, such as 'The Enemy Sees Your Life'; all Germany would witness the same idea rather than a chorus of discordant voices.[59] Control was extreme – groups were told they must 'follow precisely the plans of the propaganda central'.[60] Even by the end of the 1920s there was already a stress on the central release of literature, because if each local group self-produced then 'propaganda would be dissipated and the unified strength of the movement, which above all should be expressed in its propaganda, would suffer'.[61] Local groups could only distribute the official leaflets from the propaganda department of the national party. The corporate control displayed here was intense. If the local group wanted a particular kind of leaflet it had to be submitted in draft form and could only be printed with national party approval.[62] An image system which is ad hoc, locally produced and subject to variation cannot have that consistent, all-crushing quality which the Nazis sought. Already the planning and precise organisation for May Day in the town of Northeim had been ordained from on high, 'the first instance during the Nazi seizure of power when the higher offices of the party intervene decisively in the local organisation of mass propaganda. National propaganda headquarters sent out comprehensive and detailed instructions – the entire programme of the day, co-ordinating it with the pre-planned national radio schedule.'[63] By 1935 the party had forgotten any residual arguments for localism, and the propaganda imperative engendered an implacable national bureaucracy: 'for example, a directive sent to the town of Northeim in November 1935 concerning a forthcoming meeting contained three pages of detail on how it was to be staged, including a step-by-step programme, and down to the last exact words in introducing the Speaker'.[64]

Market research

The Nazis were market leaders in political consumer research, for the operation of the propaganda bureaucracy did not rest on the edifice of intuition or ideology alone: one source of information on public opinion was the security service of the SS as well as the reports of the Reich Propaganda Offices. Characteristic of Goebbels's approach 'was the system of monthly reports on grass roots sentiment which he demanded from the Gauleiters, urging them to send agents into the bakeries, butchers' shops, grocery stores and taverns, to find out what people were saying, material which the RPL then used in developing its campaign literature'.[65] And Hitler appreciated the value of political intelligence, endorsing the analysis of rumours and the opinions held by one group or another 'in order to appreciate the relative value of these elements of information'.[66] More generally, new market research techniques were emergent that might inform opinion research, and new schools of study were formed after 1933 such as the Institute for Market Research, the Society for Consumer Research and the Institute of Economic Research.[67]

The SD reported back to Goebbels and sought out the temperature of public opinion. Germans came to believe 'Germany is conquering herself to death', and 'England loses all the battles but wins the war.'[68] Goebbels knew this. The Nazis were enthusiastic public opinion researchers given the important constraint that, in a police state, people were naturally reluctant to talk freely.[69] This meant that Nazi propagandists had to find other ways of assessing public feedback, using cunning methods such as cinema ticket receipts so that although public opinion could not be quantified, it could at least be roughly gauged.[70] And the system was also capable at some level of actually responding to public opinion within the constraints, again, of totalitarian control and the straitjacket of ideology. Public opinion research under the Nazi regime presented a special set of demands, namely the interpretation of nuance, alertness to vague signals and the recognition that formal statements of opinion might conceal as much as they reveal. There were spies everywhere – a kind of Nazi version of mass observation, reporting on people's comments such as their response to films and newsreels; reports therefore functioned as market research since they recorded public reaction. Their methods may have been crude, and restricted by the overall intimidation of the population, but the important point is that some kind of primitive feedback loop existed (at one stage Hitler's Chancellery was receiving more than one thousand letters and petitions per working day).[71] There was often investigation of some sort. For example, on 7 December 1944 Goebbels screened *Kolberg* to an audience of around 150 Nazi leaders, and their responses to the film provided market research data for the rough cut and changes were made.[72]

One of Goebbels's market research experts became a leading post-war authority on opinion research. Elisabeth Noelle-Neumann had a fellowship at the University of Missouri in 1937, which she used to study American polling techniques; she was 'very proud that she was invited to a tea party all alone with Hitler before she went over to perform her patriotic task in America'.[73] She would later write a book, *The Spiral of Silence*, which articulated what became a foundational concept in political opinion research (she quoted an animal psychologist – 'To a wolf, the howling of another wolf is a powerful stimulant to follow suit').[74] She also advised a subsequent German leader: 'In the 1990s Noelle's influence became even greater. She was a prominent political adviser to Chancellor Helmut Kohl. Her book was constantly praised and commented upon in the UNESCO-funded *International Journal of Public Opinion Research*, which she co-edited.'[75]

Tactical opportunism The propaganda culture – partly because of the level of personal control exercised by Goebbels himself – had an inherent flexibility and could respond opportunistically. For example, the tone and content of the films evolved, moving as the war continued towards light relief and pure escapism for war-weary publics in such vehicles as the *Adventures of Baron Münchausen*. The Third Reich, in other words, was neither entrepreneur nor rigid bureaucracy but in fact combined elements of both, sometimes in creative, sometimes destructive tension; it operated without a pre-determinate and micro-ideological route-map, only vague precepts. Ideas both could and sometimes did rise from below. For example, the Edelweiss case:

> Speer describes a women's delegation wanting to meet Hitler and asking what his favourite flowers were. No one knew; but since the question was likely to arise again it was decided that an answer must be found. In the end one of Hitler's aides, completely on the spur of the moment, said it was Edelweiss. The only reason for that choice was that it came from the Bavarian mountains. From then on the Edelweiss was the Führer's flower.[76]

There was no pre-invented libretto. There existed, for instance, neither concept nor master plan for a euthanasia programme; the idea was originally inspired by a letter to a senior Nazi minister (Bouhler) from the father of a severely disabled son.[77] The basic, non-negotiable demand was total loyalty to Hitler himself: everything else, providing he did not object, was invented.

Some party literature in the early days would even self-define as 'The Hitler Movement' as well as 'National Socialist', for it was a charismatic movement as well as a political party. The Nazi message was responsive, an interpretation of citizen wants. Gellately argues that 'Nazi propaganda couldn't be crude, on the contrary it was meant to appeal to the Germans, match up with everyday German understandings', and thus 'far from forcing unwanted or repellent messages down the throats of the population, Hitler and the Nazis carefully tailored what they said, wrote, and especially what they did, in order to win and hold the support of the people'.[78] The NSDAP polemicist had to immerse himself in mass consciousness to be an effective persuader and acquire the ability to see the world as the people saw it: 'it is above all essential that the propaganda warden does not follow advice coming from a desktop, but rather that he is and remains in close contact with the people'.[79] And they add

> only he who understands everyday life, and who is familiar with events in political life, will be able to speak effectively to the people he wishes to persuade. Without that contact, advertising speaks in a dead language. To see with the eyes of the masses – that is the whole secret of effective propaganda.[80]

They recognised the importance of neighbourhood, that is, all politics is local.

Segmentation and targets

The formula was a propaganda assault, and segmentation: 'we delivered an election newspaper to every house in every village, adjusting it to the audience. One version was directed to the rural population, another to the industrial districts.'[81] Von Wilucki speaks of the different letters to people they knew to be Marxists, farmers, retirees, women and so forth (again, the citation of Marxists as target group): 'determining success is naturally possible only in a few cases. But many stories testify that such letters achieve their goal'.[82] They wanted their propaganda to convert the enemy, even the Communists. But they therefore rejected the idea of an undifferentiated text for a homogenous market: 'the text can be cruder in working-class districts, more subtle in the style of the Berlin democratic papers in middle-class neighbourhoods'.[83] Astonishingly they observed, three years before the assumption of power, that 'the swastika should be used sparingly at first, particularly in middle-class districts': again, the acute sensitivity to market segmentation (and an interesting piece of advice, given the organisation that was proffering it).[84] What intrigues is the depth of manipulation; the Nazis in other words did not simply proceed with a propaganda steamroller, though that was part of the show, as they were also capable of deftness, nuance and surprise. Evans has summarised thus:

> beyond this very general level, the Nazi propaganda apparatus skilfully targeted specific groups in the German electorate, giving campaigners training in addressing different kinds of audiences, advertising meetings extensively in advance, providing topics for particular venues and picking the speaker to suit the occasion. Sometimes local non-Nazis and prominent sympathisers from conservative backgrounds shared the platform with the main Nazi speaker. The elaborate organisation of the party's subdivisions recognized the growing divisions of German society into competing interest groups in the course of the depression and tailored their message to their particular constituency. Anti-Semitic slogans would be used when addressing groups to whom they might have an appeal; where they were clearly not working, they were abandoned.

The Nazis adapted according to the response they received; they paid close attention to their audiences, producing a whole range of posters and leaflets designed to win over different parts of the electorate. They put on film shows, rallies, songs, brass bands, demonstrations and parades.[85]

Originally the worker was specifically solicited and thus in 1930 'The Nazi propaganda effort, indeed, was directed in particular at workers, borrowing images and slogans from the Social Democrats, attacking "reaction" as well as "Marxism", and presenting the party as heir to Germany's socialist tradition.'[86] By 1932 it was the middle class, the bedrock of Nazi support: for by now sixty per cent of their vote was middle-class, and the remaining forty per cent were manual workers and their families.[87] Apart from with the Communists, they succeeded least with Germany's Catholic population (only fourteen per cent of Catholic voters supported them).[88] As Sheridan Allen observes in his town study of Northeim, 'Nazi propaganda went beyond pure acting. The system driving it was coupled with a shrewd appreciation of what was needed at the time for each element in the population.'[89] The desire was for an internalised and not a purchased loyalty, one which would forgive the party its sins. In marketing terms, the Nazis also stressed personal selling or what they called a face-to-face propaganda. This was a very serious business – 'only in this way can we prevent false opinions and therefore nip the resulting morale problems in the bud ...'.[90] Face-to-face 'is the best way to deal with rumours, which must be answered by propagandists immediately with the appropriate information'.[91]

Segmentation was also pursued via another marketing innovation, personal direct mail. Targeted and political direct mail at that stage in history was rare. Although used by the radio demagogue Father Charles Coughlin in pre-war America, it did not really enter the American political arsenal until the direct mail entrepreneur Richard Viguerie succoured the New Right in the post-Watergate era. So the Nazis were innovators; they did not merely borrow and internalise some handbook of propaganda but completely re-wrote the text. Thus 'following the example of one local group, we use personal letters. The letters were provided to local groups. The letters were then reproduced either by hand or by machine, with personal address. Two days before the election, they were delivered to all voters, not only our supporters'.[92] The Nazis offered something for everyone. But every political party now adopted its own political language and imagery to distinguish itself from rivals in the most significant medium of the Weimar Republic, print, and they framed their appeals at clearly defined occupational groups.[93] And there were different projections of Hitler for different target markets – for example, a 'trained' Hitler for the old elite, a fighting Hitler for ex-servicemen, a thoughtful Hitler for the scholarly. The party had many masks for different audiences. Hitler's skill according to contemporary observers was to address each member of his audience separately in understandable language. There were numerous different sections of the party, for example for teachers, lawyers, doctors and students.[94] Nevertheless it was with the middle class that the Nazis really succeeded:

'Programmatically both anti-capitalist and anti-proletarian, conservative and revolutionary, the NSDAP appealed to a middle class threatened by modern capitalism, fighting off proletarianisation, and hoping for "any kind" of change. Proletarianised classes sought to win back their lost prestige in the fight against a changing world.'[95]

The Nazis then intuitively recognised that no market, including a political market, is an amorphous mass accessible via an undifferentiated appeal, but rather a fragmentation of subgroups, each of which has to be addressed in terms of its own interests and through the medium of its own emotional discourse. So the posters targeted women, but in surprisingly sensitive ways, in some cases bereft of Nazi imagery and Nazi tone. Workers were another segment/target market, via the posters for example, since Communism was a rival brand. There was no monolithic German consciousness and therefore appeals were modulated to the needs and prejudices of the different social groupings; hence farmers were a distinct market subset and they had their own National Socialist journal, the *Rural Post*. The local political marketing of the Nazi Party really was based on a finely tuned market segmentation strategy, with provincial meetings for businessmen, civil servants, pensioners, workmen and other target groups. Local context was observed. For example, anti-Semitism was downplayed if there was no real regional tradition. Think national, act local – the ability to interpret and apply a national template to local conditions – was thus recognised in the original Nazi push for power (although subsequently, as we have seen, local sensitivities were not indulged). They might acknowledge the importance of local agency, who has the most direct contact 'with the manifold changes in the moods and attitudes of the various circles within the population'.[96] Party analysts, for instance, clearly understood the importance of orators knowledgeable about country matters: 'changes in the political attitudes of the rural population can result only from using methods that can be understood by them and are consistent with their psychology'.[97] They were not, however, able to persuade the party to develop a separate cadre of agricultural speakers confident in rural affairs. Nevertheless, after 1929 the party succeeded in Protestant rural areas most, and least in the cities.[98]

Youth The National Socialists specialised in youth recruitment, with Hess creating their student organisation in 1921: the new party was 'seductively adventurous' for young males – the sloganeering, fights, parades, trips, planning of attacks.[99] They were the expression even of a generational alienation, its discontent with a somnambulant status quo incapable of confronting the employment crisis.[100] The Nazis became, almost, the youth party: 'in 1931, almost 40% of the members were under 30, compared with 20% in the SPD [Social Democratic Party of Germany]'; and it was thus in the universities, with their professoriates indifferent to democracy and their toxic sludge of Nazi propaganda (as with the campaigns against 'Jewification'), that the Nazis had their best 'storm', their greatest impact.[101] The Nazis exploited what has been called an 'ideology of adolescence';[102] the emphasis was as much beguilement as discipline, for it was the soul, the internalised commitment, that the Nazi sought. Youth was the delighted object of enchantment, offered a 'dazzling array' of programmes, their energy released, their curiosity intoxicated. The aim was capture, to harness the incontinent idealism and soaring imagination of the young. An SS article claims that the Nazis offer youth 'room for creative fantasy' (the word 'creative' became one of their favourite terms at this time), it speaks of:

> the opportunity to transform great thoughts to reality outside the lecture hall. We offer the realisation of dreams on a world scale, a common Germanic will, a common European will. We fill the spiritual vacuum left by liberalism with the magic of a worldview that draws self-confidence and meaning to life from race and the blood of one's ancestors.[103]

Thus the popular youth 'film hours' at local cinemas, preceded by a march in formation, always included the weekly newsreels.[104] It was a political education with 11.2 million youth visits to cinemas in 1942/3 to watch 45,000 performances, and 2.5 million of these visits were outside the urban parameters in rural church halls and similar venues.[105] The focus on youth was to pay a grim dividend in Normandy, where the Hitler youth division, the Twelfth SS Panzer, lost 10,000 of their force;[106] and the Panzerfaust boy was a staple of the battle of Berlin.

Women Women became very important in the Nazi calculus, and by 1932 'Goebbels's propaganda apparatus targeted specific groups of voters with greater precision than ever before, above all women.'[107] But posters aimed at women are entirely different in feel from those aimed at, say, farmers or unemployed working-class males. They emphasise nurture, and there is no militaristic or violent imagery. One poster shows a baby suckling the breast of a large blonde woman and behind her is the relief of an old medieval German town: the mother appears to be formed from the earth, and the baby with her, she is silhouetted against a huge bright sky.[108] The baby is of course fair and extremely big. The mother has no kind of decoration or jewels or makeup. The meaning of this is certainly not obscure: she represents and is symbolic of the fecund German Reich, a kind of metaphor.

Under Nazism the right to work would not exist for women, that at least is what other parties were telling them, and they said that Nazis would harvest their sons for future wars.[109] So the party faced an interesting problem in convincing women. It is quite extraordinary that even a 1927 Social Democrat poster could depict and therefore anticipate the classic post-war porno-kitsch image of a terrified young woman cringing before a uniformed, jackbooted Nazi brandishing a whip.[110] Even then, the notion of Nazi depravity was sufficiently established to be turned into popular political coinage. Specific invocations by the other parties to 'women's issues' had limited impact, however – the KPD (the Communist Party of Germany), for example, promised most and benefited least.[111] But while the Nazis were increasingly convincing women from 1930 they did not yet actively target them, and yet by 1932 they were garnering more votes from women than men in Protestant areas.[112] So they began to flood the female voter market with propaganda, their promise, a husband for every woman and a job for every husband; and this resonated, a claim to emancipate women from employment not from man, to emancipate women from emancipation.[113] At

FIGURE 3.1 German mother

the Sports Palace, Hitler asserted that while women were men's life companions, it was men's responsibility to earn the daily bread: the 'moist and glistening eyes' of the front row women were noted.[114] And there were now various National Socialist women's organisations – the German Women's Order Red Swastika (1923), the Nazi Women's Association (1931); and in power Mother's Day became a major public occasion, and then there were those Mothers' Crosses.[115]

Targets: anti-Semite Anti-Semitism in much of the mainstream media of the Third Reich was less visible than we might imagine. The *Berliner Illustrirte Zeitung*, for example, or films like *Kolberg*, lack sinister Jewish characters or

FIGURE 3.2 Women's labour service

indeed any significant reference to the Jews at all. One might tentatively suggest that what the Nazis were really doing was again engaging the very modern consumer access method of market segmentation: the anti-Semites were a distinct target market and thus anti-Semitism was appropriated by particular media and particular media vehicles, particularly the paper *Der Stürmer* of Julius Streicher. The 'Toadstool' series of cartoon books, for example, published by *Der Stürmer*, showed images of grotesque Jews and their wickedness, such as the story of how 'Little Hans' refuses a sweet from a fat (pederastic?) Jew.[116] Such images were disgusting to more than a few Germans, and it is questionable how far

FIGURE 3.3 Nazi women voters pre-1933 poster

they deliberately sought them or actively chose to watch films such as *Jew Süss* or *The Eternal Jew* or *The Rothschilds' Shares in Waterloo*. These media texts were labelled anti-Semitic and the audience knew what it would get. But it was not, necessarily, a national audience. It was an audience which constituted a particular market, namely those citizens of the Third Reich who had a particular appetite for incendiary anti-Semitic imagery: 'Anti-Semitism, by contrast, was of significance only for a minority, and for a good proportion of these it was only incidental. The younger they were, the less important ideology was at all …'.[117] However, this point is controversial and could not be confidently asserted without an exhaustive content analysis of media in the Third Reich.

Communists Communists were an enemy to be fought, but, crucially, they were also potential converts to the Nazis, hence the ambivalence which qualifies the antagonism. Communists and socialists functioned both as a rival brand and as a market to be won. The Marxist was treated with respect by writers such as Fritz Oerter, and sound advice was offered on the rhetorical arts of ideological conversion:[118] Oerter fears that 'we do not impact their worldview' – a crucial aim for a Nazi – and that they were not gaining Marxist converts. 'Marxist' (i.e. SDP) propaganda was effective at defending market share. The view on Marxists was that they were deviant folk comrades who just needed convincing arguments – hence the importance of persuading and targeting Marxist workers (in marketing argot, suspects must be made prospects). The Nazis would supply rhetorical ammunition for post-hoc rationalisation of emotional choice, but they recognised that the workers seek a rational as well as an emotional justification. The Nazi view of Marxism was that it privileged rational materialism over emotion and heart, but Nazi speakers were ordered to have a thorough understanding of their perspective in order to win Marxist converts:

> the movement speaker has the task of making it easier for Marxist workers to break with the past. He must be ready and able to give these citizens a logical base for the emotional longing of National Socialism. He can do that only by knowing the Marxist world view as well as he knows his own.[119]

They recognised that the erudite Marxist speakers were tough adversaries. There was always hope of redemption. Hence in 'How Worker Hartmann became a National Socialist' (another *Der Stürmer* story for children), the Hitler Youth, out on a hike, are told by Worker Hartmann how years ago he was unemployed and became a Communist and then realised its leaders were Jewish. Worker Hartmann interrupted a Jewish agitator and asked him why he always talked about Russia – '"we want to do something about Germany not Russia". Later, I found my way to Adolf Hitler.'[120] But as for its efforts with the working class, the Nazis succeeded not with organised labour but with the unemployed, targeting unemployment offices and recruiting young Communists from here into the SA.[121] Yet they remained concerned about proletarian loyalty after the assumption of power and for the rest of the life of the regime (for example, the worker was now to be mollified by new post-work light radio programmes).[122]

Part 2: A darker darkness: fraud and deceit

Neumann argued for the opportunism of National Socialism – it takes or discards theory in so far as the situation determines: 'National Socialism is both capitalistic and anti-capitalist. It is authoritarian and anti-authoritarian.'[123] Surely that was because it was primarily driven by the need to exploit propaganda opportunities, and hence the ideological incoherence which so many have remarked upon. Neumann claimed Nazism ingratiated with any official force that was amenable to it 'but it will not hesitate to flatter anti-authoritarian movements when that is more expedient', and 'it will promise liberation for racial minorities and will sacrifice any minority if the government of the country involved is ready to co-operate with Germany. National Socialism is for agrarian reform and against it, for private property and against it, for idealism and against it'. However, he argues that 'what National Socialism has done and is doing with its propaganda is to take advantage of the soft spots in the social body'. It exploited tensions and antagonisms which were pre-existing. National Socialism had two aspects – 'the destruction of whatever remnants of spontaneity are left and the incorporation of the population into a super machine'.[124] And thus another scholar observes 'at the moment of growing economic, social, and political crisis, the instruments were ready for offering up a melange of seemingly plausible stereotyped explanations, solutions, and cures and simultaneously holding them in check politically'.[125] The Nazis, it appears, were pragmatists.

Tactics: manipulation

Spin The opportunities for what we have since come to call 'spin', for creating an instant interpretive framework for fluid events, were considerable. For example, the Germans were reluctant to fight another war but Hitler sought to justify that event 'ex post facto', and this was a challenge for Nazi propaganda – to make the war intelligible, to promote an unpopular appeal within the context of an existing value set.[126] Thus the pact with the Soviet Union was 'spun' with all the artifice the Reich could muster. *Signal* tried to justify the Soviet alliance by claiming that Germany, and previously Prussia, was Russia's historic friend, whereas England was its antagonist. Molotov's November 1940 visit was accorded three pages of evasive text, and imagery.[127] The meeting was evoked in fatuous verbiage – 'to deepen by a personal and renewed contact the current communication of the ideas within the framework of the friendly relations between the two countries'.[128] But by June 1941 *Signal* had proclaimed the USSR as the enemy, the famous pact being just a cynical time-buy, a Soviet Russia that sought Germany's and then the world's subjugation.[129]

Goebbels's operational thesis of propaganda anticipated the voguish idea of being on and off message. Thus Goebbels was the universal media enforcer of ideological rectitude who would give an official a dressing-down 'because he has allowed the magazines to stray too far from the correct line'.[130] The powers of hyperbole and assertion were supplemented tactically with unverifiable claims, the manufacture of threats and the massaging of data. The Nazis were opportunistic, devious, cynical and manipulative in every conceivable way. This was of course a world without ethics, but it did not mean communication, marketing and propaganda could operate without restraints; far from it. Nothing therefore was truly true about the communications of the Reich, but rarely was the distortion fully false either. For example, one of their greatest charges, the equation of Judaism with Bolshevism, could be made credible by the existence of residual Jewish involvement with the Russian Revolution (and intelligible in the context of the *ancien régime*'s revival of ethno-nationalism). Even the lies about the war's causality contained a particle of truth. Some Volksdeutsch had been killed by Poles; Poland had been granted German lands at Versailles; the Norwegian annexation may have frustrated the British move (Germany argued that the assault on Narvik was pre-emptive); and though improbable, the USSR might have attacked at some opportune future moment. Paranoia would conjure into fact the very enemies it feared in theory.

Tactical opportunism The Nazis' methods evolved out of the streets. Flexible and innovative, they betray their revolutionary paternity, they hit hard, exploit any opportunity. The propaganda organisation exhibited the two typical and in many ways antithetical characteristics of the Third Reich – that it was both a highly centralised bureaucracy, and yet could on occasion demonstrate surprising plasticity; they had a tactical approach, not a strategic one, as would befit a party originating in the beer halls. And a proselytising organisation arose from a market context, that is to say, the political marketing techniques of the rival parties such as the Communists and the SDP were observed by the Nazis, borrowed for the purposes of their propaganda and re-engineered. The Germany of those early days was a laboratory, a learning tutorial where the Nazi was the tutor as well as the taught. So Nazis could admire the SDP's grasp of the role of symbols and their clever manufacture of a rival icon to the swastika (the three arrows of the Iron Front).[131] It was a competitive process. Their intelligence-gathering enabled them to 'anticipate the best slogan and use it in advance' – thus 'the SPD had planned to use the slogan "for the welfare state of millions against the welfare state of the millionaires"'.[132] The Nazis pre-empted this by circulating a similar one. The parties copied each other because of their mutual visibility: during the rise to power propaganda activists were supplying local groups with brief summaries of the latest arguments used by opposition parties, plus recommended counter-arguments. Party newspaper deliveries over the last ten days of one campaign 'allowed us to refute the opponents' lies each day, and remind readers of our goals and previous accomplishments'.[133] Thus rapid rebuttal was their technique against the socialists, against the Weimar government, the Communists, then later against the British press and the British government during the war. The aim was to sabotage Allied broadcasts by alacrity of response, thus for example Goebbels: 'my Paris interview grossly distorted by agency: I have a denial rushed out for foreign consumption'.[134]

Tactics: deceit and fraud

Fraud The new Reich signalled how it intended to proceed right at the beginning of the regime. The appointment of Hitler as chancellor was greeted with the inevitable torchlight parade but the crowd was a small one. So it was simply repeated:

> the world has often seen photos and films of that torchlight parade, but the marchers they saw did not parade on the night of 30 January 1933. It was

much too dark that night, the marchers were ragged, and no searchlights had been positioned. The whole parade was re-staged a day later by Goebbels, with floodlights and cameras in place and film directors to channel the brown-shirted, torch-carrying marchers. It was the first typical Third Reich propaganda fabrication.[135]

Honesty was never an objective:

> a democracy can never completely divorce propaganda from truth because there are competing propaganda machines and they must ultimately prove their value by actual performance in the social life of the nation. National Socialism has no political or social theory. It has no philosophy and no concern for the truth.[136]

The frauds and fabrications of the Nazi regime were of course on a lavish scale, everything from the deceitfulness of Munich to the bogus prospectus on which the invasion of Poland was justified, to the distortions of the final months. There were the straight lies, such as those of Goebbels in the autumn of 1944 when he referred to 'brave fighting divisions, which are constantly being strengthened, and which are receiving ever better weapons'.[137] Indeed, the ideology of the regime was built on an earlier forgery, the Protocols of the Elders of Zion, which supposedly furnished evidence of an international Jewish conspiracy. The International Olympics Committee was one such target for Nazi fraud, an epic swindle: Avery Brundage was shown documents allegedly proving the rights of Jews to engage in sport, and he also concluded 'America can learn much from Germany.'[138] International pressure was always cynically manipulated, for example the 1934 Jewish ritual murder edition of *Der Stürmer* provoked international outrage; most copies had been sold when Hitler finally banned it.[139] And during the war neutral nations could be fed an image of British atrocity (e.g. 'mass murderer' Harris, head of Bomber Command).[140] And as Leonard Doob reminds us, Nazis, especially, understood the power of shameless denial and assertion.[141] Thus Ambassador Henderson described how he raised the question of the concentration camps with Göring:

> His answer was typical. After listening to all I had to say, he got up without a word and went to a book case from which he took a volume of the German encyclopaedia. Opening it at *Konzentrationslager* (concentration camps) he read out 'first used by the British in the South African War'.[142]

And for Nazis of course the camera could certainly lie; a photograph was not a historic record but a persuasive device, and if it failed to make its point with sufficient clarity it could be doctored and the features enhanced. Thus photographs of alleged Jews might not be horrible enough for *Der Stürmer*, and so images were manipulated by for example 'undressing' a photograph of a woman standing next to a 'Jewish' man; another little deceit was the post-hoc Judaisation of non-Jewish figures in American public life, for example a photograph of boxer Jimmy Durante's nose was compared to that of a monkey in *Der Stürmer*.[143] But the attempt to sanitise the international image of a nation so thoroughly toxified with anti-Semitism could never succeed. Information leaks. For example, *The Manchester Guardian* photographed a 'Jews forbidden' notice in the Bavarian village hosting the Winter Olympics; even a regime as efficient as this one had not managed to remove all signs and Count Baillet-Latour threatened to cancel the Olympics.[144]

The propaganda system was a structure of organised public deception that could manufacture a logic and an explicandum for any state initiative, however criminal, notably in justifying the extrajudicial exterminations of 1934. Journalists in the Third Reich 'became transmission belts for the lie'.[145] The propaganda regime was flexible enough to accommodate events as they arose and provide a plausible rationale which the public could accept. The serious test of this was the so-called Night of the Long Knives, in effect, a mass murder of elite individuals, carried out by the regime itself with no recourse to judicial decision, something astonishing among such a process-minded, bureaucratic and juridically obsessed people. The Nazis achieved this by talking up the threat to the state itself. And the Second World War began, not with the German invasion of Poland, but with a propaganda fraud, the bogus Polish assault on Gleiwitz radio station (Upper Silesia). The cosmetics of this fraud included clothing the corpses of murdered concentration camp victims in German army uniforms.[146] Hitler then proceeded to roar to the assembled Reichstag that 'fire has been returned' and that 'bomb will be met with bomb'. Editors were ordered not to speak of war but of a 'response to [the] Polish attack'.[147] During the war itself, German assertions were often deceitful: one leaflet claimed the German town of Freiburg was bombed by the Royal Air Force on 10 May 1940. But this was untrue. The Germans bombed their own town, mistaking it for a French one.[148] The Nazis said this 'treacherous attack' left fifty-seven civilians including thirteen children dead.[149] Later, V1-distributed literature referenced a book published about the deliberate bombing of civilians (even citing the book's code). But no such book existed.[150] Nor had there been a BBC report that 6,000 houses in Hastings had been destroyed, or a United Press one that Folkestone had lost over 5,000 homes.[151]

Foreign commentators could easily fall victim to Nazi frauds. On 1 September 1939, for instance, the American radio commentator R.G. Swing claimed there had been twenty-one Polish penetrations of Germany on 31 August and repeated the lie about Gleiwitz, turning the murdered prisoners into Polish insurgents.[152] At every point in the Nazi expansion, atrocity was used as an alibi for assault: 'Goebbels was authorised to launch a propaganda offensive to show how miserably treated the Sudeten were' and he would 'fill the papers with atrocities carried out by the Czechs against ethnic Germans'.[153] A Sudeten Nazi was murdered by another Sudeten German: 'the German radio jumped on the story right away. More Czech brutality it thundered.'[154] There were, then, deceits, straight lies, but also the device of suggestion, eschewing categorical statement. For example, a cartoon showed a rocket with a human face actually chasing a soldier on a motorbike, and this leaflet invokes third-generation terror weapons which would be able to target individuals (i.e. anticipating the smart bomb by over half a century).[155]

For international consumption the socio-pathology of the regime, its murderous subtext, were rinsed in emollient language and imagery: 'Until now researchers always held as an established fact that *Signal* represented a "sweet" version of Nazi propaganda, and that anti-Semitism and racism – which otherwise so principally characterise the Hitlerian ideology – were missing. Admittedly, a cursory glance at the magazine tends to give such an impression.'[156] But a more rigorous reading discovers the artifice: 'Closer examination, however, cannot support this opinion: a thorough reading of *Signal* reveals a magazine strongly tinted by racism, this notion being gradually eclipsed and replaced by less and less dissimulated anti-Semitism as the outcome of the war is becoming more and more clear.' This was achieved via a rhetoric that was allusive and elusive, the light plantation of dangerous ideas almost below the threshold of consciousness. Thus the 'idea of the subhuman is alluded to indirectly in certain phrases like "primitive beings, half savages", towns and cities "devoid of any trace of civilization" and thus in the Russian war it is "civilisation itself which fights against cruelty. It is a question of life and death."'[157]

Fantasy Of the Nazis' ability to concoct a pure fantasy, there can be no doubt. Rumour was a tactic in the closing months. The illusions persisted to the end of the regime, with graffiti proclaiming the imminent arrival of General Wenck's army; and, it is often forgotten, even beyond the end, not merely with the threat of the 'werewolf' campaign, but also the appearance of Nazi graffiti in areas which had already been captured by the Allies. Even in March 1945 newsreels were still showing a radiant Goebbels, and German troops heroically retaking towns captured by the Russians. Goebbels continued to insist on ultimate victory, and his wonderful idiosyncrasy, the 'Volkssturm' or People's Storm – note again the facility for branding – was willed into existence. Finally, illusion and reality became co-mingled and it was difficult to disentangle the two. For example, there were the bogus statistics, such as the claim that rapes in the United States increased threefold between 1942 and 1943, thereby proving 'that Americanism has reached its limits'.[158] Military threats could always be argued away, not with emotion but via a credible parody of logic as the crutch for belief. Jansen, for example, argued in July 1944 that much of the British air force had to be redirected to attack V1 launch pads and therefore could no longer support ground forces – 'it is this spirit, and German genius, that will determine the outcome of this war for our existence'.[159] And in October 1944 *Berliner Morgenpost* asserted that since March the German air force's flak units had shot down 5,000 enemy planes,[160] while earlier in the war (1942) Winkelnkemper claimed a British air force 'expert' had said they could not replace their air losses.[161]

Misguided missiles: using the enemy's propaganda against them

Their art lay also in turning the enemy's polemics against them, to conscript Allied vitriol as Axis propaganda; since these were open societies their citizens could publicly express a range of views, some of them frankly murderous. The Reich gave these venomous, often provincial tractarians a German, even a global audience. For example, their claim was that the British nurtured a fanatic hatred of the German Volk, from the governing elite and media to ordinary people writing letters to papers, and to the clergy. And many such opinions were supplied, from H.G. Wells himself to a Miss Ida Turnbull from Cambridge to a Mrs H. McRae Smith to a Mr H. Foster of Linton to Miss Dot Critshlay of Newtonfield – all pretty ordinary Britons writing to their newspapers lusting for the obliteration of Germany.[162] The Revd F.O. Baker, for example, demanded the instant extinction of twelve German cities. Another clergyman says 'the orders to the bombers of the British air force should be: wipe the Germans out! ... If I could, I would wipe Germany off the map. The Germans are an evil race.' Hence also *The Manchester Guardian* – 'it is necessary to kill as many Germans as one can, whether they are wearing the uniform or not'.[163] Winkelnkemper concludes 'The British were and are in bloody earnest about annihilating the entire German people.'[164]

Theodore Kaufman During the war itself a Newark (New Jersey) businessman, Theodore N. Kaufman, wrote a book advocating the sterilisation of all Germans; but finding no publisher he produced it privately.[165] Goebbels subsequently printed a version (five million copies, he claimed): 'Kaufman remained a mainstay of German propaganda for the remainder of the war, his last major appearance coming in a late-1944 pamphlet titled *Never!* which collected every manner of allied threat against Germany.'[166] Kaufman checked every box – he was Jewish, American and proposed the kind of tactics and rhetoric the Nazis employed themselves:

> it is the bounden duty of the present generation to those yet unborn, to make certain that the vicious fangs of the German serpent shall never strike again ... for to the German, Nazi or not, the mailed fist is as stimulating and meaningful a symbol of all the aims and aspirations of his nation as the Statue of Liberty is to the American.[167]

Naturally the Nazis inflated this local flea into a global dragon. Thus a poster proclaiming 'Germany Must Die!' illustrates Kaufman's proposal to redistribute German territory, showing him alongside Roosevelt, Stalin and Churchill.[168] This fitted satisfactorily into the idea of an existential threat propagated by Hitler himself, the ethos of apocalyptic anti-Semitism and the myth of the hidden Jewish manipulator; here was the evidence they needed. Whether this was actually believed is irrelevant, since it helped to sustain a political climate. As ever with Nazi propaganda there is a faint sliver of truth on which to rest the baroque edifice of illusion, for subsequently the 'Morgenthau Plan' actually did discuss returning Germany to an exclusively agricultural state after the war. It got nowhere. Thus 'the American Jew Morgenthau' proposes turning 'the industrial land of Germany into a potato field'.[169] But Morgenthau was a member of Roosevelt's cabinet, so the true Morgenthau plan could validate the false Kaufman plan; if this had been intentional it was a masterful piece of psychological prestidigitation. While the idea of unconditional surrender emanated from Roosevelt, the 'disastrous' consequences of that decision were exacerbated by the Morgenthau plan, since Goebbels exploited these things to fire German morale.[170]

Projection Projection was one of the principal devices of Nazi rhetoric, for their propaganda was an uncannily accurate chronicle/double image of the record of Nazi malfeasance. They made their enemies enact their crimes. Thus in 1941 Wolfgang Diewerge imagined the vengeful implementation of the 'Kaufman Plan' in language and imagery that exactly captured the sense and reality of the concentration camps:

> Slowly, column after column is taken into the barracks and tents where mocking Jewish doctors carelessly sterilise them. Each German soldier has to pay the Jews for the operation. Then the troops march, under Jewish and Soviet supervision, to forced labour in the wild mountains of the Balkans, to Siberia or the Arctic Sea. There, the heroes of this war, the Führer's soldiers who bear the Knight's Cross, will be tortured with the 'tested' methods of Soviet forced labour, serving as slaves under miserable conditions, until starvation releases them from this life. Meanwhile Jewish doctors will be set loose on German women and children. Whatever perverse lusts have been imagined in the dark minds of the Jewish people will be unleashed on defenceless German women and children. All the bestial horrors that were previously conducted in the dungeons of the GPU, far from public view, can then be carried out in the 'offices' of Jewish humanitarians ...[171]

Similarly with the film *Ohm Krüger*'s climax, the concentration camp scene, which was plagiarised from a great rhetorical moment in Eisenstein's *Battleship Potemkin*: Boer women inmates complain about the maggot-ridden food, as the Potemkin sailors had done. As in *Potemkin* the protest leader is shot. And the biggest fantasy of all was Radio Berlin's claims late in October 1941 that the Soviet Union had exterminated four million Muslims.[172] This assertion of an Islamic Holocaust is another example of projection, a claim of course impossible for the people in the Middle East to verify – the main criteria in the Berlin factory of fibs.[173] And Kaufman's rhetoric was reminiscent of Goebbels's, so by circulating it the Nazis were promulgating the identikit of their own practice. It was the language of the Third Reich in reverse – right down to the use of the rhetoric of disease ('immunize itself forever against the virus of Germanism' etc.), and advocacy of a final solution to a racially sourced existential threat: 'sterilisation has become a byword of science, as the best means of ridding the human race of its misfits: the degenerate, the insane, the hereditary criminal'.[174] Their problem was also a rising global awareness of the dark side of Nazism. They responded to this in various ways, for example in Stanley McClatchie's *Look to Germany* through the device of satirical admission, an interesting example of manipulative technique since here the target was the English-speaking and American world. Always the Nazis suggest the outline of their crimes, in this case by publicly admitting the suspicions and ridiculing them. Yet these crimes were, or became, true: the Nazi propaganda text therefore is invariably a kind of shadowland, a make-believe world where, via such devices as projection or satire, the reality of what they truly did is hinted at. Thus the book carries headings like HITLER SAYS THAT GERMANY NEEDS THE RICH LANDS OF THE SOVIETS. BUT WHAT DID THE FÜHRER REALLY SAY?[175] It offers a picture of a craftsman absurdly burdened with clocks and components, following the heading 'NAZI SECRET AGENT ... dressed as a watchmaker ...' And we are shown A TWENTIETH CENTURY TORTURE CHAMBER where 'the victim of the Nazis is strapped into this horrible looking machine. Then, by means of mysterious rays invented by a German named Röntgen, his body is rendered totally transparent. Such methods are resorted to daily in every German hospital.' Then there is 'the victim who has become transparent' (i.e. an anatomical model). Their propaganda becomes in fact a history of Nazi misdeeds which they attributed to others – to Jews or the English; the manipulation, the murderousness, is not their enemy's but their own.

Intellectual subversion Unobtrusively, a new language began to take hold of people's minds. The Nazis had a gift for banality, for making workaday and acceptable what was in effect profoundly radical and a portal to atrocity. The new values were un-interrogated because they were made to appear universally shared. A good example is the film *I Accuse*, a response to the campaign by the Catholic Church against the euthanasia programme and specifically Cardinal Galen's pulpit denunciation where he publicly and tearfully reproached the regime. This pseudo-intellectual story was cast as a courtroom drama, with the jury seeking to pronounce on the fate of a professor whose wife was crippled by multiple sclerosis, and whose doctor had refused her a painless death; at her request, the husband gives her the lethal medicines. A friend, however, denounces him.

And it was a plausible film, with ostensibly balanced debate among the jury members, but also the subtly subversive moments (such as when the elderly hunter on the jury recounts how it is necessary to kill the dogs he loves when they are old, and in great pain). *I Accuse* reveals how important a public pseudo-discourse of ethical rationality was in the Third Reich. So the Nazi response to the forced (and only partial) abandonment of their euthanasia programme had been to make a movie. *I Accuse* had a deep impact. It was seen by eighteen million people,[176] and stands comparison with modern television documentaries on the subject, certainly using much the same argumentative formula and rhetorical construction. It offers insight into the way the propaganda regime operated – sow doubt, create ambivalence. A mature and balanced argument, eloquently articulating all perspectives, was seductive to the kind of people who would have been appalled by, for example, the grotesque anti-Semitism. It also illuminates the propaganda uses of sophistication and indeed of sophistry. By restricting the terms of the debate to the most extreme cases imaginable, the Nazis engaged in a mystification strategy, and by creating that fictitious story they contaminated objectivity. In this confusion, the narrative of *I Accuse* serves as an alibi for more radical forms of euthanasia: for licensed murder. The image of the wife's end is artfully contrived, the elixir of death makes her feel 'light and happy' as cadences of Beethoven waft from a downstairs room.[177] Euthanasia, sold with the saccharine bathos of a soft drink advertisement.

Battlefield weapon

Under the Third Reich, propaganda was an offensive war weapon. It cajoled the domestic civil population but it also sought to afflict the enemy both on the battlefield and at home (i.e. their army and their people). To a quite remarkable degree, the regime believed that language as well as guns and soldiers were tools of war, and hence language too was a conscript. This was undoubtedly a response to the First World War. Behind it indeed lies an unarticulated model of war as a branch of persuasion; if Clausewitz could see war as a branch of politics, the Nazis were certainly capable of developing this thesis to its logical conclusion: 'The world can be manipulated by techniques and formulas; in fact, if properly used these techniques and words automatically change things.'[178]

The Nazis saw propaganda as an instrument of conflict in all its forms – ideological but also physical. It was particularly significant in determining the trajectory that led to the fall of France. For while the 'phoney war' was quiet, its parallel propaganda war was noisy: 'across the Rhine, huge rival hoardings and loud speakers confronted one another' and such machinery was inviolate, not strafed by the enemy.[179] But the French were tragically inept propagandists – the wrong ideas articulated via the wrong messages. In contrast German propaganda was tart, smart and remorseless. They offered excellent musical programmes, resonant slogans and crude cartoons.[180] True to the notion of going for your adversary's weakest point, they sought to exploit French anglophobia and they succeeded. Sensing a French aversion to this war, they pretended to a truce – 'you remain in your Maginot line, we will stay in the West Wall'.[181] The French too were spooked by the Germans' revealed awareness of French deployments, and the intimacy of this knowledge: one broadcast, for example, informed a French commander that the wives and girlfriends of his officers were enjoying weekends with them in nearby towns (apparently true).[182] And in classic Third Reich propaganda tradition, the sentiments proffered by the Germans were repeated over and over.[183] In France itself the neo-Fascist press was given licence to indulge its anglophobia/anti-Semitism, making for a form of subversive home front propaganda whose messages were indistinguishable from those of the Germans.[184]

Propaganda was thus a battlefield weapon, a kind of psychological artillery designed in its more basic forms to demoralise enemy troops. But its more devious expressions had the intent of deceiving even the generals, and propaganda became strategically relevant at points of high fluidity, particularly the earlier and later stages of the Second World War. It was relevant again as Allied armies hovered over a collapsing German Reich, when the dexterity of Goebbels's fibs became a menace to Allied grand strategy. Thus an Austrian general, Rendulic, forbade the destruction of bridges in those areas near Vienna towards which the American armies were driving:[185]

> [Rendulic] at the time made no mention of the reasons for that decision, but it may very well have been due to a propaganda story spread by Goebbels. The propaganda minister disseminated the lie that the armies of the Western allies were about to join forces with the German army, and that together the Anglo-US-German forces would drive back the Red Army and win the war. Only a lie of such proportions coming from such a senior source could have influenced the actions which Rendulic carried out ... A great many other senior German commanders also believed that propaganda story. In their opinion it was the logical step which Britain and America had to make if they were not to stand idly by as Europe passed under Communist hegemony.[186]

The situation became surreal:

> both sides were using the Salzburg–Linz autobahn and were not firing a shot at each other. It was a ludicrous situation, and the more Rendulic pondered on it the more convinced he became that there was substance in Goebbels's 'split' story. The Americans were not firing at the German columns because they would soon be allies.[187]

After Hitler's death a German general asked Patton to permit the passage of German units through American lines to reinforce the Eastern Front – 'together we can fling the exhausted Russians back across their own frontiers'.[188] The Soviets meanwhile had constructed a defence system behind their eastern Austrian front, and this was inexplicable until Russian loudspeakers announced the imminence of 'the greatest betrayal in the history of the world'. They had fallen for Goebbels's lie about a forthcoming Western–German alliance against Russia; and another marketable lie was that the Germans were building an Alpine fortress, and the Americans believing this then diverted the thrust of their armies within Germany.[189]

The final solution

Welch observes that:

> It is interesting to note that films which were explicitly anti-Semitic scarcely existed before the war. Anti-Semitism was propagated chiefly by means of the educational system and the press. It was only after the final solution to the Jewish problem had been decided ... that the propaganda minister instructed filmmakers to produce anti-Semitic works.[190]

Thus in the *Völkische Beobachter* anti-Semitic propaganda was significant but not dominant. Of the more than 2,000 daily editions from 1939 to 1945, only eighty-four headlines were anti-Semitic (the exception is the Holocaust, 1943, when it ran fifty of the anti-Semitic headlines).[191] Yet the early intimations of genocide in the propaganda are there if we seek them; exterminating the Jews was presented as the terminus of an inexorable train of logic. In *Der Stürmer* children's book *The Poisonous Serpent*, one of the characters, a farmer, remarks: 'to protect against these creatures, there is only one real solution … I know what it is father, Elsa interrupts. One has to destroy the poisonous snakes. The farmer nods grimly.' That is to say, the final solution: 'one must find them, wherever one can. One must make their offspring harmless. One must hunt them down without pity and exterminate them in all the nations of the world. If we do not kill the poisonous snakes, they will kill us.'[192] This is the language of the SS. Another *Der Stürmer* children's story is the parable of the drones: 'each individual needs to learn that the drones are a threat to us. Then we have to ruthlessly destroy the drones. If we do not destroy them, they will destroy us and our children.' The bees conclude that they must educate the whole people. Then the people rise in uproar and fight – that is to say, the Third Reich.[193] According to Klemperer, while the word 'to exterminate' is part of the general vocabulary of the LTI (Language of the Third Reich), it finds its home in the Jewish section.[194]

At the end of the film *Jew Süss* the words of the jury chairman merge with the hangman's voice and the scene is set: the beating of the drum, the screaming Süss, the bald hangman and the columns of soldiers and the silent ranks of citizenry. And then the signal. Then the terrible drop of the cage and the abrupt and awful quiet; a Jewish life has been snuffed out, a costume-drama anticipation of the real extinction of millions more. Such a scene, the chronicling of the judicial killing of a single Jew, goes beyond mere ideology or propaganda; it is in fact both a preamble and an advertisement. It announces in terms entirely symbolic the commencement of the Holocaust. Increasingly the official language also offered, at least for the alert, intimations of a finality for the Jews, of genocide in fact, manifest in a rhetorical journey from mere anti-Semitism to apocalyptic anti-Semitism and embodied in a lexicon that migrated from a language of exclusion to one of existential threat. Such rhetoric was the harbinger of genocide. The imminence of the Solution was telegraphed by poster as well as other media. Between 1936 and 1940 posters were seldom anti-Semitic; for example, in 1940 only three of the 'wall newspapers' were. But from 1941 to 1943 twenty-five per cent of wall posters included an anti-Semitic theme.[195]

The management of imagery was crucial since concentration camps in particular were the Achilles heel of the regime, precipitating negative international publicity. So the government opted for a counter-intuitive strategy, giving the camps plenty of exposure; that which would be most hidden was most promoted: they wanted local people, Germans, and the world, to know. There were even testimonials from democratic countries praising the camps. Nazis sought to 'position' the camps cognitively via the rhetoric and imagery of reform/re-education: that the merely thuggish and brutalised return as good citizens, but with the implication that the delinquents were in some way not fully German. There was always the British precedent for concentration camps in the Boer War, and the Nazi camps were of course far more humane! But liberals, socialists, conservatives and other democrats had also been interned (subsequent inmates included members of the crypto-Fascist Austrian government).[196] Nazis had apparently saved the nation from itself; it was well known that Communists were among the camps' inmates, and they threatened the murderous horrors of Bolshevism already inflicted on Russia. The idea promulgated was of this being a mere temporary measure in a situation critical to the nation. Thus the antecedents of the Holocaust were managed as a public relations exercise. As Klemperer and his Jewish friends noted before the war, people came back from the camps, and these were not equated with extermination. It was an inspired PR move to close down most of the camps in the mid-1930s before stealthily re-opening them, this time not for the civic threat but the existential one, Jews.

Public impact Gellately has made a detailed study of the methodology of concentration camp marketing:[197] The Germans he says 'swallowed the propaganda about the increasing number of dangerous criminals who had to be locked up and guarded'. Or they were indifferent, and propaganda supplied them with an excuse for their inertia. Guilt was self-confirmatory: 'some even realise that these are not real criminals but on the other hand think that there is something vaguely wrong with them'. Many became convinced believers:

> some praise for the camps came from unexpected quarters like a Catholic bishop who paid an official visit to a camp in 1936. He is quoted in the press as saying that those who still doubt the constructive work of the Third Reich should be here. What was earlier neglected is today being undertaken. The Bishop uses the image of the Sleeping Beauty being awakened by the Prince and he concludes that the Prince was Adolf Hitler.[198]

Gellately portrays the Gestapo as a savvy PR-conscious organisation. Positive publicity and positive imagery were something which the Nazi government strove for on every occasion, the default method of the regime quite simply, the SS as PR agency: 'the Gestapo seemed to be as interested in the public relations side of their operations as they were in other aspects of the terror'. Himmler was a public relations enthusiast, especially in connection with his camps, approving a list in March 1938 of forty-six journalists to be shown around and addressed by him. In one case 'a week after the camp was founded, no less than seventeen daily newspapers from the region and one national published accounts of it often simply repeating verbatim the official news release'. The local press and public figures were welcome, and local communities were 'proud of having a concentration camp in town'. The regime not merely admitted the existence of the camps but gloried in them, at the same time refuting any suspicions of organised cruelty.

According to Gellately the celebratory journalism was formula-driven and formula-directed. The press offered cautionary parables 'crafted according to specific guidelines laid down by the Propaganda Ministry'. Stories, for example, 'must avoid describing how a certain worker or carpenter were sentenced to death, but instead tell of how a murderer or arsonist was executed'. Thus 'they write a cover-up that uses the catalogue of phrases that was already standard fare' (i.e. mechanistic/formulaic propaganda journalism). The courts became an adjunct to the PR propaganda machine. Hence the concentration camp was heavily sold. It functioned as a popular brand in the market for symbolic security, conceptualised as a spartan but dignified hive of activity amid its smiling landscape of greenery and plenty. They were, fundamentally, locations where Communists could be de-programmed and thence returned to civic society. And fear was fomented by a new technique, rumour:

> the Gestapo itself used what it called 'whisper propaganda' to spread terror-filled rumours to friends and relatives of those they sent to the camps ... Local Gestapo officials would be told, if and when Himmler ordered that prisoners be beaten in the camp, and they could then leak that information to heighten the 'deterrent effect'. As per instructions from Berlin, this 'whisper propaganda' was to be passed only to 'especially well-suited and reliable persons'.[199]

This illustrates how far the terror was married to the propaganda; terror, to function as such, needs to be visible. The aim was to ingratiate, but also to frighten. All crime was ultimately political; conversely, much that was political was now criminal. Not merely the institutions but also the personnel of the coercive state were actively 'sold' to its publics. The 'Day of the German Police' was a marketing exercise – fortifying the police brand and softening the harsh contours of policemanship (in an extra-legal totalitarian state) with a credible and friendly face. Citizens were asked to trust the police, thus Himmler: 'The police in National Socialist Germany has set for itself, to be seen as the best friend and helper of the German people, and as the worst enemy of criminals and enemies of the state.'[200] The regime projected itself as at the cutting edge of police science for the rest of the world, an exemplar for the global community; there was even a visit from the FBI in 1938.

Gellately notes how the external-imperial as well as the internal-domestic police achievements were similarly celebrated. The policing of occupied territories was publicly hailed in press and in radio interviews and events, for example the 1940 Day of the Police. German police regiments were 'exterminating bandits' and bringing law to lawless regions, guarding the army's rear: Polish criminality was 'unimaginable'. The police were 'presented as introducing better order and more humane methods. Even the Warsaw ghetto established in late 1940 for Jews was shown in terms of how it would prevent crime and the spread of disease.' Thus the Third Reich was a protracted act of advocacy where barbarity received a PR makeover, and the press reports now claimed the new territories were free of Jews (which surely raises the issue of what happened to them).

Extermination

There were essentially two kinds of functions which were often performed within the same physical space, concentration camps and, much later, starting within months of the Wannsee Conference in January 1942, death camps (at Auschwitz they were on the same site, whereas Sobibor and Treblinka and two other camps were exclusively dedicated to extermination). Lord Russell of Liverpool summarised the experience of one British victim:

> Few who reached the Jugendlager ever left it alive. One of those who did was Mary O'Shaughnessy who described the conditions there when giving evidence at the trial of members of the camp staff at the war crimes tribunal in Hamburg.[201]
>
> It was, according to her evidence, a small camp consisting of about ten huts, smaller than those in the main camp. On arrival the women were made to stand about for three or four hours before they were allocated to their 'rooms'. These 'rooms' were just partitioned areas in each hut. There were no beds but the floor was littered with bags filled with straw. Each 'room' was so overcrowded that it was impossible for all to lie down at the same time. It was not even possible for all to sit down in comfort. No food was handed out until 5 p.m. on the day following arrival, nor was there anything for the inmates to drink during the first 24 hours of their stay there.
>
> Miss O'Shaughnessy spent nearly 5 weeks in the Jugendlager during which time the diet diminished, the number of 'Appells' increased and hundreds of women were picked out for gassing. Selection parades during this period were held almost daily. On one of these parades were two French girls who were sisters; only one of them was picked out for the gas chamber but her sister refused to leave her and eventually they went to their death hand-in-hand.
>
> There was also a crematorium. This was latterly not only used for disposing of dead bodies and there is evidence that some internees were thrown into the ovens while still alive. One of the inmates at the camp in April 1945 was Odette Sansom and she could see the building from the window of her cell. The ovens were working day and night from the latter part of 1944 and Mrs Sansom could hear the doors being open and shut and people screaming.

Part 3: The empire strikes back – propagandising the British and Americans

Target England

The English were always a particular target, even before the war. Thus J.C. Davidson to Stanley Baldwin: 'Germany is opening her mouth very wide, backed by a chorus of well-meaning and enthusiastic agents.'[202] A British Legion delegation visited Hitler, visited Dachau concentration camp and had tea with Himmler, an 'unassuming man anxious to do his best for his country'.[203] There was plain bribery: 'British writers and journalists were paid to produce favourable reports.'[204] Boys at Charterhouse School, according to their headmaster Robert Birley, derived their whole impression of Europe from that trip to Germany in their last year at school, one which 'was neatly arranged for [them] by Herr Goebbels'.[205] Yet there were indigenous English apologists for the Nazi movement, positive articles and so forth such as 'Herr Hitler and his Policy, March 1933' in the *English Review*.[206] There were elite British sentimentalists such as Lord Lothian and the Bishop of Gloucester (Headlam), and Bruce Bairnsfather felt that 'to my mind there is so much for England to admire, and even envy, about the Germany of today'.[207] And at Bedford School, a visiting troupe of Hitler Youth performed dances and songs to rapturous applause, the school's German department displayed posters of the Führer, and the British Union of Fascists advertised in school literature.[208] During the early part of the war British listeners found the German stations were offering up-to-date and accurate reports (and that their reporters reached the front lines): these were subversive, attacking Britain's motives for war and making invidious comparisons between the two systems, especially on unemployment.[209] There was thus the 'Anti-Lie Bureau' of the British, actually a rather Orwellian enterprise: 'the purpose of this bureau was originally to counteract supposed German propaganda lies with the truth. More often they found themselves in the position of giving the lie to rumours which were in fact true'; as in the case of a woman who had been forced to move her nursing home from London because of the blitz.[210]

British incompetence? Some British grandees despaired of the quality of their propaganda when confronted by an enemy for whom propaganda was not an instrument but a faith to live by; it needed, they felt, to be more visceral. Sir Harold Nicolson castigated Britain's Ministry of Information (3 August 1940):

> The Ministry is ill organised and mistakes are made. A Ministry of this character cannot readily be conducted efficiently if the majority of the press are out to sabotage it. And it may be true that if our propaganda is to be as effective as that of the enemy, we must have at the top people who will not only command the assent of the press, but who will be caddish and ignorant enough to tell dynamic lies. At present the ministry is too decent, educated and intellectual to imitate Goebbels. It cannot live by intelligence alone. We need crooks. Why I hate Hitler so much is that he has coined a new currency of fraudulence which he imposes by force. I am prepared to see the old world of privilege disappear. But as it goes, it will carry with it the old standards of honour.[211]

They recognised then that a world where the image, as well as the sword, was mighty, needed to shed the last vestiges of chivalry. Thus Nicolson (10 June 1941):

> the Middle East have no sense of publicity. The Admiralty is even worse. We complain that there are no photographs of the sinking of the *Bismarck*. Tripp says that the official photographer was in the *Suffolk* and that the *Suffolk* was too far away. We say, but why didn't one of our reconnaissance machines fly over the ship and take photographs? He replies: well you see, you must see,

well upon my word, well after all, an Englishman would not like to take snapshots of a fine vessel sinking. Is he right? I felt abashed when he said it. I think he is right.[212]

And then there was William Joyce, Irishman and Fascist, who attained immortality as recipient of the completely improbable soubriquet 'Lord Haw-Haw'. W.J. West describes Joyce's activity in Berlin as 'one of the most sustained outbursts of political polemic in British letters, rivalling the achievements of such masters of the political pamphlet as William Prynne in the 17th century'.[213] He had an impact: 'the propaganda was insidious, the effect cumulative', for Joyce was credible: 'What he said was taken seriously. If he seemed to threaten a raid, then preparations were made for a night in the shelter.'[214] Fiction and fact became interwoven; Joyce also wrote the scripts for the clandestine stations and up to seventy per cent of the listening public at weekends were hearing Nazi broadcasts.[215] It was not just the content, but the dramaturgy. A confidential BBC report spoke of his 'sardonic almost mephistophelian voice'; but people were fascinated with this voice, it was 'dark', 'cold' and 'virile', 'it arrested attention and stayed in the memory'.[216] The American magazine *Life* called Haw-Haw a smash hit and spoke of his 'impeccable Oxford accent', and how he 'cloaks his news and opinions with clever humour that Englishmen find irresistible'.[217] The BBC report describes Haw-Haw as 'a familiar feature of the social landscape' and recognised the popular resonance of his critique.[218] It was the credibility attributed to what Joyce said (or allegedly said) that had induced the Ministry of Information to create its 'Anti-Lie Bureau' (i.e. a formal process of riposte).[219]

Clandestine German stations There were a number of clandestine Nazi stations pretending to be indigenous, including the New British Broadcasting Station (William Joyce orchestrated this but did not speak for it), the Workers' Challenge (socialist revolutionary station that derided the Labour leadership) and the 'pacifist' station, the Christian Peace Movement (with its signature tune 'O God Our Help In Ages Past').[220] There was also the fake Radio Caledonia which insisted on a separate peace for Scotland, and even a Radio Cymru for Wales at one time; so each had a radically different persona: the NBBS used a middle-class tone, Workers' Challenge was cockney-accented. The official view was that the pacifist station was 'the most insidious of all'.[221] The methodologies of the New British Broadcasting Station were cunning, publicising some secrets such as the fifty destroyers Britain was seeking from the United States or that the Duke of Windsor was to meet Roosevelt (the plan was then abandoned), but also subtly ominous and psychologically acute: 'there was even a hint in the broadcasts that they were in some way official, that a group of senior men had realised that invasion and conquest were inevitable and this radio was to be the voice of the new administration'.[222] And thus 'as the campaign in Europe developed, the NBBS broadcasts began to resemble more and more those of an alternative official channel'.[223] The Nazis had done this with the French, and the secret 'French' channel the Voice of Peace was recommended by Peace News in Britain unaware that it was a German station; nor did the censor notice.²²⁴ In 1940 there was still a residuum of a Fascist fifth column in Britain which spread posters, stickers and handbills advertising this NBBS, printed via secret presses. The über-right were attaching gummy labels critical of the government on to lampposts.²²⁵ The NBBS offered advice for the probable invasion, and elaborated the charade, thus 'their broadcast on the 28 June extended the game of bluff by beginning to talk to alleged agents in Britain in a nonsensical code, followed by ever more urgent requests to bring about a revolution'.²²⁶ When invasion was 'postponed' they offered a new campaign, 'the People's peace', and sponsored chain letters; yet the British government often appeared impotent in the face of this 'internal' outrage, as it could not draw public attention to the existence of these stations.²²⁷

The impact

Lord Haw-Haw There was in particular a recognition that 'Haw-Haw' was succeeding because the native product was so tedious: the BBC offered hours of organ music from Sandy Macpherson, provoking Cassandra of the *Daily Mirror* to declaim 'to hear Lord Haw-Haw's diatribes shouted from Hamburg in guttural English is a lot more entertaining than listening to the canned cafe music which is almost the sole fare offered by the BBC'.²²⁸ The BBC would not broadcast the latest hard news at night on the self-limiting grounds that the print media must be allowed to publish it first, and hence people were hearing important events, such as the resignation of defence minister Leslie Hore-Belisha, from the Germans.²²⁹ Moreover, up-to-date information was abundant, domestic detail acquired through the exchange of newspapers via daily plane flights to Stockholm, Sweden and Madrid, Spain, and this was exploited: 'It is quite sufficient to tell [people] things directly related to their own environment, things happening around them, for everything else to be carried along with it, including the demoralising half-truths and embarrassing political facts.'²³⁰

People were finding the BBC heavy going and in contrast were excited, adulatory even, about Haw-Haw; to listen to him was even to appear sophisticated, and about nine million people listened daily and eighteen million every few days (about two-thirds of the total radio audience).²³¹ In a BBC survey of 34,000 people, twenty-five per cent admitted they heard Haw-Haw the previous night; fifty-eight per cent listened to his show 'because they thought his version of the news so fantastic as to be funny'; thirty per cent found 'his voice and manner amusing'; twenty-nine per cent 'listened to him because they wanted to know the German point of view'; and twenty-six per cent because 'his anecdotes made them laugh'.²³² William Joyce 'adopted a sardonic, calm persona that mesmerised British audiences'; the Haw-Haw diatribes articulated a scalding critique of English society – 'heroes of Mons or the Marne who have for so many years been waiting for justice outside your labour exchanges' and so forth.²³³ David Lloyd George commented that 'the government ought to take notice of every word this man says'.²³⁴ Observations on Haw-Haw from Goebbels's *Diaries* evince the pride the

Nazis had in their celebrity: 'Lord Haw-Haw's name is on everybody's lips. He has become a sort of worldwide celebrity and does us incalculable service ... our Broadcasts to England are having a great effect, according to all reports. We operate in tune with the principle: constant dripping wears away the stone.'[235] And then 'Everyone is talking about Lord Haw-Haw, and that's half the battle ...'. And further 'The English are lying to the heavens again but our Lord Haw-Haw is always ready with an answer for them ...'. And so 'I tell the Führer about Lord Haw-Haw's success, which is really astonishing. He praises our foreign propaganda.'[236]

Target America There were many Germany wished to convince, or at least neutralise. There were, for example, very many German Americans. But American hostility to the regime had early become evident – 'Germany Puts the Clock Back' was published in the United States in January 1933, and among Americans who actually experienced Nazi Germany support was negligible.[237] American media – not only papers but wire services and radio networks and magazines – were a major presence in Berlin until the war, with fifty journalists.[238] Yet, there was scant recognition of this regime as existential threat: 'the impact of memories of an earlier Germany encourage some observers to underestimate Nazism's potential before 1933 and others to overestimate the ability of so-called moderates to influence the new regime once it was in power'.[239] Goebbels sustained an American PR executive (Ivy Lee), much refreshed at an emolument of $30,000 a year, and the foreign journalist cadre was cherished and cosseted (as with his offer of soundproofed international telephone facilities).[240] Propaganda attachés were added to every German embassy; £20 million per year was directed to foreign propaganda – 'glossy, beautifully produced publications on the new Germany', a simple but effective piece of bribery.[241] And in America Congressmen were 'brought', cash distributed and a bogus literary agency concealed the commissioning of books and articles.[242]

American reaction Americans, aware perhaps of having had a patent on modern popular consciousness by turning mass entertainment into a global industry, were alarmed. In an epic of self-scourging, *Life* reviewed the situation in the late winter of 1943 in an article entitled 'US is Losing the War of Words':[243]

> But there was one theater of the war where Americans were still not big enough, sure enough or smart enough to challenge Axis superiority – the theater of political warfare or propaganda. ... Was the US winning or losing the war of words? ... Nobody in Washington knew better than O.W.I. [Office of War Information] Director Davis that he was still running a puny pushcart compared to the high-powered propaganda machine operated by the Nazis. The overseas branch of the O.W.I. spends only $26 million a year. Nazi Dr Goebbels spends between $ a quarter of a billion and half a billion annually. The chief US foreign propaganda magazine *Victory*, over which a Congressional economy storm blew up last month, is but a pallid imitation of the German *Signal*. *Victory* has less than half the circulation of *Signal*, contains

no terrific propaganda sock like its Nazi counterpart. The reason for this difference in wallop can be seen in the examples of US ... and Axis propaganda ... The O.W.I. sticks to facts, shuns exaggerations, tries to bring the peoples of the world messages about our leaders, our war aims, our growing armed might. The Axis harangues, scoffs, falsifies, attempts to divide. The best propaganda is based on truth but it must be forceful, inventive, consistent. In the last war Allied propaganda was so effective that it broke down German morale. But in this war the US lacks a clear-cut policy in the verbal ammunition it fires at peoples of occupied Europe, in printed promises it drops to Germans or Italians or Japs. For example, from month to month neither our propagandists nor the Axis people who receive their propaganda know for sure what American policy will be when the US has won the war. On one occasion the propaganda line is that the enemy will be destroyed, the next time that conquered peoples will be clothed and fed ... Although they are the world's masters of advertising and publicity, Americans as a people have always resented propaganda by government. Since it is now a necessary weapon of political warfare, the US, through the O.W.I., is slowly trying to master it. Their handicaps are shortages of training and funds, and the lack of a single credo, typical in a democratic nation.[244]

It was not entirely a farrago of incompetence by any means, however:

The Nazis had invariably employed 'the strategy of terror' to invade the enemy's mind. Elmer Davis and the O.W.I. have been trying to counteract this with 'the strategy of truth'. The results, some of which are reproduced on these pages, are not always as slashing or colorful as those of the Axis ... But with typical Yankee ingenuity the O.W.I. has added a few new propaganda wrinkles. American leaflets and pamphlets are dropped from the air over occupied areas, hidden in babies' diapers, printed on the inside of badly wanted matchboxes, or attached to a needle and thread.

They add that:

Lies are sent around the world by a smooth, high-powered machine. Long before the war, Berlin, Rome and Tokyo perfected great, intricate and effective propaganda machines. Today the crafty men who cast the Axis line from Singapore to Valparaiso are far ahead of the US. They have talent, experience, almost unlimited funds and no compunctions about honesty. In 18 languages they spread their lies, fomenting hatred against the United Nations, scoffing at our war aims and leaders. On these pages are examples of their work. The deadliest weapon in the vast Axis propaganda arsenal is *Signal* ... a German twice-a-month picture magazine patterned after *Life*. Each issue of one million copies is translated into all major languages, distributed in 23 countries. Signal costs 2½ million dollars a year. The Japs have at least eight periodicals and use every journalistic line, including 'cheese-cake'. Nine Italian magazines boast of the peaceful, prosperous and beautiful life in sunny Fascist Italy.[245]

Enemy learning/ riposte

Limitations of German propaganda: the culture of terror And yet the international resentments aroused by the insane terror could not be mollified by even the most therapeutic propaganda. The enemies soon included foreign publics; hence *Picture Post*'s photographs of Jewish shops smashed at Crystal Night precipitated an appalled public reaction.[246] And the Pope was now an enemy, warning in March 1937 against making any human being godlike: he 'denounced as idolatrous the Third Reich propaganda in favour of a race-god'.[247] Whatever the cunning of Lord Haw-Haw, nothing could disguise the reality of a regime so gloatingly cruel. For example, images of the dead of Coventry, frozen in the shape of their final agony (and concealed from the British people), were transmitted to the United States.[248] The Reich's operational thesis may have been that people are intimidated by terror, but neglected to recognise that at some point a terror of such magnitude teaches people to lose their fear of death: that, anger apart, it assassinates all other emotion. Ziegler suggests that even schools seemed to be a deliberate target of the German air force, and describes an incident in 1943 where a fighter-bomber eluded London defences and (ineffectually) machine-gunned a school in Woolwich, then dropped a 1,100 lb bomb on Sandhurst Road School in Catford. Thirty-eight children and six teachers died. This raid's leader, Captain Schumann, bragged in a broadcast from Paris that 'the bombs fell just where we wanted them to'.[249] The hubristic boasts of Nazi media remained their vulnerable point, as with the assertion that Britain lost over 1,500 aircraft in the summer and autumn of 1941 without hurting the Germans.[250]

A competitive context And German propaganda functioned of course in a competitive context; against it were arrayed the various public information, or propaganda, departments of the Allies, and these became powerful adversaries after Hitler declared war on the United States at the end of 1941. But crucially there was the impressment into war propaganda of the Allied media systems, everything from the Crown Film Unit to Hollywood itself. Thus the broadcasts of Ed Murrow painted 'an affectionate picture of a crusty liberal Britain muddling through the war, congenitally incapable of efficient propaganda and insistent on preserving the rights of genuine conscientious objectors'.[251] The film *Foreign Correspondent*, for example, offered a dramatic view of the blitz:

> I can't read the rest of this speech because the lights have gone out. So I'll just have to talk off-the-cuff. All that noise you hear isn't static, it's death coming to London. Yes, they're coming here now. You can hear the bombs falling on the streets and homes … America, hang on to your lights, they're the only lights left in the world.

Goebbels called this film a 'masterpiece of propaganda'.[252]

Counter-propaganda There was of course demoralising counter-propaganda against Germany from various sources, for example German maladroitness could be exploited, as with a map they had created as a 'propaganda device drawn up to tempt the larger Latin American countries towards Hitler's new order'.[253] This map's deliberate redistribution of South American territory was exaggerated by the Allies to frighten other regional nations.[254] And the impact of Bishop Galen's sermon was manifest in people refusing X-rays even though these are hardly likely to be a conduit to euthanasia.[255] But propaganda needs a kernel of truth to be credible; and the RAF dropped copies of the sermon, while the BBC promoted it.[256] German soldiers were also dismayed by the stories about Anglo-American bombing and the Allied propaganda claims, and it was found necessary to issue figures for the Hamburg firestorm deaths (eighteen and a half thousand, the bulletins claimed).[257]

And German propaganda itself could be turned into Allied counter-propaganda, as with Capra's incorporation of imagery from *Triumph of the Will* into his 'Why We Fight' series.[258] Those self-same qualities of menace and militarist balletics were turned against their original authors, and what made German propaganda effective at home transformed it into counter-propaganda abroad: its regimented vistas, the darkly brooding Nazi brow, the automaton-like people. And, satirically, Pathé News set marching images (forward/abruptly reverse) from *Triumph of the Will* to the jaunty rhythm of 'The Lambeth Walk'.[259] The British did have one 'master stroke of censorship policy' and permitted intercepted German propaganda material to enter America.[260] These included documentaries about the attack on Poland and the celebration of Blitzkrieg. Cull argues that:

> in so doing, they permitted the Germans to commit an appalling policy error ... Goebbels believed that scenes of the Polish army being routed, set to the strains of a jolly German male voice choir, would build an image of the Wehrmacht's invincibility in the Americas. But they did little to impress the people of the United States.

And in 1940 March of Time included elements of Campaign in Poland as part of their film *The Ramparts We Watch*.[261]

Learned response The British were, briefly, hysterical about the operation of a 'fifth column' and the ubiquity of German agents. 'Lord Haw-Haw', who was credited with such omniscience that he apparently knew when town clocks stopped, played to the gallery on this, publicly issuing fake orders among many other things.[262] However, the British riposte to Joyce (Haw-Haw) had embodied 'one of the most successful counter propaganda campaigns of modern times', via this inspired soubriquet that evoked an effete, sneering dilettante-traitor.[263] But the real Joyce was none of these things and yet the fiction sabotaged the reality. The image stuck, it fired public imagination and turned Joyce into one of the greatest celebrities in the entire history of British media. But it also connected satisfyingly with popular superstitions about upper-class traitors as presented for example in the film *Went the Day Well* (Ealing Studios 1942). British newspapers revelled in the opportunity to commend Nazi broadcasts to their readers. The *Daily Express* asserted: 'the more people who tune in to the foreign radio impropaganda experts, the greater the joy and laughter'; *The People* thought that to 'remove him from the air and our nightly black out will be intolerable'.[264] Commerce and entertainment got in on the act. Phillips sold radios featuring the Germany Calling broadcasting schedule in their advertisements, and there was a theatre show called *Haw-Haw* with Max Miller and even a spoof biography.[265] William Joyce heard about the spoofs and created two characters, Schmidt, the smart German, and Smith, a silly member of the British upper class.[266] Later in the war Joyce formally assumed the Haw-Haw soubriquet in a new programme.[267] Originally the journalist Barrington had created the character of Lord Haw-Haw of Zeesen by the post-ascription of lordly characteristics on to a conglomerate of Nazi speakers who gradually congealed into the one. William Joyce: 'from his accent and personality I imagine him with a receding chin, a questing nose, thin, yellow hair brushed back, a monocle, a vacant eye, a gardenia in his buttonhole. Rather like P.G. Wodehouse's Bertie Wooster.'[268] *The Mail*'s Charles Graves evolved the conceit further: 'I am willing to have a small bet that he is a fat, elderly Shakespearean actor, probably deported from England and until war broke out a professor of elocution at some small German institute.'[269] Lord Donegal in *The Mail* thought 'whoever writes Lord Haw-Haw's stuff is a genius in the art of being unconsciously funny. At times he drops his monocle (I'm sure he has one) and becomes endearing.'[270] He was the 'rollicking rake of the Reich', the 'humbug of Hamburg', who was 'all rather county and very well off, this Oxford and Cambridge and Teutonic toff' according to the English comedy duo, the Weston Brothers.

Conclusions

The global impact of Nazi propaganda was realised not only because, intellectually, Nazis recognised this as a priority, but also because they implemented it as such. For example, during the Olympics there was a vast expansion of the Zeesen transmission: there were now eight transmitters, and Zeesen became the most powerful station in the world, with free access for foreign correspondents.[271]

And no regime ordained its imagistic legacy more completely than the Third Reich: it is remembered through the prism of its own self-imagining, for example the imagery distilled from *Triumph of the Will*, a film which can actually be seen to function as an imagistic pool in which all subsequent documentaries on this era are baptised. Imagery was the way the regime operated, and how it created its public story. The problem was that all this entailed 'hollowing out democratic conceptions of the modern public from the very centre. The rising tide of posters, slogans, flags, and insignia reflected an understanding of the voter more akin to the "controllable customer" than the rational citizen.'[272] The propaganda represents not the Reich as it really was but the Reich as it wished to be, and to be seen. Film, documentary and newsreel hand down to us a self-edited public persona and not the proximate truth of obese, superannuated storm troopers; the media's truth in a sense becomes really real, the historically accepted narrative.

Notes

1. Ross, *Media*.
2. Neumann, *Structure and Practice*.
3. Bracher, *German Dictatorship*.
4. Ibid.
5. Huber, *Propaganda Primer*.
6. Stark, *Political Propaganda*.
7. Ibid.
8. Ibid.
9. Ibid.
10. Ibid.
11. Ibid.
12. Evans, *Third Reich*.
13. Bracher, *German Dictatorship*.
14. Fest, *Hitler*.
15. William Sheridan Allen, *The Nazi Seizure of Power*, New York: Franklin Watts Inc., 1984.
16. Ibid.
17. Huber, *Propaganda Primer*.
18. Ibid.
19. Stark, *Political Propaganda*.
20. Ibid.
21. Ibid.
22. Ibid.
23. Ibid.
24. Ibid.
25. Bytwerk, *Bending Spines*.
26. Gustav Staebe, 'The Coming Tasks Of Rural Propaganda', *Unser Wille Und Weg* 2 (1932), Calvin College German Propaganda Archive.
27. Helmut von Wilucki, 'Tested Methods of Modern Propaganda', *Unser Wille und Weg* 2 (1932), Calvin College German Propaganda Archive.
28. Huber, *Propaganda Primer*.
29. Ibid.
30. Bullock, *Hitler and Stalin*.
31. Ibid.
32. Allen, *Power*.
33. Ibid.
34. Klemperer, *Language*.
35. Stark, *Political Propaganda*.
36. Bracher, *German Dictatorship*.
37. Allen, *Power*.
38. Ibid.
39. Ross, *Media*.
40. Ibid.
41. Bytwerk, *Bending Spines*.
42. Ross, *Media*.
43. Ibid.

44 Ibid.
45 Ibid.
46 Hoffmann, *Triumph*.
47 Ross, *Media*.
48 Herzstein, *War*.
49 Ibid.
50 Ibid.
51 Bytwerk, *Bending Spines*.
52 Herf, *Jewish Enemy*.
53 Herf, *Arab World*.
54 Ibid.
55 Ibid.
56 Rutherford, *Hitler's Propaganda*.
57 Herzstein, *War*.
58 Rutherford, *Hitler's Propaganda*.
59 Burleigh, *Third Reich*.
60 Stark, *Political Propaganda*.
61 Ibid.
62 Ibid.
63 Allen, *Power*.
64 Ibid.
65 Bullock, *Hitler and Stalin*.
66 Martin Bormann, 30 October 1941 in Hugh Trevor-Roper (ed.), *Hitler's Table Talk 1941–1944*, Oxford: Oxford University Press, 1988.
67 Ross, *Media*.
68 Herzstein, *War*.
69 Rutherford, *Hitler's Propaganda*.
70 Allen, *Power*.
71 Robert Gellately, *Backing Hitler: Consent and Coercion in Nazi Germany*, New York: Oxford University Press, 2001.
72 Culbert, 'Kolberg'.
73 Lee Bogart, *Finding Out: Personal Adventures in Social Research*, Chicago: Ivan Dee Inc., 2003.
74 Ibid.
75 Ibid.
76 Rutherford, *Hitler's Propaganda*.
77 Rees, *Warning*.
78 Gellately, *Consent*.
79 Stark, *Political Propaganda*.
80 Ibid.
81 von Wilucki, 'Tested Methods'.
82 Ibid.
83 Stark, *Political Propaganda*.
84 Ibid.
85 Evans, *Third Reich*.
86 Ibid.
87 Ibid.
88 Ibid.
89 Allen, *Power*.
90 Huber, *Propaganda Primer*.
91 Ibid.
92 von Wilucki, 'Tested Methods'.
93 Helen Boak, 'Mobilising Women For Hitler' in Anthony McElligott and Tim Kirk (eds), *Working Towards The Führer: Essays in Honour of Sir Ian Kershaw*, Manchester: Manchester University Press, 2004.
94 Bracher, *German Dictatorship*.

95 Ibid.
96 Huber, *Propaganda Primer*.
97 Staebe, 'Tasks'.
98 Bracher, *German Dictatorship*.
99 Ibid.
100 Ibid.
101 Ibid.
102 Hoffmann, *Triumph*.
103 *Das Schwarze Korps*, 14 March 1944, Calvin College German Propaganda Archive.
104 Hoffmann, *Triumph*.
105 Ibid.
106 Ibid.
107 Evans, *Third Reich*.
108 Calvin College German Propaganda Archive, Posters 1933–39, no. 39.
109 Boak, 'Women'.
110 Ibid.
111 Ibid.
112 Ibid.
113 Ibid.
114 Ibid.
115 Ibid.
116 Ernst Hiemer, 'The Experience of Hans and Elsa with a Strange Man', *Der Giftpilz* 1938; Calvin College German Propaganda Archive.
117 Ross, *Media*.
118 Fritz Oerter, 'Our Speakers In The Anti-Marxist Battle', *Unser Wille Und Weg* 2 (1932); Calvin College German Propaganda Archive.
119 Ibid.
120 Ernst Hiemer, 'How Worker Hartmann became a National Socialist', *Der Giftpilz* 1938; Calvin College German Propaganda Archive.
121 Bracher, *German Dictatorship*.
122 Ross, *Media*.
123 Neumann, *Structure and Practice*.
124 Ibid.
125 Bracher, *German Dictatorship*.
126 Kallis, *Nazi Propaganda*.
127 *Signal*, 'Why Germany and Russia? Lessons of History', London: Bison Publishing, 1976.
128 Saur, 'Signal'.
129 Ibid.
130 *Goebbels Diaries*, 15 December 1940.
131 von Wilucki, 'Tested Methods'.
132 Ibid.
133 Ibid.
134 *Goebbels Diaries*, 12 December 1940.
135 John Weitz, *Hitler's Diplomat: Joachim Von Ribbentrop*, London: Orion Books, 1997.
136 Neumann, *Structure and Practice*.
137 *Berliner Morgenpost*, 5 October 1944; Calvin College German Propaganda Archive.
138 Guy Walters, *Berlin Games: How Hitler Stole the Olympic Dream*, London: John Murray, 2006.
139 Randall Bytwerk, *Julius Streicher: Nazi Editor of the Notorious Anti-Semitic Newspaper Der Stürmer*, New York: Cooper Square Press, 2001.
140 Giles MacDonogh, *1938: Hitler's Gamble*, London: Constable, 2009.
141 Leonard W. Doob, 'Goebbels's Principles of Propaganda', *Public Opinion Quarterly*, 14 (3) (1950): 419–442.
142 Kallis, *Nazi Propaganda*.

143 Bytwerk, *Bending Spines*.
144 Walters, *Berlin Games*.
145 Louis L. Snyder, *Hitler's German Enemies: Portraits of Heroes Who Fought the Nazis*, London: Robert Hale London, 1991.
146 Stanley Newcourt-Nowodworski, *Black Propaganda in World War Two*, Stroud, Gloucester: Sutton, 2005.
147 Herf, *Jewish Enemy*.
148 Herbert Friedman, 'The German V1 Rocket Leaflet Campaign', www.psywarrior.com/V1RocketLeaf.html.
149 Toni Winkelnkemper, 'The Attack on Cologne', Berlin: Franz Eher, 1942.
150 Friedman, 'V1 Rocket.'
151 Ibid.
152 West, *Truth Betrayed*.
153 MacDonogh, *Gamble*.
154 Sir Geoffrey Cox, *Countdown to War*, London: William Kimber and Co. Ltd, 1988.
155 Friedman, 'V1 Rocket'.
156 Saur, 'Signal'.
157 Ibid.
158 *Das Schwarze Korps*, 14 March 1944; Calvin College German Propaganda Archive.
159 Harald Jansen, 'First Results of the V1', *Das Reich*, 2 July 1944; Calvin College German Propaganda Archive.
160 *Berliner Morgenpost*, 5 October 1944.
161 Winkelnkemper, 'Cologne'.
162 Ibid.
163 Ibid.
164 Ibid.
165 Randall Bytwerk, 'Introduction to the War Goal of World Plutocracy', 1941, Calvin College German Propaganda Archive.
166 Wolfgang Diewerge, *The War Goal of World Plutocracy*, Berlin: Zentral Verlag der NSDAP, 1941; Commentary by Randall L. Bytwerk. Calvin College German Propaganda Archive.
167 Ibid.
168 Calvin College German Propaganda Archive, Posters 1939–45, no. 14.
169 *Berliner Morgenpost*, 5 October 1944.
170 MacDonogh, *Good German*.
171 Diewerge, *Plutocracy*.
172 Herf, *Arab World*.
173 Ibid.
174 Diewerge, *Plutocracy*.
175 Stanley McClatchie, *Look to Germany: The Heart of Europe*, Berlin: Heinrich Hoffmann,1938.
176 Welch, *Propaganda*.
177 Ibid.
178 Neumann, *Structure and Practice*.
179 Alistair Horne, *To Lose a Battle: France 1940*, London: Papermac, 1990.
180 Ibid.
181 Ibid.
182 Ibid.
183 Ibid.
184 Ibid.
185 James Lucas, *Hitler's Enforcers: Leaders of the German War Machine, 1933–1945*, London: Brockhampton Press, 1999.
186 Ibid.
187 Ibid.
188 Ibid.

189 Ibid.
190 Welch, *Propaganda*.
191 Herf, *Arab World*.
192 'The Poisonous Serpent' in Ernst Hiemer, *Der Pudelmopsdackelpinscher*, Nuremberg, *Der Stürmer-Verlag* 1940. Calvin College German Propaganda Archive.
193 'The Parable of the Bees', ibid.
194 Klemperer, *Language*.
195 Herf, *Arab World*.
196 MacDonogh, *Gamble*.
197 Gellately, *Consent*.
198 Ibid.
199 Ibid.
200 Ibid.
201 Lord Russell of Liverpool, *The Scourge of the Swastika: A Short History of Nazi War Crimes*, Bath: Chivers Press, 1989.
202 Richard Griffiths, *Fellow Travellers of the Right*, Oxford: Oxford University Press, 1983.
203 Ibid.
204 Ibid.
205 Ibid.
206 Ibid.
207 Ibid.
208 De La Noy, *Bedford School*.
209 West, *Truth Betrayed*.
210 Ibid.
211 Harold Nicolson, *Diaries; The War Years 1939–1945*, New York: Athenaeum Book Club, 1967; 3 August 1940.
212 Nicolson, *Diaries*; 10 June 1941.
213 West, *Truth Betrayed*.
214 Philip Ziegler, *London At War 1939–1945*, London: Mandarin Paperbacks, 1996.
215 West, *Truth Betrayed*.
216 Farndale, *Tragedy*.
217 Ibid.
218 Ibid.
219 West, *Truth Betrayed*.
220 Ibid.
221 Ibid.
222 Ibid.
223 Ibid.
224 Ibid.
225 Farndale, *Tragedy*.
226 West, *Truth Betrayed*.
227 Ibid.
228 Farndale, *Tragedy*.
229 Ibid.
230 West, *Truth Betrayed*.
231 Farndale, *Tragedy*.
232 Ibid.
233 Ibid.
234 Ibid.
235 Ibid.
236 Ibid.
237 James Sheehan, 'Hello to Berlin', *New York Review of Books*, 8 November 2012.
238 Ibid.
239 Ibid.
240 Rutherford, *Hitler's Propaganda*.

241 Ibid.
242 Cull, *Selling War*.
243 'US Is Losing The War of Words', *Life*, 22 March 1943, vol. 14 (12).
244 Ibid.
245 Ibid.
246 Andrew Roberts, *The Holy Fox: The Life of Lord Halifax*, London: Papermac, 1991.
247 West, *Truth Betrayed*.
248 Cull, *Selling War*.
249 Ziegler, *London*.
250 Winkelnkemper, 'Cologne'.
251 Cull, *Selling War*.
252 Ibid.
253 Ibid.
254 Ibid.
255 Burleigh, *Third Reich*.
256 Ibid.
257 Baird, *Die for Germany*.
258 Garth S. Jowett and Victoria O'Donnell, *Propaganda and Persuasion* (second edn), London: Sage, 1992.
259 British Library, 'Propaganda, Power and Persuasion', Exhibition: 17 May – 17 September 2013.
260 Cull, *Selling War*.
261 Ibid.
262 West, *Truth Betrayed*.
263 Ibid.
264 Farndale, *Tragedy*.
265 Ibid.
266 Ibid.
267 West, *Truth Betrayed*.
268 Farndale, *Tragedy*.
269 Ibid.
270 Ibid.
271 West, *Truth Betrayed*.
272 Ross, *Media*.

4

PRODUCT, ADOLF HITLER

The ersatz kaiser

> Our Führer is the most unique man in history. I believe unreservedly in him and in his movement. He is my religion.
>
> – German soldier

Introduction

By the early 1930s the Nazis looked unbeatable. In 1932 they had run an American-style presidential campaign, one which was better financed and managed than that of 1930, focusing on the personality of Hitler as the embodiment of all Germany,[1] and hence the equation between Hitler and the Nazis was now absolute. The party internally was a totalising dictatorship based on the Führerprinzip, the leader principle. European Fascism enshrined this as its market differentiator, its core idea. Hitler was Nazism, not just the surface but the essence, and everything had to be taken on trust from this – that he would deliver the right policies, for example. It was a leap of faith which the Nazis asked the German people to make. So to imagine that in, say, 1932, people were merely or even primarily voting on a Nazi manifesto would be a serious misreading of history: what was being sold was Hitler the man, then and afterwards; all countersigns, the visible negativities of life under the regime, could be self-argued away as a passing phase, or the work of recalcitrant subordinates ('if only the Führer knew').

The kind of supremacy enjoyed by Fascist leaders did not derive primarily from the legitimacy of election process or from coercion, but from charisma:

> a mysterious direct communication with the *Volk* or *razza* that needs no mediation by priests or party chieftains. Their charisma resembled celebrity stardom (raised to a higher plane by its associations with war and death). It

rested on a claim to a unique and mystical status as the incarnation of the people's will and the bearer of the people's destiny.[2]

Charisma was the exclusive foundation of the Fascist state. There was nothing else. This is reflected in the fact that no part of any Fascist domain was passed on to a political inheritor.[3] According to Le Bon, charismatic leaders are 'specially recruited from the ranks of those morbidly nervous, excitable, half-deranged persons who are bordering on madness': Fascist supremacy arises from unmediated charisma.[4]

The political science literature still perpetuates the notion that voter decisions are rational and that individuals weight each component of a political programme to determine their final electoral choices (i.e. rational choice theory). Such a paradigm, like the multi-attribute model in consumer research, exists more to lend academic research a patina of rigour than to capture those elusive truths of cognitive process. Did German voters think carefully about the various parties' policies in 1932–3? Some surely did. But for many, the Hitler image was evidently enough; imagination could embroider what that image really meant, so he became the creature of private fictions. What sufficed was faith that this man was a patriot, that he was a moral man, that he would reverse the painful verdict of Versailles, heal internecine strife and banish the red menace; that he would return pride to Germans and staunch the bleeding wound of mass unemployment. None of these aims were inherently evil, or even wrong, and the vast majority of Germans certainly agreed with them. Of the byways of the Nazi product, the fierce anti-Semitic rhetoric, for example, or the brutality of the language, there was always an ad hoc rescue hypothesis: high office would tame them, the rituals of government of a mighty country would civilise and satiate these soldier-bohemian revolutionaries. Sir Nevile Henderson, Britain's last ambassador to Nazi Germany, described asking those around Hitler what his chief quality was and being told almost unanimously that it was his 'tip of a finger feeling', *Fingerspitzengefühl* (i.e. instinct), that is to say, a sense of opportunity and clarity of purpose, as with his decision to reoccupy the Rhineland in 1936 which was taken against the warnings of his general staff.[5] He was instinctual, and the consequence of his reckless disregard for caution was accumulated prestige. Sir Horace Rumbold argued that Hitler would seek to lull adversaries 'into such a state of coma that they will allow themselves to be engaged one by one'.[6]

All that mattered was belief. Yet at one time belief in Hitler did not seem irrational, as there was evidence, of a kind; Hitler reminded people in April 1939 that he had:

> created the thousand year historic unity of the German living space … without spilling blood and without inflicting on my people or on others the suffering of war. I have managed this from my own strength, as one who 21 years ago was an unknown worker and soldier of my people.[7]

In the mid-1930s Hitler recognised that public enthusiasm could only be nourished by multiple and stunning success, and this is what he perpetually delivered until the end of 1941. As Bullock observes, his popularity 'also reflected genuine approval of the achievements for which he claimed credit in foreign policy and the successful campaigns of the earlier part of the war'.[8]

Stature

The 'greatness' of Hitler subsists in the narrow sense of an event-making man, greatness here being an academic formulary that excludes (as it does not in its vernacular sense) any idea of moral status. But any effective explanation of his success must recognise his bizarre talents. The stature of Hitler was as a rhetorical performer and propagandist visionary, one of the greatest actors of all time, who conceptualised the world, crudely, brilliantly, as a stage set. Writers naturally fear superlatives such as these because of the long shadows of the nihilist homicidal psychopathology he represented. Yet the phenomenon of Nazism cannot be understood without acknowledging both his dramaturgic and his propagandistic skills. As the private conversations recorded in *Table Talk* reveal, his was the curse of the lazy, untutored, pseudo-intellectual mind: yet he possessed a sense of the grand sweep of history, the millennia, the ends, the rise and fall of nations. The idea of evil genius is something we can accept in science fiction, in comics, novels and movies. However, in politics, in history, this is not admissible, and the relation between talent and virtue is the connection that we instinctively but irrationally make.

Hitler was the actor-manager of the Reich, the central character in its pageant, the author of its script, the conceptualiser of its stage set; he dominated the rest of the cast in this melodrama and vigorously rehearsed and evolved his stage role. Spotts argues for the thespianism of the Führer: everything was planned, nothing left to chance in a pre-packaged dramaturgy of performance, and these effects were not just personal-histrionic but mechanised-technical, for he 'even ordered equipment to be installed in the Speaker's podium allowing him to control the lighting and signal precisely when cameras should photograph him'.[9] Part of this pre-planning was the choice of venue to optimise the effects and the atmosphere; shape, size, acoustics and appearance dictated the selection.[10] A Hitler speech was an orchestrated public performance that would lead the crowd in a mutual hallucination of delight and rage: pathos, bathos and euphoria. First, bands would prepare the crowd. This atmosphere, part carnival, part church, was not just 'there', but created. Hitler had written, re-drafted and struggled until the speech was right, and it would be printed in a large font so that he did not have to wear glasses.[11] Such speeches were a carousel of 'stock themes', and emotional arousal was achieved not through remorseless logic (has it ever been?), but via 'moody induction ... trance-like repetition'.[12] Hitler spoke of what he called the wrestling bout between speaker and audience. He said 'at night however they succumb more easily to the dominating force of a stronger will'.[13] Night is 'the realm of the senses rather than reason'.[14]

The photo opportunity was something the Nazis cultivated to perfection: Hitler with small children, Hitler's role as father of the nation supplanting that of Hindenburg the grandfather, Hitler as first soldier and brooding philosopher-king. Thus Hubert Lanzinger's 'The Flag-Bearer', a popular print, depicts Hitler as a Teutonic warrior, a medieval knight on horseback.[15] Hitler was created as a free-floating symbol of national greatness, detached from the daily realities of the regime. Part of this was the resurrection of the ancient idea that 'the king can do no wrong', only the evil advisers. Such an idea was flexible and could be changed or at least nuanced as circumstances dictated. As Kershaw explains, it was only after Stalingrad that its magnetism began to fail. The greatest impersonator of Hitler was Hitler; ultimately the Nazis were selling Hitler, not the Nazis. He was, in the end, a political brand: 'the packaging – the skilful manipulation of his public image – was just as important as the contents. In many ways Hitler served as a political brand name, invoking a sense of loyalty, continuity, and trust among a highly diverse "market" of constituents.'[16] And then there was the evolution of the Hitler brand into that of the Führer.[17] Another aspect of the psychology of Nazism and of Fascism in general was the attribution of heroic and indeed superhuman qualities to a single man who became, more than the embodiment of the nation, the embodiment of its consciousness. To Germans this was by no means unnatural, for before Hitler there was Hindenburg, Bismarck, William the First and Frederick the Great. To condense the virtues of the regime into a single man had merit: as we have seen, the image could be quarantined from the party that sustained him, and the party could be the locus of blame.

Moreover, it meant that each citizen could invent a private relationship with Hitler which bore very little connection to the real man. The rise of leader worship from the early days was to become the most effective part of a propaganda which offered not merely victory, but salvation.[18] Bullock points out that 'Goebbels was later to claim, with some justification, that the creation of the Hitler myth was his greatest propaganda achievement'.[19] But this dependence on the idea of a single man also speaks of a wish to regress to some childlike state of dependence. Hitler, and the steroidal patriarchy he represented, was the creation of collective insecurities or a kind of mass hallucination. Hitler was pre-invented as well as self-invented, the emanation of a collective yearning for romantic-heroic leadership which assumed radical form after 1918 and was evoked in the language of the charismatic, 'the bearer of godly power of destiny and grace'.[20] Others have seen the success of the Hitler discourse as illuminating something dark and primitive within human nature itself: 'Hitler raised the secret chills people feel when they admire brutal solutions. He appealed to the hidden thug which can be found behind many civilised facades.'[21] Bullock has argued that Hitler did not *ab initio* perceive himself as the long heralded leader, or messiah, but as the 'drummer' (i.e. propagandist), and only the saga of his imprisonment and public reactions to his imprisonment realised this destiny.[22]

The Hitler speech

Speech: the actor and the act

Hitler was the general manager of the spectacular, the dark lord of political gimmickry. He styled himself the greatest actor in Europe; his perverted brilliance as a professional communicator was such that no other politician in the twentieth century identified politics with performance so extensively.²³ How fresh the act seemed to its neophyte German spectators. The endless comedic parodies from *The Great Dictator* (1940) onwards capture surface but not essence, yet parody should not blind us to how well it was originally done. The photo-journalism of papers such as the *Berliner Illustrirte Zeitung* record, often in full-page images, the public dramaturgy of a professional actor – folded arms, eager face, gesticulating to his key ministers or relaxing by a lake, accordionist at hand. Heinrich Hoffmann, Hitler's personal photographer, helped him to develop his public persona and physical dramaturgy, and published over twelve photo-journal volumes.²⁴ By as early as the autumn of 1922, the British consul general was reporting that Hitler 'had developed into something much more than a scurrilous and rather comic agitator', and had formed 'an efficient and active organisation'.²⁵

His dramaturgy was a novelty for those on the political right,²⁶ eschewing the pomposities of the old conservative ruminators and inspired by the rhetoricians of the left, Eisner for instance:²⁷

> He gained much of his oratorical success by giving audiences what they wanted. He used simple, straightforward language the ordinary people could understand, short sentences, powerful, emotive slogans. Often beginning a speech quietly, to capture his audience's attention, he would gradually build to a climax, his deep, rather hoarse voice would rise in pitch, chiming in a crescendo to a ranting and screaming finale, accompanied by carefully rehearsed dramatic gestures, his face glistening with sweat, his lank, dark hair falling forward over his face as he worked his audience into a frenzy of emotion ... Everything was absolute, uncompromising, irrevocable, undeviating, unalterable, final. He seemed, as many who listened to his early speeches testified, to speak straight from the heart, and to express their own deepest fears and desires ... His speeches began with an account of his own poverty-stricken early life, to which he drew an implicit parallel with the downcast, downtrodden and desperate state of Germany after the First World War, then, his voice rising, he would describe his own political awakening, and point to its counterpart in Germany's future recovery and return to glory. Without necessarily using overtly religious language, Hitler appealed to religious archetypes of suffering, humiliation, redemption and resurrection lodged deep within his listeners' psyche; and in the circumstances of post-war and post-revolutionary Bavaria, he found a ready response.²⁸

Charm: the Hitler act In the early years of his search for power, the Hitler 'act' was performed up to five times a night to different audiences: a remorseless torrent of words emphasised by a symphony of gestures, now fey, now harsh, all packaged together in five or so key themes. Thus rhetorical force was projected not only through the use of potent metaphors or verbal formulae but also via performance, an expressive physical articulation of the idea.

Many intellectuals such as Thomas Mann were predictably dismissive of Hitler. Mann said he offered 'politics in the grotesque style with salvation-army attractions, mass fits, showground-stall bell ringing, hallelujahs, and dervish-like repetition of monotonous slogans till everyone is foaming at the mouth'.[29] It is certainly true, as Wistrich argues, that 'when you look for some essential core at the heart of the Nazi phenomenon, rational explanations begin to break down'.[30] Sir Nevile Henderson thought Hitler was 'or at least began by being, a visionary of genius and a man who was able to tell the German people what it was they wanted';[31] yet anxieties began to rise with his handling of the Sudeten question. An earlier British ambassador, Horace Rumbold, thought Hitler 'an uncommonly clever and audacious demagogue and fully alive to every popular instinct'.[32] Foreign contemporaries like Henderson recognised Hitler's great talent, yet they lacked an explanation for the revolutionary impact of the Hitler performance:

> Many Germans, women in particular, used to descant to me upon the radiance of his expression and his remarkable eyes. When I looked into the latter they were generally hot and angry. That was possibly my misfortune, since I only saw him on official occasions ... He never ... gave me any impression of greatness. He was spellbinder to his own people. That is self-evident; nor was there any doubt about his capacity to charm, if he set himself out to do so.[33]

Henderson recognised the existence, at some level, of a rational Hitler, or at least a Hitler who could converse with a parody of rationality: 'In his reasonable moods I was often disconcerted by the sanity and logic of his arguments.' But he adds 'to the last I continued to ask myself how he had risen to what he was and how he maintained his ascendancy over the German people'.[34] Others, such as the French ambassador, André François-Poncet, claimed to have 'read' Hitler, but it is hard to discern how much of this was via the prism/post-hoc imposition of events and images. The French ambassador perceived:

> a pale face, globular eyes, the faraway look of a medium or a somnambulist. At other times, animated, colourful, swept away with passion and violence. Impatient of control, bold, cynical, energetic. Sometimes a 'Storm and Assault' face, the face of a lunatic! At other times naive, rustic, dull, vulgar, easily amused, a thigh-slapper, a face like a thousand other faces ... Sometimes he was all three in one conversation. He ranted on for 10 minutes, a half hour, three-quarters of an hour. Then he was exhausted. At that time one could speak, and he would even smile. He was no normal human being, but a morbid, quasi-mad Dostoevsky figure, a man possessed.[35]

The source of Hitler's extraordinary persuasiveness is perhaps elusive for later generations unfamiliar with German narratives in the years following the First World War: 'Its power lay in its appeal to an explosive mixture of archaic myths, irrational cravings and specifically modern anxieties. Hitler's uncanny ability to act as the screen or medium for the secret fears and desires of millions of Germans provided the psychological foundations for his initial appeal.'[36] The torrent of verbalisations resonated with many:

Somehow, Adolf Hitler frequently found the energy to explain himself to listeners by pouring out his views, his dreams, his arguments in a massive and hours long, drama-filled barrage of words. These 'lectures', dissertations, verbal assaults were always aimed, quite instinctively, at the vulnerable core of the audience, which might range in size from 10,000 to one person sitting in front of him.[37]

Hitler offers the paradox of being both tyrant and vox populi, an articulated public consciousness; thus William Shirer: 'for the last three or four years the Nazi regime has expressed something very deep in the German nature and in that respect has been representative of the people it rules'.[38]

Speech: train/prepare Germans were simply unfortunate in that they were victims of the greatest seducer of the people who ever lived. Hitler experimented with various appeals, polemical thrusts and theatrical poses. His focus was pragmatic – on what works: nothing was spontaneous, the practised and rehearsed gestures were a mere pretence of spontaneity. He disgorged entire passages 'as if he were an actor going up on stage, every gesture calculated with the utmost precision'.[39] Goebbels also engaged in intensive training by preparing his speeches and trying out new gestures in front of a three-sided mirror specially bought for that purpose.[40] Hitler's speeches were self-authored and themselves miniature epics of struggle. The themes were formulaic, and the focus never rational persuasion. But for the act to work, the context also had to work. He was absorbed in the detail – the hall must be slightly too small and thus create the effects of crowd and excitement, there had to be pre-practice, the acoustics had to be tested.[41] The great illusionist also needed the right equipment to project the great illusion. Here Sir Geoffrey Cox describes the theatre of a Hitler Nuremberg speech:

> a mother in front of me turned to her teenage son, her eyes bright with tears. No one seemed to notice the stage management behind it all. As Hitler worked towards a climax the arc lights came on, one after another, until he rounded off his sentence, fist in the air, in a blaze of purplish light. When he brought his fist down on the rostrum, and turned to his text again, every light would go out except one beside him, illuminating his face. At his feet crouched cameramen, and a film camera on a moving trolley moved up and down the aisle.[42]

Speech: the physical act

Speer described how he first heard Hitler at the University of Berlin, dressed in a suit and beginning quietly, softly, talking of his concerns about the future before graduating to a tone of urgency which galvanised all who heard him. The Führer would woo his audience gently, as a seduction in the Latin sense, *se-ducere*, a leading to oneself. The tempo would increase, the relaxed muscles tensed: momentum. There were actorly tricks such as staring unblinking, deep into people's eyes, suddenly dropping the voice. All the rhetorician's fabulous arts, charm, mystical posturing, humour, courtesy, elegance even, would congeal into a rising torrent of invective, driving inexorably towards the foreordained crescendo ever nearer in sight. It was a convulsive narrowing, a harshening, hectoring idée fixe. Words would tumble and cascade in an avalanche of sarcasm, rage, brutal irony and sardonic abuse; the voice now rapidly spitting out dreams and accusations in high pitch – this was the 'hysterical' Hitler of doctored war and post-war imagery.[43] His characteristic pose was of head thrown back, his arm stretched forth and with his index finger jabbing at the ground as he roared his demands for revenge.[44] Fest speaks of 'the constant alternation between rehearsed self-control and attacks of literally senseless rage, between Caesarenistic postures and lax stupefaction, between his artificial and his natural existence'.[45] Mussolini gave himself to the flow; Klemperer says that 'Hitler on the other hand, regardless of whether he was playing up the unctuousness or the sarcasm – the two tones between which he always liked to alternate – Hitler always spoke, or rather screamed, convulsively'. Then finally there was the Hitler climax, 'screaming and spitting out resentment, knowing it was not merely his own emotion, but also that of his audience'.[46]

The rhetoric of some of Hitler's speeches was actually quite bland and it was often the gestural and symbolic that carried the real message. The language of Hitler could be vacuous, a kind of mood music and content-free. But every communication carries a tone as well as a content, and here that tone was formed by a physical elaboration of a verbal script – the performance art of Adolf Hitler. A close analysis of Hitler's style and dramaturgy would emphasise the initial economy of gestures; they were neither random, nor repetitive. They could become sweeping and violent, but the control of performance was absolute – no hesitations and unscripted gestures/vocalisation. Henderson comments 'I once watched Hitler review his black and brown shirted army. The march past lasted for four hours, and practically throughout he remained with his right arm stretched out at the Nazi salute. I asked him afterwards how he managed to do it. His reply was, "willpower".'[47] Then there was that direct and unblinking stare, the eyes have it, portholes on to an inner inferno of pure rage. What distinguishes him from any other politician of that era was the eye contact: a Hitler who read from notes would not be Hitler, not without the sense that he was looking at you personally, a retained interest stimulated by continual staring, a kind of mesmerism.

Speech: content Hitler himself was a convinced believer in the raw power of the spoken word over literary exposition, criticising academic emphasis on the written word: 'the power which has always started the greatest religious and political avalanches in history rolling has from time immemorial been the magic of the spoken word, and that alone'. Bolshevik literature contained nothing in comparison with 'the glittering heaven which thousands of agitators, themselves, to be sure, all in the service of an idea, talked into people'.[48] Rutherford suggests that his style was to reminisce, about the struggle, about comradeship, about enemies, and he rejected a rational appeal. He prophesies and he abuses, 'sometimes incorporated into the fabric of his address in such a way as to give them an almost conversational air as a man might confide his feeling to a friend'.[49] There might be shouting, and the raising of fists, but even the apparently innocuous could also be fraught with menace such as the phrase 'my patience is exhausted', said in tones of a vindictive entreaty: the fist was of course presented as the normal, naturalised, as just, with terms like hate, ruthless, smash, force.[50] These principles had been laid out in *Mein Kampf*:

> it was the application of the idea of releasing an uncompromising assault upon adversaries, disdaining to offer any qualification and presenting all this using sharp contrasts, as one might say, in the strident hues of the Nazi flag. Moderation implied uncertainty; the speaker 'must impart the total justice of his cause'.[51]

Goebbels on the other hand would also use these words but defended them as made necessary by context, and only for the time being:[52] Le Bon had claimed that crowds suffer from magnified emotions; they are only persuaded by excess: 'an orator wishing to move a crowd must make an abusive use of violent affirmations. To exaggerate, to affirm, to resort to repetitions, and never to attempt to prove anything by reasoning are methods of argument well-known to speakers at public meetings.'[53] This of course is an accurate description of the rhetorical technique of Adolf Hitler.

Hitler's speeches featured a carousel of themes, such as German humiliation, the debauched commercialised West, the smearing of Germany's past, the Weimar Republic as a Western imposition, the Versailles disgrace, black music, bobbed hair, modern art, lack of work and security.[54] A series of mini-conclusions pointed inexorably to a grand conclusion. There were the memorable phrases such as 'Germany is starving on democracy'; metaphor and mythic allusions created a pseudo-profundity: as Fest argues, 'the general view of Hitler as an unprincipled opportunist does not do justice either to his daring or his originality'.[55] For the charismatic leader (in Weber's sense) to succeed, he has to continue to deliver, and until Stalingrad he did. Hitler was:

> one of those 'terrible simplifiers' who had the gift of reducing complex problems to their elemental foundations. Whether he was dealing with culture, economics or politics, his powerful if limited mind was able to grasp the broad sweep of history and analyse the available choices with ice-cold calculation. Rarely can so much mediocrity, vulgarity, cruelty and dogmatism have coincided in the same individual with such political skill and propagandist genius. Rarely can one find such self-consciously criminal barbarism mixed to the same degree with an obsessive concern for the state of the arts.[56]

Speech: seduction

Meaning was not meant to be understood merely via clarity of exposition, but inferred obliquely via gesture, tone and metaphor. Britain's Foreign Secretary Lord

Halifax commented 'I can quite see why he is a popular speaker. The play of emotion, sardonic humour, scorn, something almost wistful – is very rapid.'[57] Hitler could seek out and explore the multi-layered feelings of the audience and engage vanity and appeal to raw prejudice:[58] he possessed 'a psychic ability to connect with an audience and mesmerise it. What resulted was not a mere speech, it was a *Gesamtkunstwerk*, a total artwork.' Hitler was able to sense 'what his listeners felt, not what they thought. ... Then he told them what to think.'[59]

The charismatic is endowed with the mysterious facility of interpreting the masses: ostensibly a brave leader articulating a shining vision, but in fact deftly returning to them their old ideas in new packaging. What is apparently leadership is in fact a kind of followership. All, leader and led, are partners in the same fantasy. Hitler therefore was as much led as leader, self-created and other-created, a kind of national super-ego of the German people. Rutherford even makes the unorthodox claim that Hitler was lackadaisical in the preparation of his great speeches, and that he relied on interpreting his audience through an instinctual feel, an appreciation of human motives and sensing of popular mood.[60] He knew their unconscious hatreds. The dictator craves acclaim, but his power flows from the mob which may turn against him and this is a paradox: Speer thinks that 'in a deeper sense they derive their whole existence from the reactions of the audiences'.[61] There was some stress on participation, always a powerful appeal if we want to internalise commitment. Hitler would ask the audience to regurgitate the oath of loyalty and chant the word 'Germany' to a swelling choric echo from the crowd; he read the audience and translated its inchoate feelings and wildly confused rages and dreams into coherent, impassioned language and ideas, sucking in the atmosphere.[62] There was a sense of clairvoyant intuition and mesmerism; he was medium and hypnotist in one according to Christa Schroeder, his secretary, who subsequently spoke of his 'gift of a rare magnetic power to reach people' and a 'sixth sense' that 'in some mysterious way foretell the subconscious reactions of the masses and in some inexplicable manner mesmerize his interlocutors'.[63]

The imagined Hitler speech is an immensely crude affair; but in fact he had command of the finer nuances of the German language.[64] In *Mein Kampf*, Hitler conceptualised audiences as female, that is to say, a parodic version of allegedly 'feminine' characteristics (i.e. submissive, impressionable, hysterical). He was a 'mere' ranter to the democratic world. But much is ignored in this caricature, so much so in fact that Hitler's success becomes attributed to the perversity of German culture or the wicked DNA of the German race. The rant was only ever the terminus of a long preamble and its rapt reception was conditioned also by the contrivances of packaging/context – time of day, darkness, burning torches – which legitimated a more theatrical style. But it was also charm, and the ability to project it, which gave Fascist dictators their affinity with the masses; for example, the cover of Heinrich Hoffmann's photo book about the Anschluss shows Hitler quite literally 'blessing', touching the head, of an ecstatic young man whose arms are outstretched in supplicant prayerful posture. The point is neglected in studies of Hitler's success and its underpinning of charisma: the Hitler of modern memory is the ranting demagogue of History Channel documentaries, yet such demagoguery was only ever the summit of a more protracted oration, of a process. It is here that our public memory of Hitler so actively misleads because it forgets the smiling Führer, one adored by crowds of women. The point could perhaps even be proven empirically with a laborious content analysis of the thousands of surviving magazines, photojournalist literature and so forth, as the Hitler of the print media is a very beguiling man indeed. By ignoring this, the explanation of Hitler's success in power is seriously impoverished.

The impact

Crowds

Nazi ideology had two components: a belief system and a proselytisation system – a credo and a method. The big political meeting remained the core of the Nazi evangelism, even more so after the ascent to power and despite their newly acquired ownership of other mediums such as radio.[65] A festive atmosphere was created, carnivalesque, and the raw edge of anticipation stimulated by the bands and all the excitement, the air alive. As Goebbels described it, the 'Sports Palace roared and raved for a whole hour in a delirium of unconsciousness'.[66] Here is how he saw Hitler making an early war speech to munitions workers. Goebbels captures the mood, the moment, the popular enthusiasm: 'then the Führer speaks: the contrast between plutocracy and our system. Brilliantly human phrases. The applause is deafening … The Führer speaks as a man of the people. The scene is a glorious one: the Führer before his workers, flanked by monster weapons.'[67] Here then the stage-setting, the building up of a scene in a theatrical way and evoking the bond between Führer and people. 'The Führer speech will put backbone into our entire nation': again, Goebbels's notion of rhetoric is as a kind of medicine, or a hypodermic stimulus-response model. Goebbels adds 'we shall now be able to make it through a few crucial weeks with some grace'. Rhetoric and persuasion were the integuments of his worldview. He believed that a single speech by Hitler could totally refresh the national atmosphere, at least for a short time.

Here is another Goebbels description of a speech by Hitler at the Sports Palace:

> The seething ocean of humanity. Frenetic rejoicing. Fantastic storms of applause even during my introductory speech. Then the Führer speaks. Withering attacks on London and Paris. Resolute will to victory. Most unshakeable confidence. The people respond exultantly. Real Sports Palace atmosphere. The England song at the finish. The Führer is very satisfied.[68]

The speech was then broadcast to the world: 'London and Paris are stuttering embarrassed slogans.' In a factory speech to workers, apparently what received most applause was when 'the Führer said that he wanted no prestige successes at the expense of human life':[69] an extraordinary boast given Hitler's real views. This charade, this ability to play the human, amplified the power of his message. Then Goebbels adds 'the Führer is absolutely full of his speech. He now intends to speak more often.' That is to say, Hitler is drunk with rhetoric and its creation, script and performance; it was the fulcrum of his mode of leadership, almost in fact an end in itself. In contrast, Stalin, according to Hitler, represented the anti-rhetorical approach to governance (i.e. reliance on coercion alone), for he 'began as a small clerk, and he has never stopped being a clerk. Stalin owes nothing to rhetoric. He governs from his office, thanks to a bureaucracy that obeys his every nod and gesture.'[70]

It was a form of what we would today call experiential consumption. The meeting would be framed by a street parade, the preparatory overture before entering a banner-draped hall with its uniformed stewards, the air heady with anticipation and scarcely-controlled aggression, and singing and shouting of 'Heil!':[71] 'the most terrifying aspect of all was how the architects of Nazism were able to calculate the way in which such effects were achieved'.[72]

The audience for Hitler was electronic as well as live. Radio had given the ancient art of oratory a new relevance as it had ceased to be primarily living theatre and was now a phenomenon of the airwaves, hence replicating the excitement of a real event. Klemperer thus describes the public broadcast of a Hitler speech: 'for a huge animated crowd jostled in front of the illuminated hotel facade. Next to the main railway station in Dresden, from which a loudspeaker relayed the speech, storm troopers stood on the balcony with large flags bearing swastikas and a torchlight procession approached from the Bismarck Platz.'[73] In fact, between January 1940 and June 1941, Hitler broadcasted nine major speeches, an interesting comparator to Churchill who likewise grasped radio as a key interlocutor to wartime audiences.[74]

Fanatical loyalty

In many instances the impact of the propaganda created an intimacy of perceived connection between each German and Adolf Hitler, sometimes bizarrely so, as with the thousands of letters from women wanting Hitler to father their children:

> some try to touch Hitler, as though he were endowed with thaumaturgic powers. Others built little domestic shrines to him. Widows sent him small gifts. But a tubercular party member gazed at the Führer's portrait for hours 'to gain strength'; schoolgirls painted swastikas on their fingernails, and one group of blonde-maidens vowed to Heil Hitler and give the Nazi salute at the point of orgasm.[75]

In 1933 less than half of voters had supported Hitler, yet he proceeded to win over the majority.[76] The effect of the propaganda was to turn large numbers of people into true believers, and to inoculate against defeatism when Germany actually was being defeated. The propaganda – the strategic successes and the marketing that rhapsodised those successes – created legions of faithful prepared to follow their Führer to the ends of the earth. It is a question of belief, its acquisition and its impermeability, for such a belief once acquired is, by many, never discarded whatever the evidence; and all events are viewed and distorted through the prism of that belief. As an upholsterer told Klemperer at the end of the war, 'understanding has nothing to do with it, you have to have faith'.[77] This faith was not just confined to the credulous and the dull-witted. It was a mood, pervasive if not universal, including, perhaps especially, those whose training should have guarded them against it. Thus Grunberger claims that 'the abject obeisance made by many intellectuals to Hitler can be explained only in terms of the capitulation of bankrupt rationalists before the principle of irrationality incarnate'.[78]

Klemperer's portraits of the doggedly, stupidly, blindly loyal, are unforgettable, as with his portrait of an aristocratic secretary ('the Führer brought us home'). An educated woman, she nevertheless represents the abasement of rationality before the throne of feeling: 'It is something you have to feel, and you must abandon yourself to your feelings, you must always focus on the Führer's greatness, rather than the discomfort which you are experiencing at present ...'. Klemperer recalls walking into a bank in Dresden one day, where, to his surprise, he saw everyone standing attentively listening to a declamatory voice on radio. It was booming out Hitler's proclamation of Anschluss; amid the outstretched arms, and in the front row, was 'Paula von B' – 'she was in a state of total ecstasy, her eyes sparkled, she was not simply standing to attention like the others, the rigidity of her posture and salute was more of a convulsion, a moment of rapture'. She was harmless, not malicious, just utterly enthusiastic: 'their faith communicates itself to more than just old maids, for Paula is educated and sensible and should have been immune to mass psychosis'.[79] Klemperer conversed with a German army corporal near the very end of the war who believed that Hitler had only let the enemy in thus far so as to destroy them more effectively: 'he said we'd win, he never lied'. And then there was the upholsterer upbraiding Klemperer's defeatism: 'as if we'd lost the war, just because the Yanks have broken through ... The Führer won't give in.' Klemperer also gives an account of an impenitent ex-Nazi who he found (post-war) as a labourer, and who refused to be rehabilitated 'because I believed in him'. It was a very curious kind of integrity – the man would not repent because 'I still believe in him'. As for Hitler's crimes, 'others betrayed him'.[80]

Morale Kershaw argues that the continuity of the Hitler myth remained strongest in the German Army, the last group to lose its faith, and clearly some never did: ordinary soldiers were critical of poor morale in the homeland. It is significant that often their letters home continued to express faith in the Führer, frequently buttressed by overtly Nazi sentiments.[81] Moreover, the questioning of German prisoners of war who had been captured in Europe in 1944–5 also demonstrated the continuity of dedication to Hitler, almost until the last moment. Hitler's voice on the radio boosted the morale of SS soldiers on the Eastern Front more than letters from home.[82] So he managed to retain loyalty to the end in 1945, this was not 1918 again. Germany was often defended street by street against the much more powerful Allied forces. The effect of the propaganda campaign among the civilians too was to strengthen Hitler's appeal; this is uncontroversial – the central, and ultimately non-measurable question, is how far. Popularity was his critical political asset since it assured the survival of the regime at its most vulnerable, and earlier this same quality had been instrumental in cajoling non-Nazi elites to accept Hitler's regime in the transitional period immediately following the seizure of power.[83] News of his 1944 'death' elicited a traumatic reaction; his survival a delighted one. Speer apparently terminated his assassination plot after overhearing workers on the West Wall affirming their loyalty to Hitler.[84] This was an achievement of the dramaturgy.

Symbolism

Everything Hitler did was dressed in the symbolic, and he understood the role of symbolism in structuring a public meaning as few politicians have ever done, before or since. A representative example of this is the state funeral accorded to the workers who had been killed building the Berlin subway, announcing to Germans that the lives of individual workers were valued by the new state in ways that the old class-bound and monarchic society never could.

Hitler's stage props were the integuments of many a Second World War cartoon – the flop of hair, Iron Cross, brown shirt, a 'Caesar with a lederhose';[85] the abbreviated moustache of the First World War trench soldier whose symbolism was instantly intelligible to veterans – 'I am one of you'. Yet in the context of Germany in the 1930s such semiosis mattered and had meaning. The simplicity of dressing contrasted with the gaudy wedding cakes around him and emphasised the idealised man of the people in party uniform. Thus Speer describes Hitler's Italian journey of 1938: 'resplendent uniforms were designed for the entourage and shown to Hitler. He loved such pomp; that his own dress was modest was a matter of careful strategy. "My surroundings must look magnificent. Then my simplicity makes a striking effect."'[86] Hitler 'always wore a simple brown tunic without any decorations except the Iron Cross of the second class which he had won in the Great War ... Hitler's simplicity was one of the sheet anchors of his hold on the people.'[87] Hitler remarked in private conversation 'in my capacity of the Führer and head of the state, I am obliged to stand out clearly from amongst all the people around me. If my close associates glitter with decorations, I can distinguish myself from them only by wearing none at all.'[88] It was not just a matter of dress but of context, the showcase, as it were, for the Führer; there had to be a gilded frame, and thus in 1941 Hitler said 'whoever visits the Reich Chancellor must have the feeling that he is before the master of the world'.[89] Art and furniture were part of the stage props, the scene setting for a world-historical encounter, and they were carefully chosen for their symbolism – the portrait of Frederick the Great, the picture of Teutonic tribes vanquishing Roman legions. Hitler emerged packaged, swathed in an aesthetic so contrived that an office became a propaganda tool.[90]

Sartorial Image was both a means to further ends and an end in itself, the celebration of the pomp and grandeur of the regime. Hitler gloried in his role of theatre entrepreneur; Speer also discusses Hitler's supervision of the regime's style and his preoccupation with its public imagery, especially on the sartorial front. According to Speer:

> Hitler turned to the stage designer Benno von Arent, known for his sets for opera and operettas, and had him design new uniforms for diplomats. He was pleased by the frock coats laden with gold braid. But wits remarked: 'they look like a scene from Die Fledermaus'. Arent also designed medals for Hitler; those too would have looked great on stage. Thereafter I used to call Arent: 'tinsmith of the Third Reich'.[91]

He was the image editor; never for example pictured publicly in glasses, and never with Eva Braun. The story of the putative wartime assassin Axel von dem Bussche is well known (Obituary, *The Independent*, 20 February 1993): this young officer had been selected to model new uniforms before Hitler and was prepared to trigger hidden grenades (i.e. self-detonate; the train carrying the uniforms was strafed before the event, however). Yet could we imagine Churchill, say, or Roosevelt, attending the catwalk, transfixed by the new experiments in military fashion? Merely to pose the question thus is to answer it. The projection of Hitler was also material/artefactual – the buildings he ordained and used, the mighty Mercedes cars, the planes and trains, and above all the Reich Chancellery and the Berghof. These were essential stage props to the role of Führer, totemic of omnipotence. It is impossible to imagine the execution of such a role without them, and though it is true that they are the hackneyed bricolage of dictatordom (Shelley's 'Ozymandias' springs to mind), both the scale and stylisation of the Nazi public theatre have never been rivalled. They were physical evocations of the hubris which precedes nemesis.

Function

Legitimacy Hitler's role was also as the image of legitimacy in a post-monarchical culture. The displacement of monarchy as traditional symbol of allegiance created a gap in symbolism and ritual filled first by Hindenburg then Hitler, so for example 'Kaiser weather' (i.e. beautiful weather which in some mystical way was attributable to the monarch) became 'Hitler weather'. But there was also need for democratic legitimacy in a legalistic culture which had been based on a synthesis of oligarchy and parliamentary democracy. Hitler was not positioned in the political market as a dictator but as 'executor of the people's will', almost a kind of public medium, the 'People's Chancellor' concept:[92] 'the true leader comes from the people and represents the people. He forges the opinions and this is the source of his power – he is the personification of public opinion.'[93] The loss of monarchy had been so sudden,[94] the fixed point in the civic compass gone overnight; many even beyond the social elites were unnerved. This was a vacuum for Hitler to fill. But there were also non-monarchical precedents, Bismarck obviously, but also the Hindenburg of the First World War as well as the post-war Republic. More generally there was yearning for romantic/charismatic national leadership.

Absent ideology Nazism was bereft of deep ideological coherence, but it had the compensatory comfort blanket of the myth: even for most of those who supported the Nazis, Hitler's ideological preoccupations had more of a symbolic than a tangible meaning.[95] Ideology was subordinated to image and to an extent a means of its production; symbolism and mythology filled the space vacated by tangible belief.[96] There was thus a conscious devising of the Hitler myth as integrating force, a crazy ideological witches' brew given apparent clarity by the projection of Hitler's persona.

Gap between projection of Hitler and party Why was the projection of Hitler so successful and that of the party so ineffective? It is a measure of what can and cannot be achieved by propaganda. On the one hand, we cannot deny the everyday reality before us – the gap between propaganda and lived experience; on the other, we may be accepting of some overall vision and attribute the performance gap to failings in operationalisation, of perverse or inept subordinates. Hitler became, for each individual German, the receptacle of projection: a moderate among extremists, protector of religion and so forth. All this was a conscious objective of the propaganda.[97] The appeal of the leader, Goebbels understood, could exist independent of ideology, thus Hitler seemed as if he were willing to repress the revolutionary fanaticism of the party zealots and the stormtroopers.[98] As for public ownership of the Führer, there was even a 'Christian' Hitler for Christians despite all the contrary evidence. Thus Cardinal Faulhaber: 'he doesn't let matters drift, the Chancellor, there is no doubt, lives in a state of belief in God'; Hitler was elevated to a spiritual realm.[99] Goebbels's rhetoric was ecclesiastical, 'we feel him in us and around us'.[100]

Multiple roles

The regime had many masks for different audiences; Hitler's compound persona, which blended the functions of a politician, priest, artist and Wagnerian mythic hero, has often been noted.[101] Yet he remained a two-dimensional symbol, accorded scant individuation.[102] In power, posters projected many facets of the Hitler persona – warlord, ex-soldier, simple brown shirt, be-suited motivational speaker. Hitler appeared at Nuremberg as 'both Caesar and Comrade'.[103] The Nazi propaganda machine claimed a Hitler who really had emerged from the mass (a photograph of Munich crowds greeting war in 1914 revealed his face as one among a thousand anonymous faces).[104] Women were invisible in this mythology, the absence of wife or girlfriend part of the act, part also of a more general imagining of Hitler as an austere, humble man,[105] even, perhaps especially, the image of compassion such as his visiting a dying 'old fighter'. Pseudo-modesty and gentleness, on occasion, were a constructed part of this script, as with the various 'Hitler days' in his private apartment. One *Illustrierter Beobachter* feature, 'In the

Führer's House' (1938), for instance, includes interplay between Hitler and Göring and the dramaturgy between them (Hitler is shown cheerfully giving the Reichsmarschall a baton).[106] Otto Dietrich described the evolving components of Hitler serial role-playing/self-mythologising – fighter for unity, statesman, supreme leader.[107] Germans were made to feel inferior to this fanatical altruist-patriot, this 'abstemious half monk half soldier' who 'denied himself in the service of his country', who had allegedly lost eyesight in a gas attack:[108] he was successfully marketed as a man of the people, a true 'People's Chancellor'.[109]

Leader

Leader image is no mere abstraction. Even in democratic times the leader is of supreme importance since party policy itself is often ambivalent and contested; elections today are leadership contests and even Westminster-model parliamentary systems have evolved a presidential character. This, now as indeed then, is to satisfy the demands of mass media, its hunger for drama, its privileging of personality over abstraction and visuality over dry detail.

Persona As I have argued, much of the propaganda was concerned with projecting Hitler personally and the leaderly imagistics associated with him. This is a central edifice of this book's argument: it was hail Hitler, not hail Germany. When Germans voted in the elections of the early 1930s the ballot card sometimes referred not to the NSDAP but to the 'Hitler Movement'.[110] And everywhere, even the car industry, a new verbal coinage emerged – 'leader' and its related vocabulary;[111] the introduction of this title was the inspiration of Goebbels in 1931, who had demanded that it was instituted throughout the party.[112] The Führer principle seemed to transcend mere parody: 'the Führer demands the unity of the whole German cyclists' movement', and bowls players 'were informed that they owed it to the Führer that this sport had now received the recognition due to it'.[113] The myth was nourished both via manipulation but also from genuine popular belief, for Hitler could emerge as embodiment of a national unity arising above the sectarian interests represented in over thirty parties, a zealous guardian of Germany's honour and rights against enemies within and without.[114] Hitler claimed to symbolise and interpret the national will and community,[115] he was the anti-sectarian, the voice of the united nation. Moreover, in the absence of a cohesive programme, Hitler's personality was the main attraction in terms of gaining voters and new party members, one greatly underestimated by Nazism's contemporary adversaries.[116]

Behind the image was the story. Hitler had to be explained and his life set forth in populist, luminous terms: who was this man who had arisen from the ranks of the people to save Germany? Thus the public narrative sought a coherent story about the Führer's outsize life, about how he came to be. How then to make credible, how to construct, an ordinary/extraordinary biographic narrative of a being simultaneously both man and superman, mechanic and messiah? *Berliner Illustrirte Zeitung* (20 April 1939) tried to do so, retailing the life of the Führer as a

FIGURE 4.1 Ja! Referendum poster

kind of sophisticated comic strip.[117] A colour portrait of Hitler filled the entire front cover – 'The Leader of the Greater German Reich'. On the back are further rich colour images: 'Leader of the Greater German States' (he is seen receiving people and legations at a diplomatic reception); then 'Leader of the Party' (this time they are at Nuremberg); then he is seen looking out from the great (*c.* twenty-five foot) picture window over the Berghof mountains and forests in classic 'Führer' pose.

Product, Adolf Hitler 123

FIGURE 4.2 Ja! Referendum poster

Soldierly visionary Formal portrait art was a key part of Hitler's image-building since it could both ornament public places and be endlessly reproduced in magazines. It gave a classical-historical 'feel' to the image, as if Germans were walking with destiny in some hyper-historicised time. These were essays in the construction of a soldier-leader-visionary: the focus of his gaze was always something beyond the immediate vicinity (i.e. the notion of a journey, a place to take Germany to). In a typical product of this kind, 'The Führer and Commander-in-Chief of the Army' (Great German Art Exhibition, 1940), he stands in romantic posture wearing a greatcoat over his shoulder as a kind of cape, in full field-grey military uniform, a backdrop of concrete fortifications and a massively brooding sky.[118] Hitler is staring with intense concentration into the middle distance, as is usual, his mode reflective rather than aggressive. This is all in a long tradition of dictator art; it could, for example, be the cover of an insipid novel, or a propaganda poster, but these categories are really dissolved in the case of much of the art of Nazi Germany.

Mystic

Religion Many have since ascribed to Nazism the pre-conditions of a religion, and while this is an exaggeration, the credo certainly contained cultic and indeed quasi-religious elements. For many it was an experience of secular conversion to an essentially material creed, one that felt like a private encounter with the mystical – sublime, an epiphany in fact.[119] All rhetoric of uplift aspires ultimately to the condition of religion, and this is what Goebbels gave them, a ritual and a quasi-sacerdotal language, with words like 'mission' and 'miracle'. One author speaks of the 'mystical resonances' surrounding certain words such as blood and soil, folk, community, fatherland.[120] Goebbels described an address by Hitler about the Rhine plebiscite 'as if Germany had been transformed into one big church embracing all classes and creeds'.[121] Riefenstahl similarly describes hearing Hitler and being transfixed by the vision: her description of the event is as an eruption.[122] And here is Albert Speer's private epiphany and embrace of Nazi truth, a Damascene conversion:

> three hours later I left that same beer garden a changed person. I saw the same posters on the dirty advertising columns, but looked at them with different eyes. A blown-up picture of Adolf Hitler in a martial pose that I had regarded with a touch of amusement on the way there had suddenly lost all its ridiculousness.[123]

He was an emanation, almost a *deus ex machina*. Bracher speaks of the 'submissive fatalism of both membership and bureaucracy which was given direction by the consummate exploitation of the pseudo-religious, mystical, providential role of the one and only Leader'.[124]

The mystical aspects of Hitler's leadership are undeniable. The public relationship to him was one of faith: he was, in some extra-religious way, an instrument of fate or Providence. In towns suffering from air attacks, for instance, it was even believed that the wall containing Hitler's portrait would survive the destruction of the house.[125] The cultist aspects of the Hitler image regularly surface: it is the hagiography of sainthood. For example, one magazine from April 1939 devotes a half page to 'the hands of the Führer' and another half page to 'the handwriting of the Führer'.[126] There is scant evidence that the German people felt any loathing of him even amid obliteration: 'this may have had less to do with a persistent sense of identification with him, than with the impression that he was a supernatural phenomenon, eerie rather than hateful'.[127] Thus when Goebbels at the height of the war exhorted all Germans to pray for Hitler, 'those who responded by lighting candles in the Hitler corners of their homes included many who had never bought a votive candle for any other saint'.[128]

Pseudo-religious sentimentality suffused the artistic celebration of Hitler. Thus the aesthetic of a painting entitled *In the Beginning was the Word*, by Hermann Otto Hoyer

(1937), owes to religious hagiography as well as Bolshevik political proselytisation (Lenin addressing his early followers).[129] There is a nondescript room, tables, chairs, no decoration, swastika flag. The faces are lit, faces of innocence, they are dressed austerely and the women are not made up; the glow of light suggests something quasi-mystical is in fact happening. Hitler is on a slightly raised platform, arm on his hip, gesticulating, his face visionary, transfigured before his credulous listeners. Another painting, *Hitler at the Front*, by Emil Scheibe (1942), is a composition with Hitler surrounded by dense rows of enraptured soldiers.[130] The strains of war define their faces, and the rear is dominated by a figure beckoning to his comrades to come and join them. The suggestion is that Hitler has just dropped in, and this is somehow the kind of thing he generally does to inspire morale. In an artistic journeyman sense it is well done, the author has striven to give soldiers individual characters, precisely etched, rather than simply replicating the same sequence of faces. There is present, and probably unintentional, some kind of intimation of idiocy on the part of these men: some of them are in a trance-like state. The aim was to show the huge popularity of Hitler and the way his charisma was indispensable to the war effort. The effect is quasi-sacerdotal, evoking half-remembered images of Christ and other messianic figures.

Hitler, it will surprise some at least to know, was also conceptualised by his propaganda machine as the avenging sword of the Prophet Muhammad. The prophet was 'an enemy of the Jews'; Hitler had 'arrived to purify the world ... A sword has been sent into the world with the command, destroy evil, the hypocrites, the selfish, so that the world can again breathe freely and be pure. Awaken, oh Arabs ...'. Himmler was interested in the project.[131]

Priest-King Hitler's strategy could be described as the messiah position, invoking messianic rhetoric, a climactic struggle and a journey to a promised land. Sir Nevile Henderson, for instance, describes how the adulation shown towards Hitler almost amounted to idolatry.[132] This attributed status was popularly endorsed, and explicitly so in the propaganda, most notably with *Triumph of the Will*, where Hitler in his plane descends from the clouds.[133] And Hitler also managed to convey the image of the Unknown Soldier, simultaneously belonging to the dead as well as to the living. The clever idea was to connect Hitler with the dead of the First World War: he was their representative, their vice-regent on earth and the everyman of the Western Front, and the avenger of their spilled blood. But there are deficiencies in the messiah position; if the messiah ceases to work miracles he ceases to be messiah. Stalin by contrast chose a more sustainable positioning strategy, that of apostle: the key idea was that Hitler was lucky, under the protection of 'Providence', hence his own self-portrayal as 'the sleepwalker blindly executing a higher mission'.[134]

Superman

Hitler was a self-proclaimed, self-believing visionary who consciously sought the symbolic appurtenances of genius. According to Le Bon, the crowd demands superhuman qualities from its hero, superlatives, virtue and courage, things which do not actually exist in reality. So another integument of the Hitler image was that of superman, and this involved association with mythical figures like Lohengrin, or mythologised figures like Frederick the Great or Bismarck. Hence the ending of the film *The Great King* (1942), where King Frederick's face gazes down from the clouds, watching over his people. And like the Kaiser had done, Hitler had himself portrayed as Lohengrin. As earlier suggested, the essence of Max Weber's definition of charisma is the continued delivery of success:[135] and for the major part of a decade, Hitler gave Germans one triumph after another – abandonment of the Versailles limitations on army and air force, the Anglo-German Naval Treaty, refusal of reparations (by that stage a mere lingering ghost anyway), re-occupation of the Rhineland (Hitler 'walked into his own backyard' in the words of the appeasers). But such a strategy is self-limiting: it demands the delivery of new triumphs, fresh sacrifices on the altars of the deities of charisma. Again Le Bon had offered at the end of the previous century what could have been a description of Hitler, and a premonition: for crowds reject the weak and flatter the strong, and it is the despots they like: 'their sympathies have never been bestowed on easy-going masters, but on tyrants who vigorously oppressed them. It is to these latter that they will always erect the loftiest statues.' They will reject the despot who has lost power because they despise weakness – crowds like a Caesar, 'his insignia attracts them, his authority overawes them, and his sword instils them with fear'.[136]

The paternal signifier was important too, for he was also father of the nation: Hitler was always being photographed with children. A 1940 poster, 'Youth Serves the Führer: All 10-Year-Olds into the Hitler Youth',[137] uses the familiar technique of photomontage where the image of Hitler or some other Nazi emblem is pasted on to an image of general or ordinary Germandom. The featureless boy's face contrasts with the muscular contortions of Hitler's, the untutored youth of the bland, blonde boy sets off the wisdom of the Führer. Both are staring in the same direction: there is also an imputed paternity – a sense in which Hitler is some kind of universal father in this picture, the father in fact of this boy. And, not for the first time in history nor the last, a dictator began to believe his own propaganda: 'from my part, I must say that when I meet children, I think of them as if they were my own. They all belong to me.'[138]

Evolution of the role Behind Hitler's early stylistic confusions lay the aim of defining his role, his awkward, fumbling essays in sartorial gaucherie and serial experiments in the rearrangement of props represented the search for coherence;[139] now bohemian artiste, now insurance salesman, now the tiny gilded peasant who springs forth erect from the Swiss cuckoo clock. The Hitler image was quite consciously constructed as a commercial brand, his face first being used extensively in the 1932 spring elections.[140] What followed was an image structured around ideas of forcefulness, moderation, dynamism, trust; but also evolutionary (i.e. the conceptual movement from agitator to statesman).[141] Moreover, Hitler did not become absolute dictator of the Nazi Party, let alone Germany, until 1933, and so before then the Nazi leadership hosted multiple perspectives.[142]

Later evolution Kershaw conceives the image of Hitler as one which was never static but fluid and evolving, with the later war necessitating deep revision as a regime hitherto drunk with success adjusted to the costs of serial catastrophic failure and, increasingly, glimpses of the chasm of utter defeat and ruin.[143] According to Kershaw,

FIGURE 4.3 Hitler Youth wartime poster

Hitler's very visibility had been a surrogate and substitute for democracy. Now he was almost invisible, the remote commander of imperilled fighting legions. Hitler's speeches were infrequent after 1942 – seldom now 'the direct experience of contact with the Führer through his major speeches which for years had served as the ritualistic form of plebiscite; meeting between the leader and his people'.[144] For now he was increasingly the remote, enigmatic warlord of distant frontiers, glimpsed but rarely.[145] This graduated change in role from presence to absence was represented by the limiting of his screen appearance to occasional 'war leader' shots where he would be

128 Operational: implementing the Nazi brand

FIGURE 4.4 Motivational speaker pre-1933 poster

shown bending over maps surrounded by obliging members of his general staff.[146] Yet the Hitler myth continued to inspire loyalty and the Nazi concept, so holding the party and nation together.[147]

Defender of Europe Hitler was also, or became, the defender of Europe and the first citizen in the global struggle against the satanic might of Communism. He was self-cast as the first Europhile. There was a Nazi alternative to the vapid proposals for European Union even then being promulgated, which was German hegemony – the European problem is being solved 'essentially today by the self-same

FIGURE 4.5 Hitler floating head pre-1933 poster

central powers, which in those days were the helpless objects of one-sided lifeless political schemes'.[148]

Humanitarian

Germans had feared war and invested their trust in 'peaceful' Hitler: they had admired his foreign policy triumphs because they were bloodless victories.[149] This image was never discarded but rather supplemented by the defensive war argument, according to which benevolence would no longer suffice given the irrational malevolence of the fatherland's enemies. The Armistice offered to Britain and

France on 6 October 1939 was a cunning and influential propaganda ploy and refreshed this 'peaceful' image positioning.[150] Thus one propaganda article describes how 'Churchill rejected this last chance to unite with Europe. He responded to the Führer's peace proposal with insults and air terror.'[151] Hitler, we are constantly reminded by his hagiographers, is a leading international humanitarian: 'Even during the current struggle, how often did the Führer extend his hand of peace, not because of defeats, but after brilliant victories! Each time the Jews spat on the hand that offered peace.'[152] According to Winkelnkemper, practical suggestions for disarmament and for more humanitarian warfare 'were always ignored', for had not the Führer avowed 'I do not want to wage war against women and children'?[153] And on 1 September 1939 the German air force was particularly instructed in choice of targets, with Hitler proclaiming to the Reichstag 'I do not want to wage war against women and children. I have given my Luftwaffe the order to limit their attacks to military targets.' And later: 'you know that I have proposed to the world for years the cessation of bombing warfare, especially against civilian populations ... I waited over three months, but then one day I gave the order. I will take up the battle.' Winkelnkemper describes Hitler's 'knightly approach' and praises the 'almost mathematical accuracy' of the Stuka dive-bomber, 'a model for the world'.[154] The bombing of Britain was thus presented exclusively in terms of necessary self-defence:

> For three months, the Führer watched the criminal insanity of British air pirates. He gave the English people time to come to their senses and their catastrophic politicians time to see reason. But when finally the terror became ever more bold and their demands ever more impudent, the Führer gave the order to strike back.[155]

Cause Hitler was a man with a 'moral' cause. It is easy to neglect this fact and to see only his preposterous bellowing, the self-aggrandising calls to Lebensraum, to conquest and to racial dominion; yet if this had been the exclusive content of his rhetorical oeuvre he would have got nowhere. The real key to his rhetorical success was much more credible, residing in the more contemporary idea of the politics of victimhood. It was this that touched the hearts of his beer hall and auditorium audiences, this which fired the emotions alternately of sentimentality and rage, for what he offered was no less than a hallucination of injustice – the trigger in fact of a collective psychosis.

While the essence of the propaganda projection of Hitler lay in his rhetoric (defined by both the script and the performance, or dramatic expression), the core of this rhetoric was the manufacture of grievance. His story is an essay – relevant to our own times – in how grievance can be surfaced, packaged and politicised. This should not obscure the fact that many such grievances were indeed genuine, such as the loss of territory post-Versailles, the separation of East Prussia, the Danzig corridor to Poland, the French occupation of the Ruhr, the de-militarisation of the Rhine, the multi-billion reparation demanded though only partly exacted (and

Germany today is still bereft of Pomerania, Silesia and East Prussia and towns such as Kolberg and Königsberg, now Kaliningrad). Such were the raw materials of rhetorical conflagration at which the young Hitler excelled, and that is why they called him 'the drummer'. Part of the contemporary relevance of the phenomenon of the marketing of Hitler is that it reminds us how the dexterous manipulation of tribal or national grievance, legitimate and illegitimate, can inflame nihilistic aggression against the claimed perpetrators of the injustice. This has usefulness, for example, to the study even of terrorism today: a sense of injustice can be talked into people. Commitment does not pre-exist as an antecedent state, but is argued into being, the rhetorical creation of conviction: a vision of rebirth, an enemy to hate, the righting of historical wrongs, a job, a home, bread on the table and cash in the pocket.

Global Hitler

Then there was global Hitler, the Hitler who enchanted powerful foreign visitors, including those from the Anglosphere such as General Sir Ian Hamilton, the Hitler who mesmerised English hagiographers. No small part of the German global propaganda effort resided in the self-conscription of naïve – or dangerous – foreign verbalisers whose euphoria exhaled a thick mist of unreason. The English historian Arthur Bryant (who subsequently became the author of such books as *The Years of Endurance* and *Our Island Story*) offered a lavish encomium to Adolf Hitler – the unknown soldier of the Great War and so forth: 'the man who alone among the leaders of mankind, has endured all the sufferings and trials of a common soldier – and who to my eyes seemed almost like the German Unknown Warrior risen from the grave'.[156] The writer Henry Williamson admired the Führer in terms similar to German contemporaries:

> a man who had served in the ranks of the infantry, been wounded, and blinded by mustard gas, a man who loved Beethoven and lived only for the resurrection of his country's happiness – a nation's honour – a man who was the ideal of youth, was one who not only knew the truth, but could speak it and convey it to the minds of others. He was the corner-stone for the new, the realistic pacification of Europe.

Hitler according to Williamson was a 'truth perceiving father of his people'; he was 'the only pacifist in Europe'.[157] There were potentially more heavyweight recruits. T.E. Lawrence was approached about meeting Hitler, and had his fatal crash when returning from telegraphing Williamson agreeing to discuss the idea.[158] And Hitler knew how to flatter as well as convince: thus to Lloyd George: 'it was not in the first place the soldiers to whom victory was due, but to one great statesman, and that yourself, Mr Lloyd George'. The endorsement was reciprocated, with Lloyd George calling Hitler 'the greatest German of the age' and publishing a famous article in the *Daily Express* on his return and an interview in the *News Chronicle* praising Hitler.[159] There were also English rhapsodies such as Michael Fry's *Hitler's Wonderland* (1934) which says 'there is a magnetic fluid emanating from Hitler which seems supernatural', and James Murphy's *Adolf Hitler* (1934) (Murphy was a member of the German Propaganda Ministry for four years).[160] Books were also targeted at British schoolchildren, while school visits to Germany were actively encouraged. Thus Harrop's *Plain Texts in German* (1935) included 'Adolf Hitler ... a short account of his life and works'; this was a celebration of Hitler, his noble life and defence of children against bullies, and a paean to the greatness of the Nazi movement:

> the new Weltanschauung permeates all spheres of life, and everyone recognizes that National Socialism has not brought a change of government or of system, but a complete renewal of the conception of life. One can confirm with pride that the whole revolution took its course bloodlessly thanks to the outstanding discipline of the troops.[161]

German products like *Mein Kampf* in 1933 and books such as *Germany's Hitler*, and *For the Fatherland* (in 1934) were also published in English; the last of these concludes that 'later generations will consider the period of Marxian socialism as an interlude out of which purgatory the world emerged into the truer and beneficent conception of – ADOLF HITLER'.[162]

Conclusions

Thus one of the great points of utility in Nazi propaganda was the making of Hitler and not the party the core of the offer. This deflected critics: people think about politics in personality not ideological terms, and it is this insight that Hitler and the Nazis grasped. The leader was the brand. The leader was the party as well as the face of the party and the party's success did not exist independently from that of the leader. He was both other-communicated and self-communicated; he self-rhetoricised his image via the system of public auditoria, and the subcontractors did it for him via film, hagiographical text and so on. This goes to the heart of Fascism and why propaganda was so essential to its success, that is, it was a charismatic movement.

Notes

1 Evans, *Third Reich*.
2 Robert O. Paxton, *The Anatomy of Fascism*, London: Allen Lane, 2004.
3 Ibid.
4 Herzstein, *War*.
5 Sir Nevile Henderson, *Failure of a Mission*, London: Hodder and Stoughton, 1940.
6 Ian Kershaw, *Making Friends With Hitler*, London: Penguin, 2005.
7 Wistrich, *Weekend*.
8 Bullock, *Hitler and Stalin*.

9 Spotts, *Hitler and the Power*.
10 Ibid.
11 Ibid.
12 Ibid.
13 Ibid.
14 Ibid.
15 Peter Adam, *The Arts of the Third Reich*, London: Thames and Hudson, 1992.
16 Ross, *Media*.
17 Ibid.
18 Bracher, *German Dictatorship*.
19 Bullock, *Hitler and Stalin*.
20 Ibid.
21 John Weitz, *Hitler's Diplomat*, London: Phoenix (Orion Books), 1997.
22 Bullock, *Hitler and Stalin*.
23 Spotts, *Hitler and the Power*.
24 Bytwerk, *Bending Spines*.
25 Kershaw, *Making*.
26 Evans, *Third Reich*.
27 Ibid.
28 Ibid.
29 Piers Brendon, *The Dark Valley*, London: Jonathan Cape, 2000.
30 Wistrich, *Weekend*.
31 Henderson, *Failure*.
32 Kershaw, *Making*.
33 Henderson, *Failure*.
34 Ibid.
35 Weitz, *Hitler's Diplomat*.
36 Wistrich, *Weekend*.
37 Weitz, *Hitler's Diplomat*.
38 Sheehan, 'Hello'.
39 Spotts, *Hitler and the Power*.
40 Rutherford, *Hitler's Propaganda*.
41 Spotts, *Hitler and the Power*.
42 Cox, *Countdown*.
43 Kershaw, *Hitler Myth*.
44 Fest, *Hitler*.
45 Ibid.
46 Rutherford, *Hitler's Propaganda*.
47 Henderson, *Failure*.
48 *Mein Kampf* cited in Michael Blain, 'Fighting Words: What We Can Learn from Hitler's Hyperbole', *Symbolic Interaction*, 11 (1988).
49 Rutherford, *Hitler's Propaganda*.
50 Ibid.
51 Ibid.
52 Fest, *Hitler*.
53 Gustave Le Bon, *The Crowd*, n.p.: Filiquarian Publishing LLC, 2005.
54 Fest, *Hitler*.
55 Ibid.
56 Wistrich, *Weekend*.
57 Roberts, *Fox*.
58 Rutherford, *Hitler's Propaganda*.
59 Spotts, *Hitler and the Power*.
60 Rutherford, *Hitler's Propaganda*.
61 Ibid.
62 Fest, *Hitler*.

63 Spotts, *Hitler and the Power*.
64 Ibid.
65 Rutherford, *Hitler's Propaganda*.
66 Grunberger, *Social*.
67 *Goebbels Diaries*, 31 January 1940.
68 Ibid.
69 Ibid., 11 December 1940.
70 Bormann, *Hitler's Table Talk*, 11–12 July 1941.
71 Rutherford, *Hitler's Propaganda*.
72 Ibid.
73 Klemperer, *Language*.
74 Kershaw, *Hitler Myth*.
75 Brendon, *Dark Valley*.
76 Kershaw, *Hitler Myth*.
77 Klemperer, *Language*.
78 Grunberger, *Social*.
79 Klemperer, *Language*.
80 Ibid.
81 Kershaw, *Hitler Myth*.
82 Ibid.
83 Welch, *Propaganda*.
84 Grunberger, *Social*.
85 Fest, *Hitler*.
86 Speer, *Memoirs*.
87 Henderson, *Failure*.
88 Bormann, *Hitler's Table Talk*, 21–2 October 1941.
89 Petropoulos, *Art*.
90 Ibid.
91 Speer, *Memoirs*.
92 Kershaw, *Hitler Myth*.
93 Walter Schulze-Wechsungen, 'Political Propaganda', *Unser Wille Und Weg*, 4, Munich: Zentralverlag der NSDAP, 1934.
94 David Welch, 'Working Towards the Führer: Charismatic Leadership and the Image of Adolf Hitler in Nazi Propaganda' in A. McElligott and T. Kirk (eds), *Working Towards the Führer. Essays in Honour of Sir Ian Kershaw*, Manchester: Manchester University Press, 2004.
95 Kershaw, *Hitler Myth*.
96 Ibid.
97 Evans, *Third Reich*.
98 Burleigh, *Third Reich*.
99 Grunberger, *Social*.
100 Bytwerk, *Bending Spines*.
101 Wistrich, *Weekend*.
102 Hoffmann, *Triumph*.
103 Rutherford, *Hitler's Propaganda*.
104 McClatchie, *Look*.
105 Kershaw, *Hitler Myth*.
106 *Illustrierter Beobachter*, 1938, Folge 10.
107 Kershaw, *Hitler Myth*.
108 Grunberger, *Social*.
109 Wistrich, *Weekend*.
110 Welch, 'Charismatic'.
111 Kershaw, *Hitler Myth*.
112 Rutherford, *Hitler's Propaganda*.
113 Grunberger, *Social*.

114 Bullock, *Hitler and Stalin*.
115 Bracher, *German Dictatorship*.
116 Bullock, *Hitler and Stalin*.
117 *Berliner Illustrirte Zeitung*, 20 April 1939.
118 Adam, *Arts*.
119 Rutherford, *Hitler's Propaganda*.
120 Ibid.
121 Ibid.
122 Spotts, *Hitler and the Power*.
123 Herzstein, *War*.
124 Bracher, *German Dictatorship*.
125 Grunberger, *Social*.
126 *Berliner Illustrirte Zeitung*, 20 April 1939.
127 Grunberger, *Social*.
128 Ibid.
129 Adam, *Arts*.
130 Ibid.
131 Herf, *Arab World*.
132 Henderson, *Failure*.
133 Burleigh, *Third Reich*.
134 Rutherford, *Hitler's Propaganda*.
135 Kershaw, *Hitler Myth*.
136 Le Bon, *Crowd*.
137 Calvin College, German Propaganda Archive, Posters 1939–45, no. 1.
138 Bormann, *Hitler's Table Talk*, 27–8 July 1941.
139 Fest, *Hitler*.
140 Ross, *Media*.
141 Ibid.
142 Ibid.
143 Kershaw, *Hitler Myth*.
144 Ibid.
145 Ibid.
146 Roger Manvell, *Films and the Second World War*, London: J.M. Dent and Sons, 1974.
147 Bullock, *Hitler and Stalin*.
148 Max Clauss, 'The False Path of Pan-Europe', *Signal*, London: Bison Publishing, 1976.
149 Ross, *Media*.
150 Ibid.
151 Winkelnkemper, 'Cologne'.
152 Diewerge, *Plutocracy*.
153 Winkelnkemper, 'Cologne'.
154 Ibid.
155 Ibid.
156 Roberts, *Fox*.
157 Griffiths, *Fellow Travellers*.
158 Ibid.
159 Ibid.
160 Ibid.
161 Ibid.
162 Ibid.

5

PACKAGING OF THE REICH

The politics of consumption and the consumption of politics

> *No man however civilized can listen very long to African drumming, or Indian chanting, or Welsh hymn singing, and retain intact his critical and self-conscious personality. If exposed long enough to the tom toms and the singing, every one of our philosophers would end by capering and howling with the savages.*
> – Aldous Huxley, appendix to The Devils of Loudun *(1952)*

> *Films of the Third Reich emanated from Ministry of Illusion, not the Ministry of Fear.*
> – Eric Rentschler

> *National Socialism understood how to tackle the soulless framework of technology and fit it with the rhythm and hot impulses of our time.*
> – Joseph Goebbels

Introduction

Fascists were distinguished from other political movements via their proclaimed 'access to the crowd'. That crowd was won by a public dramaturgy of spectacle and publicity, and the exercise of charismatic authority; disciplined via paramilitary organisation; and deceived by the substitute of plebiscite for democratic electoral caprice.[1] This was a governing concept that was dependent on packaging both as a means and as an end. Blaring sound and screaming posters would announce a great public demonstration:

> elements of spectacle borrowed from circus and grand opera were cleverly combined with edifying ceremonial reminiscent of Church rituals. Parades of banners, much music, welcoming slogans, communal singing, and repeated cries of heil formed the framework for the Führer's speech. All these histrionic

elements built up the suspense and made the speech seem a kind of Annunciation.[2]

Even the SS were packaged. There is, for example, a well-known colour image of SS Reichsführer Heinrich Himmler picking flowers amid a glowing meadow[3] (one is grotesquely reminded of the policemen's song from *Pirates of Penzance*, 'When a felon's not engaged in his employment, Or maturing his felonious little plans, His capacity for innocent enjoyment, Is just as great as any honest man's'). In February 1939, Dr Goebbels commented that 'National Socialism understood how to tackle the soulless framework of technology and fit it with the rhythm and hot impulses of our time.'[4] But in reality, 'the goal of mass persuasion was to conceal the vacuousness of all those things that had been made an official part of the political landscape ...'.[5] The stress was on celebration in National Socialist propaganda – on people visibly and greedily enjoying themselves. National Socialism was a continuous sequence of triumphant action and an experience of a decade of chronic euphoria; a bustle of war films, uniforms, fast cars, the cult of the aeroplane, and trivia. Thus one observer:

> Nazism, more than perhaps any other regime, was literally obsessed by its own self representation ... They knew the power of visual bombardment in overcoming the average person's resistance and critical resolve. They realised how easily the normal recipient can mistake the illusion he or she is being offered for an authentic experience.[6]

The packaging was an important part of the instrumentality of Fascism: 'Fascism could well seem to offer to the opponents of the Left efficacious new techniques for controlling, managing, and channelling the nationalisation of the masses, at a moment when the Left threatened to enlist a majority of the population around two non-national poles: class and international pacifism.'[7] The decoration was the content. Siegfried Kracauer even, controversially, declared German Fascism a pseudo-reality.[8] In 1921, *Berliner Illustrirte Zeitung* had commented: 'what interests the masses of people are matters of sensory perception. The formation of their opinions proceeds from the visual appearance of life and its occurrences, not through intellectual consideration and speculation.'[9] Thus the 'deceptively beautiful sheen' of the Third Reich ultimately helped to conceal the murderous cruelty that lay at its heart,[10] since the Nazis fully recognised the sensual allure of modern popular culture.[11]

Symbols

Visual To invoke as a descriptor of this regime the word 'package' would surely seem an anachronism. Even today, the very idea of a political party or a politician being 'packaged' would receive a contumelious sneer from some political scientists. Yet it is possible to argue that Nazism was represented by a totalising symbol system and that therefore the package was indeed the message. The broader system of public rituals took many forms. In general there is what we might call a gimcrack Prussianism, where elements of archaic Prussian military culture were reimagined, distorted and dissolved into the texture of everyday life. The defunct imperial ceremonials of the *ancien régime* were replaced with a new ritual, celebratory not of monarchy and empire but of race and supremacy. But the militarism was also a way of retrieving lost pride, as for example in the Tannenberg Memorial ceremonies of October 1935.[12] This was a nation in uniform, clad in essentially an updated imperial sartorial of the old Wilhelmine armies, cavalry boots, gold braid, insignia gleaming against its mounting on field grey cloth background. This represented a sustained appeal to male vanity; the smart, even spectacular costumery, the swathes of SS black, the glittering orders and decorations and hierarchies, and the highest of heights remotely glimpsed – the Knight's Cross with Oak Leaves, Swords and Diamonds. The pictography of the regime was much enhanced by its support cast of thousands in their elaborate costumes and plumage. Brian Leigh Davis and Pierre Turner depict around 240 different uniforms from the Third Reich period, from Führer to Pimpfe to Stahlhelm to Post Office to falconry official to cabinet minister; sixteen ranks are listed for Hitler Youth, seventeen for Organisation Todt, eighteen for NSFK (National Socialist Flyers' Corps), seventeen for Stahlhelm.[13]

The packaging embraced an entire structure of symbols from small badges to giant buildings: the same messages were being communicated. The regime pioneered a distinctive style in all of its public manifestations, for example architectural structures such as the Air Ministry, and sundry exercises in gigantism and extroversion. The statement they made was often the same – that this was the new Rome. The imagery associated with this packaging was brought to life by the *Illustrierter Beobachter* of March 1939 with its big photograph of Berlin.[14] The city is shown in a swirling mass of lightness and dark – ranks of searchlights illuminate the sky, seething crowds, bright street lights, swastikas, classical buildings; all are decorated by a distinctive gift-wrapping such as the long red banners trailing much of the length of the buildings. Then there are the action shots of Hitler with his dynamic gestures acting the self-conceived role of Führer.

Spatial Public buildings were an integument of the packaging, a visible index of a political ethos and an expression of bombast. In 1929 Hitler remarked that 'out of our new ideology and our political will to power we will create stone documents'.[15] They had a use function but they also had an imagistic function. No leader who ever lived was perhaps more obsessed by architecture than Adolf Hitler, and for him architecture was always a political act. So architecture was packaging in a very direct way, a protection – the regime lived inside these very buildings – and a projection. Hitler's sense of political mission and his architectural ambitions were inseparable; only through political success could he have fulfilled himself artistically.[16] Significant buildings included the two temples to the Munich martyrs designed by Paul Ludwig Troost; his House of German Art (Hitler influenced this design); Speer's German Pavilion at the 1937 Paris Exposition; and Speer's Reich Chancellery.[17] Hitler thought that buildings should be 'erected with the aim of

FIGURE 5.1 Labour service poster

strengthening ... Authority'.[18] The packaging of the regime was embodied in the new Chancellery, hyperbole in stone. *Signal* lovingly chronicled the stupendous detail: the door of Hitler's study was twenty foot high and made of mahogany and German marble and decorated with his initials; the west portal of the Chancellery was 'crowned with the emblem of the great German Empire'.[19] A colour picture shows the long hall. The same article then goes on to describe Hitler's study itself: 'The walls are composed of dark red marble from the East marches and the

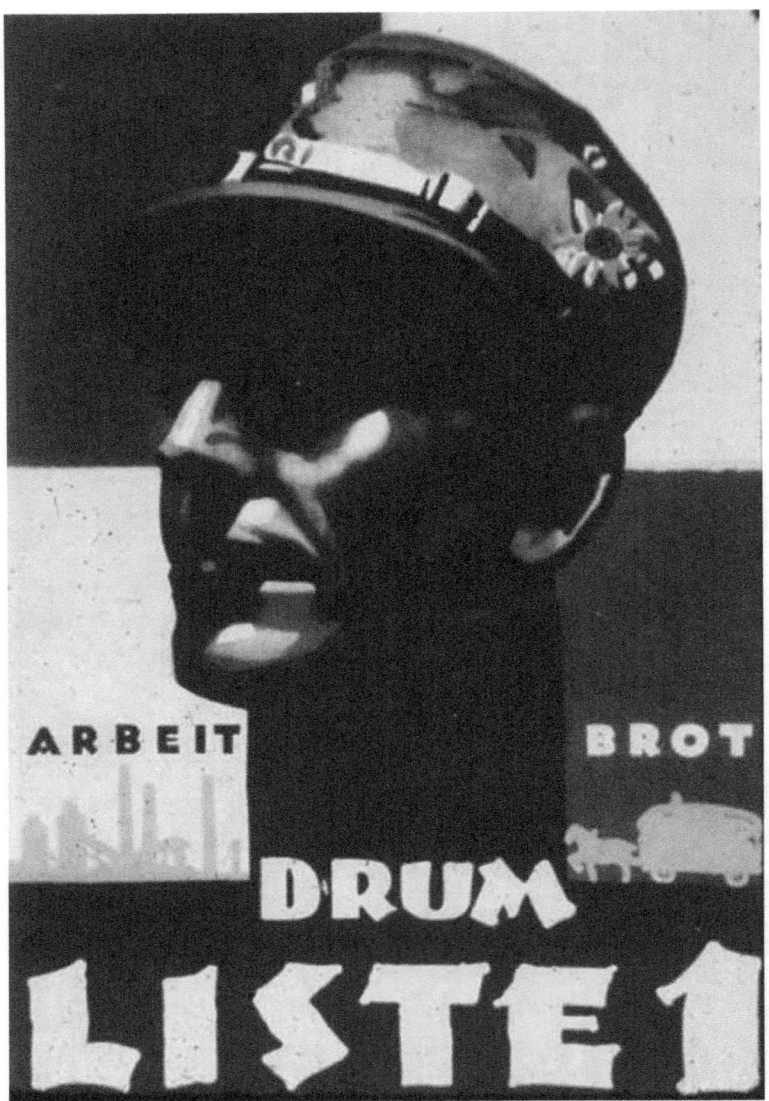

FIGURE 5.2 Storm trooper poster pre-1933

wainscot is a dark brown ebony. The floor is made of marble, and a half ceiling of rosewood.'[20]

Architecture was only one part of the broader theatre of public construction, as everything from motorways to ocean liners were also part of the packaging. 'Master Builder of the Reich' (April 1939) is a serial tableau from the *Berliner Illustrirte Zeitung* that seeks to imagine in one great image the new Germany: it pictures a teeming, outsize world, a land of pullulating energy.[21] There is a licensed cacophony – Bismarck's tomb and a wreath and sunbeams, crowds, more crowds. People are living in a legendary time, a world reinvented with ceaseless toil, the new bridges, muscular workmen, scaffolding, motorways: the shape of greater Germany is emerging, with squadrons in the air, ships, factories, horse-ploughing farmers. Mythology and technology coexist as two naked giants peruse the scene, a hyper-real and debased romantic ideological geo-scape. One author refers to the dynamism which so much construction suggested and which was in itself a propaganda device.[22] Like much else in the Third Reich, the aim even of the technology was not only effectiveness (i.e. direct instrumentality), but to impress (i.e. packaging).

Buildings had coherence with the rest of this palimpsest. A classic idiom recaptured not only the scale of ancient structures but such details as the quality of the stone and granite selected. This public propaganda of architecture was ongoing, as manifest for example in the plans for 'Germania'. Hitler said:

> At that time I lived in palaces of the imagination. And it was precisely at the time that I conceived the plans for the new Berlin ... Berlin will one day be the capital of the world.[23]

And thus:

> One will arrive there along wide avenues containing the triumphal arch, the pantheon of the army, the square of the people – things to take your breath away! It's only thus that we shall succeed in eclipsing our only rival in the world, Rome. Let it be built on such a scale that St Peter's and its square will seem like toys in comparison![24]

Germania would be an amalgam of ancient Rome, Paris, Washington, but on a superlative scale, epic poetry in stone. Thus the Fascist monumentalism of Hitler's great projects – his arch of triumph, for example, would be double the size of the Arc de Triomphe in Paris; the great hall in Berlin would be the tallest building in the world.[25] Features were borrowed from Paris – the arch of course, and the majestic boulevard, like the Champs-Élysées; and a dome like Washington's Congress (but much bigger with, reputedly, an internal climate). Water features and a lake would shimmer and reflect the grandiloquence of the place. Arenas, huge parade grounds including the Adolf Hitler Platz, and great fleets of administrative offices would make everything else, including Edwin Lutyens's recently completed New Delhi, seem stunted. There would be thirty-three theatres and a swimming pool to rival ancient Rome's Baths of Caracalla.[26] As one Nazi hagiographer proclaimed, 'the buildings of the Third Reich are the catechism of this secular faith put in stone and steel, concrete and iron!'[27] And then there was the continuous year-on-year construction of the Nuremberg stadium.

However, this trend 'did not exclude the selective adaptation of parts of the architectural heritage of modernism – technical rationality, economy, sobriety and functionalism ...'.[28] Bauhaus was not embraced but neither was Gropius entirely dismissed, and thus Troost adopted a minimalist approach that melded ancient and modern and Hitler was open to the idea of architecture being contemporary, nor did he interfere with the efficient and functional building style favoured by architects employed within the German Labour Front.[29] There was one truly modernist element in the Nazi aesthetic, albeit an unintentional one – the concrete gun emplacements of the Atlantic Wall that had been constructed by the Todt Organisation. These massively brutal slabs of concrete, whose gun slits resembled cruel eyes, were the signature of occupied coastal Europe (and the harbinger of what was to come in many a post-war European city centre). The party's art magazine also had a secondary edition with material on architecture included as well. Hitler 'knew the persuasive power of stone',[30] arguing in *Mein Kampf* that the large cities of Germany lacked a domineering monumentalism that symbolised the age, and that this separated them from the cities of the ancient world which all had their own special monument.[31] The ancient city excelled not in the private but in the public sphere, it was communalist and historicist – things which, in Hitler's words, were made 'not for the moment but for eternity'.[32] The objective of architecture was to transmit its spirit to posterity.[33] Speer entertained the bizarre concept of the 'ruin value' approach to architecture, making drawings of how Nazi buildings might look after the Reich had passed a thousand years hence. Although Hitler's retinue found this somewhat discomfiting, the Führer himself was apparently rather pleased by the idea.[34]

Ephemera

A theory of packaging

The package is a dress rehearsal for the consumption experience. There is a definitional meaning to this term, and beyond this it is in fact a metaphor. The packaging carries an idealised and hyperbolic image of the core product. It is a prior, antecedent idea of the product which defines expectations and anticipates the consumption experience. Package is, therefore, a separate medium. It is in fact an arrangement of the symbols into a unitary structure of meaning; but the idea is of accent, the aim not to convey the truth but to accentuate the most positive features. Packaging is thus a branch of advocacy, the way in which something is made more attractive, and hence we speak of the 'packaging' of a politician. But it carries with it an idea of inauthenticity in that certain things are hidden from view. The package is a kind of corset, holding the stuff in, giving visibility and pleasingness of form. The regime was indeed packaged, and such language in this context cannot be anachronistic:

> The party flag was everywhere in evidence. Huge posters, pictorial homilies, and Nazi slogans screamed from windows and kiosks, blazoning forth messages about honour and duty, national solidarity and social justice, bread, liberty and the beauty of sacrifice – all proclaiming the consummate skill with which

Hitler had been leavening the masses. Passers-by wore tiny lapel emblems; uniformed men elbowed their way through the crowds, the swastika circling their brawny arms. On every news stand the *Beobachter* and *Angriff* were piled high.[35]

Tangible The ephemera were packaging in a more literal way, the confetti, the tat, the regime's collectibles and knick-knacks. A weight of buttons, medals and badges facilitated self-aggrandisement, as did the various kinds of ceremonial knife. Swastika pennants, wine glasses and teacups were available to transmit the swastika brand to every conceivable social function. Kitsch abounded, such as Hitler Youth dolls, postcards of heroes and party events, cigarette cards and photographs of the regime figures; ubiquitous pamphlets, gilded volumes, stamps, photo-journalism essays by authors such as Hoffmann, with a high production quality for the more self-commemorative of these works. There were celebrity texts in elaborate binding, journals hailing achievements of the Reich such as technology and autobahns, commemorative books on the SA, the army, navy and air force, and beautifully illustrated manuals for Hitler Youth. Nevertheless, the tat of the regime was an important instrument of its popularity. To buy an object is to make a commitment, however trivial. It is part of the process of value exchange. The vulgarity, bright colours and brassy surfaces magnetised an urge to collect and thus an identification, however unconscious; since they were indeed ephemeral, it is often possible to forget about them and their significance. Insignia such as the hero mother medal for matrons of large families were also a way of connecting people to the Reich. All of these were public identity definers and ways of creating a civic adhesive which would bind rulers and ruled.

Intangible: style However, the idea of packaging has to mean more than its constituent elements. It also includes the intangible as well as tangible ways in which the Reich represented its idea of itself. Beyond even cultural ethos, it covers a certain social style, a sardonic extraversion, and a new kind of man: the Reich was a social mannerism, a look, a stare. Style was also an attitude, a swagger, embodied in the characteristic Nazi physical posture. The facial expression, part sneer/part leer, has been widely caricatured on film, but these things were actual enough, the aim was to intimidate. Nazi style offered vainglorious appeal: the long leather coats, high black boots; putting a man in uniform places him within a larger collective to which he assigns his identity. The style has been refracted through a thousand television and film performances, with the result that it has lost its historical moorings and has blended into a fictional world alongside intergalactic troopers, cybermen and so on. But at the time it was real enough, in the flesh, brutal, angry. Every storm trooper, every SS and party-uniformed official was a walking billboard for the party and the regime. They telegraphed its style and its primary notes of preening narcissism. The imagery of course was all of a piece – regime figures in pseudo-mystical, sham heroic poses; the intimations of euphoria; of scowling oligarchs and their alert henchmen, the cheerful youth, soldiery, the usual happy crowd. And, always, an idea of dynamism: their characteristic pose of alertness, action. They enthuse, brim-full of energy. The sinister aura of so much Reich

FIGURE 5.3 SA Mann poster

imagery can hardly be accidental and it too was part of the package and the packaging. These were not normal men. They seemed to have arisen from the dusks and the liminal spaces of history, sometime between the collapse of Rome and the rise of the Renaissance. The Nazi soldier himself was a cyborg, his 'coal scuttle' Stahlhelm, helmet, darkening part of his face in shadow, something other than, or less than, human.

Nazi media, particularly the illustrated magazines, were an idiosyncratic blend of consumerism and frivolity, ideology and regime symbolism. Their stress was on visual narrative via photographic essays. Germans had enjoyed a leading international position in photo-journalism and the illustrated magazines were its showcase, the Nazis were particular enthusiasts of this medium since the photograph reveals what is 'really there'.[36] A photograph is ostensibly a facsimile of an event as it occurred, and therefore valued as a propaganda medium since it is a capture of 'truth'. The magazines' garish front cover pictures are an invitation to view a drama. Everything is made like a movie, the image, action, sequence of striking photographs such as a night cockpit shot,[37] or a view over Alpine scenery from the glass nose cone of a bomber.[38] These cover pictures were full-page, such as an Allied ship framed by the propeller of a German plane in an edition of *Adler* from 1942.[39]

The composition of the photograph was constructed to elucidate meaning, the quality of the photo-journalism consistently good and an anticipation of television. There was a cult of personality, of intimacy, and readers would learn every detail of their military. Focus was also placed on Moscow with maps, planes and pictures and analysis of defensive structures with many technical images.[40] *Adler* in particular is about the machinery of war with diagrams of their internal workings, for example a Stuka dive-bomber;[41] or a photo spread of the Gigant aircraft, a mighty monster of the skies with its six engines.[42] This is war as process; all elements of war are here such as the factory with its production line of bombers. The interest is also in the preparatory part of military existence, such as life on an air base, with officers mimicking fighter plane motions and men examining the huge hole in a fuselage, and the backstage, for example the training of a Fahnenjunker or the teaching of parachutists to land properly.

And there was *Signal*, a visually stunning encomium to German power whose colour photographs and shameless prose were supposed to dazzle those living in the Reich's new imperium, and the speakers of the twenty or so languages in which it was published.[43] Thus, Germans were depicted as the conquerors of Paris, now the jewel in the Nazi crown. The image of Paris was cherished and embellished, with Germanisation simply absorbed into its traditional character, an authentic self returning to its elegantly egotistical ways.[44] The Nazis were self-presented as coming not as conquerors but as friends; their journalism focused on the fiction of an everyday world unaffected by the imperium of the Third Reich and the granite face of its ambition. Paris, twenty-four hours after the occupation, and a Parisian who fought in the war of 1870 is shown conversing with a German corporal; German soldiers become German tourists in a Paris 'which has been left intact' while traffic policeman peruse their new military tenants with intense curiosity.[45] *Signal* specialised in the kind of frivolous journalistic essay that is ostensibly apolitical, full of the hack journalist's bogus bonhomie and posturing curiosity before the world. Thus an article entitled 'Paris on Wheels' features a chic cyclist who 'keeps her reputation for smartness, even on a bicycle'; like all such journalism it revels in incongruities such as the pedal-powered cycle-car, and never fails to refresh a stereotype such as the pipe-smoking, cycling professor.[46] *Signal* also adores the mystique of Vichy; the ubiquitous portrait of Petain 'seems to watch with ironical eyes all those who come to Vichy for a few days to intrigue, to spy and to whisper ...'.[47] Everything, even the institutions of war, are made to seem normal, as with the images of Maurice Chevalier singing in a prisoner of war camp.

The physical extinction of the Allies was chronicled in vivid prose and photo-sets, the battered machines of the enemy shown strewn across the burned landscapes like smashed baubles. It was a visual poetry of mastery and of nihilism, for this is the exultation of demolition: 'ruined ... tanks cover the field as far as the eye can see'.[48] Another *Signal* photo-set purports to be 'the first coloured photographs of the great battle in the West'; Sedan is depicted in flames, its buildings set against a burning sky. In a two-page colour photo spread (as if from *Saving Private Ryan*) the blasted French town is framed by the silhouette of a steel-helmeted German soldier staring down from a church tower.[49]

Frivolity

The Reich was constructed through its media. Nazi Germany never seemed like Nazi Germany, the imagined Reich of folk memory: the prolific cartoons in *Adler*, the smiling, happy faces of the men, the projection of a lightweight world, evoke even a frivolous Reich where the gentle touch was determinedly manufactured, and projected through the many illustrated weekly magazines:

> The point is rather that, like the popular cinema, their political utility lay not in shouting the virtues of a Nazi-led Germany from the rooftops but in conveying a reassuring sense of cosmopolitanism and social harmony by means of visual pleasure, thus teaching readers to look away from the brutality of the regime.[50]

There is atmosphere and action footage in Nazi propaganda, but, also, a remorseless tone of the light and optimistic such as the German soldiers with camels;[51] the birdie and her chicks; men wrestling and pulling funny faces.[52] The humour of the Reich could also be unintentional: garden workers in Potsdam marching solemnly with their watering cans on top of poles, a po-faced legion of serious men doing silly things.[53] The cartoons were another facet – a woman in a bath is surprised when loads of little boys with small boats open the bathroom door, while an anti-Semitic cartoon features a fat 'Jew' speaking to a worried Teuton housewife.[54] The cartoons represent the Reich's idea of humour, such as men returning to their wives and girlfriends from Africa with monkeys and crocodiles as pets.[55] Propaganda is, prima facie, an explicit symbol system with no secondary definer, but actually the Nazis did often conceal their propaganda. Newspapers looked and felt as they had done before the seizure of power.[56]

Editors are ever alert for the idiosyncratic, such as the picture of a British Army band in gas masks,[57] or incongruity, as with the seat carved out of a huge bomb with a fellow sitting inside it,[58] or the Luftwaffe airman mounted on a donkey.[59] The magazines sought to interest their readers in the sights and stories of a vast and exotic world, even if the perspective on that world was a parochial one. A global gaze features the (Islamic) world of North Africa;[60] Argentina; tanks in Moscow;[61] circus animals; flying to Rio and Buenos Aires; middle-class black people in South Africa;[62] and Ibn Saud of Saudi Arabia.[63] Other articles show the Westminster Coronation;[64] glamorous shows; adverts for Atikah Turkish cigarettes; a curious spread on Albania with its burka-clad women.[65] Readers are offered various scenes in Alexandria of women in Western bathing suits, women in burkas, and women, confusingly, in both. There are standard images, for example material on Gay Paris,[66] but also a very un-Nazi spread on über-modernist buildings in Tripoli[67] (thus other ideas, other aesthetics, were progressing within the world-Fascist order).

The journals were a kind of smorgasbord of divergent images, a sort of visually arrested stream of consciousness, designed to amuse, divert and entertain: imagery of stage shows, chapters from novels, pictures of actors and actresses, celebrity culture. Thus an edition of *Das Reich* from 20 January 1941 is organised under the headline 'Ist England zu retten?' and a big action-shot of Mussolini; but follows this with a set of images and stories which seem to derive as much from the realms of aesthetic kitsch and celebrity as they do from politics.[68] Photos of films, shows, theatre scenes jostle alongside new sculpture and images of the men of the day – Victor Lutze of the SA, Lord Halifax and so forth. The rituals of state are also visually recorded, such as an article depicting the Führer in white tie at the opera from March 1939.[69] What they lack are any kind of coherence or unitary message – old cars contrasted with the modern VW, a feature on the fall of a corrupt American politician, Roman finds, a canvas boat, advertising, pretty girls with their long legs showing seductively;[70] the delights of an oasis resort in the desert expressed visually and lyrically; and life at the US Military Academy of West Point. Other scenes include the Japanese at Heidelberg, and of course the record of the giant ceremonials of the Third Reich such as Nuremberg.[71] But there is no design to this tumult of lucid images: bare-chested Africans feature, latterly becoming French colonial soldiers,[72] and there is an essay on ancestry, while in another issue Bund Deutscher Mädel girls visit a 104-year-old woman.[73] Fortifications, immense, brooding, are seen guarding Germany's coast in the North Sea, the nautical ramparts of the Reich. There is a two-page spread on Westminster Abbey, where a craftsman is seen cleaning the memorial to Admiral Sir Cloudesley Shovell.[74]

The onrush of images from an exotic Fascist world

The magazines offered readers a world viewed from a provincial German prism, but a perspective that often seemed merely surprised and curious rather than bigoted: from Texas farm boys, quaint in their straw hats (shades of Tom Sawyer) to a shepherdess in traditional costume, to the image of half-naked showgirls reminiscent of the old Windmill Theatre.[75] Sensation was still an important part of the media in the Reich and lurid tales were permissible if they were not actually subversive, a retreat once more from ideological austerity.[76] But there were also vistas of a gracious world, such as the ballet or the day at the races where the gentry of the Reich assembled, the old and new elites meet, old elegance and brash new symbols – Prince George but also Gauleiter Wagner, Max Amman, Otto Dietrich; the contrast of top hats and party uniforms.[77] At its core, however, was a Fascist world, a political geography that teemed with ideological confrères and allies in the new credo and its aesthetics of ritual.

But the magazines can sometimes seem contemporary, almost, in fact, of our era: there is for example a feature in one article on Count Ciano, bare-chested on the beach or clad in a polo shirt standing next to a car, the relaxed modern politician on vacation.[78] The image-building usually reflects a propaganda-constructed world, though on occasion, as with the pictures of dead civilians in the Sino-Japanese conflict, a real one. But some parts of the propaganda construction were more deceitful (i.e. pure fable) than others, such as the images of inter-racial harmony over the Olympic period – white, Sikh and black cheerfully together, or separate but on equal terms; happy Indians; ladies of all races meeting; an Indian yogi; women, one of them Asian, linking arms and so forth.[79] These images are 'real' enough in that they have occurred historically, but at a deeper level they are a false construction, that is, the public and temporary claim of the racial state to be a supra-racial state.

Mobility The magazines seem mesmerised by the idea of mobility and they introduced this earth for their readers via travelogue, for example *Die Woche*'s big photo-journalist spread on German seaplanes flying around South America.[80] The magazine's cover invites perusal via the bizarre image of a cowboy contemplating the German plane, and Rio is seen from its windows and, *en passant*, a Zeppelin in the distance; 'Condor über Sudamerika' also delivers us exciting views of the Andes. The illustrated magazines offer then perspectives on to a broader world, epic even, but also tragic, the dazed world of the 1930s with such horrors as Shanghai – Germans must therefore have been familiar with modern war and its consequences for civilians.[81] It is a global order lacerated with conflict and still dominated by the senescent British Empire. Thus in October 1937 the cover of *Berliner Illustrirte Zeitung* shows an Arab holding aloft the swastika flag while perched on the bonnet of an open-top Mercedes, and within its pages a photo spread of the British occupation of Palestine, British troops in riot gear looking over the city-scape and so forth.[82]

Celebrity showcase The magazines were a celebrity showcase, especially rhapsodising the images of regime favourites (but also almost anyone else in the world who had become famous). Thus an article from 1943 contains a full front-page photograph of General Dietl in his sheepskin garment,[83] while another offers masses of material on Mussolini with a photo-journal history of his career and a mighty colour photograph.[84] There were also features on Marshal Balbo in Libya,[85] and a photo spread of the Labour leader Constantine Hierl.[86] But there were differences of emphasis between the illustrated magazines. So *Berliner Illustrirte Zeitung* used an 'established formula of eye-catching photos and illustrations that spoke for themselves with little explanatory text', and it also 'continued to serve up the same diet of celebrity portraits, fashion, high society, Royals, serialised novels, recent inventions, natural catastrophes, and all manner of human interest stories that had packed its pages for decades'.[87] In contrast, the *Illustrierter Beobachter* 'specialised in the visual portrayal of the Führer and the Nazi movement' (the *Illustrirte* had projected regime titans 'in a personal rather than an iconic manner, for instance Hitler walking his dogs in the Alps, or Goebbels on holiday with his children').[88] Hitler storms through all these illustrated pages, the vortex of regime imagery, receiving and being received by the king of Italy on alternate state visits, contemplating vast fleets, his colour photographs adorning front covers.[89] Such covers are an invitation to continue the journey, to seek within. They were the packaging of the packaging and offered images which were visually arresting, for example the Hitler birthday edition of *Berliner Illustrirte Zeitung* from 27 April 1939 with its precision geometric vistas of marching troops. War when it comes manufactures a new, more youthful and ebullient set of heroes such as the fighter ace Lieutenant Marseille.[90] The Knight's Cross winners, astonishingly young and not invariably radiating the 'sunny' disposition favoured by the regime, process across these pages with who knows what impact on readers; comrades in flying suits, dashing, smiling, arms around each other (*Adler* cover, 1943) – the customary camaraderie shot from all the air forces of the Second World War.[91] Inevitably in such a world, the final peak of celebrity is heroic death, the glory and the fame extinguished, the gallant deeds chronicled in the farewell valedictions such as the obituaries of Mölders and Udet from December 1941.[92]

Arts

Wistrich points out that politics and ideology invaded aesthetics in the 1930s. The arts were inevitably heavily politicised and the illusion of pure aestheticism was impossible: in this decade, according to one observer, 'propaganda in some form or other lurks in every book'.[93] Art was another way the regime sought to package itself, another conduit or means of propagation. Its function was to reinforce imagery generated by primary media – of Hitler for example – but also to expand the range of such imagery and endow it with the dignity of classical portraiture. Oils and watercolours were not intended merely for the galleries or private consumption, but to be endlessly reproduced as posters, cards or images in magazines. The aesthetic of the Nazis looked to early models such as Dürer or Bruegel, and rather more generally the aesthetic was petrified in a kind of mid-nineteenth-century agrarian romanticism: all experiment was banned. Hitler wrote 'if the creative spirit of the age be manifested in the Parthenon, then the Bolshevist era is manifested through its Cubist grimace';[94] but this is precisely what Communism did not do. Moreover, although some banned artists had been political critics, Dix for example, others had not (e.g. Nolde).[95] So this was simply another branch of propaganda, nothing more, nothing less: thick-set villagers, ideal families, horses and folk festivals. And of course, virile combat soldiers, especially after the war had begun. The Roman idiom was a constant theme, from the Roman salute of the parade ground to the style of the buildings and kitschified revelries of the sculptors such as Arno Breker, scowling male nudes with tiny penises, mighty, muscular, their bodies an act of violence. The anatomy of Nazi sculpture was outsized to an extreme degree, so that much of the (internal) muscular system of the body was visible (external). It is what postmodernists would call hyper-real, taking us beyond photographic truth to something which is exaggerated to the point of caricature. These statues really were self-parodic. Emphases in music were of a similar martial dimension.

Hence although the artistic technique of Nazi art shares many of the characteristics of the style of the previous centuries, the presence of ideology is also felt. This is not to say that, for example, similar group portraits, in similar manner, were not done throughout Europe and the United States in the 1930s. The group sequence of individuals at work and play portrayed in a hyper-realist mode and frozen in stylised or even ritualised form was a familiar aesthetic signature of the decade. But the Nazis could not entirely excise modernist accents although they wanted to, even where the rigours of neo-classicism were applied with totalitarian frenzy, literally so with the Führer personally objecting to some entries for the Great German Art Exhibition at the House of German Art in 1939 (even though the exhibits had been vetted by the formidable Frau Troost). There was a seepage of abstraction and impressionism and caricature into even the most deracinated artistic culture and its product.

Music was an important part of the packaging; indeed, the Reich resembled a musical, so invasive was the melodious background. Music functioned as propaganda at many levels. It was expressive of an aesthetic of martial heroism of course, but it also acted as static propaganda. That is, its very ubiquity buttressed notions of the Reich as the cultured nation, evidenced for example by the number of opera houses it possessed. The aesthetic mobilised in Nazi song was partially derivative from hymn-signing as well as antique folkish tunes and ballads, or the sentimental dirges or saccharine patriotic airs of the nineteenth century. In this as much else, the Nazi aesthetic was a synthesis and repackaging of heritage elements within German culture. But the principal origins and inspiration lay in traditional German military music; in fact songs such as 'Watch on the Rhine' (as sung by Major Strasser and his cronies in the film *Casablanca* (1942)), usually imputed to Nazis, often date from much earlier. Yet the grandiloquence of the martial was difficult to reconcile with the popular cultural embrace of voguish nightclub acts, or the semi-submersible jazz scene, but all of this was part of the same cultural conundrum. Germans simply possessed a public political and private domestic sphere and learned to distinguish the two. Each had its separate cultural props.

Hence there was an operatic quality to the Third Reich itself, one reinforced by this starring role of music, brisk and melodic military marches or pseudo-sacerdotal and hymn-like, a significant dualism. This musical background was a constant; images were not simply projected but elevated through the playing of jaunty airs or solemn tunes (behind this lay a great infrastructure of local band training and music production). Music was a part of Fascist monumentalism – over the airwaves, but also live at every kind of event. The invasion of the Soviet Union, for example, was serenaded by radio's bombastic music with recorded battle sounds, the boom of artillery, the banshee wail of the Stuka dive-bombers.[96] Fascists recognised the power of music to illuminate emotional interiority, to evoke atmosphere without tedious ideological didacticism. Words commit, words describe, but music merely feels. Ideas may resonate but music haunts.

Modernism

Nazism was a deviant version of modernism, a default path. The scientists themselves were willing conscripts in the continuous search for a scientific base for the ideology, everything from the exposition of 'German physics' and archaeology into Teutonic prehistory to the Ahnenerbe's Tibetan expedition with its measurement of Tibetan heads to discover traces of proto-Aryans. But there was also a continuous invocation of pseudoscience in any particular social domain. The futurism of the process was manifest obviously in the civil constructions like the autobahns, and in military hardware too, rockets, jets and so forth. Hence even the motor car was a propaganda instrument and a highly effective one, with the subsidising of Grand Prix teams – 'millions of Europeans got their first close-up of Blitzkrieg style action by watching Germany's 600 hp Mercedes or Auto Union's racing cars thunder past their cowed opponents'.[97] At Donington Park in 1937 'the British crowds were awed; they had never seen such a display of massive power'.[98] Then there was Ambassador Ribbentrop in London – 'yet London crowds were impressed by that long black Mercedes with its swastika flag and London licence plate CYF3 rolling into Buckingham Palace, arriving at Westminster Abbey or at 10 Downing St'.[99]

The effectiveness of Nazi propaganda was intimately connected with a historic coincidence. The Nazi Party, its ideology of race chauvinism and methodology of propaganda, entered the great stage of history at exactly the moment when the moving image ceases to be silent and staccato and flows, vocalised and assured. In 1931, Goebbels himself boasted that Nazism 'uses all the means of modern technology. Leaflets, and ... posters, mass demonstrations, the press, stage, film and radio – these are tools of propaganda.'[100]

The modernist packaging fulfilled important propaganda functions. It anchored Nazism in the contemporary, its claim to be the latest, best. Consumerism was a key part of this 'modernity' packaging, of course, and a key differentiator from the ideological competitor brand, Bolshevism. Thus there was the 'modern, consumer oriented lifestyle on display in hit comedies', films which 'exuded an almost hedonistic attraction amidst the constant appeals to discipline and heroic self-sacrifice'.[101] The magazines evoked a romantic world, elegant, dreamy and, at the margin, erotic: the cover of *Die Woche* in October 1933 offered the pastel colours of autumn leaves, a young man and girl on bikes in the country, casual, innocence in sweetness – bland girl, floppy-haired boy.[102] The latent hedonism of the Reich's world is instantly recognisable to modern consciousness, a world of film, actors, advertising and beautiful women and girls in swimsuits. The Nazis were acutely aware of American-style consumerism, and indeed attacked it, as with the article criticising American advertising or what they called the 'Kitschified mass soul'; but while abusing it, they also replicated. Advertising, the poetry of consumption, was a significant part of the packaging of the Reich. Indeed, the Nazis made the fateful decision to continue with an essentially consumer economy until the later years of the Second World War, until in fact Goebbels's Total War speech of 1943. Social aspiration, the quest for status, the longing for identity-bearing and identity-defining goods, these things were intuitively understood by the Nazi Party and its ideologues.

Thus *Signal* was more than the propaganda magazine of the German army (it was a condominium, controlled also by the Propaganda and Foreign Ministries). The magazine discusses the major themes of war, such as military and economic matters, but in addition to that there are rather surprising topics, such as art, fashion, history or cinema. Far from merely being a collection of excellent photographs from the war, *Signal* constitutes a mirror of a certain vision of the life in Europe during the last World War, which truly makes it a fabulous subject of research.[103]

The stylisation of *Signal* was a significant influence long after the demise of the Reich, since it had been the world's first colour news magazine, for example publishing almost 160 colour images of Operation Barbarossa.[104] Post-war *Paris Match* 'drew heavily from the layout, conception and design of *Signal*. In 1956 a *Paris Match* reporter claimed: "our role model is *Signal*. You know, they were already publishing color pictures at that time. We kept those old volumes. It's something you can learn from."'[105] It was indeed lavish, with a Polish print-run of 100,000 copies, as well as Spanish, Swedish, Finnish and Turkish editions. There was even a Russian version, of which one recently discovered edition significantly contains images of peace not war on both its covers.[106] The height of *Signal*'s circulation was 2,500,000 copies per issue; and in its vigorous promotion of the Pax Germanica appears to have impacted the European Volunteer Movement.[107]

The key stylistic influences on Nazi communications were commercial aesthetics. They borrowed from a world of consumerist imagery: magazines, advertisements, book illustrations, cinema posters. These located Nazi imagery in terms already well understood: 'Party propagandists made little attempt to hide the influence of commercial advertising on their key techniques, from the use of lighting to poster design to the development of concise symbols.'[108] Posters, for example, mimicked commercial forms and therefore served to de-toxify the Nazi message: by placing something in the public space you make it part of the social landscape, you naturalise it. For example, the poster for the film *SA Mann Brand* is a stylised storm trooper holding aloft a swastika flag, the upper part of his face in shadow as he looks towards the distance.[109] It is an image of controlled ferocity and murderous intent. The effect is sensational in the manner of film posters, but it seems to make Nazism just another media event, to normalise the abnormal, to legitimate the perverse. Nazi posters were still in the tradition of popular illustrators, melodramatic, with only certain things brought into sharp focus (face and hands and knuckles, since hands in the image were often clenched). Bodies are shown taut for action: square jaws and lined faces and not an ounce of spare flesh, veined hands on belt buckle, eyes pierce the middle distance. But, again, the values are those of the upmarket comic book or the popular retail novel.

Packaging of the Reich 153

The physical, vigorous posters contrast with the moribund art. An aspect of the posters is their modernist and abstract aesthetic, a style specifically banned in formal art as 'degenerate' and yet justified in a propaganda context, enhancing also the contemporary feel of the regime: Rutherford concludes 'at the same time, in their design the posters were models of the art, using techniques well in advance of their times – which is why they always stood out from the others'.[110] They were also 'never overloaded with texts; their drawings simple, straightforward …'.[111] For an image to sustain either extinction, or exhibition, was entirely governed therefore

FIGURE 5.4 SA Mann Brand film poster

FIGURE 5.5 Wounded storm trooper pre-1933 poster

by the designation of the format; but such internal contradictions never seemed to matter in Nazi ideology. Take, for instance, a poster for the 1935 Saar referendum.[112] The figure is an abstract one of a male form, the face rutted with anxiety and holding forth his arm and hand, not so much in greeting as in a plea for help. He is bathed in shadows; the idea is of someone coming out of the darkness and into sunshine; he is wearing a light-coloured tunic. It is highly effective, and again would have merited the exhibition of Degenerate Art. In fact commercial advertisers praised Nazi propaganda efforts and moreover businesses

FIGURE 5.6 Work and fight wartime poster

sometimes imitated Goebbels's publicity extravaganzas, as for example with the launch of the newspaper *Tempo* in 1928 which plagiarised the advertising campaign for *Der Angriff* a year earlier.[113]

There was a co-existence of the extreme tyranny of the regime with easy-going, sensually charged media products which could have been manufactured by a democracy. This was not accidental: 'realising that loyalty could not be sustained by brute force and terror alone, the Nazis struck a bargain with the German people, satisfying appetites and stimulating imaginations'.[114] Thus German film makers of that era profoundly admired the professionalism, craft and technical

FIGURE 5.7 Saar referendum poster

excellence of the American product; and so the film *Habanera* for example consciously adopts American forms of recognition.[115] The regime did not seek a monopoly of entertainment. This was not Russia; Nazi audiences were watching many of the same Hollywood movies, maybe by some of the eminent Jewish producers of the era, as Americans. The social grammar of such movies is democratic and demotic, an idea of normality in a civil society, the antithesis of the Nazi state.

What is often neglected in the public remembering of the Third Reich is the illusion of normalcy which the dictatorship was able to create. It looked and felt, despite all the uniforms, like the modern world: the world of movie posters, magazines piled at newsstands, foreign movies, international magazines and newspapers, foreign radio broadcasts. There was *Das Reich*, the 'quality' newspaper founded by Goebbels in mimicry of Britain's *Observer* and an illustration of the Nazi talent for producing facsimiles of the symbols of a sophisticated Western democracy. All this changed with the war, but before then many of the movies shown in the Third Reich were from Hollywood, and they had a marked impact, audiences sometimes groaning when the Teutonic product appeared on the screen. The Reich was not a sealed information system. Fashions, styles, attitudes from outside Nazi Germany were buzzing within, even to the extent of the Nazi cultural system itself seeking to imitate them, as with the re-make of the film *It Happened One Night*, re-imagined, recast, as the German film *Lucky Kids*. German audiences loved Disney: Goebbels noted in his diary on 20 December 1937 'I present the Führer with thirty of the best films from the last four years and eighteen *Mickey Mouse* films for Christmas.'[116] The films were particularly appreciated by their recipient: 'he is very pleased about it, delighted with this treasure'.[117] Goebbels later spoke of 'the magnificent artistic achievements' of *Snow White and the Seven Dwarfs*. Busby Berkeley was an influence on Nazi musicals. Germans also loved Westerns, and *Lives of Bengal Lancer*, that 'primer of manly vigor', was particularly influential.[118]

The aura, this look and feel of an ordinary society, was sustained in every way possible. It was perpetuated, for example, by the social character of Nazi journalism with its easy-going, gossipy, mildly inquisitive and even comedic ethos, and its slight raising of the veil on the management of the regime – such as a *Signal* article entitled 'A Day in the Life of the Propaganda Ministry', with a cast of official cars, international communications, the office of Goebbels and so on.[119] There was a cult of the light, the trivial and the everyday, the idle chatter of the ordinary, of an innocent parish. This was further refined by very powerful appeals to altruism and the civic sense, for how could a regime which had stressed the love of others be murdering people? In the continuity of its consumer culture, and in colour movies, action films, press and radio programmes, foreign tourists and an ostensible openness to the world, the regime sought to mask itself and its true drivers towards authoritarian control and the obliteration of the individual critical mind. Few actually went on a Strength Through Joy cruise to Madeira or obtained the Strength Through Joy Car (de-Nazified as the Volkswagen Beetle, the most successful car of all time). But radio became a general feature and so did movie-going. The ostensible modernity of the Reich is an important explanatory factor in assessing its appeal, the fact that it in some way managed to seem relevant, to tap into the international zeitgeist of the time – what was in the air. The relationship between a Busby Berkeley extravaganza and the human geometrics of a Nuremberg rally may seem to stretch comparative semiotics to extremes, but, obvious or not, a relationship exists.

The Nazi world was at many levels strangely seductive. It was emphatically not the image post-war cinema has encumbered it with: the caustic bark of command, the inhuman grimace, the rigidities of hierarchy. The reductivism of humans to automata functions as an appropriate metaphor for aspects of the Nazi state. But to describe what it truly felt like, and seek some explanatory richness for the way it captivated the minds of so many, we must look elsewhere. The Hitler Jugend, for example, was not self-presented as a rigid exoskeleton of discipline, regimentation and organised bullying. Whatever the truth, the organisation was actively marketed as a sort of uniformed adventure holiday, the fun of the vigorous collective free of the invasiveness of a pompous adult world.

Thus in *Hitler Youth* (Gustav Memminger) the delightful world of the Hitler Youth is revealed. Despite the publication date (1942) there are only a few casual visual references to war (collecting tin cans): a year of shadows for the Reich, yet complacency reigns and civic participation is limited and ritualised.[120] No intellectual pursuit is inscribed in the text such as reading or art for the boys, but sunlit open-air vistas often near water and with plenty of sunshine, and there are over twelve beach scenes. We graduate in ages from the little 'Pimpfe' to the senior sea cadets. The book is full of images of camp life – throwing someone in the air, lots of hiking, pitching tents, canoeing, the rituals. It is exhilarating and the boys laugh with their eyes; they seem deeply, profoundly happy. The focus is on action, such as making an aeroplane or holding a model warship, and repose is only the suspense of action. But it is the antithesis of what a totalitarian system should look and feel like: nothing commanded, the rule system invisible, everything spontaneous. What we have here is the capture of a world, de-individuated, but warm, a constructed boys' world liberated from parent and pedagogue, indulgent and sentimental. Scattered throughout the book are charming marginalia cartoons and drawings, often of bemused figures, humorous, with castles and cottages and pieces of heritage, objects of equipment such as shaving kits, tools such as water cans. All this is enhanced by the use of different styles of print and multiple colours so that attention is maintained.

Entertainment – film

Power of the medium

Film in the words of one critic was 'the genuine mother tongue of humankind'[121] (belatedly recognising this, the old imperial state had increasingly intervened in film). The twentieth century had seen the creation of a cinematic language which was visual and universal;[122] there was a new psychology of the cinema, the actor swells to giant size (television diminishes, a difference, the one small and private, the other public and shared). Hence the new notion of 'stars', literally the lights we gaze up at. Hitler was part of this, star of shows, newsreels and the cinematic operetta *Triumph of the Will*. Rutherford comments 'paradoxically, the projected images of light and shadow made to move by the phenomenon of the persistence of vision have a strange kind of immediate conviction lacking in the other arts'.[123] The venom created is 'as likely to destroy those who produce it as those who consume it'. The cinematic experience provides flow and blurs transitions in time and space; it heightens sensations of reality and immediacy and has a comprehensive range.[124] Being viewed communally with others, it offers a connection between collective thoughts and feelings, while the cunning angle of photography can manipulate perception.[125] Filmgoers are hypnotised persons, 'voluntary captives'.[126] This is a free surrender of intellectual autonomy. The viewer 'cannot help succumbing to the suggestions that invade the blank of his mind', and thus film is a unique instrument of propaganda.[127] And there is film as a physiological experience, tears and so forth, 'an unconscious sense of liberation from the rational control we normally exercise'.[128] Nazi film offers a scale of values, and one is 'apparently' invited to choose sides.

Weimar had been a world leader in the film industry and a potential rival to Hollywood. Films such as *The Cabinet of Dr Caligari, Nosferatu*, Fritz Lang's *Metropolis, The Blue Angel* and *The Golem* were, and remain, among the greatest classics of the silent era; and actors whose names would subsequently become world famous – Dietrich, Lorre and so on – ornamented the industry. The Nazis did not invent a Nazi cinema *ab initio*. These films both resemble their historic predecessors and also their successors, and they have a collective 'feel' of the pre-war Hollywood cinema and its European imitators. Indeed, there is little that is obviously 'Nazi' about them – but that was part of the master plan. Even an overtly Nazi film like *HJ Quex* can shamelessly plunder the imagistic legacy of its predecessors (in this case, the Weimar proletarian film). It is clearly part of a cultural continuity, a default path but still within an established tradition. Hence Nazi culture came forth to the German people as neither entirely, or even mainly, new or shocking.

Importance of film to the Nazis The use of entertainment to persuade was not of course invented by the Nazis. But persuasion through cultural gatherings was a generic category of propaganda according to the propaganda theorist G. Stark, and this included theatre and conference, and film, and he cited the influence of Bolshevik propaganda on the Nazis as a model – such as *Battleship Potemkin*.[129] He applauds the success of the NS Volksbühne and NS Filmbühne and suggests attempting to 'supplement political speeches with films in the suburbs'.[130] Cinema was to become a very significant component of regime projection and the essence of its packaging. New groups were also converted to cinema-going, the less well-off now 'spending roughly twice as much on cinema in 1937'.[131] It wrapped the regime in the clingfilm of modernity, the dream factory of Babelsberg, a sunset boulevard for Teutons. There was of course no Nazi *Gone with the Wind, Casablanca* or *Grapes of Wrath*; the Nazis could not reach the heights of war/pre-war Hollywood either in their craftsmanship, that slick putting together, or the sense of epic. They could seldom dazzle an audience, but they could captivate it. Quality now overrode quantity, fewer, better films sustained the rising production costs.[132] The Volk loved the 'capitalist made dream worlds churned out by UFA and MGM'.[133] Hitler had said to his visitors 'one cannot deprive people of distractions; they need them, and that is why I cannot reduce the activity of the theatres and studios. The best relaxation is that provided by the theatre and the cinema.'[134]

Hitler was a media phenomenon both as producer and consumer, an avid watcher of media of every kind both traditional, such as grand opera, and popular, mainly talking pictures. He understood that media was not just another instrument for the gaining and sustaining of political power. It was in fact both the means and the end as well, a life form in which he lived, moved and had his being. Goebbels defended cinema to the hilt as the most important medium of public entertainment and morale, receiving assurance that all other forms, music halls, restaurants, theatres, would be closed down first: Goebbels's argument was accepted, for example in privileging raw material.[135] The importance of film to the Nazis is suggested by the fact that even at the end of the war 2,000 men within the industry had draft deferments.[136] For example, in late 1944 the *Berliner Morgenpost* even recorded that the Academy of Visual Arts in Vienna had appointed set designer Gustav Abel to teach film set building under the leadership of Professor Birchan, and that this was the first time this had been taught at the university level.[137] For Goebbels, film was the essential mass art and its production one of the core functions of the ideological state:

> popular art must present in artistic form the joys and sorrows of the masses. There is no art that is self-supporting: material sacrifices made in the services of art bring a return in ideal values. For every government it is a matter of course to finance great state buildings ... theatres ... art galleries ... It must be the same with film ...[138]

The discipline of distraction

The post-Great War citizen was the delighted target of sensory stimulation, a constant low-voltage bombardment. Introverted villages and towns were now part of one vast communications metropolis or indeed, since film was international, a media supra-state as well as super-state. But this was a disguised media: the Nazis had a greater appreciation of the apoliticality of most people, especially after the failures of 1933. So the films continued to look and feel like the pre-Nazi ones, there was a sense of uninterrupted flow.

Nazi films were a way of talking about the Reich itself. Costume drama was a transposition of message on to history. The Reich offered 'a politicised entertainment and an entertaining politics'.[139] This was stealth propaganda: all films, Goebbels was fond of saying, were political, and his ambition was to re-invent film as a 'discipline of distraction'.[140] The plot lines discreetly map the ideology and the heroes and heroines represent ideological rectitude. The Nazi film seemed to have been removed to an extra-political sphere, admission card to a utopia of fun, drama and historical epic, a realm in effect sanitised of moral depravity in the oppressive shadowland of a powerful state. But this ostensible de-politicisation, far from representing some feeble energy of cultural resistance, was part of the grand design of Nazi propaganda.[141] The Frankfurt School view was that all entertainment is propaganda, gratifying to the masses yet contributing to their further enslavement; while that is perhaps not generally true, in the case of the Third Reich it certainly was, and that was the intent. Hitler himself thought that all cinema should be embody the leadership purposes of the state.[142]

The best Nazi films are of equivalent quality to the good Hollywood films of their generation, while the power of the gripping military action movie was a recruiter in Germany then as today for the US armed services. The skill, contrivance, artifice and actorly qualities surprise: 'The shrill, insurrectionary propaganda of the "period of struggle" was increasingly out of place. What was needed was not the divisive techniques of electioneering but a more consensual form of "state publicity". This was all part of the general shift from "revolution" to "evolution", as Hitler repeatedly put it.'[143] The focus, usually, was on escapism (*The Adventures of Baron Münchausen*), and ostensibly 'pure' entertainment: the greatest box-office triumph during the war was the completely escapist *Grosse Liebe* (the Great Love), a film about a soldier's love.[144] *Great Love* was viewed by 28 million; only enemy casualties were seen on the screen.[145] Film was a laxative, the natural history *Kulturfilms* for example – 'these wonders of nature that could be seen ever more frequently during the war on the screens of an ever more ravaged country were designed to distract'.[146]

Many Germans led a double life, a ritual performance in the public sphere and a retreat in the private one.[147] Rentschler suggests that films such as *Lucky Kids* 'would appear to pose a radical extension of what Schaefer calls a "split consciousness": an UFA film made with official sanction which deferred to the culture and conventions of one's fiercest foreign competitor'. And this was not so much a matter of 'split consciousness' as it was a double identity: 'as with the vast majority of films made under Dr Goebbels, we encounter neither steel bodies, triumphant wills, no racial slurs, state slogans, or party emblems'. Fascism's visage was both sinister and seductive – and cinema embodied the latter: National Socialism was made more acceptable via the imagined private life it offered as well as the sense of inclusion it bestowed; under Dr Goebbels, the aim of film was to nurture an imaginary community, a *Volksgemeinschaft*.[148]

American competition Not least, there was the problem of American competition, something Nazism permitted – but it was a form of self-scourging, surfacing the deficiencies of the indigenous, government product: displeased with what one had, envious of what one had not.[149] Thus of the 150 to 200 films distributed each year in the Reich from 1933 to 1939, slightly over half were German, while around twenty per cent were imported from the United States.[150] Moreover, 'the actual market share of Hollywood films far exceeded their proportion of titles. In each of the years from 1935 to 1937 Hollywood accounted for four of the top 10.'[151] So German audiences and critics delighted in *Test Pilot, Broadway Melody of 1936, Our*

Daily Bread, Cavalcade, Desire, San Francisco and many others.[152] In 1935, for example, ninety-two German films competed with forty-one American ones, and Disney cartoons at the Marmorhaus delighted crowd and critic alike every Christmas.[153] More generally, Germans appreciated the cultural populism of the United States, and this cohered with the Nazi aspiration to an entertainment that was artful, commercial and socially inclusive.[154] Berlin's favourite film in the first winter of the war was *China Seas* with Clark Gable and Jean Harlow.[155]

While the Nazis borrowed extensively from other cinemas, Hollywood in general was more than an influence, it was a model even to the extent of mimicry, for example *It Happened One Night* with Clark Gable and Claudette Colbert was transformed via the witchery of Babelsberg into *Lucky Kids*. Thus in pursuing their aim of a normative/essentialist film theatre Goebbels and his acolytes looked to Hollywood: and this 1936 movie is a Nazi plagiarism of the American screwball comedy.[156] But it was not in any sense subversive,[157] and its function goes to the conceptual heart of the Nazi propaganda and entertainment idea. The world of slapstick, laughter and frivolity it evokes, an American world that is both homely and smart, gauche and urbane, did not arise by chance. It is a commentary on the Nazis' wish to construct a parallel universe, the one fun-loving and metropolitan, the other regimented and coercive, existing side by side: the one cannot breathe without the other.[158] *Lucky Kids* 'relied on foreign forms of recognition yet still proudly bore the appellation Made in Germany'; this film was 'imitating a generic pleasure made in a foreign dream factory, in effect creating the illusion of an already illusory world'.[159] The SS journal *The Black Corps* attacked the film vociferously. This fact is an interesting one as it shows that there was actually a pseudo-public debate in Nazi Germany; but the appearance of *Lucky Kids* was a definitive moment in the Reich's popular culture, scripted by a writer admired by Goebbels, acclaimed by pundit and public, placed in Hitler's private collection.[160]

Film and ideology Originally the Propaganda Ministry itself tried film production. But the ministry soon stopped being a cinematic entrepreneur. Failures in Nazi propaganda were failures of pure propaganda – the disaster of *The Eternal Jew*, the limitations of the 1933 party films. But the use of entertainment to muffle ideology became the core of the Nazi propaganda method: Hoffmann claims that only five per cent of feature films after 1933 (perhaps less) were overtly propagandist. Their narratives were principally historical or war and love stories and romances were often the foreground.[161] Others offer a higher figure, but such numbers obscure the latent politicality of every film the German public ever watched;[162] by the mid-fifties only three hundred remained repressed on ideological grounds.[163]

Yet the filmic message was uncompromising. There was never any subtle aspersion or nuance, and no interrogation or introspection. The films detached the violence from its human impact, as did the documentaries. One might, for example, contrast this with a contemporary Hollywood epic, *Dawn Patrol* with Errol Flynn and David Niven (Warner Brothers 1938). Though a classic action movie about aviators set in the First World War, it had to pay homage to the pacifist ethos of its era, and the emotional consequences of the gross loss of life on the

Western Front. It is impossible to imagine a product of the Nazi media machine being similarly ambivalent. The early war period carried the highest number of overtly propaganda films (one company in 1940 was told by Goebbels that half of its product for the next year would be political in orientation).[164] Later the Propaganda Ministry focused the politics on the few large-scale productions and there was a surfeit of love stories and operettas such as *Frauen Sind Doch Bessere Diplomaten*, *Bel Ami*, *Liebe Und Die Erste Eisenbahn* and *Die Grosse Liebe*.[165] The parallels are with the Gainsborough films, romantic drama in later wartime Britain where love and history are present and war absent, as with such 'bodice rippers' as *Fanny by Gaslight* (1944) and their new generation of stars with no pre-existent profile in war movies, such as James Mason or Stuart Grainger.

The ideological touches were often discreet – for example, in both *Kolberg* (with the French), and in *The Rothschilds* (with the English), black footmen are in attendance wearing turbans. The black footman was a signifier of the metropolitan decadence of Germany's enemies, and the fact that they were insensitive to the ideal of racial purity. In *Kolberg* the pacifist violin-playing Claus (the farmer's son) has been corrupted by French culture in Strasbourg.[166] Again, in the film *Jew Süss*, the clever idea is not to show imagery of allegedly contemporary Jews (as was done in the box office failure, *The Eternal Jew*), but rather costume the Jewish enemy in the garb of the eighteenth century. This time Goebbels's media apparatus presented the Jew as sophisticated. But it was nevertheless the same story: the Jews can change shape. The insidious message was that the real danger lay not with obviously Jewish figures but with the polished 'court Jew', who insinuated himself into polite society. By proceeding thus, the Nazis attacked an audience when its cognitive defences were relaxed, because the entertainment package did not come with the label 'political rant' attached, or resemble a jeremiad from a Nazi Party official. But audience research showed that viewers got the idea.

Yet sometimes these films could be crude, as in *The Rothschilds' Shares in Waterloo*, or *Soldiers of Tomorrow* where the English elite are degenerate and implicitly homosexual. Even in the better films there can be an ideologically laboured element, as with the speech of Gneisenau in the town square of Kolberg, where he harangues and hectors the assembled masses not only in the tone, but with the very language of Goebbels himself.

The film *Request Concert* was the perfect ideological vehicle for the Nazi government since it cleverly conveyed a core message, that is, the unity between front and homeland. Based on a real radio programme that was broadcast live with a studio audience, where civilians could request tunes and songs for family and lovers in the military (i.e. an ideological schemata), it is the story of an airman and his girlfriend who meet at the Olympics and lose touch after he goes to fight in the Spanish Civil War in the Condor Legion. They are reunited when she requests a tune on this programme, and he is there to hear it. The film finishes with the airman off to fight again, this time at the beginning of the Second World War. Ideology is integrated into the fabric of the story, the message absorbed without conscious awareness, the pleasures of narrative leading unobtrusively to renewed political consciousness: for example, the heroine is amazed by her aunt's reflections on her own love in the Kaiser's time for a young man of higher class; they could not marry.[167] Hence important films 'demonstrate a common recipe of interweaving the central love story with a wider set of social relations, in which the resolution of group tensions goes hand-in-hand with the fulfilment of individual desires', and thus 'insofar as there was anything distinctive about them, it was the degree to which they fused personal happiness with social harmony'.[168]

Kolberg: the celluloid victory The message/form of this film demonstrates how the propaganda was adjusted to suit changing contexts, for this is a movie about courage when surrounded, the encircled Kolberg of the Napoleonic Wars. It is packed with imagery of obliteration, of blasted homes and buildings, a level of destruction in fact that would have been unknown in the Napoleonic Wars. It is, actually, the costume drama disguise of Germany at the end of the Second World War. The director of *Kolberg*, Veit Harlan, stated 'Hitler and Goebbels must have been possessed by the thought that such a film might do them more good than, for instance, a victory in Russia.'[169] The film and its making illustrate how far the Nazis relied on the medium to hold the home front together.

Kolberg is a good film, the scene for example between the new commander, Gneisenau, and the citizens' leader (Heinrich George) is convincing, with its little deceit (Gneisenau intends defending the town, but provocatively suggests its surrender). Harlan claimed misleadingly that 187,000 soldiers were involved in the making of the film, taken from the front to work as extras:[170] Burleigh echoes Harlan's claim,[171] while others have given widely different figures (Hoffmann suggests 20,000).[172] But the employment of even 20,000 still represents a significant deployment of manpower mid-war. With the brooding presence of George, the sentimentality, this film is a compendium of the clichés of old Hollywood. Noteworthy, also, was its self-conscious contrast between an old and a new military style. Like many media products of the Third Reich, it is among other things a leadership training manual with a focus on resourceful leadership which is visionary and risk-taking. Yet the film was conceived too early for it to have been specifically intended as Folk Storm propaganda – although Goebbels remarked that the film 'fits exactly the military and political landscape that we shall probably have to record by the time the film is shown', an extraordinary point.[173] In the high tradition of Nazi film, the history, character and costume drama are an indirect way of talking about modern Germany and justifying the Nazi raj. The language of exotic old clothes, carriages, cavalry, elaborate manners, shimmering ballrooms and elegant banquets was in fact one of the Third Reich's principal methods of self-advertisement, a world very far removed from concrete gun emplacements, jet fighters, Gestapo, yellow stars and field-grey uniforms. Yet the symbols and rituals of the past were conscripted in the attempt to explain the present. One could not, for example, condemn Hitler's generals in a speech, or humiliate them in a newsreel. But one could in a history movie. So the movies were also an important part of the internal political and institutional struggles within the Third Reich. Moreover, mass publics are easily fatigued by an overt political diet, and it is this, the capacity for cognitive exhaustion, which taught the regime that it needed to find a fresh and refreshed grammar of political expression which bypassed traditional forms of proselytisation altogether. *Kolberg* is a rhapsody to the ideology of the regime: the idea of the folk community, of the unity of all Germans, of heroic death and ultimate sacrifice and the unflinching confrontation of impossible odds.

The significance of this film is that it is a storehouse of Nazi cinema archetypes. Goebbels sought to show that the people themselves, not the army, embodied the will to resist. The mayor, Nettelbeck, wants to fight; the original commander, Lucadou, wants to surrender – the analogy is with the contemporary German army. This film is a working museum of Third Reich rhetoric. According to the director, many of the speeches were written by Goebbels – the call for a great sacrifice and suicidal courage, the acceptance that an irrational act is legitimised by a higher level of reference.[174] Thus Goebbels himself wrote the final oration in which the people are roused to fight; and he was now officially defender of Berlin.[175] *Kolberg* is Hollywoodesque and could easily have been a prestige studio product with its choruses, its superior Agfacolor and its re-imagining of history (the real Kolberg fell to Napoleon), and in the best Babelsberg/Hollywood tradition there is the contrivance of a love story for mass appeal. It is alternately glamorous and sentimental in the dream-confectionery tradition of narrative epic movie. At the heart of the film lies a petition (to replace the garrison commander), and a drama between two women, a humble farmer's daughter and a majestic queen. The people solicit the powerful, and the powerful hear them, royalty and peasant united in purpose. For the people are not alone in their struggle. The film premiered in Berlin on 30 January 1945, with a copy dropped simultaneously on the besieged fortress of La Rochelle 'to lift the morale of the defendants and encourage them to hold out to the bitter end';[176] the commanding vice admiral's reply was broadcast on German radio.[177]

The ending of *Kolberg* is an invocation to immortality. It is perfumed with pseudo-celestial choruses, but Nettelbeck's (George's) speech to Söderbaum is actually deeply moving – we have done all we could, and so forth: it is 'a speech of resignation for the Nazi elite',[178] and an example of self-propagandising. Goebbels turned to his assembled guests after *Kolberg*'s first showing: 'Gentlemen, in a hundred years' time, they will be showing another fine colour film describing the terrible days we're living through. Don't you want to play a part in this film, to be pulled back to life in a hundred years' time?'[179] *Kolberg* offered the regime a kind of afterlife, the hope that generations yet unborn would one day see their film and be inspired: 'by 1944 Goebbels was making propaganda as much for himself and the leadership as the masses'.[180] They had come to believe in a self-created myth. This was truly the last testament of the regime and serviced the psychological needs of the leadership in its final days. Few ever saw *Kolberg* then, or have seen it now. Audiences in the cinemas that remained intact were nervous and beyond persuasion; Manvell even claimed that 'the film was, however, completed so late it was never released in Germany', but this suggestion seems improbable (one youth, a future journalist, claimed to have seen it in Croatia before war's end).[181]

Radio

As with film, so radio. The chronicle is similar; just as the methodology of the three 'party films' of 1933 was abandoned, so too did radio jettison its hectoring tone of the early years, the harangues and the martial music and the dutiful high seriousness of the 'cultural pedagogy' (lectures made up less than six per cent of airtime by 1937).[182] Goebbels asserted 'the vast majority of radio listeners lead lives of unceasing toil and therefore have a right to genuine relaxation ... In contrast, the small minority who want to subsist on Kant and Hegel are hardly of consequence.'[183] The most successful innovation in the Nazi entrepreneurship of the airwaves was its variety programmes, that medley of song, comic turn and 'big number' which Germans found irresistible (research showed eighty-seven per cent of respondents listened to them).[184] Radio became a de-Nazified zone (with only trace elements of ideology, e.g. the concern for a more inclusive folk culture), a realm of popular song, of dance music, of the very 'asphalt culture' Nazis had claimed to hate.[185]

Consumerism

Part of the political function of the artist in a Fascist state was consumerist. As Rentschler has argued, 'I came to recognize how much of the cinema's fatal appeal derives from a modern society's not altogether illegitimate desires for a better life. Utopian energies tapped by the feature films of the Third Reich in a crucial manner resembled, indeed at times consciously emulated, the American dream.'[186] The Nazis he says promulgated a synthetic popular culture replete with shows, film cultists, magazines, fashion, marketisation and mass consumption, and a film industry that quietly parodied Hollywood conventions, techniques and genres. Hitler's Germany was similar to Huxley's *Brave New World* as it was also an exercise in emotional engineering, a political order that proffered consumerism and recreation 'as dialectical compliments to law, order, and restriction'.[187] He also argues that America shaped consumer habits and affected daily behaviour every whit as strongly as party doctrine – in 1939, for instance, Coca-Cola had more than 2,000 German distributors as well as fifty bottlers. Ocean liners left Hamburg for New York. Domestic labour-saving devices – coffee makers, stoves, refrigerators, washing machines – vacated the world of the American film and entered the Reich household; and there were American and international journals, newspapers and other publications freely available. Hollywood stars smirked from the covers of German magazines, their pages advertised American cosmetics, jazz music breathed its aromas of freedom. American mass culture, its consumer items and popular icons, offered designs for living in a modern world: 'the Fordist vision of a mass consumer society plainly resonated with National Socialist dreams of social integration and material entitlement for all "national comrades"; a kind of consumer Volksgemeinschaft'.[188]

The SS were worried by this, but even they offered permission for the battle-weary soldier to refresh himself with the captured contraband of the American anti-culture:[189]

> we do not wish to deny this culture of nothingness its right to exist. It can even, rightly used, be good, just as it is sometimes a pleasure to do nothing. Should a German soldier happen to find a portable record player and jazz records in the deserted quarters of British or American soldiers, he does not smash them against the wall. Instead, he takes them along and thinks he has a great treasure. We don't want to suggest excessive cultural disaster here. There are times when he wants a vacation from himself, from us, from the whole world. He needs to relax, and certainly does not wish to ponder intellectual matters. Nothing is better suited to take him out of the normal world than the complete nonsense of this hot music, this cacophony of animal howls, wild instruments and foot-stomping Negro lust. It takes him away from human concerns back to the depths of pre-human apedom, returning him to the time when people did not need to think because there was no past and no future ... He is immune to the danger of confusing this rhythmic pig grunting with good music, much less art or culture. He cannot meet his higher standards.[190]

The advertising was a very important part of the illusion of normalcy and consumerist banality (see, for example, the *Berliner Illustrirte Zeitung* from 9 July 1936): the elegant women in glowing gowns, the hand creams and cigarettes, Palmolive and red lips and shiny blonde beauties, Blendox, boys admiring a speeding Mercedes car, mature gentlemen and smart ladies seated in a summer garden – members of the upper classes, handsome bottles, Nivea cream, ladies in swimsuits, cameras, binoculars, Zeiss film, cigarette boxes and distinguished senior men, bras, compact powder boxes, more cream, more Nivea, unclothed kids and yet more cream. Then there are the English lavender fields of Long Melford, set out in a pseudo-medieval manuscript style in the full glory of summer. Cologne, shoes and increasingly the domestic technology such as the vacuum cleaner, and fridges; more cigarettes, radiograms and above all the blonde hair dye and yet more blonde shampoo advertisements, Trislyn hair tonic, Cutex nail polish, Odol toothpaste, Eukotol, Chlorodont, box advertisements for away weekends and the happy image of an international hotel beckoning you to the island of Capri. Advertising was, moreover, the beneficiary of technical advances in photography and thus more visually enticing than ever before, colour for example was now freely available.[191] But advertisements (such as for the Sparta brand) were not overtly 'Nazi', only that for Opel Cars shows imagery consistent with Nazi ideology: and only one in all the samples I looked at was overtly anti-Semitic, linking Jews with blood and gold (*Illustrierter Beobachter*, 11 August 1938).

The effect is to package the Reich as a kind of granary of consumer delight, solving the minor problems of everyday domestic life and also introducing a tone of technological mastery and the gloss of pure luxury. Not least also, the message is to facilitate self-presentation to the world, a social image as clean, blonde, scented and crisply elegant. There is still a gentry in Nazi Germany whose ways we can emulate through the agency of informed advertising and the products of German manufacturing. The impact of course is to position the Third Reich as a kind of crucible of ordinariness, what is clearly an emergent consumer culture offering the spoils and trophies of industry for everyday folk to live their lives more efficiently; and in this it is distinct from Communism with its stress on collective ownership. Under Nazism the individual could aspire to the possession of property and the blessings of consumer goods.

The appeal was to mobility, geographic but also social – the two ideas elide, as, for example, with a stylised poster in *Signal* of an Italian lake captioned 'A Dream becomes Reality'. The poster asks who was able to travel to Italy except the privileged few, and yet now via the Strength Through Joy organisation one could 'spend one's vacation on the Riviera or on even more distant shores'.[192] Indeed. Another poster showcases a huge yacht, with the caption 'Yachting – An Exclusive Sport?'[193] This is no longer the case in Germany, since anyone can do it, just as they can take up any other sport. The key idea was that the perquisites of an old elite were now a general right of citizenship, and one should never underrate the persuasive power of this idea in a socially stratified society: 'Nazi social propaganda latched onto potent desires for social recognition, upward mobility, and equal opportunity that had swelled during the post-war years. Although the underlying aim remained unambiguously productivist, the manner of presentation was unabashedly consumer oriented'; thus this integration propaganda was characterised 'not only by calls for common sacrifice but also by the promise of consumption and pleasure'.[194] Nothing was too good for the Volk. In October 1939 a *Signal* heading was 'Recreation Every Evening', showing high-style programmes of the Berlin Variety Theatre – 'instead of cheap printed programmes in two colours, the best is just good enough for the audience. Not a few keep and collect these programmes in memory of happy hours.'[195] Another poster is rather naughty, an exotic lady in tight leathers and silks pertly rested, whip in hand, as a huge white polar bear drinks placidly in front of her; an image then of Nazi German recreation.[196] Personal mobility was the aspirational core of the offer, a key ingredient of Nazi packaging, no longer was the individual bonded to the parish but could aspire to physical mobility (and cultural, via the airwaves). One advert from around 1939 showcases the VW, with the text 'Save five marks a week and you will drive your own car', the image a front view of the VW Beetle (in photomontage) against a massive coin.[197] The message works through simple association, the five marks and the car. One can only speculate on how far it appealed to a society principally governed by public transport, the tram and the bicycle. And a 1936 poster urges people to vote for Hitler by noting what he has done to promote automobile ownership in Germany.[198] The caption – 'The Führer Promised to Motorise Germany'. It finishes 'The leader gave 250,000 people's comrades jobs in the auto industry and its suppliers. German people: Thank the Führer on March the 29th!

Give him your vote!' Then there was radio, another new consumer durable. 'All Germany has the Führer of the People's Receiver' is a poster that again uses the device of photomontage, where a giant People's Receiver dwarfs the surrounding crowds of ordinary Germans (crowds are frequently represented in the posters to create a sense of social admiration and social consensus).[199] The consumerism of the Reich was as much conceptual as applied and its products held high symbolic meaning. An autobahn, for example, was not just a road but was a resonant symbol of progress, of the future, of freedom.

FIGURE 5.8 Volkswagen advertisement

In his diaries Klemperer does not speak of propaganda but of advertising, and he describes the Nazis as the best advertisers the world had yet seen. The Nazis 'not only plundered the latest ideas on reputation and imagery but were also well versed in brand technique'.[200] There was an intimate connection between Nazi propaganda and consumer culture: a world in which both advertising and marketing have high visibility as the essential lubricant to the exchange of goods in a sophisticated, modern economy, logically entails a political parallelism – the exchange of value, persona and promise. Thus 'just as advertisers were recognizing how better to tap the human craving for acceptance, Nazi propagandists similarly sought to harness the yearning for social harmony and belonging'.[201]

Was Hitler an adman? The idea is fanciful but not incredible. Indeed, it would have been strange if he had not scrutinised the advertising industry very closely. Fest describes several (remote) possibilities from the Viennese years:

> Meanwhile, reputedly through Greiner's mediation, he produced a poster advertising a hair tonic, another poster for a bed-feathers shop, another for an antiperspirant sold under the brand name 'Teddy'. A copy of this last poster, with Hitler's signature in a corner, has been found. It shows two rather stiff, clumsily drawn figures of letter carriers; one has sat down in exhaustion wringing heavy blue drops of sweat out of his sock; the other is informing his 'dear brother' that 10,000 steps a day are 'a pleasure with Teddy powder'. In another poster that has come down to us the tower of St Stephan's Cathedral rises majestically above a mountain of soap.[202]

And then there is 'the story of the woman who sold a hair growing lotion by means of false testimonials'. Thus:

> for almost an hour, Greiner's story goes, Hitler waxed enthusiastic about the woman's skill and the vast potentialities of psychological persuasion. Propaganda, propaganda he is supposed to have raved, you must keep it up until it creates a faith and people no longer know what is imagination and what reality.[203]

Propaganda, he is quoted as saying, is 'the fundamental essence of every religion … whether of heaven or hair tonic'. But Fest adds 'these accounts are dubious'.

Vistas of material possibility were as much part of life in the Third Reich as Nuremberg rallies, and materialism performed an essential role, with products, films and magazines sustaining a private realm of individual enjoyment in which the political/public world could be forgotten. Packaging in its more literal sense protects and facilitates distribution. In a metaphoric sense it also does this, making the credo more attractive; the new world of consumer choice pre-empts political resistance (or confines it to minimal compliance and 'dumb insolence'). For example, there were cruises to the Azores on the Nazi liners (cruises e.g. to Norway could cost only 5–7 marks per day on a KdF [Strength Through Joy] ship);[204] these were all part of this idea of entitlement. Here then, under the auspices of the Nazi state, was emerging a new social order, the culture of consumption:

> by overcoming geographical barriers and traditional hierarchies of taste, modern advertising sought to construct new consumer identities centred on participation in the burgeoning world of commodities. As a self-declared People's party that claimed to rise above sectional interests, the Nazis similarly sought to open up new constituencies by breaking down older class and regionally based allegiances and constructing new political identities revolving around social entitlement based on the nation and race.[205]

Much of this material world was of course a chimaera; for example, workers had paid into an instalment scheme for the Strength Through Joy cars but none were ever delivered (full production had been designated for September 1939).[206]

While the promise to make the luxuries of the higher classes attainable to the masses was also a part of symbolic socialism, it could equally be construed as an anticipation of post-war consumer culture; the Reich was an emporium as well as an imperium. The magazines were protracted paeans to the glories of consumerism mixed with the serious and political vistas of that foreboding 1930s world. Hence in *Illustrierter Beobachter* Franco's cabinet, dour, remorseless, feature alongside German advertising icons such as the American frontier ghost who represents Dollar Cigarettes and the sailor boy of Blendox and the cartoonish housewife, her head simply a wooden 'O', who is the icon of FEWA (a brand of detergent).[207] Palmolive is well advertised, and blonde hair dye is as ever ubiquitous. In *Die Woche* there was an advertisement for radios featuring uniformed militia from all the nations and with their national flags.[208] Its thrust is clear – get access to foreign channels (the Reich was a dystopia but it is not until the war a hermetically sealed one). During the war, the old nightmare, that the workers might 'return to their old etiolated Marxism', began to trouble Nazi dreams; the obtainability of consumer goods was thus perceived as an essential guarantor of loyalty to the regime.[209]

War as consumerism

War was consumption, a media event and a vigorous branch of the consumer economy: 'From a 21st-century vantage point, the synergies between the Nazi war machine and the mass media seem anything but surprising.'[210] Goebbels remarked 'entertainment is nowadays politically crucial, perhaps even decisive for the war'; as one scholar has suggested 'it was not the cinema that mobilised the populace for the war, but the war that mobilised the populace for the cinema'.[211] But the vagaries of the conflict could dictate the course of production and distribution, for example withdrawing from circulation *Garrison Dora*, a film about a German unit fighting in Africa, France and Russia (1942–3).[212]

The magazine series *Berlin Rom Tokyo* is a lavish salutation to the Axis which blends heroic imagery of friends and the victimhood of enemies with vistas of

Axis cultures and lucid colour advertising to tantalise the most jaded Third Reich consumer.[213] We see the Japanese in action in Corregidor and Philippines via the conventions of war photography such as the fording of a river; a self-described racial state then, honouring a multiracial alliance. There are decorous shots of Croatian girls, and Japanese women in ceremonies, and a mighty colour image of the falcon (Polarfalke) of the Reich Marshal. The colour advertising cascades from this issue: a big beer advert is a luminous melange of ashtray and cigarettes, the glowering photograph of a postman exudes vague menace. The golf gloves commercial offers nice colour drawings of elegant women; and a couple seem to have been displaced from another era, say from *The New Yorker* of the 1950s – smart, contented, they evoke a mellifluous world far removed from the Third Reich, urban, urbane. And a mother and her beautiful children evangelise for a brand of socks: again, a colour drawing that suggests social savvy and class and wit.

The narrative of the war was retailed through images and print, popular cultural products that were parasitic on the brave and the dead with their synthetic rhetoric – 'The men were filled with an iron will as they flew toward their goal' and so on – and their paint-by-numbers journalism. Short sentences embedded in tiny paragraphs celebrate the stereotype, spat out in staccato style. Everything is hackneyed; the two-dimensional warrior sitting in his cockpit 'had made a name for himself during the Spanish Civil War' inevitably as 'Iron Gustav'; this is of course a 'mission for tough guys' who can 'look danger straight in the eye'. Then we are told 'the Germans have been seen' and then 'peppery greetings rise to meet them. The English pirate quickly receives his "just reward".' For here in the early spring of 1940 complacency has set in: 'the illegal weapons must naturally be punished. Down … dive … the button is pressed and the first bombs follow the path, hitting the English ship dead centre!' There is an exultant nihilism about such writing – 'down there, a smoking wreck! Two pillars of flame rise, mixing with white and black smoke to form a splendid symphony of colour! … Searchlights illuminate the English coast once again. Their deadly fingers reach into the heavens, searching with wide and narrow beams. In vain.' And then again 'a worthwhile flight. It's great to hunt English pirates in the channel!'[214] The stories also function as homilies, epistolary little morality tales:

> I yelled in his ear: 'Land! Land! He finally heard me, and pulled himself back from death, opening his eyes … as if in a dream, he took the controls and put his foot on the rudder control. With a weak smile, he began to land the plane … His smile spread a little as he felt that we were on the ground, but then his smile faded. We sat motionless in the machine for a long while, hardly daring to take the life he had given to us, until the ground crew hurried to us. God grant me such a death!'[215]

Such was the alabaster heroism of the Third Reich. They attempted to convey tension but readers always knew that everyone would generally get home safely; the edginess was muffled since Germans inhabited a propaganda world and thus the best of all possible outcomes. It was the Orwell Ministry of Truth style, for example the enemy Spitfire's two cockades 'glittered like the eyes of a beautiful butterfly', and the narrative thrust is laboured ('another Spitfire to the right!'); like a computer game, action-packed and mindless. Will the wounded plane return safely? There is manufactured drama: a huge sheet of water entirely conceals the plane for a few seconds, 'then as I looked down I saw the plane at rest in calm water, with the Old Man standing on the wing'.[216]

And then there was the desert. But journalism on the desert war was more about the desert than the war (e.g. *Signal*, 'The Four Plagues of the Desert').[217] Here at last was a gentleman's campaign: genocidal ambition, the murder of prisoners, concentration camps, the SS, are all absent from the scene. It is the mutual enemy and the vividness of its assault that obsesses, the desert itself, its imagery and symbolism and the unflinching harshness of its physical realities. Its cruelties are chronicled in detail. This is in fact an effective literary evocation of the desert war. Nazi journalism was good at the level of surfaces, it fondled the superficial: its limitations, prescribed by the ideology, lay in failing to penetrate beyond the level of appearance. Significant military detail was actually provided, such as the ingenious slit trenches which allowed reconnaissance parties to disappear, apparently completely, in the desert sands. There was of course the hubris; readers are told of the gun, which went from Poland to France and is now in Africa – 'the aim of this old warrior is as good as it was on the very first day'.[218]

Germans win, of course, and the enemy is inferior, but such narratives also humanise the war and make it less an abstract clash of massed armies and machines. 'His First Strike in Africa' is a *Signal* photo-journalistic essay on the shooting down and happy survival of an American fighter, and shows the bomber crashing, the explosion, descent by parachute and the image of him surrendering, dragging his parachute in behind.[219] It concludes with a picture of his wrecked machine. Here is the face of the enemy and his knightly German conqueror. It makes war like a game, without human suffering, this enemy is alive, physically intact and conqueror and conquered exchange pleasantries. Invariably the German soldier is smiling and humane. But the real foe is the desert: 'the raging inferno of sand and yellow light which the eye cannot penetrate' where 'dripping with perspiration, tortured by thirst and flies, and almost suffocated by dust, we curse every desert on the face of the earth'.[220] The extremes of physical deprivation are well evoked: 'the company that is lucky enough to have sweet water within its reach is the envy of the whole front'. The intense heat and absence of shade goad men to hide under their coats, but then 'it becomes like a Turkish bath'. It is the barbarities of nature, not man, that preoccupy.

'The Attack on Cologne' Yet the content of much of the literary output, much of the press in the Third Reich, was constructed according to an ideological/rhetorical template. Thus Winkelnkemper's 'The Attack on Cologne' (1942) is an article about a great air raid on a major German city which is formulated according to a rigid schemata.[221] It is all ferociously 'on-message' at the cost of nuance, individuation and therefore interest: the same catechistical lessons are constantly driven home – the unity of party, people and army, the party as the repository of all civic

value and so on and so forth. Events and characters are always glimpsed but dimly through a miasma of hyperbole; these people, this city, this party, are not really real but simply a symbol. Cologne is credited with remarkable powers of self-renewal – as if a massive air raid could just be flicked off with sufficient determination. Thus 'the work continued tirelessly. Ever more piles of rubble turned into construction sites overnight ... More than 90% of Cologne's workers showed up for work on Monday morning.' Such texts always read like an advertisement for the NSDAP. In the first place, they give all credit to the organisation and leadership, during and after the raid, to the Nazi Party and its officials, the party is shown to be a paragon of efficiency and exhibits 'a refreshing ability to do new things. This rapid and unbureaucratic assistance was possible thanks to the foresight and generosity of the relevant Reich and provincial offices.' Thus 'by dawn, by order of the Gau economic director and the city administration, temporary shops were functioning in every part of the city to provide essential food items'. The party is human, and humane: 'The Party had taken care to be able to transport the homeless to the countryside and to neighbouring cities, and had columns of buses, trucks and special trains for this purpose in readiness.'[222] Alongside this there is the pursuit of a populist theatric, a vivid dramaturgy that disguises what is always a pedagogic exercise: thus the attack on Cologne was evoked in the lurid anthropomorphism of a cheap novel – 'the insectlike buzzing of their airplanes sounds ever more menacing, and the dreadful sounds of exploding shells and detonating bombs, mixed with the chattering of machine guns aimed at the civilian population, grows ever louder'. Sentimentality is not a quality we associate with the Third Reich, yet the Reich was a Niagara of sentimentality and its scribes were masters of the manufactured human touch: here, a lawyer rescues his grand piano from the rubble and his daughter plays a little children's melody: 'For a moment, it sounded like a fairytale in the midst of the smoke and fume-filled night. People listened for a moment, deeply moved – then got back to work.' And over this broken city loom the shadows of the East: 'the thoughts of the sorrowing wandered over the borders of their great Fatherland to the wide spaces of the East, where sons, fathers and brothers stood against a pitiless enemy ...'.[223]

The newsreels absorbed the techniques for sensationalising war. For example, Manvell, citing Kracauer, describes their compression of an entire blitz campaign into a 'crescendo of continuity', with realities or pauses edited out:[224]

> The German development of blitzkrieg thus occurs like some kind of irresistible magic, of which the ministers are the screaming, dive-bombing stukas, plunging down from the sky like avenging thunderbolts. Maps were used with stabbing arrows showing the overwhelming advances of the invading armies. Nazi territory was shown gleaming white, while enemy territory was symbolically black, the powers of light opposed to those of darkness. Nazi newsreels were not informative, they were Impressionist, emotive, all-conquering – a blitz in themselves of sound and image. The enemy always appeared to be humiliated to the point of absurdity, or at least utter, frozen inactivity – he was

a mere gaping observer of the all-conquering armies which rolled swiftly and unopposed along his roads, his streets, or crept hideously on caterpillar tracts over his fields. Meanwhile music, bombastic, Wagnerian, hymnlike or merely gay and tuneful, mocked the civilian and soldier alike who failed to stem this onslaught by the Führer.[225]

Spectacle

The Reich specialised in pageantry: that much is cliché, the *panem et circuses* formula of the Caesars and Caesarism. There were the rituals and red-letter days like Heroes' Memorial Day and Bückeburg; they were both a pastiche of the saints' days and feasts of the Christian religion, but also a kind of politicised Fascist version of the English Season, a whirligig of social events where one could see and be seen. Then, towering above them all, the magnificent rhetorical edifice, the Grand Opera of the Nuremberg rallies (the final Nuremberg Rally was held in 1938). This cult of the spectacular also represented a direct symbolic appeal to tradition, and also its re-imagining, a pastiche and synthetic reworking of the celebratory militarism of the Prussian monarchy. While the Nazis did not invent the symbolic strategy in politics, they took it further than any regime before or since. Dr Goebbels claimed in 1941 that his two notable propaganda achievements were, first:

> the style and techniques of the party's public ceremonies; the ceremonial of the mass demonstrations, the ritual of the great party occasion, and, second, that through his creation of the Führer myth, Hitler had been given the halo of infallibility, with the result that many people who just glanced at the party after 1933 had now complete confidence in Hitler.[226]

Part of this was the stage-management of Hitler's public presence: 'But then transfiguration would occur. Arriving late in the night to enhance the dramatic effect, the noisy, flimsy aircraft would descend in darkness and sometimes storm, its lights blinking, as though Hitler were "the incarnation of Siegfried the light-God."'[227] Here was a substitute for democracy via a new and seductive magic: 'whereas citizens in a parliamentary democracy voted to choose a few fellow-citizens to serve as their representatives, Fascists expressed their citizenship directly by participating in ceremonies of mass assent'.[228] Hence the 'propagandistic manipulation of public opinion' became the motor of government quite simply; it replaced 'debate about complicated issues among a small group of legislators'.[229]

It was an outsize world, a gigantic stage awash with mythic creatures. This – the gothicity of the regime – owes something to the role of grand opera in Hitler's thinking, since it was for him so much more than a recreation or cultural interest. It was a passion; a consumptive obsession such that the division between the fictive/stage world and the political/actual world became for him a dissolving boundary. If grand opera could function at some level as politics, then politics could also become grand opera:

> The ... orchestration ... of the great Nazi festivals owe[s] much to Wagner's sense of the communal function of art. His attraction to heroic virtues and to a mythical Germanic world, his skill in staging and dramatic effects, his ability to create a hypnotic, delusionary spell of suspended reality, were ideally suited to Nazi manipulation.[230]

People were being invited to participate in an epic adventure: 'The style of public ceremonies in the Third Reich is inconceivable without this operatic tradition, without the essentially demagogic art of Richard Wagner.'[231] Television documentaries, with titles like *The Third Reich in Colour* (2001),[232] have surfaced the ornamentalism and the lucidity of the Third Reich (the monochromatic of the black/white footage dignifies but it also distances, in effect conjuring not a living world of the blood-flushed cheek, but a land of grey shadows).

The Third Reich was literally spectacular, a land of spectacles, with the great set piece national liturgical events, the special occasions and the weight of local and parish ceremonial. These rituals of regime visibility were also important elements of the packaging, and as such consciously aimed to excite but also to communicate key ideological propositions and to reinforce regime imagery/leader cultism. Their constituent elements – the music, the symbols and banners and torches, the disciplined geometry of the massed human formations – constituted a form of militarised carnival that was both seductive and threatening. No regime ever hitherto paid such constant attention to the theatrical: 'a Hitler rally in the early 1930s was an event judged well worth the cost of admission, with its singing, marching, flags, military music – and Hitler, portrayed as the one man who could save Germany and lead Germans to the promised land of the Third Reich'.[233] And thus 'there standing before him was this authoritative public figure, putting into words, making not merely permissible but actually laudable, that which hitherto had lain in the realm of the half-shameful, and un-confessed fantasy. And here, about him, fantasy was being acted out.'[234]

The rally was a living medium and vortex of Nazi propaganda, a theatre of mass affirmation wherein those attending could internalise the new values: 'Hitler's competitors in post-defeat Germany did not know how to arouse a crowd or build a catch-all party.'[235] The function of the big parade, the big rally, was a collective recognition of solidarity, and there were many of them. When Speer first listened to Hitler addressing a university audience, he arrived expecting to be hostile and was astonished by the moderation and rationality of Hitler's tone; apparently everyone appeared to be taken in. Yet this was an academic audience, this 'was an audience by training critical, claiming to exalt reason over emotion'.[236] They left the meeting enthralled; an atmosphere such as this destroyed all scepticism, speaker and listeners becoming united in one cause, a completeness, so that the speaker 'appeared to be no more than the articulation of the mind of the hall'. Then there is Speer's description of the crowd leaving the Sportpalast and taking over the entire street and moving down it, a massive mobile throng, intoxicated with a sense of its omnipotence: he perceives that this could become a permanent condition.[237]

Hitler was a skilled propagandist from the very beginning, which is really to say a talented manipulator of the symbolic realm. The claim is that what Stalin accomplished through terror, Hitler achieved through seduction and therefore realised a mysterious grip on German people: 'using a new style of politics, mediated through symbols, myths, rites, spectacles and personal dramatics, he reached the masses as did no other leader of his time'.[238] Germans became participants in National Socialist theatre. Others have seen in the superficialities of the packaging not the ancillary to the message but the core of the message itself. Partly of course this 'blatant reliance' was used to 'cover up basic weaknesses, this medley of pagan, ritual and music-hall elements anticipated the era of mass hypnosis',[239] since successful Fascist leaders rejected (ideological) purity.[240] Other critics have argued that 'the fascist aesthetic itself reflected the needs and hopes of contemporary society, that what we brush aside as the so-called superstructure was in reality the means through which most people grasp the fascist message, transforming politics into a civic religion'.[241] Fest states 'repeatedly we will be tempted to ask whether politics ever meant more to him than the means he employed to practise it'.[242] For Hitler therefore means and ends amounted to much the same thing, that is to say the theatre of politics was an instrument to realise the ideology, but it had an independent function as well. 'Packaging' was in and of itself an aim with the 'rhetorical overpowering of his enemies, for example; the histrionics of processions, parades and party days; the spectacle of military force applied in war'.[243]

Pictorial essence

The pictography of Nazism was not then an aspect but Nazism's core essence: 'the aesthetic of fascism ... was not merely a medium ... rather, the medium was the message'.[244] The fabulous ceremonies, the generated imagery, the nation bathed in rhetoric was not just going on a journey. It was also to a significant extent the destination. For Walter Benjamin, Fascist propaganda was 'less about the politicization of art than about the aestheticization of politics. This is why it was left to Riefenstahl's genius to do the impossible and to popularise the negative aesthetic of the state by means of a positive film aesthetic ...'.[245] Thus Henderson, the British ambassador: 'nobody who has not witnessed the various displays given at Nuremberg during the week's Rally, or been subjected to the atmosphere thereat, can be said to be fully acquainted with the Nazi movement in Germany'.[246] Fest argues:

> his doctrine then was that of the aesthetician who would subordinate life entirely to the dictates of the artist. The state was to be raised to the heights of a work of art; politics would be renewed and perfected by the spirit inherent in art. Elements of this programme are clearly visible in the theatricalisation of public life in the Third Reich, the regime's passion for histrionics, the staginess of its practical politics – a staginess that often appeared to be the sole end of the politics.[247]

Thus Sir David Low: 'his political conceptions were the artist's conceptions, seen in shapes, laid on in wide sweeps, errors painted out and details left until later, the bold approach and no fumbling. Essentially a simple mind, uncomplicated by pity.'[248] There was then a duality of purpose in the dramaturgy of the Third Reich. One aspect was political theatre not as the route but as the terminus, politics subordinated to aesthetics: 'Propaganda was a substitute for ideology. Propaganda itself was the message, down to and including school textbooks.'[249] The other aspect of that duality was tactical in that it helped the Nazis realise their goals. For example, the generation of powerful imagery and propaganda were important tools in the battle with the Communists. Fest repeatedly asks whether Hitler was anything but an artist – did politics really mean more than rhetoric and histrionics? The answer is no, according to Speer, who says Hitler was essentially an artist.[250] This role of spectacle, of the spectacular, is obviously going to be more important in societies which lack alternative distractions, which unlike the modern era lack immediate consumption choices and possibilities. Society was simply more dreary, with less on offer to use up time. Nazi street theatre must then have seemed compelling, this repeated staging of national moments when Hitler's speeches would be broadcast simultaneously throughout the Reich and every activity would halt.[251] Nazis also understood the more nebulous concept of atmosphere, that what they offered was not merely a speech, or a symbol, but immersion, an absolute experience from which the individual would re-emerge re-created. This experience was akin to a religious conversion and was evoked in the terms of the sacerdotal, an abject surrender to a sensual mysticism. The Nazi effect was an assault on the consciousness.[252]

Hitler's use of lighting was derivative from opera; he knew that light could literally turn night black. The naked flame, primitive and primordial, blazed and flickered, it was another piece of stagecraft: bonfires, torches, fireworks. Hitler according to Spotts had intuitive recognition of the psychological effect of darkness, where he could play with controlled lighting effects: there was ceremony and theatre and close regulation of every platform appearance, march and salute.[253] Sir Nevile Henderson remarked that Hitler's arrival at Nuremberg

> was theatrically notified by the sudden turning into the air of the 300 or more searchlights with which the stadium was surrounded. The blue tinged light from these met thousands of feet up in the sky at the top to make a kind of square roof, to which a chance cloud gave added realism. The effect, which was both solemn and beautiful, was like being inside a cathedral of ice.[254]

He goes on to describe the advance of the standard bearers: some of these standards apparently had electric lights; he evoked the spectacle of 'five rivers of red and gold rippling forward under the dome of blue light, in complete silence, through the massed formations of brownshirts'. This was 'indescribably picturesque. I had spent six years in St Petersburg before the War in the best days of the old Russian Ballet, but for grandiose beauty I have never seen a ballet to compare with it.'[255] And such foreigners and the nations they represented were an important target: British grandees attending Nuremberg rallies as guests of honour were greeted by Hitler's

ADCs, grandly housed and taken to meet the Führer and the paladins of the Reich.[256]

From 1933 Albert Speer was the designer of party rallies and their conceptualiser, structuring the public aesthetic via flags, standards, lighting, backdrops, and hence his commission to build the Zeppelin Field stadium to accommodate 340,000 spectators; the famous 'cathedral of light' at Nuremberg was his creation[257] (and, in parallel, his Beauty of Labour Office was seeking to 'make industry beautiful').[258] The drama was reinforced via percussion – cannon, rifles; church bells, sirens, drum, fanfare – all these were integuments of the orchestration. There were other tricks like making a crowd wait for several hours. It was about 'transforming the rituals of the rally with its boring speeches and uniform parades into a hedonistic feast, into an easily saleable art product'.[259] Elite Britons recorded their reactions; for Sir Arnold Wilson, Nuremberg was all 'so simple, so solemn, so moving and so sincere as to merit, better than many customary religious rites, the title of worship ... Such a ceremony would have satisfied the early Saints.'[260] One British academic felt 'it seemed as though, on this night, the prophecy had been fulfilled. Barbarossa, Germany, the spirit of the Fatherland, was re-arisen.' He spoke of:

> a country that in the truest sense of the word was a nation; a living whole of concordant wills; a people regenerate and restored, physically and morally sound, and set firmly and resolutely on the way towards grandiose masteries and achievements ... Everywhere health, character and order, and a virtual absence of the evils that are their negation.[261]

The contrasts with England were shameful, its 'louts and hooligans and wastrels, sinister or feckless toughs or softies ...'. By comparison, in Germany 'the physical well-being of the nation's youth is a pleasure to see'.[262] This development of party ritual, the theatre of politics, was lugubrious and amateur in the early years.[263] Yet a methodology of the spectacular had to be acquired, Nazi public theatre was an operational competence which had to be evolved and matured. Instructions stress music; martial melodies are to serenade the larger meetings, especially during the entrance of the flags: 'whether or not there is music has an important impact on the mood of the meeting, and therefore of the speaker'.[264] Flags must only be brought on in massed, serried ranks, and if the band is not available, formations such as Hitler Youth can sing. The ending had to be visually powerful as well – no closing remarks by the chairman, only a short 'Sieg Heil' and the national and party anthem. Reporting back to HQ was essential (again the importance of feedback), within three days at the most, a detailed scrutiny. Hence the quality of spectacle was achieved by orchestration; Pfeffer (the party's master of ceremonies) understood the psychology of ornamental drill and his orders for meetings are a pedagogy of mass persuasion: 'the only form in which the SA displays itself to the public must be en masse. This is one of the most powerful forms of propaganda.'[265]

Effects could be almost surreal – such as the colour image of hundreds of swastika banners held aloft by their bearers in various party uniforms, a forest of flags each surmounted by a silver eagle at Innsbruck on 21 May 1942.[266] Ceremonialism was a feature of the illustrated papers, which hail monarchic and imperial ritual both in Germany and other countries with Fascist or imperial regimes: the ornamentalism of the Reich.[267] Naturally attention focuses on the Nuremberg rally with its blazing light.[268] But there were the harvest rites of Bückeburg;[269] and others such as the Tannenberg Memorial ceremonies with their congregations costumed in the ritual garb of tradition – nuns, generals of the old order in the anachronistic pickelhaube helmets, the gothic, living figurine of Field Marshal von Mackensen. It was not only a matter of ornamentalism but also architecturalism; the human ceremonies are partnered by ceremonial frozen in stone. The pseudo-classic architecture of the Reich and the design of its symbolic structures constituted a sort of public street furniture. Illuminations lit the Unter den Linden, swathing its regiments of classical columns in the ribbonry of lightness and darkness. And of course, as ever, the Reichsmarschall, for Göring always seems to be around in these public displays; the one constant, always at Hitler's side (for example with Hitler on the front cover of *Flug Und Werft*, 17 August 1936). Göring is the genial uncle of the Third Reich and his role is quite unique and differentiated from the other paladins. One cannot just pay homage to a superman, the regime needs a human face and that face is Göring's, the nation's friend. His ubiquity, the dramatics of his act and the theatre of his self-presentation, are not accidental; in fact, his public role was critical to broaden and lighten the appeal of the regime.

Great occasions

Potsdam

The past, history and tradition were a constant theatrical present in the Third Reich and a rich source of its symbolism and packaging. It generated stage props for the Nazi pageant; they celebrate a new ideology in old language.

The inauguration of the Third Reich, Potsdam 1933 The inauguration of the Third Reich at the Garrison Church in Potsdam was an occasion packaged with grandiloquent symbolism, and indulgently chronicled by the illustrated photo-journals with overblown visual images.[270] Thus *Die Woche* carried a cartoon of Old Fritz himself as the front cover.[271] Vivid imagery of the various ceremonies follows, the Hindenburg address amid the splendours of the Garrison Church itself, the Hitler address. Hindenburg is still head of state, not Hitler, and hence it is he who stands at the head of the congregation and who addresses it as a pseudo-monarch. It is indeed curious to see how Merry Widow operatic uniforms combine with the brown shirts; masses of top hats mix and swell with storm trooper shakos. The sartorial contradictions are naturally not commented upon, but the brown shirts are agents of menace. There is the usual Nazi formulaic of delirious crowds and burning torches, youthful and pushed back by happy policeman. Pictures of the new cabinet (most of whom were not Nazis, who possessed only three cabinet posts) offer a contrast of face and physiognomy; members of the old regime represent, if not a touch of class, then a touch of caste, such as Crown Prince William and elderly generals and other princes suitably ensconced in steel helmets. Artillery fire, youth march boldly with flowing flags and there is an entire page surreally filled with what appear to be mere strutting steel helmets; and the baroque vistas of Potsdam are backdrop to this. Then the scene moves to Berlin and the night: torch-lit streets, troops, the Brandenburg Gate, Hitler in his opera box decked out in white tie (whereas Göring is, somewhat incongruously, in party brown shirt uniform), and the Reichstag with its masses of brown-shirted members. There is very little written comment – the essay is purely visual, an exercise in regime packaging.

Funerals in Berlin

The state funeral of President Hindenburg was not long in coming; it was the first of the great funerals of the Third Reich, though the Nazis were already practised masters of this symbolism, the great dying-in-state and neo-state funeral of Horst Wessel, for example. The early funerals had developed the concept and set the tone. The funeral (little more than a year after Potsdam) was also similarly a pastiche of the old national and the new ideological imagery.[272] Nazi insignia were prominent at the ceremony, but the old order presides over the photo-journal record. At the Tannenberg Memorial the admirals, superannuated generals in pickelhauben, soldiers with flaming torches, cavalry, all congregate alongside dragoons with swords; women are in black veils; officers carry Hindenburg's medals. A mighty Iron Cross banner dominates, and foregrounded were such sights as Field Marshal Mackensen in full plumage against the backdrop of the cod-medievalism of the Memorial. The photojournalist essay then follows Hindenburg's funereal journey from family and home and village, and the masses of eagle flags and the Iron Crosses are made haunting by the effects of night, of the smoke-edged torch-lit nocturnal. And then the funeral in Berlin, the grandeur of its cathedral, solemn crowds in place, the face of Hindenburg in death. The dignity of these occasions was not entirely synthetic or produced.

Other funerals – and there were of course a great many both of the grand and the ordinary – were indeed formulaic, like much else in the public persona of the Reich. Typically (such as with the funeral of an airman at Tannenberg) there were stage props such as a massive Iron Cross, generals seated, uniforms and flashing medals, alert black-uniformed Hitler Youth to attention.[273] Colour images of the funeral of Gauleiter Wagner of Upper Bavaria in April 1944 elaborate the basic recyclable funereal paradigm: the usual red carpets and steps, the pleated red curtains, pomp and pageantry celebrated in foliage and flowers.[274] But there are also refinements, the kitschified symbols of status-recognition for the deceased: a brazier and an effigy of a mighty gold eagle, rows of standards and banners, coffin guarded by men in various uniforms with their legs apart in aggressive stance. And similarly with the images of the funeral of Adolf Hühnlein, head of the Nazi Motor Corps. For bomb victims there could be a mass funeral with the usual death-packaging and the legions of swastika-draped coffins.[275]

And the burial of a senior Nazi in the autumn of 1944 was thus described by the *Berliner Morgenpost*:

> the Gauleiter's coffin rested on the flower-strewn platform, surrounded by black pillars and the flags of the Gau. The honour guard consisted of leaders of the party and the Wehrmacht. While Beethoven's Coriolanus overture was played, the Führer's massive wreath of red roses and white chrysanthemums was carried in by two SS men. The family entered, greeted silently by the gathering. The Gauleiter's wife was accompanied by Reichsleiter Rosenberg.[276]

The speech of Rosenberg concludes 'the Führer has authorised me, party comrade Bürckel, to express to you his thanks for your complete loyalty to him and to the movement'. He keeps repeating this word 'loyalty' three more times in a few sentences. And then:

> Rosenberg presented, at the Führer's instruction, the German Order with Swords. Alfred Rosenberg then placed the Führer's wreath on the Gauleiter's coffin. The party ceremony ended with the moving second movement of Beethoven's Eroica. On Wednesday morning, the mortal remains of Gauleiter Bürckel were laid to rest in his native soil of the Neustadt cemetery.[277]

Then there were the obsequies for Rommel. Hitler had ordered national mourning and a burial with full military honours:

> the body lay in state in the town hall at Ulm, with Rommel's Marshal's baton, helmet, sword and jewelled decorations placed on a velvet cushion. A large crowd gathered in the square, which was festooned with banners and flags. Field Marshal von Rundstedt gave the funeral oration: 'I have been called here by the Führer to say farewell to his Field Marshal fallen on the field of honour. This tireless fighter in the cause of the Führer and the Reich was imbued with the National Socialist spirit and it was this which gave him his power and has been the mainspring of all his actions. His heart belonged to the Führer.'[278]

The funeral of Rommel was a protracted homage to the criminality of the regime and, even in that wasteland of shamelessness, it still stands out (and in March 1945 Rommel's wife received a letter saying that Hitler had ordered a monument to the Field Marshal).[279]

Olympics

The 1936 Olympics represented the acme of Third Reich packaging, this time for a global audience as well as a national one, for the whole purpose was to portray the Reich as validated by the global community. They revealed just how far perceptions of reality can be managed, and the willingness of people to prefer the elation of falsehood to the sobriety of truth. This was not a regime that was, yet, fully in the business of massacre, but it did deny Jews the right to participate in the public service and, increasingly, the professions, it did incarcerate political opponents in brutalising camps and was happy to beat them up and indeed kill them – 'shot while trying to escape'. The *New Statesman* commented 'terrorism for a few and megaphone propaganda from the many provide the essentials in this new technique of government'.[280]

And the world knew this. It is a convincing testament to the power of effective political packaging and propaganda that so many in the community of nations were happy enough to masticate the pre-digested chimaera of self-delusion that the Nazis had fed to them: visitors were even welcome at Dachau concentration camp, 'where they will be convinced that we're detaining nothing but gangsters'.[281] The strategy was to charm the oligarchs of the IOC, and parade the tokens, German athletes of some Jewish descent who could be cajoled into participating – for example, because their relatives had still not escaped Germany.[282] The Berlin Olympics were the Reich's embassy to the world, its painted face, its false face. It was a sanitised Reich, with endless help for the international journalist cadre, multiple phone banks and legions of staff; the Reich pampered them. Germany had a friendly countenance. Some of the illustrated weekly reports are even written in English to oblige the tourist. Arnold Lunn (the British businessmen) saw the Winter Olympics that preceded them as an advertisement for a new system of government: 'the young skiers were encouraged to believe that a ski race is a competition in which Germans race to prove, not that they were better skiers than other people, but that Nazism was better than democracy'.[283]

The Olympic Stadium was in fact sunken so 'the effect is like entering a mighty and partially subterranean cave',[284] and within, the taut figures and the human geometrics, fresh-faced youth (30,000 of them) and the tramp of marching feet. In the air the *Hindenburg* floated, above the garlands and myriad ribbonries and bunting; the bands played, soldiers stood to attention and uniforms glittered with the insignia of rank and regiment. So the ceremonies began, the stirring opening overtures, and Hitler's arrival according to one American was 'something like the wind across the field of grass' as the crowd reacted.[285] The commencement ritual was magnificent even by the baroque standards of the Reich (one symbolic innovation became a permanent part of the Olympic panoply – the Olympic torch).[286] A symphony of symbolic imagery: the playing of Wagner's *Great March of Allegiance*, the five-year-old girl in the white dress with flowers; Hitler's arrival and then the orchestra play the German national anthem and the Horst Wessel song, and the German team enter dressed in white and yachting caps as the crowd rises.[287] And finally the lithe torch-bearer races into the Olympic Stadium; silence as he runs round the southern half of the track in front of Hitler's box, up the steps, pauses before the brazier, more silence, and then he sets the brazier alight. A mighty roar arises from 100,000 hearty throats; and then the taking of the Olympic oath.[288]

But nothing perhaps in this imperfect world captures perfection, not even in the Reich. The release of the 80,000 pigeons would have been a potent image. But, tragically, their fright at the artillery barrage precipitated their mass defecation all over the assembled athletes as hubris became nemesis.[289] With the closing, the standard formulaic of the ornamental state again applied; 130,000 people gazed as guns boomed, with a regiment at attention, midshipmen running national flags up the poles, Göring and Goebbels watching as Germany took second place. Searchlights illuminated the sky in the usual fashion. William Shirer thought 'the Nazis have done a wonderful propaganda job'.[290] The 1936 Berlin Olympics were probably (apart from the 1934 Nuremberg Rally, also immortalised by Leni Riefenstahl) the pre-eminent public event of the Third Reich: perhaps more famous than notorious given the extent to which Nazi symbolism is subverted by the glorious victories of Jesse Owens, making Leni Riefenstahl's filmic tribute, *Olympiad*, which gives Owens's achievement full weight, therefore a much more complex form of propaganda. Any 'master race' message of the games, though not overt, was nevertheless sabotaged both at the games and necessarily (as it could not deny too much authenticity) in the film. *Olympiad* showcases the multiple triumphs of a black man (Hitler does not congratulate Owens but on the other hand he congratulates hardly anyone else either).[291] But the race message was anyway deliberately muffled; a regime based on the notion of the supremacy of blood showed it was adept at a 'multi-culti' symbolic strategy when political necessity called, for example the photo-journalism of the *Berliner Illustrirte Zeitung* on 23 July 1936.

Olympiad was a visual poem to the athlete's body, not a crude drumbeat of physical prowess but almost balletic in its grace. Riefenstahl's technique in *Triumph of the Will* was perfected here – the alert face in half-profile, heavily shadowed, making bodies and faces appear to be sculpted out of light and shade, thus lending them tangibility and weight. The final effects took two years of editorial diligence. The relation of the Olympics to Olympia and the ancient games was the explicit master-narrative of the film, commencing with vistas of classical Greece. Nazi Germany is revealed as the inheritor of Sparta. The play of light on inanimate sculptures transforms them into living bodies, a vision of muscular antiquity. The camera slowly focuses on Myron's discus thrower and, by means of low angle shooting, creates the impression of power and movement; suddenly the Greek statue dissolves into the modern 'aryan' athlete.[292] All this imagery of young people performing supreme physical feats was propaganda for the regime ideology, but indirectly: for it necessarily celebrated character and physical performance, not art or intellect, and this is typical of the way Nazism only 'got' part of human existence and excluded so much else. The film's message has merit for propaganda purposes since its ethos is both universal (at least in the Eurocentric world), and parochial, definitely Nazi in its evocation of concepts like Strength Through Joy and the idealised Aryan body (the records demonstrate that the film was commissioned by Goebbels's ministry).[293]

Anschluss

The Anschluss, a meld of conquest and coup d'état, and the triumphal entry into Vienna that represented it, was a master class in symbol manipulation.[294] Hitler's imperial journey from the German border to the new Ostmark was greeted by a facsimile of universal Austrian ecstasy, massed ranks of happy faces. Central Vienna became another Hitlerite auditorium and this backdrop, the magnificent imperial city, its statuary and palaces, suggested the apparent blessing of accumulated history: a stage set for Hitler's new imperium to replace the old. The maintenance of the fiction of benevolent invasion was continued as, behind the scenes, key members of Austria's (far-right) regime were shoved into concentration camps.[295] The Anschluss is structured in Hoffmann's photo-journal 'Hitler in his Homeland' as a royal progress whose symbols telegraph basic messages about the nature of Hitler's rule and, specifically, the meaning of this Anschluss (or union with Austria).[296] It is a pictorial narrative of the progress of the anointed and his enactment of a priest-king ritual: 'teutonic kings, again, in the old heathen days seem to have stood in the position, and to have exercised the powers, of high priests'.[297] The rear end of the photo-chronicle is an image of an old man in high pointed hat, cardigan, long beard and extraordinarily long pipe, the iconography of folk tradition. And talking to this Gandalf figure is an eager young German soldier in austere uniform. Again, this frames the photo-narrative; and its message is that the venerable and folkish elements, the citizens of the soil, welcome their conquerors and their deathless invasion. This is heritage Hitler, an offer of the benison of history and tradition. His image is carefully crafted throughout – the technique of close-up, intensive portrait shots juxtaposed with the reactions of publics, or his silhouette, or his serial 'leader' poses. This then is also a 'lone' Führer: he stands above everyone in the composition of these images, his head framed against a white sky or a church steeple. Here also is a ritualised script, recording the formal balletics of Hitler's rule such as the usual 'German greeting', the delirious crowd shots or the floral tributes. Thus a woman, barely held back by the military, thrusts flowers at the Führer as his armoured car rolls past. And on his return floral tributes again, this time from a BDM (Bund Deutscher Mädel) girl at the airfield.[298]

Fiftieth birthday

Hitler's fiftieth birthday in April 1939 was another of the set piece occasions.[299] This was the aesthetic essence of militarism: the canon becomes an object of art, the whole thing a crudely effective display of power and might for all the world since the target market was international as well as domestic. It was a bricolage of tradition and technology, the usual Nazi formulary, horse-cavalry and the latest tanks. Organised as a theatre set, it was a play with a structure, beginning with the band serenade and the Führer's receipt of bouquets from children (a sort of official signature in Hitler's Third Reich but also a 'monarchical' sign – the kind of thing royalty does); then the great crowd singing and the serried ranks of veterans. The fleet of Mercedes appears, the bands belting out Preussen's Gloria as the mighty cars roar down the Unter den Linden to the admiration of gazing crowds, and then entry through the Brandenburg Gate. Hitler leaves the car to take his high place on the dais in front of the serried ranks of generals and admirals, seated in fact upon a big throne. The symbolism is unambiguous. And then the parade, not so much an event as an emotional condition: the almost trance-like state induced by the rhythmic choreographed movements of thousands of high stepping feet, the drill, the rigour. Hitler seems elated, arm outstretched, finally returning to his balcony surrounded by excited aides. The display of cavalry struck a quixotic note, as did the final act of the drama, when all the banners are rushed forward in a great dash. This is the house style of many dictatorships and totalitarian regimes, of course, but the Nazis did it best, on the biggest scale and with the finest choreography. The backdrop is official, public Berlin, the standard Heritage Europe metropolitan landscape of the high nineteenth century.

The symbolism of this exercise in Caesarism is indeed of Hitler as Roman emperor, as absolute ruler, source of ultimate knowledge in a perplexing mid-century world, the certainty at the centre of the maelstrom of uncertainty. The idea of the military might of Germany is delivered via the icons of that might, the hardness of the hardware, the rigid discipline of its troops, the vast numbers of both. It is situated in history very near the end of the Spanish Civil War, that great symbolic clash, but also a few months before the beginning of the Second World War. The message, conveyed through imagery rather than other means, is clear to Germans and others: the spirit of Versailles is finally exorcised, we are back in business. Thus the regime established its internal public dominance via military renewal, and its external hegemony via merchandising the symbols of war.

Conclusions

Paxton argues that Fascism's combination of a high-tech look with attacks upon modern society, along with its scorn for conventional bourgeoisie tastes, was pleasing aesthetically and emotionally. The Nazis literally packaged the ideology, turning it from abstraction into story, and facilitating neglect of the dark side of a regime that hid its private content beneath a public idea. They were creating a narrative, an explanation. Their worldview was self-validating and obvious, everything connecting and all the elements integrated into a universal explanatory framework. As a result, no great intellectual tax was necessary to understand the meaning of the regime as it offered something for everybody, including simplicity for the simple-minded. The packaging, moreover, conveyed the illusion, rather than the truth, of hyper-efficiency. The production of imagery of immense assertive power and on an industrial scale was matched by rhetorical overdrive. The mighty swarm of violent machines hid much incompetence; the anachronism for example that the army's transport often used horses and it still retained cavalry regiments.[300] There is actually a dualism to the German imagery of the Second World War – here was a regime which hurled gigantic rockets against its enemy and yet much of its artillery remained still horse-drawn; but historical memory, the publicly imagined Third Reich, neglects this – for what movie ever showed the great German army of the Second World War, the Wehrmacht, in thrall to a four-legged animal?

Was Klemperer right? Were the Nazis the finest admen in history? That the true talent of the regime lay in packaging, its true depth lay in surface? But Klemperer later revised his view about the creativity of National Socialist advertising, their art was moribund, their motion pictures epics of maudlin sentimentality.[301] National Socialism's real creative strength lay in its political and cultural ephemera – slogans, posters: 'the most self-consciously visible of all political forms, Fascism presents itself in vivid primary images'.[302] Nazism's core competence, as it were, was the ability to force heterogeneous elements together and impose structure;[303] and it achieved this through propaganda. And the point, surely, about the 'packaging', then, was its novelty, but to us how different: our knowledge makes all those proud symbols, artefacts, blazing colours, seem contaminated and worse. Totemic of genocide, they evoke a conditioned reflex. The memories, the monochrome images of cattle trucks bursting with people, the women in headscarves, the children, the pallor of the faces bewildered or petrified, these intrude and reconfigure perception. To perceive this packaging, as it were, *ab initio*, requires an extraordinary act of imagination, perhaps an impossible one. And even the concentration camps, subsequently instruments of genocide, were as we have seen an invited subject of press interest, far from being hidden in remote forests. The public were told fresh air, exercise and skills training were on offer. There was of course the 'model' concentration camp, Theresienstadt, an image almost of 1950s Butlin's. The sinews of the Nazi state were set forth as something you could admire and even regard with affection; they were the public musculature of your tribe.[304]

Notes

1 Paxton, *Anatomy*.
2 Fest, *Hitler*.
3 Wistrich, *Weekend*.
4 Ibid.
5 Hoffmann, *Triumph*.
6 Wistrich, *Weekend*. He also speaks of the manipulated collective representation of German history.
7 Paxton, *Anatomy*.
8 Hoffmann, *Triumph*.
9 Ross, *Media*.
10 Ibid., citing Reichel.
11 Ross, *Media*.
12 *Berliner Illustrirte Zeitung*, 10 October 1935.
13 B.L. Davis and P. Turner, *German Uniforms of the Third Reich*, London: Arms and Armour Press, 1997.
14 *Illustrierter Beobachter*, March 1939.
15 Wistrich, *Weekend*.
16 Spotts, *Hitler and the Power*.
17 Wistrich, *Weekend*.
18 Ibid.

19 *Signal*, 'The New Reich Chancellery', London: Bison Publishing, 1976.
20 Ibid.
21 *Berliner Illustrirte Zeitung*, 20 April 1939.
22 Rutherford, *Hitler's Propaganda*.
23 Bormann, *Hitler's Table Talk*, 25–6 September 1941.
24 Ibid., 21–2 October 1941.
25 Wistrich, *Weekend*.
26 Rutherford, *Hitler's Propaganda*.
27 Bytwerk, *Bending Spines*.
28 Wistrich, *Weekend*.
29 Ibid.
30 Bytwerk, *Bending Spines*.
31 Ibid.
32 Ibid.
33 Wistrich, *Weekend*.
34 Bytwerk, *Bending Spines*.
35 Brendon, *Dark Valley*.
36 Ross, *Media*.
37 *Adler*, 9 November 1943.
38 Ibid., 19 January 1943.
39 Ibid., 28 April 1942.
40 *Die Wehrmacht*, 3 December 1941.
41 *Adler*, 27 April 1943.
42 Ibid., 9 November 1943.
43 Rutherford, *Hitler's Propaganda*.
44 *Signal*, 'Paris 24 Hours after the Occupation', London: Bison Publishing, 1976.
45 Ibid.
46 *Signal*, 'Paris on Wheels', London: Bison Publishing, 1976.
47 *Signal*, 'Vichy – Pictures from a Quiet Residence', London: Bison Publishing, 1976.
48 *Signal*, 'The Great Tank Battle in France', London: Bison Publishing, 1976.
49 *Signal*, 'Historical Hours Around Paris', London: Bison Publishing, 1976.
50 Ross, *Media*.
51 *Adler*, 31 March 1942.
52 *Berliner Illustrirte Zeitung*, 9 July 1936.
53 *Die Woche*, 28 October 1933.
54 Ibid.
55 *Adler*, 21 July 1942.
56 Ross, *Media*.
57 *Berliner Illustrirte Zeitung*, 27 April 1939.
58 *Adler*, 28 April 1942.
59 Ibid., 23 June 1942.
60 *Berliner Illustrirte Zeitung*, 22 July 1934 and 7 November 1935.
61 Ibid., 25 February 1934.
62 Ibid., 28 July 1938.
63 Ibid., 22 July 1934.
64 *Die Woche*, 14 April 1937.
65 *Berliner Illustrirte Zeitung*, 16 September 1937.
66 Ibid.
67 *Die Woche*, 14 April 1937.
68 *Das Reich*, 20 January 1941.
69 *Illustrierte Beobachter*, 23 March 1939.
70 Ibid.
71 *Berliner Illustrirte Zeitung*, 9 July 1936.
72 Ibid., 28 April 1938.
73 *Berliner Illustrirte Zeitung*, 25 February 1934.

74 *Die Woche*, October 1933.
75 *Illustrierte Beobachter*, 11 August 1938.
76 Ross, *Media*.
77 *Illustrierte Beobachter*, 11 August 1938.
78 Ibid.
79 *Berliner Illustrirte Zeitung*, 23 July 1936.
80 *Die Woche*, 14 April 1937.
81 *Berliner Illustrirte Zeitung*, 16 September 1937.
82 Ibid., 14 October 1937.
83 *Die Wehrmacht*, 5 May 1943.
84 *Berliner Illustrirte Zeitung*, 16 September 1937.
85 Ibid., 23 July 1936.
86 Ibid.
87 Ross, *Media*.
88 Ibid.
89 *Berliner Illustrirte Zeitung*, 12 May 1938.
90 Photo spread, *Adler*, 29 September 1942.
91 *Adler* cover, 4 August 1943.
92 *Die Wehrmacht*, 3 December 1941.
93 Wistrich, *Weekend*.
94 Ibid.
95 Weitz, *Hitler's Diplomat*.
96 Herzstein, *War*.
97 Weitz, *Hitler's Diplomat*.
98 Ibid.
99 Ibid.
100 Joseph Goebbels, in *Wille und Weg* (1931), pp. 2–5 (first issue, lead article), Central Office for Propaganda, NSDAP, Calvin College German Propaganda Archive.
101 Ross, *Media*.
102 *Die Woche*, 28 October 1933.
103 Saur, 'Signal'.
104 Ibid.
105 Ibid.
106 Ibid.
107 Ibid.
108 Ross, *Media*.
109 Calvin College, German Propaganda Archive, Posters 1933–39 no. 8.
110 Rutherford, *Hitler's Propaganda*.
111 Ibid.
112 Calvin College, German Propaganda Archive, Posters 1933–39, no. 20.
113 Ross, *Media*.
114 Rentschler, *Ministry*.
115 Ibid.
116 Ibid.
117 Manvell, *Films*.
118 Rentschler, *Ministry*.
119 *Signal*, 'A Day in the Life of the Propaganda Ministry', London: Bison Publishing, 1976.
120 Gustav Memminger, *Hitler Jugend: Das Erlebnis Einer Grossen Kameradschaft*, Munich: Carl Röhrig-Verlag, Kom.-ges, 1942.
121 Ross, *Media*.
122 Baruch Gitlis, *Cinema of Hate: Nazi Film in the War against the Jews*, Bnei Brak, Israel: Alfa Communication, 1996.
123 Rutherford, *Hitler's Propaganda*.
124 Gitlis, *Cinema*.

125 Ibid.
126 Ibid.
127 Ibid.
128 Ibid.
129 Stark, *Political Propaganda*.
130 Ibid.
131 Ross, *Media*.
132 Ibid.
133 Ibid.
134 Bormann, *Hitler's Table Talk*, 18 October 1941.
135 Kallis, *Nazi Propaganda*.
136 Herzstein, *War*.
137 *Berliner Morgenpost*, 5 October 1944, Calvin College German Propaganda Archive.
138 Welch, *Propaganda*.
139 Ross, *Media*.
140 Rentschler, *Ministry*.
141 Ibid.
142 Ibid.
143 Ross, *Media*.
144 Jowett and O'Donnell, *Propaganda and Persuasion*.
145 Oliver Thomson, *Easily Led. A History of Propaganda*, Stroud: Sutton Publishing, 1999.
146 Hoffmann, *Triumph*.
147 Rentschler, *Ministry*.
148 Ibid.
149 Ibid.
150 Ross, *Media*.
151 Ibid.
152 Rentschler, *Ministry*.
153 Ibid.
154 Ross, *Media*.
155 Farndale, *Tragedy*.
156 Rentschler, *Ministry*.
157 Ibid.
158 Ibid.
159 Ibid.
160 Ibid.
161 Hoffmann, *Triumph*.
162 Rentschler, *Ministry*.
163 Ibid.
164 Welch, *Propaganda*.
165 Ibid.
166 Culbert, 'Kolberg'.
167 Herzstein, *War*.
168 Ross, *Media*.
169 Paret, 'Kolberg'.
170 Ibid.
171 Burleigh, *Third Reich*.
172 Hoffmann, *Triumph*.
173 Paret, 'Kolberg'.
174 Welch, *Propaganda*.
175 Manvell, *Films*.
176 Hoffmann, *Triumph*.
177 Welch, *Propaganda*.
178 Herzstein, *War*.
179 Ibid.

180 Ibid.
181 Manvell, *Films* (the journalist was Christopher Cviic, an Anglo-Yugoslav contributor to *The Economist* who gave this information to the author in 2010).
182 Ross, *Media*.
183 Ibid.
184 Ibid.
185 Ibid.
186 Rentschler, *Ministry*.
187 Ibid.
188 Ross, *Media*.
189 *Das Schwarze Korps*, 14 March 1944, Calvin College German Propaganda Archive.
190 Ibid.
191 Ross, *Media*.
192 *Signal*, 'Hitler's Wartime Picture Magazine', London: Bison Publishing, 1976.
193 Ibid.
194 Ross, *Media*.
195 *Signal*, 1976.
196 Ibid.
197 Calvin College, German Propaganda Archive, Posters 1933–39, no. 54.
198 Ibid., no. 42.
199 Ibid., no. 38.
200 Ross, *Media*.
201 Ibid.
202 Fest, *Hitler*.
203 Ibid.
204 George Forty, *Germany at War*, London: Carlton Books, 2003.
205 Ross, *Media*.
206 www.pre67vw.com/history/
207 *Illustrierte Beobachter*, 1938, Folge 10.
208 *Die Woche*, 7 October 1933.
209 Herzstein, *War*.
210 Ross, *Media*.
211 Ibid.
212 Manvell, *Films*.
213 *Berlin Rom Tokyo*, August 1942.
214 'Hunting Pirates in the Channel', Kleine Kriegshefte No. 2, Zentralverlag der NSDAP Munich 1940, Calvin College German Propaganda Archive.
215 'Landing as if in a Dream', Zentralverlag der NSDAP Munich 1940, Calvin College German Propaganda Archive.
216 Oskar Lachmann, 'Alarm in Birmingham, Noise and Fire – An Aircraft Factory Destroyed', Munich: Zentral Verlag der NSDAP 1940, Calvin College German Propaganda Archive.
217 *Signal*, 'The Four Plagues of the Desert', London: Bison Publishing, 1976.
218 Ibid.
219 *Signal*, 'His First Strike in Africa', London: Bison Publishing, 1976.
220 *Signal*, 'The Four Plagues of the Desert', London: Bison Publishing, 1976.
221 Winkelnkemper, 'Cologne'.
222 Ibid.
223 Ibid.
224 Manvell, *Films*.
225 Ibid.
226 Welch, 'Charismatic'.
227 Brendon, *Dark Valley*.
228 Paxton, *Anatomy*.
229 Ibid.

230 Wistrich, *Weekend*.
231 Fest, *Hitler*.
232 *The Third Reich in Colour*, Simply Media, May, 2001.
233 Boak, 'Women'.
234 Rutherford, *Hitler's Propaganda*.
235 Paxton, *Anatomy*.
236 Rutherford, *Hitler's Propaganda*.
237 Ibid.
238 Spotts, *Hitler and the Power*.
239 Fest, *Hitler*.
240 Paxton, *Anatomy*.
241 Spotts, *Hitler and the Power*.
242 Fest, *Hitler*.
243 Ibid.
244 Hoffmann, *Triumph*.
245 Ibid.
246 Henderson, *Failure*.
247 Fest, *Hitler*.
248 Wistrich, *Weekend*.
249 Hoffmann, *Triumph*.
250 Spotts, *Hitler and the Power*.
251 Welch, *Propaganda*.
252 Spotts, *Hitler and the Power*.
253 Ibid.
254 Henderson, *Failure*.
255 Ibid.
256 Griffiths, *Fellow Travellers*.
257 Wistrich, *Weekend*.
258 Ibid.
259 Hoffmann, *Triumph*.
260 Griffiths, *Fellow Travellers*.
261 Ibid.
262 Ibid.
263 Fest, *Hitler*.
264 Huber, *Propaganda Primer*.
265 Fest, *Hitler*.
266 Forty, *Germany*, pp. 190, 191.
267 *Illustrierter Beobachter*, 11 August 1938.
268 *Berliner Illustrirte Zeitung*, 16 September 1937.
269 Ibid., 10 October 1935.
270 *Die Woche*, 21 March 1933.
271 *Die Woche*, 21 March 1933.
272 *Das Illustrierter Blatt*, 14 August 1934.
273 Forty, *Germany*, photograph p. 176.
274 Ibid.
275 Ibid., p. 178.
276 *Berliner Morgenpost*, 'The Reich Minister Speaks to Workers in a City in Western Germany Near the Front', 5 October 1944; Calvin College German Propaganda Archive.
277 Ibid.
278 Snyder, *Enemies*.
279 Ibid.
280 Guy Walters, *Berlin Games: How Hitler Stole the Olympic Dream*, London: John Murray, 2006.
281 Ibid.
282 Ibid.

283 Ibid.
284 Ibid.
285 Ibid.
286 Ibid.
287 Ibid.
288 Ibid.
289 Ibid.
290 Ibid.
291 Ibid.
292 Walters, *Berlin*.
293 Ibid.
294 Heinrich Hoffmann, *Hitler in his Homeland*, Berlin: Zeitgeschichte-Verlag, 1938.
295 MacDonogh, *Gamble*.
296 Hoffmann, *Hitler*.
297 Sir James Frazer, *The Golden Bough: A Study of Magic and Religion*, London: Macmillan and Co., 1922.
298 Hoffmann, *Hitler*.
299 *Hitler's 1939 Birthday Parade*, International Historic Films, Chicago, 2004 (fiftieth birthday in April 1939).
300 Janusz Piekalkiewicz, *The Cavalry 1939–1945*, Harrisburg: Historical Times Inc., 1987.
301 Klemperer, *Language*.
302 Paxton, *Anatomy*.
303 Ibid.
304 Burleigh, *Third Reich*.

6

PLACE: POLITICAL MARKETING CHANNELS

The entrepreneurship of the public space

> *The average Englander is not nearly as well educated as the German, but he is more mature and sure of his opinions. He therefore does not need the same permanent political schooling as we do.*
>
> — Dr Josef Wells, 1936

The probing intellect of Nazi propaganda was always searching for new ways of communicating. But this facility of technique was also part of their self-promotion: a display of the regime's virtuosity, it projected the idea of their slickness, cutting-edge mastery. To contemporary observers, the Third Reich often looked like a commercial production, one which was assured, business-like and superbly organised. The fluency and confidence of self-presentation both intimidated and impressed: 'The most intriguing aspect of the extension of American-style marketing techniques in the mid-1930s was their affinity with many of the Nazis' own ideas about advertising.'[1] People often assume that external impressions provide evidence for the internal (i.e. that competent self-articulation implies competent administration). In the view of the Communist propaganda entrepreneur Willi Munzenberg, the Nazis had employed 'all of the refined methods of large-scale advertising in the 20th century'.[2] Bracher observed that 'the party owed its growth to the application of commercial advertising techniques to political recruitment, which, violating the rules of good taste and acceptable levels of noise, began an assault on the collective subconscious'.[3] Nazi advertising advice paralleled Madison Avenue's – 'do not just propagate the name, but also the product – do not merely place an ad for the producer, but also for the consumer – do not simply write, but also explain and convince'.[4] Until 1933, Germany was a democracy: the Nazis were therefore competing in the political marketplace of ideas through their techniques of political evangelism, and they were competing, in a dynamic environment, with other parties. And other parties responded competitively: 'in a futile effort to counteract Hitler the Social Democrats opened a school of oratory'.[5] But the efforts of other parties were not trivial. The Communists, for example, enjoyed the services of their maestro Munzenberg, the 'maverick mastermind of Communist propaganda in interwar Germany'.[6] And the Nazis needed to conceive a methodology to fight the great Hindenburg. Thus:

> Goebbels's propaganda machine found a way of them combatting Hindenburg without insulting him: he had done a great service to the nation, but now was the time for him finally to step aside in favour of a younger man, otherwise the drift into economic chaos and political anarchy would continue.[7]

The Nazis had to differentiate their offer, as it were. Their chosen method of doing this was what is today called negative campaigning, and they certainly have a share in its paternity even if they did not invent it. They were moreover political, in the sense that all parties are political, in their preference at strategic moments for the impressionistic over the tangible – thus one speaker declaimed 'we don't want lower bread prices, we don't want higher bread prices, we don't want unchanged bread prices – we want National Socialist bread prices!'[8] The vigour of evangelism lacked all precedent. Thus Goebbels 'on a scale never before seen … deployed the arts of mass suggestion – posters, gramophone records, films, leaflets (some flung from aeroplanes), and advertisements revealing that Hindenburg was the candidate of the Jews'.[9]

The imagery was lurid and crude, but arresting; it involved comic caricatures as well as menacing vistas of their various enemies and gloriously sanitised images of themselves. Their opponents were depicted as tiny beetle-like little men, Disneyesque creatures representing the religious parties, the conservatives, the Jews and Communists and Old Reaction (the forces of tradition). But it was the vigour of the Nazi assault and consequent ubiquity of their imagery that most impresses, for example the 1930 Goebbels campaign exhausted the twenty-three rival parties: 'He distributed millions of brochures. He stuck posters everywhere. He organised thousands of mass meetings, many of them in the open, where they were lit by phalanxes of blazing torches.'[10] Goebbels once said 'he who conquers the streets conquers the masses; and he who conquers the masses conquers the state'.[11] Invariably, of course, their opponents were shown as in league with the Jews. One set of posters juxtaposes photographs of the Nazi leadership against photographs of various Jewish public figures; and offers a celebrity assortment such as Einstein, Hindenburg and Hitler, asking who is the most important man in the world?[12] And they had an eye for the latest visual techniques such as photomontage, cruelly satirising Bernhard ('Isidore') Weiss, the deputy Berlin police chief, by showing serial images of him at social functions with buxom ladies, with the aim of stereotyping him as the decadent Jew of Nazi mythology.[13]

Nazi propaganda was based on a bestiary of hyphenated entities such as the Jewish-Bolshevik, Old Reaction, greedy Anglo-Saxon capitalism, all painted in luminous colours. But the comic-pulp nature of Nazi lies should not blind us to their effectiveness. However, while the Nazi narrative was condensed and articulated via symbolic imagery inscribed in posters, this imagery drew from a common stock: 'many of the symbols in the opposing political arsenals were strikingly similar, as was the dynamic, naturalistic style in which they were conveyed'.[14] They were now shared as common property among the agitational parties – the colours, the movement in the images, the similar generous use of red with its 'insurrectionary connotations', all of which became 'images of anti-establishment subversion, of fundamental opposition to the Weimar system'.[15] And thus:

> All over Germany, electors were confronted with violent images of giant workers slashing their opponents to pieces, kicking them aside, yanking them out of parliament, or looming over frock coated and top hatted politicians who were almost universally portrayed as insignificant and quarrelsome pygmies.[16]

This 'hyper-masculine, musclebound proletarian giant' was the antithesis of the socialist's florid, flaccid capitalist (an image the Nazis would Judaise) and indeed of the political symbols of an earlier generation.[17] But the universal symbol system was not static but flexible, capable of evolution:

> Yet, given the Nazis' need to reassure the middle classes, the giant worker was now in some instances portrayed in a benevolent pose, no longer wild and aggressive, but wearing a shirt and handing tools of work to the unemployed instead of wielding them as weapons to destroy his opponents; the Nazis were prepared for responsible government.[18]

More generally, in any system, even in a venerable democracy, real imaginativeness is by definition rare, even among 'creatives'. Thus once in power the great crisis in Nazi propaganda, its internal contradiction, was never fully negotiated: sometimes it is the sheer quantity, rather than the quality, which truly impresses. Bullock observed that the:

> non-Nazi papers – the *Frankfurter Zeitung*, for example – were tolerated in order to preserve some variety of style and so avoid a dull uniformity which would lose readers and so reduce the impact of the propaganda message; Goebbels's instructions to all the media were to 'be more monoform in will, polyform in the expression of it'.[19]

But the press in Germany had collectively lost one million in sales by 1934, and in part this is attributable to its stupefying mediocrity; for Goebbels the press was 'our problem child'.[20] A publishers' trade journal article analysed the situation in 1934:

> One newspaper was just like another since complete articles were delivered by the state and party news apparatus with specific instructions to print. Party

officials and agencies at all levels appointed press representatives and these gentlemen expected their 'news releases' to be printed in full in the local press. Every tiresome crank in the party now demanded that his views be aired.[21]

People were simply ceasing to read newspapers.

Part 1: New media

Channels: new media – radio

Communications channels were an assemblage of new (electric/cinematic) and old (print) media. The new media were particularly important channels of evangelism, and it is no accident that the Hitler phenomenon is coexistent with their maturity. Apparently a Hitler extravaganza only had limited impact in the years prior to 1933, such were the technical imperfections; until the end of the 1920s cinema productions were soundless.[22] German publics had certainly not then been sold the idea of political film as artwork, nor were the cinemas interested.[23] Yet these were mediums that could create life, capture its breath; no longer the static page alone, or the ephemera of campaigning, but the true voice in the home and the living form in the picture-palace. Radio was just emerging from its crystal-set chrysalis into a commodious item of domestic furniture, but not a cheap one. Yet by 1932 there were 4.25 million radios in Germany.[24] Its effects were profound; above all it was nationalising, creating a national audience and the opportunity for the nation to be addressed as one body, simultaneously. The only constraint was purchase cost, a problem the Nazis solved systematically.

Goebbels first commandeered radio in the election campaigns of February and March 1933; the Nazis were in a strong position since although they possessed only three cabinet seats, one of these was the Interior Ministry which had responsibility for radio.[25] Goebbels remarked 'we make no bones about the fact that radio belongs to us and to no one else. And we will place the radio in the service of our ideology, and no other ideology will find expression there.'[26] Since the coalition arrogated a monopoly of the airwaves, the opposition voices were completely excluded.[27] And like cinema, the radio was the beneficiary of technical and organisational innovation: 'there were technical improvements in radio transmission which helped rural areas, reception improved, and by 1938 broadcasting was 20 hours a day as distinct from 14 hours in 1933'.[28] For Nazis, radio was the 'single most important means of mass communication'.[29] It possessed the attributes of innovation, centralisation and simultaneity, a centrally controlled apparatus that touched much of the nation instantly. Radio ownership more than doubled in five years, to 9.6 million in 1938.[30]

As the years went by, Goebbels proved himself right in that radio became by far the regime's most effective propaganda tool. As William Shirer recalled:

> it was surprising and sometimes consternating to find that notwithstanding the opportunities I had to learn the facts and despite one's inherent distrust of

what one learned from Nazi sources, a steady diet over the years of falsifications and distortions made a certain impression on one's mind and often misled it. No one who has not lived for years in a totalitarian land can possibly conceive how difficult it is to escape the dread consequences of a regime's calculated and incessant propaganda.[31]

Wistrich speaks of the tribal resonance of radio: Hitler 'knew how to play on this tribal drum to awaken profound, archaic forces'. He also cites the observation of another authority on 'its power to turn the psyche and society into a single echo chamber'.[32]

Historical Movies and radio bought a new intensity and immediacy to communication. And new they were: radio, for instance, was still a novel and expensive medium when the Nazis came to power in 1933, and the use of sound in films only really began, despite earlier experiments, in 1928. Radio itself had been in an experimental state – since the Marconi wireless demonstration of 1897 – until the years following on from the end of the First World War. In Germany, radio transmissions began in 1915 with a more general system from 1923, a mere decade before the coming of the Reich.[33] Thus radio was in its technological adolescence during Weimar and was an extra-political realm, barred from use as a political medium.[34] In the elections of March 1933, following Hitler's appointment as chancellor, forty per cent of voters were still anti-Nazi, but the party now enjoyed a monopoly and Goebbels told station managers to 'make public opinion'.[35] What had formerly been a regional service was now national,[36] and the print press information oligopoly was challenged by the new radio medium which proceeded to flourish under the aegis of Goebbels. Radio was decentralised in Weimar and so the Nazis centralised it.[37] Hitler was the first politician to make major use of radio,[38] and Goebbels asserted: 'I profess to see the day when every factory, every cinema, theatre, marketplace and square, railway station and every home will be within range of the Führer's voice.'[39] Thus Hitler himself was a radio personality, speaking almost every week and becoming in other words an intimate domestic voice familiar in every German home. Nazi Germany created a universal communications system, a fluid stream of thought and ideas and entertainment and music which flowed through almost every house in the land and every person within that house. The Nazis, in other words, ultimately succeeded in colonising the domestic space which had hitherto been the last refuge from tyranny and indoctrination. Now no more.

Goebbels had also initiated the People's Receiver (a smaller, half-price version was later introduced). The People's Receiver was the Nazi special bargain to the German people, available within a year of Hitler's election victory; even the radio brand – 301 – was propaganda, since it commemorated 30 January 1933, 'the most important day in German history!'[40] In psychological terms, the state mobilised the 'reciprocity principle': people 'owed' the regime for a magical piece of domestic technology which linked them to every other German, an electronic folk community. Three million cheap radio sets were sold, and overall listening rose from

FIGURE 6.1 German People's Receiver

4.5 million to 16 million between 1933 and 1942.[41] The importance of the German People's Receiver is often only glanced at in the literature, yet it was critical to the global receipt of message, the doctored news and its pre-ordained response.

And Goebbels had a switch in his office whereby he could intrude his own urgent announcements into all radio programmes. A further refinement was the installation of radios with loudspeakers in public places such as cafés, as well as the careful control of domestic listeners via radio wardens charged with organising, encouraging and policing radio use.[42] A total of 6,000 radios was placed in these public spaces.⁴³ This was significant, as it made listening not only a private but also a communal act, a ritual of collective approbation. Public address systems, their music and their exhortations, became a feature of the urban topography. Then there were the big factory radios, alternately hectoring and soothing their captive crowds. Also, radio is a medium we inhabit, one that does not demand concentration because it is heard not watched; this is more analogous to breathing than anything else, and the consumption of message is often unconscious. Its propaganda uses exemplify the notion of 'low involvement learning', for radio insinuates, we are persuaded without necessarily being aware of the persuasion. Moreover, as an aural medium it can stimulate engagement since visual imagination makes pictures out of sound. But radio also functioned in a competitive market arena, for example from German-language shortwave broadcasts from outside Germany, and the radio magazines carried foreign radio schedules until the war began.⁴⁴ The BBC claimed that by the end of 1944 it had ten million German listeners, forcing German radio to respond; so the context was still a competitive one, an astonishing struggle unique in history between embattled nations for the domestic audience.⁴⁵

Customer response Goebbels's focus was also on the analysis of listeners and their preferences via a survey system, and he used the national group of radio wardens to gather evidence and feedback.⁴⁶ As time went on, the regime saw that radio had to be refreshed and reinvented with less political content. In this policy shift, the Nazis introduced new notes of frivolity after initially failing with their formal party propaganda with its fanfares and martial music, and they substituted classical music and light entertainment for the original ideological digest.⁴⁷ Bullock makes interesting comparisons with Soviet Russia; Germany was economically and culturally more sophisticated and so the Nazis could use 'indirect methods', that is to say the propaganda could be hidden and made implicit in other activities.⁴⁸

Export Nazi radio propaganda was also exportable, with its first target being (for Germany was not just a nation but a pan-European tribe) the German minorities elsewhere in Europe:⁴⁹ for example with the radio campaign urging Austrians to overthrow their regime in 1933. Radio had also helped Hitler in the 1936 Saar plebiscite.⁵⁰ There was a significant vote in favour of Hitler, and it was comparatively (though not absolutely) free:

> the problem was that, in the propaganda war with the stations broadcasting from Germany, the French-German stations lost hands down. Their programmes aimed at the Saarlanders and the Germans as a whole were regarded as almost as bad as those aimed at Germany from Russia. It was said to be impossible for a German with even mildly patriotic feelings to listen to them without anger. The result of the war by 'Ether Waves' was indeed helped on by the radio propaganda from Germany, but it was the help given by the exposure of an issue as a stark one between patriotism and sophistry.⁵¹

And incendiary German broadcasts to Austria proclaiming the imminence of revolution by bloodthirsty Bolshevists helped foment the Anschluss crisis – that, and the impotence of the Austrian leadership (Schuschnigg ordered non-resistance; then the Führer broadcast followed).[52]

By universalising radio, the Nazis incorporated small and isolated communities into a national airwave culture. The novelty must have astonished, but it projected a Nazi presence into every home, not occasionally or periodically but as a constant of their being: the radio was a fixture, and the arbiter of popular culture. While this monopoly of the airwaves was never absolute, not even in war when they tried to attain this via diktat, most people nevertheless listened and what they heard was propaganda. Moreover, they were talking to provincial communities, whose cares and tribulations for hundreds of years were the petty and parochial. Now, national and international agendas could open up for them a real, mediatised national community knitted from its fragments by radio and celluloid. These were new truths of both politics and entertainment and, in the new order, the merging of both. Charisma in a large industrial nation state needs more than just an assembly hall to work its universal magic, and with these new media the entire nation could and in Germany's case did become an auditorium. The seductive potential of radio resided in the fact that message-reception required no effort, and all of it, the music, the roars of the crowd, the sonorous rhetoric, could be enjoyed in the comfort of a deep armchair; or in the beer hall, well lubricated and among comrades.

Global radio propaganda

Nazi foreign propaganda had a distinct methodology, founded on its exploitation of particularised knowledge of local events and the appeal to the tangible over the abstract, perhaps via focus on a specific individual as representative of a classification or cause.[53] A general characteristic of Nazi proselytisation overseas seems to have been a mastery of the pseudo-rational exposition, that is, to construct plausible-sounding arguments, the exposure of which would have required a mind more analytic, and situation-specific knowledge of a greater depth, than most targets of that propaganda actually possessed. And there was a radical difference in philosophy between a regime whose entire ethos was nourished by the idea of communication as the wellspring of power, and their democratic opponents, for whom information was not a tool to be used but a private property to be rationed. Thus in Lisbon, an important and neutral European capital, the German government literally retailed propaganda; it possessed a store in the picturesque Chiado shopping district of the city, merchandising its ideology.[54] During the Battle of France, for example, Goebbels indulged the international journalist cadre, bribed them with luxury hotels, full access to the front and interviews with soldiers.[55] This contrasted with the British and the French, as both states were more bureaucratic and timorous, allergic to any notion of journalists on the front line.[56]

But external global radio propaganda was the main international conduit for the Nazi message. The Funkhaus station in Berlin offered a full orchestra and broadcast in thirty languages, and around 500 people worked in its foreign-language department;[57] languages included Slovak, Turkish and even Afrikaans.[58] Radio was an agency of conquest and the BBC regarded German radio propaganda as a

FIGURE 6.2 SS Netherlands recruiting poster

significant actor in the assault on the Netherlands and France. Flemish and Breton nationalists were also targeted.[59] Over 100 English-speaking people, most of whom were British, worked for the German English-language stations.[60] There was, for example, the radio station Irland-Redaktion. William Joyce, 'Lord Haw-Haw', gave three broadcasts a week for America, with his audiences ranging from Canada and the United States to South Africa, New Zealand and Australia.[61]

The colonial world The Nazis were essentially probing for the soft tissue in their enemies' political body, that is, those points at which their social and imperial systems were failing. By targeting aggrieved groups, by surfacing contradictions and hypocrisies, they could even build a superficially plausible case. They sought to sabotage morale and to foment discord, and they did so globally since they were fighting global powers. Hitler was an unlikely champion of colonial liberation, particularly as his Italian allies ruled a North African empire, as did the Vichy French. But ideology in the Third Reich was malleable yet also of course context-sensitive. Thus there was the new rhetoric designed for North Africa and the Middle East, one that rested on a set of blatantly deceptive propositions, which spoke 'in the name of freedom, liberty, dignity, justice ...' – an ironic appeal in the light of Nazi values – and purported to draw a distinction between 'false democracy' and the democracy of Muhammad.[62] The Nazis, as we have observed, were experts in the rhetoricising of war, with advertising as a battlefield adjunct, and effort was made to make that literature compelling – colour drawings, even cartoons – and fresh formats such as postcards. Nazi leaflets had titles such as 'Rommel, the Lion of the Desert' (with half a million copies) or 'England, Master of Lies' and 'Green is the Colour of the Muslims'. The radio station VFA pretended to be located 'in the heart of the Arab world', and 'The Free Voice of Egypt' allegedly broadcast from near that country's borders.[63]

But Goebbels took pleasure at his 'grandest recruit', the president of the Indian Congress party, Subhas Chandra Bose. Goebbels was delighted: 'we are doing everything possible to pour oil on the fire' and thus 'Free India Radio' began broadcasting daily to India and 'provided a more reliable and entertaining alternative to British controlled stations in India'.[64] The broadcasts were in half a dozen Indian languages and included culture as well as politics, and the station also re-broadcast Indian classical music from the BBC Indian service; the news tried to be accurate for the sake of credibility, with the political message subtly integrated.[65] These broadcasts from Berlin were constantly re-transmitted on at least twelve Axis stations, and communicated via the journal *Free India*, which had a circulation of 5,000.[66] Bose demanded instant freedom for India and charged the British with hypocrisy – how could one imperialism invoke moral superiority over another? His status as Congress party president (from February 1938) was high, and erroneous reports of his death were greeted with 'an outburst of national emotion and grief'.[67] Bose expressed the hope that India and Japan would work together in 'the noble task of creating a great Asia that will be free, happy and prosperous', and his message was that Indians had 'nothing to gain by compromising with a crumbling empire'.[68] But all of this was based on the assumption that Japan would ultimately emerge victorious.

Marketing versus ideology However, the appeal of the Nazi 'product' was inevitably limited in the Middle East and elsewhere by the fact that the Nazis were white supremacists in a world where Caucasians were a small minority. Race ideology was of course an industrial relations disaster in that it outraged Russian slave-workers in Germany as well as sub-national groups who had gravitated towards the Axis.[69] Goebbels navigated away, substituting ideology for race (i.e. the anti-Communist crusade): towards the end of 1941 there were new orders for films to explain Germany to Russia.[70]

Channels – new media: documentary and newsreel

Newsreel and documentary represented another key channel of communication whose maturation is coincident with the success of Hitler, and again this is no random occurrence. The Nazis had been leaders in the employment of sound documentary before their ascent to power: by that time they had already made over 100 films.[71] There were Nazi films even in the 1920s, but they were amateur and cheap, as was the case with their film depicting the 1926 party conference for instance.[72] Hoffmann, who has extensively discussed the history of the moving image in Germany in the period prior to Hitler, observes that 'as early as 1925, Hitler had noted in his book *Mein Kampf* that visual images transmit information instantly, unlike the written word that requires slow reading'.[73] The Reich Film Office was established in November 1930, and Nazis had some impact with their pre-assumption of power films like *Problems of the Time* (1931), *How the Worker Lives* (1931), and *Hitler Over Germany* (1932),[74] which offered 'straight polemics'. But they were part of a broader political ecology of partisan political film. Everyone was doing it. The media celebration of Hindenburg in fact anticipated Hitler. Thus there was *Our Hindenburg* (1927) ('tired hagiographics'): 'It marketed the hero of the battle of Tannenberg in World War I as an image of steel that transcended the ages. This was not history writing the script, but historicising manipulation.'[75]

Yet Hoffmann says that newsreels were no new fetish. They had appeared in Germany before the First World War, and the filmic celebration of autocracy went back to the Kaiser himself (e.g. *The German Emperor in Film* (1912)). There had already been an official memorandum on film as propaganda, and heroic newsreels and their 'bullying chauvinism' long predated Hitler. By 1914 there were 2,446 cinemas. The German government began to take a serious interest in propaganda as the First World War rolled on inconclusively, starting its own film company, DLG. The Royal Picture and Film Office followed in 1917 and they in turn evolved into UFA which became a quasi-government operation charged with advertising Germany's greatness.[76] Ludendorff himself spoke of seeking 'a more systematic and stronger influence on the great mass of the people in the interests of the state by using general standardised themes', and wanted central controls of film. Government directives now asked for unambiguous screen propaganda (such as the 1917 propaganda film *Those Responsible for the World War*).[77]

Newsreels and documentaries were different from other media. They had to be viewed at an appointed place, the cinema. It was an inadvertent audience, however. They had come to watch the movies, and the newsreels were the compulsory prologue. Such audiences were huge as cinema-going had become the leisure activity of the 1930s. And various technical developments now emerged such as the standardisation of sound and projection speeds;[78] the first newsreel with sound was broadcast in Germany in September 1930.[79] The coming of sound had added an entire new level of immediacy to the experience, while the cinemas themselves became increasingly grand, literally palaces of the people designed to augment the celluloid fantasies of escape and wish-fulfilment.

It is here that Nazism's most luminous dreams were merchandised; film technologies in Adorno's view standardise the production of ideas.[80] The newsreels with their fanfares and excited, vigorous commentary were a concentrated burst of propaganda. In fact, they had nothing to do with news in any objective sense. Their target audiences (cinema-goers) were vulnerable to the casual absorption of message because at the cinema our cognitive defences relax. To Goebbels 'newsreels were make-believe reality'.[81] Films could apparently create reality rather than its facsimile – real voices, real declamatory speakers, real columns of marching men. Charismatic leadership could be experienced by every single citizen with vivid immediacy. Never before had this been possible. The documentary was also a valuable format for the Nazis, as images of reality that were photographically authentic could be subtly manipulated for the purposes of propaganda. Thus:

> Nazi propaganda knew how to exploit for its purposes this widespread illusion concerning the facticity of what was being presented as documents. The contemporary viewer and Volksgenosse took at face value what in fact was merely presented as an extract of reality. The dramaturgy of lies to be found in the Nazi newsreel is based on this insight.[82]

The idea was that fabricated images could be 'politically true' when they had a resemblance to what had actually occurred. But film is inherently selective, 'the camera eye represents camera truth'.[83] In a cinema, the camera's view possesses a monopoly of truth and thus the audience is more credulous than is the case with other mediums.[84] Gitlis speaks of visual 'truth', 'based on the widespread misconception held by the public that a picture cannot lie'.[85]

In 1932 Goebbels created the Nazi Film Theatre Owners Association, and during the elections (according to von Wilucki) 'despite limited time, we succeeded in arranging about 200 performances in 70 places. Sometimes, we were able to have film shown during the regular shows.'[86] In political terms, this was a revolution – compare it to the United States, for example, where film was not fully exploited until the 1936 California gubernatorial campaign against Upton Sinclair:[87] '25,000 fellow citizens saw outdoors showing of "The Führer Speaks" and "German Arms – German Honour" ... We can already tell some films are a valuable addition to our propaganda activity, particularly when lower rental costs will give local groups the chance to make a small profit.'[88] So the process was happily self-reinforcing: again we see the concern with fundraising economics. Von Wilucki suggested that 'sound films will have a major role from now on' in helping to 'win back the German people ...'.[89] The role of sound film was obviously significant in these 1932 elections; 200 performances, some in regular movie theatres, is impressive. The tradition continued in power: 'in 1935 some 140 shorts, dealing with party and governmental topics, were made and shown through mobile cinemas'.[90]

Documentaries

Hence overt propaganda – propaganda that is self-announced – found its principal expression in newsreel and documentary. They are a record of the regime's public content, but also an idealisation; they provide two of the things essential to effective packaging – they capture the core imagery of the product, and they focus attention on what is attractive and away from what disquiets: 'the media in totalitarian societies have catechetical functions. Their goal is to present people with convincing accounts of what they cannot know first-hand – the reality beyond their everyday lives. That is, what is presented must agree with the reigning worldview.'[91]

The documentaries in particular project the regime's ideal self. They helped create its public persona and provided a reservoir of images which could be re-used, replenished and recycled. In such films the diktat of imagery prevails, with melodramatic action, penetration, fighting; the visual rhetoric of progress and advance: 'Such scenes are supplemented by shots of the soldiers behind the scenes', the handsome young protagonists in Hitler's drama, 'idealistic and upward-looking with the sky reflected in their eyes'.[92] The realities of high command and strategy, details of planning and organisation, were excised from the record, there was the absence of death or even wounds in these films and their structure was 'essentially dramatic, even epic, dependent on emotional drive from climax to climax, pausing now and then for "rests" with peaceful, even idyllic, "by-play"'.[93]

Feature films used documentary components: 'these films put the moviegoer directly within the experiential vicinity of events ... There are scenes that plainly showed the close connection of this film genre to the newsreel.'[94] And members of the Nazi leadership might appear in movies. At the end of *Baptism of Fire*, for instance, 'Göring himself addresses the theatre audience, declaring, what the air force has promised in Poland, it will make good in England and France'; similarly *U-Boats Westward* includes an appearance by Admiral Dönitz.[95] But the imagery of German military aggression preceded the actuality, cheering the domestic audience and demoralising the foreign one; the symbols of potency anticipated its delivery. Images of Blitzkrieg were used 'to devastating effect' in Norwegian cinemas in 1939.[96] And the film *Campaign in Poland* was shown to the generals of neutral nations.[97] Such films were shown to invited guests in capitals such as Oslo, Belgrade, Bucharest, Ankara, Sofia. These included the film *Front Im Himmel* (1940) about air defence and the blitzing of Britain.[98] There were also three feature film tributes to the Luftwaffe in 1941, for example *Stukas*, the narrative of which was set during the fall of France.[99]

Triumph of the Will The documentaries were also a visual and symbolic expression of the ideology of the regime – their stiff choreography and obsessive-compulsive arrangement of massed human beings says something about the official view of man in society. One cannot, Rentschler argues, separate form and function, or aesthetics and politics.[100] He quotes Susan Sontag on how political relations reappear in aesthetic patterns, that is to say again the surface is also the essence. Citing Karsten Witte, he says the films of the Third Reich:

> recycle and transform in a peculiar fashion, converting the concrete into the abstract, movement into static pattern, open space into bound compositions, overwhelming viewers with 'extreme perspectives of extreme uniformity'. An example is the film *We're Dancing around the World* (1939), its female dancers offering 'exhibitions of regimentation and discipline every bit as uncompromising as those in *Triumph of the Will*'.[101]

Documentary film technique was highly innovative. Riefenstahl, one of the most inventive of all cinematographers ever, created a 'perfect symbiosis' of propaganda and aesthetics.[102] *Triumph of the Will*, a record of the 1934 Nuremberg Party Rally, set new standards in cinematography: odd angles heighten emotional involvement, powerful music synchronises with the action to emphasise dramatic points and foreshortened figures suggest the heroic/historical/transcendent.[103] Riefenstahl was 'developing a workable aesthetic formula to elevate the mundane into an apotheosis of the nation'.[104] Thus there was the innovation of the 'fluid travelling shot', that is, 'induced movement intended to set inanimate matter into waving motion and make human masses ... into stone blocks'.[105] During the wreath-laying scene the Nazi crowds 'appear to be lifeless geometric figures'.[106] The film is about celebrating Hitler's 'wedding fantasies with the masses'.[107] It is an experiment in style, technique and technology: for example, the reactive close-up shot, whereby the individual face, very often in half profile, responds to some piece of public drama; the naïve emotional response is thereby chronicled whether of farmers in traditional dress, Hitler Youth, soldiers, SS men, storm troopers or the adoring women. Riefenstahl's 'accelerated dynamic rhythm, which drives the images forward, does not give the viewers any caesuras that allow them to grasp new developments and situations; does not give them time for cogitation or room for catching their breath; in short, does not leave them any "half seconds" as formulated by cognitive psychology'.[108] Music is a core integument of the text, chosen to reflect the edited emotions placed on the screen. It is argued that the film's power derives from the sheer number of camera eyes used – not the two eyes of the individual, but thirty-two camera eyes: this 'intensifies the human capacity to see'.[109] In the hands of a criminal, such a facility becomes 'an instrument of mass murder'.[110]

Victory of Faith (1933) represented Riefenstahl's intuitive discovery of a Fascist film aesthetic.[111] But *Triumph of the Will* is like no epic that had ever gone before and it eludes precise generic categorisation. It is described as a documentary, but it might equally well be called an opera, an advertisement or a feature film. What it definitely is not is a record of the 1934 Nuremberg Party Rally. What is it? An idealised representation of Nazism through its enactment in balletic form, with waves of human beings stiffening into rigid shapes in homage to a semi-divine leader. While our idea of the Nazi documentary genre is defined by *Triumph of the*

Will, it is just the first citizen in a mighty republic of documentary films. Thus political problems could be solved at the symbolic level, grotesque injustices of a brutal ideology continue with permission because such propaganda is a lenitive. The unreality of an image-driven solution to a real world problem is clear, but for a long time the final conflict between truth and falsehood could be postponed.

Newsreels

The newsreels fulfilled a somewhat different function. They claimed of course to be news rather than a stylised interpretation of some generic theme (i.e. packaging), as in a documentary. Their business was truth. It was also action, events as they unfurled, in national culture, politics and on the battlefield. The newsreels formed a powerful coalition with the films: the news is life, the film is a fantasy about that life, it was an integrated product. But the function of the newsreels was twofold, as information and entertainment, an arrangement which anticipates the theatricalisation of television news in our own day; sensation was part of their character and thus 'audiences were attracted to them without believing everything they saw'.[112] The war newsreels wrapped 'their dramatic imagery within an aura of documentary-style accuracy. This is clearly a potent propaganda formula.'[113] In a totalitarian state, both newsreel and film were mediums of instruction and indoctrination, but in very different ways. 'News' too is about the making of images, but this time images of the moment, of the happening event. Above all they must seem an authentic account of truth, a credible facsimile, as otherwise their power vanishes: 'the manipulation of reality is perceived by the viewer as being authenticated by the documents'.[114] For Hitler reality comprised in large measure the constructed or preserved image of that reality, and hence his enthusiasm for the newsreels. As he stated in 1941:

> for the sake of the future it's important to preserve the news films of the war. They will be documents of incalculable value. New copies of these films will have to be constantly printed, and it would even be best to print them on strips of metal, so that they won't disappear ... I hope that in future news films will be made by our very best film experts ...[115]

Hitler was thus an enthusiast for the newsreels, and they were in many ways the prism through which he viewed the Second World War: 'I've been thrilled by contemporary news films. We are experiencing a heroic epic, without precedent in history.'[116] Their special historic significance, however, is twofold. First, they were the bearers of the narrative of conquest; from the invasion of Poland on 1 September 1939 to the apparent collapse of the Soviet Union in 1942, they retailed a narrative of imperial hyperbole. No empire had been created so fast in history, no country had seen so many foes crumble beneath its cruel steel; neither Rome nor Alexander nor Napoleon could stand comparison with this new Caesar and his Caesarism. And even the failure to defeat England quickly carried the compensatory image of the carnage of the blitz. Second, the Deutsche Wochenschau packaged the legacy, conveying Nazism's image to all of time; their record is a visual poem to the German soldier. They present him to history in all his ascribed heroism, possessed of an idea and an ideal, the legionnaire of a new German raj, flaxen-haired, stoic, all-conquering. This self-created image of Nazism defines public memory of the Third Reich: like some lethal virus yet slumbering in the tomb of some ancient Pharaoh, it carries within it the potential for harm once again among generations who have ceased to remember. Much of course is made of the Allied newsreels of the war and pre-war period, such well-loved institutions as the March of Time or the Pathé newsreels which have become the collective lens by which we view our own past. Yet it was the Nazis who were the true masters of this genre, of which Goebbels was both the cheerleader and the interfering micromanager. The aim was not to represent a particular infantrymen or grenadier, 'but rather the vision of the eternal German unknown soldier'.[117] The status of these films was ultimately a question of resource allocation, and therefore social priorities, derived from an ideology of propaganda.

The Deutsche Wochenschau were explicit propaganda and news only in a metaphoric sense, for they 'explained the war in the ideological terms delineated by the Nazi regime' and combined 'actualité footage and propagandistic editing'.[118] This ultimately became destructive: 'Goebbels concealed huge retreats from the public by shifting the news to reports of "victories" achieved by combat patrols, U-boats, and individual airplane and tank crews. The cumulative effect of these minor triumphs created the impression of a massive "forward defence" punctuated by occasional "tactical retreats" ...'.[119] The presentation of the Deutsche Wochenschau was no arbitrary form. They began with a fanfare; doors were closed during their showing and afterwards there was a three-minute break – mystique must be preserved.[120] Goebbels dictated the terms. According to his adjutant, Wilfred von Oven, 'the texts are examined by the Minister with extraordinary focus, and none emerges without very significant alterations'.[121] All propaganda processes resolve into a formula and the Deutsche Wochenschau were no exception – leader images, battles, human interest stories, military music. The Deutsche Wochenschau films were also for export, promptly delivered, carving out a market within and beyond the new German imperium. This material fed newsreels across Europe in multiple languages, supplying 2,540 theatres outside Germany before audiences totalling 4.5 million persons per week by June 1944.[122] The source of much of the Deutsche Wochenschau product was the Propaganda Company (PK) units. During the war itself, the PK units of the German army provided footage of the reality of war and transmitted the exhilaration of combat to everybody. They were an extraordinary achievement, and the American army's Combat Camera today is only a vague echo of what they did then. They produced the best footage of the Second World War. PK men were proper soldiers but also skilled reporters and film or photography technicians. The PK units were large, finally numbering up to 160 men with expertise in various disciplines.

Newsreels were not truth-telling devices – while the idea of the 'manufacture' of news, its social construction, is certainly admissible in democratic societies, in the case of totalitarian societies, 'news' has only a passing relation to reality. Rather, the Nazi newsreel was a symbolic device. Visualised events in that sense do not happen, but are stylised according to ideological schemata:

> The Nazis later perfected this basic pattern of manipulative tricks: they falsified facts by shifting the context in a speculative direction, by twisting causal connections through a change of chronology, by bending the visual truth with the help of corrections in the text, and used (heroicizing) music to add 'what the images were lacking in power' (Goebbels).[123]

Film of Hitler at the front during the invasion of Poland, for example, appears to show that he was personally directing and not just observing the assault. In Kracauer's view 'the effectiveness of Nazi propaganda results from the viewer's delusion that the evidence presented is genuine: everyone is inclined to believe that pictures taken on location are incapable of telling a lie'.[124] Thus all imagery was edited. Always, they were a clarion call to heroism, but a peculiarly nineteenth-century kind of heroism, one without bloodstains.

Channels – innovative new media

The Nazis were innovators, and where they were not innovators they were exploiters. They saw opportunities when others did not, as for example in the movement's use of the motor car (the SA had its own motor unit early on).[125] The Third Reich was a nexus of social regression and technological progression, a technology incubator. One could have neither ideology nor 'Führerprinzip' without the means to proselytise, and as discussed a feature of the Nazis' rise to power is that it is coexistent/coterminous with the maturing of communications media. They benefited enormously from recent technical advances such as the evolution in microphones and loudspeakers,[126] and in cinematography; sixteen colour films and features had been produced by war's end.[127] One innovation was experimental three-dimensional film, and they made a number of such films, including several in 1936.[128]

No potential propaganda medium was ignored in the Third Reich – every channel, every tool, every surface was interrogated for its propaganda potential: one magazine, *The Propagandist*, even included articles printed on the envelopes in which it was sent to subscribers.[129] The political war must never cease, even for a moment; the regime constantly sought new ways to perpetuate its imagery and ideology, on the theory that while the message would never change, the medium would and could. Even stamps were conscripted into the frenzy (postage stamps are a generally neglected medium of propagandist iconography). One 1939 issue was a sharp black-and-white image of the Führer posed as imperious tribune of the people; in 1940, with Germany at war, a kindlier image of Hitler was forthcoming, sweetly greeting a small child carrying a bouquet of flowers.[130] Another innovative method was the so-called 'wall newspapers', for that is what they were, with titles like *Word of the Week*. Blessed with an intensive distribution system, they blended language with imagery. They were 'the most ubiquitous and intrusive aspect of Nazism' and combined editorial with polemic with poster: 'every week from 1937 to spring 1943, an estimated 125,000 copies of a black and white or colour wall newspaper were displayed in the nooks and crannies of everyday life'.[131] They existed everywhere, from train stations to hospital waiting rooms.

And then there was television, decreed by Goebbels as a medium for the public space; Nazi television began in Berlin in 1935 and in Hamburg in 1941.[132] It is instructive to compare Germany and Britain: in Germany, television was conceived as a public, that is propaganda, medium, and in Britain as a private domestic one. The few private sets were 'given by manufacturers to influential people. The rest of the public in Berlin watched in public viewing rooms.'[133] Television covered the 1936 Olympics. Nazi television claimed (an exaggeration) to be 'the world's first regular television service' (the BBC's thirty-line service had in fact been launched in 1932), but every night there was a one-and-a-half-hour service from 8.30 to 10 p.m. with manufacturers' test transmissions during the day.[134] Their programmes comprised 'a weekly newsreel, studio performances and excerpts from movies and documentary films'.[135] Berlin had ten public television lounges by the beginning of the war, with television continuing until 1943.[136] Much of it was in fact typical of subsequent genre television, the usual structural banality as today, jejune, parochial: for example, the bottle-blonde young woman newsreader is, in Nazi Germany and since, a television staple. There were news interviews with politicians such as Gauleiter Wagner, arrayed in party uniforms but still clumsily affecting the folksy intimacy of television discourse. There were programmes on horse riding, gardening, music, all with a defiantly lowbrow tone – it is not the Nazi-ness of Nazi television that is noticeable here but rather its anticipation of future mediocrity.[137] Yet the surviving television archives are still revealing as they show unedited videotape versions of the Nazis, in which there is much more disorganisation, hanging around and generous bellies. The geometric rigour and the anatomical erectitude are missing; there is none of the hard polish of the documentaries.

The typeface of battle Because the ideology had two components, a belief set, a belief in belief if you will, and a methodology for evangelising that belief, it followed that every context was potentially a site for the rhetorical assault. This included the field of battle. As ever with Nazis, a physical-material war was supported by a persuasion war, not just in the obvious places, home front or troop morale, but as an offensive weapon against the enemy itself. The enemy would be remorselessly probed for its psychological vulnerabilities. Since they were fighting not a unitary state but a coalition of allies, some of whose members were imperial powers (i.e. federations of people under a loosely coercive control), this raised the possibilities of using propaganda to drive a wedge between them.

Propaganda literature was just another battlefield weapon, prepared for circumstances specific to the battles as they arose; for instance 'Facts, Figures, Faces' is a four-page news sheet for the Ardennes offensive (the Battle of the Bulge).[138] Another battlefield journal anticipated the methodology of Rupert Murdoch: but this time the leering nude always decorated the front page, an effective attention-getting device in those less erotomanic times. In this, a kind of general war magazine, stories on Japan, the weather, the draft, jostle with conventional war subjects.[139] The thrust was calculatedly idiosyncratic – astrological literature, articles about German night fighter pilots taking miracle drugs, the Soviet octopus over Europe, an image of a German pilot who claimed to have shot down 300 Soviet planes.[140] And here is a leaflet targeted at the British at Monte Cassino on 11 May 1944 – one side shows a beach and it is brightly coloured like a tourist poster, lush, a line drawing of a woman in a bathing suit with the words 'Italy wants to see you.' The other side is grey-brown and reveals a forest of crosses surmounted by British helmets, as a skull grins and gazes over them in a seigneurial way.[141]

Civilians were also now part of the battlefield and therefore also targets. For instance, the Germans prepared small gummed stickers for the Italian campaign, such as a label, bright red, featuring London Bridge and the burning city foregrounded by a German soldier.[142] If enemy troops were targets and to be reached by bizarre message delivery systems, then so also were the enemy's publics. A regime so embedded in an ideology of communication in order to promulgate an ideology of race and empire could consider means both recherché and irrational; the cost of promulgation could not necessarily justify its results. But, as an exercise in communications virtuosity, or even inspired lunacy, some of these methods impress both with their cleverness and their inanity: what did their sponsors think they were doing? Were they trying to convince themselves? Was the ante-natal memory of the street fight and the propaganda struggle against the Communists still so strong in 1944–5?

Thus one imaginative meld of technology and propaganda was the attempt to use the V1, a prototype cruise missile, as the distribution unit for leaflets and even for copies of the English-language edition of *Signal* magazine: in effect the literature was blasted out of these pilotless planes.[143] The flying bombs could be launched from Heinkel bombers as well as from ramps (for example in the Manchester Christmas Eve raid of 1944).[144] This was a direct form of propaganda, since it was actually delivering the physical product into the hands of the enemy public. As well as miniaturised versions of *Signal* magazine, atrocity leaflets were included which contained images such as corpses in a Hamburg street.[145] Hence a Home Office letter of 17 December 1946: 'after the 28th of August 1944 a proportion of all flying bombs sent over this country were found to carry propaganda leaflets, which were therefore scattered around the scene of the explosion in almost every district subject to this form of attack after that date'.[146] While Nazis were not alone in using leaflet propaganda, it was their faith in it which distinguished them. As Herbert W. Friedman recalled:

> In 1966 I published a letter from World War II German General Walter Dornberger that said his department of the Board of Ordinance, Rocket Development (WaPruef 11) designed and developed small solid-fuel rockets that could carry propaganda leaflets about 6–7 miles. The rockets had a

container tightly packed with propaganda leaflets that were fired against front-line Allied troops in Italy.[147]

This authority also cites Wilhelm Pruller (*Diary of a German Soldier*): 'We got a new gun to-day with a barrel made of cardboard. And it shoots too, as far as two kilometres. The bullets are propaganda bombs which comprise more than 100 leaflets.'[148]

The Nazis displayed virtuosity During the years of German victory, large maps were exhibited by the Reich Propaganda Office in public squares which showcased the armies' advance: enormous cartoons and charts were placed before prominent public buildings and sometimes there was a loudspeaker as well.[149] The charts explained why Germany was winning. Other methods included the production of cancellation mark slogans via the Post Office. The aim of having 'a loudspeaker pillar in every public square', the aspiration to soak the cognitive environment with political content, was actually prevented by the war.[150] One observer speaks of 'this regimentation by means of the ubiquitous loudspeaker' and notices that even arc-light standards and flagpoles 'were endowed with a mechanical voice'.[151] The technical creativity was tireless even if at times esoteric. One idea, according to Goebbels, was a huge artificial smokescreen on to which propaganda films could be projected, and other Heath Robinson devices. Not all of these things happened – certainly not the smokescreen – but they testify to a fertile technological imagination.[152]

Part 2: Old media

Channels – old media: press

Newspapers were important – and unlike radio they had negligible (illicit) foreign competition or vendors of alternate perspectives, so the attractions to the propagandist regime were considerable.

The era of struggle The press was a priority right from the start. In the early days of the movement there was the party daily newspaper, the *Völkischer Beobachter* (much of the Nazi press was merely a supplement to this), and also the *Illustrierter Beobachter* which was an illustrated weekly; and there were originally eighteen regional weekly party newspapers as well.[153] The Nazi press mimicked the sensationalism of the press in market democracies, and for commercial as well as propaganda reasons: this was a product to be sold, and Nazis favoured marketised self-reinforcing systems within their propaganda ecology. The Nazi papers were competing with non-Nazi papers before the seizure of power, and, in theory, after it: they consequently had to compete with products that owed their logic not to ideology but to the marketplace.[154]

The technique of Goebbels's *Der Angriff* was 'very much that of modern journalism'.[155] The opening invective would hurl readers into a maelstrom of polemic and the main article was made by Joseph Goebbels into a kind of verbal poster or street address. Its quality of vigour was magnetic, but 'only when the reader had been thoroughly aroused did it make its dark threats of the revenge to come'.[156] Goebbels launched *Der Angriff* to combat the Berlin police's ban in May 1927 (the word *angriff* means 'attack') and ran a teaser campaign.[157] Thus the advertising campaign posters proclaimed: (one) '*The Attack*', (two) 'When will *The Attack* happen' and (three) '*The Attack*, the German evening newspaper'.[158] Its language was 'aggressively demotic' and the wholesalers would not touch it. The familiar litany of themes included November traitors and police officials; and the cartoons of 'Mjölnir' were a feature, evoking again a depraved confederacy of stock Weimar types.[159] The scribes of these early Nazi papers were for the most part 'from the ranks of the fanatics, the salvation seekers, the rootless, and the unemployed'.[160] These papers espouse the language of violence. They were 'crude almost beyond belief':

> The worst of them scarcely resembled a weekly newspaper but rather a badly printed brochure of 10 to 20 pages filled with the wildest and meanest diatribes, poisonous, bitter, and in every way repulsive in content and appearance. These early Gau smear sheets could have been the work of juvenile delinquents.[161]

Yet this was a party under siege, impecunious, bereft of support. Their paper in Frankfurt, for example, had to be printed elsewhere as no local print firm would work with the Nazis; and there was also the exhaustive struggle to launch a Nazi daily for Hamburg.[162]

Nor was the Nazi press exactly popular. In 1928 the two Nazi daily papers had a circulation of just under 23,000, but after that there was a 'sharp surge': weeklies become dailies and newspapers were started.[163] Even then the circulation pre-1933 was not great, at three-quarters of a million, and fifty-nine daily journals, by 1932.[164] One scholar points out that the Nazi press had no more than seven per cent of total circulation even when they had achieved one-third of the votes.[165] But this represents too narrow a view of communications impact: Hitler's new allies were Hugenberg and his UFA, whose press agencies supplied the right-wing press, and Hugenberg's tabloids were just as instrumental as Goebbels's.[166] And similarly with UFA's newsreels, they were increasingly partisan – reactionary and 'geared towards discrediting the Republic'.[167]

In power: censorship and conformity The Nazi era deadened Germany's vigorous newspaper culture. The number of newspapers shrank from nearly 5,000 to 2,000 on the eve of war and to under 1,000 by the end of 1944.[168] Many newspapers disappeared, merged or were purchased by the Nazis, and these included some famous titles.[169] Ambassador Henderson could not conceal his (retrospective) contempt; speaking of the party papers he said 'no lie, however great and obvious, was too much':

> common vituperation and abuse were their main stock in trade. They were not newspapers, but emetics; and when they were really on the warpath, as for instance during the Czech and Polish crises, it was impossible to read them

without actually feeling sick. It made me sad to think of German youth being educated on such utter trash and on such complete misrepresentations of the truth.[170]

During the war, the party tried a new approach, sobriety, with Goebbels's pseudo-intellectual newspaper *Das Reich* (its circulation had climbed to 1,400,000 by 1944).[171] *Das Reich* carried Goebbels's weekly editorial, vocalised also via radio, his electronic pulpit.[172]

Yet the interest of Nazis in preserving a facade of civic culture meant that censorship, like other structures of regime oppression, was semi-submersible. Journalists self-censored; official censorship was neatly avoided by making editors legally responsible for content via the Editors' Law of 4 October 1933.[173] The Nazi world was a parody of a modern consumer economy that gave off, at a certain level, a sense that freedoms though constricted were certainly not abolished; the government was conscious that it was the government of a sophisticated European country and the Nazis therefore went to great lengths to disguise the truths, and much of the ugliness, of what they were really doing. The press, for example, was made to appear the possessor of a certain residuum of freedom – independent publishers had a broad role and continued to publish under the Third Reich; hence we may speak of 'Hitler's lip service to the alleged autonomy of the press'.[174] So Hitler 'proclaimed his adherence to the principle of a free press, the right to criticise objectively officials and policies of the state, and a positive role for the press in the conduct of public affairs'.[175] He was emollient towards the independent (non-left) publishers – he was unable to govern only with the support of his Nazi 'trumpet friends', stating that he needed 'violins and other instruments in the national orchestra'.[176] Regional titles were retained and they resembled what they had once been, traditional newspapers that Germans had grown up with. Moreover, there was an ostensible market dynamic behind the delivery of news since there was competition between the National Socialist publications and so-called bourgeois ones, and competition also among party publications.[177]

The major middle-class established papers appeared resilient and even dominant in the years after the Nazi seizure of power.[178] But 'opposition' papers became more papal than the pope, and their survival was also due to the German Foreign Office: 'they gave respectability to Nazi Germany and at the same time peddled its propaganda'.[179] Hence the *Frankfurter Zeitung* was retained as an apparently independent newspaper to present Germany as a place where freedom could at least still exist on the margin. In practice it was a useful conduit of black propaganda.[180] Henderson believed that the *Deutsche Allgemeine Zeitung*:

> attempted to preserve some, at least, of the decencies of normal journalism, as did also to a certain extent the *Börse Zeitung*, which was the organ of the Ministry of Foreign Affairs ... But the best and fairest newspaper in Germany was the *Frankfurter Zeitung*, and I often wondered how it managed, among so much censorship and corruption, to preserve its last vestiges of independence.[181]

Cinema had been another example of the Nazis' blurring of control and their confusion of private and public ownerships. By the end of the 1930s the state controlled the major production companies, but indirectly, and a film credit bank financed 75 per cent of feature film production, while cinemas remained privately owned.[182]

The press illuminated Nazi priorities. Since the coercive state was now in being, the Reich Ministry for Public Enlightenment and Propaganda (RMVP) became an agency of commission and excision: it was about creating some forms of speech and destroying others. And they had earlier stated bluntly 'the press office is a branch of the propaganda department'.[183] In other words, there was no distinction between news and propaganda. So in 1933 about 2,000 journalists were expelled, 200 Social Democratic and thirty-five Communist papers were closed and others subject to 'coordination'. There was also the establishment of the Reich League of the German Press which was accorded juridical functions.[184] The journalist in the Third Reich was officially directed to think of himself as a professional propagandist; earlier notions of professional journalism, ideas of truth and objectivity were defunct. They now serviced a higher truth, that of the values and worldview of the regime. On 3 September 1939 Otto Dietrich told journalists they were no longer only reporters but 'the soldiers of the German people. Today we build a West Wall of the soul and constitute the power that stands behind our troops fighting now in the East in Poland.'[185] The function of newspapers was advocacy, by exclusion as well as inclusion, for example the non-reportage of speeches by foreign statesmen. But the regime calibrated its influence process, from cajolery to coercion. It was capable of 'nuance', openly attacking the Jewish press, insidiously undermining the Catholic and regional media.[186]

Channels – old media: poster

In contrast to radio and newsreel, the poster is a medium of extracts, so that the art is choosing one truly resonant image rather than a fluid cascade of images, one phrase rather than a protracted rhetorical text. It is an argument edited down to its molten visual/rhetorical core. This is because of the limitations of other media, thus radio, always a state monopoly, was not available to Nazis until 1933, and overtly political film was a failure. Why posters then? Radio and cinema give us the choice of whether to participate, the poster does not; people have always tended to be apolitical and inadvertent consumers of political information, but posters trespass on our consciousness, an uninvited guest. And these posters filled the public space. Resistance was difficult. Ideas and perspectives thus seeped into the mass community.

Nazi posters, so much more lucid and arresting than those of rival parties, appealed to visceral sentiment, to what, according to Sefton Delmer, Hitler called man's inner 'Schweinehund'.[187] Collectively, the posters articulated a barely repressed fury, embodied in the physiognomy of that familiar Nazi face: taut, scowling, without an ounce of spare flesh, expressive of focused anger and race narcissism. They created a sense of menace. In the posters a scythe was not merely a scythe, for example, but a symbol of violence. Nazi propaganda worked in association with the violence which was tolerated by much of the official pre-Nazi state: 'a democratic movement cannot beat terror by counter-terror'[188] (such a perspective would in fact position propaganda as a subsidiary force). Posters were festooned with aggressive imagery, and much of their persuasive power lay not in words but in the alternative language of symbolic communication, with dragons, eagles, ploughs and spirits declaiming and decorating the message. Behind much of this was the idea of some attainable ideological utopia or perfect state, behind the demented rantings and urgings, a lust for paradise. Their posters offered colour, passion, as well as rage of course, but above all a vista – the shining future of our lives. And also, the subject of so many of the posters, Adolf Hitler – the commanding, unblinking, charismatic, pseudo-mystical stare of the marshal and the messiah. A new set appeared late war (the last) entitled 'Adolf Hitler is Victory'.[189]

It is, moreover, often conveniently forgotten that Hitler fought a long sequence of democratic elections before finally becoming German chancellor (the Nazis fought five different regional and national elections in 1932 alone). His free election propaganda anticipates modern political marketing techniques, for example he was not a German citizen until 1932, so posters stressed his patriotic credentials very much in the way modern American campaign advertising would pre-empt negative attack (they showed images of him wounded with the Iron Cross etc.).[190] Thus Adolf Hitler was, at one time, just another political candidate to be packaged and sold to sceptical voters in a democratic election, and the political marketing of Hitler had – as in any such campaign – to deal with the candidate's perceived vulnerabilities. Hence posters appeared of Hitler the frontline soldier: to fight for Germany was alibi enough for a leader. And posters responded to the vagaries of his early political career – for example, Hitler, mouth bandaged, playing the victim when temporarily silenced by the courts.[191] Later posters 'ran' Hindenburg and Hitler as a kind of dream ticket, with the two disembodied heads placed together against a black background, floating in the air; but no Nazi Party signage, just the words 'National Socialist'.[192] And another March 1933 poster: 'In the deepest need Hindenburg chose Adolf Hitler as the Reich Chancellor. You too should vote for this.' Both this time in uniform, Hitler in the brown shirt and Hindenburg in the coat and insignia of the field marshal, Hitler is shaking his hand against a backdrop of German industry and countryside. There is a mighty swastika underneath the image.[193]

In 1930 Stark claimed that posters were the best form of propaganda, that despite their cost they still constituted a relatively cheap method of 'advertising'.[194] He stressed how the Nazi house style was universally recognised: 'It is well known that our textual posters have their own style, such that the attentive observer recognizes from a distance that it is something from the Nazis.' He says large posters in red must be designed so that they stand out, a small poster is ineffective, and no one reads a poster stuffed with text: 'in general, only the name of the party should be emphasised in the text'. The top and bottom must command attention. He adds 'the headline must be large; it should dominate the poster'. This is good advice; and he also notes: 'effective posters emphasise words that create a certain mood and can be noticed from a distance'. The text poster works when there is time to read it, but if not then the picture poster – 'the effect of the picture poster lies with its capacity to be understood at a glance, to get across the spiritual attitude instantly ... The hurried city dweller does not have much time ...'.[195] In posters the Nazis liked to use 'the language of imperatives' (i.e. to demand resolute action from the viewer, or legitimate action in their name).[196] After the assumption of power their focus of course changed since the poster's function in a totalitarian

FIGURE 6.3 Farmer with scythe pre-1933 poster

FIGURE 6.4 Adolf Hitler is Victory wartime poster

system is reinforcement, not the promotion of scepticism or the refutation of criticism as would be the case in democracy.[197]

The colour of the posters was an important reason for their appeal as they lent vibrancy and brightness to a monochrome post-Great War world and the drab visual presentations of the other parties; they roar, they bleed, they explode; they were a carnivorous exercise. The creator of many of the most visible posters was 'Mjölnir':

his speciality was the German hero with cleft chin, larger than life, hard of fist and rather lower forehead, all conjuring up pictures of strength, challenge and will. It was said of him by one Nazi leader that he did far more than lengthy speeches could do by the 'glowing fanaticism of his powerful art'.[198]

FIGURE 6.5 Hitler wounded pre-1933 poster

FIGURE 6.6 Hitler frontline soldier pre-1933 poster

Another style was that of the celebrated Ludwig Hohlwein: 'looked at today, his work reminds one of nothing so much as those advertisements for seaside resorts, which used to enliven British stations in the 30s'.[199] His posters would feature 'a young Nazi, male or female, also smiling the same Cupid-like, slightly rectangular smile, often advancing with the outstretched hand in greeting. As for the beach backcloth, this has been replaced by a swirling swastika flag or some other symbol of the party.'[200] Interestingly, activists repeatedly raised the question of financial constraints. As Stark commented in 1930, 'for us, the picture poster is simply a question of money. Here too we are limited by financial weakness.'[201]

FIGURE 6.7 Hitler with sealed lips pre-1933 poster

Yet another method used recurrently in the posters was pseudo-rationality, the attempt to persuade with data, thus 'proof' was established with lavish pictograms and a hubbub of statistics. This also gave Nazi proselytisation a modernist veneer. Take, for example, a poster for the 29 March 1936 referendum: 'No German must need. 11.5 million cubic metres of coal have been provided by the Winter Relief. This is four times the volume of the great Pyramid of Cheops. That is one of the Führer's accomplishments. Give him your vote.'[202] A series of pyramids were shown, the familiar technique

FIGURE 6.8 The Marshal and the Corporal March 1933 poster

of the dramatic-pictographic representation of data to give the viewer some idea of dimension.

What strikes the observer also is the shameless political opportunism in which the posters revel. They were, for example, quite capable of showing Hindenburg as the lackey of the Jews and then shortly afterwards as the patriarchal ally of Hitler. And cunning techniques were used to pull in audiences such as the early headline 'Kaiser of America – Speaks – in Berlin', arousing curiosity by the novelty value of the claim.[203] The creation of a pseudo-folk culture, the idea of the community, even things like the focus on the overseas Germans and the unity of all Germandom, were all aspects of this enterprise. Nazism offered the modern man, rootless in an urban world, regression, and the idea of a national family that would care for him and prize his life above the alien and the other. It is not our dependence, but interdependence, which Nazi propaganda most stresses. Thus a poster captioned 'Hitler is Building. Help Him. Buy German Goods' features the usual blonde man with rolled up sleeves, placing one brick upon another, background of the swastika flag and countryside with horses pulling a cart (note the rural idiom, as so often).[204]

Other themes of the posters included didactic instruction on wartime civic behaviour of the 'careless talk costs lives' variety, or rhetorical exhortation about worker/frontline soldier interdependence. In wartime the poster added a critical educative function – how should people behave in the new onerous and restricted circumstances of war itself? And it is at this stage that the Nazi poster came to resemble its British equivalent (with similar preoccupations). One light-hearted 1940 poster was part of the Nazi energy conservation campaign and is cast in the consumer advertising tradition of personification, featuring a goblin-like little man with a sack over his shoulder.[205] According to Klemperer, 'his feet are almost amphibian, the hem of his coat looks like the stump of a tail, and with the stooping posture of the scuttling thief. He is almost a four-legged animal.'[206] The poster worked so well because of its creation of a folkloric persona and the articulation of that idea via a resonant slogan that captured both the common and the elevated: 'on the one hand, casually folksy and down-to-earth thanks to the use of "Klau" (snitch), rather than "Dieb" (thief) and on the other lifted out of the everyday and made much more poetical by the bold nominalization ... and the use of alliteration'. Then the coal thief appears framed in a hand mirror. 'Is it you?' The impact, says Klemperer, was immense – the coal thief became an image in folk consciousness: 'and if someone left the door of a heated room open there would often be the cry of "Kohlenklau's coming!"'[207]

The imagery used to depict opposition parties was typically linear, bare and without resonance. And, as typically, the Nazis offer a square-jawed blonde Aryan making a dismissive gesture to the heavy-browed, tiny men annoying him, the juxtaposition of idealised simplicity with contemptible larceny: an image of aggression and of renaissance. Above all there was the creation of enemies. Posters used cartoon figures of such enemies – Catholic parties, socialists and so on – being in some way stamped on by something giant, a huge Aryan, a massive swastika and so forth. And, especially, the inflation of the 'Jewish-Bolshevik', a hybridised monster representing an existential threat to the continued life of the 'Volk'.

The Nazi images of Jews were crude phantasmagoria, a gob of rheum spat in the face of humanity. Hence a poster released late in the war depicted a hand pulling back a curtain to reveal a burning city; and arising out of the smoke an enormous 'Jewish' face, like some evil genie.[208] In the foreground hands are shaking at this face, which is essentially a cartoon face, simply a cipher for ruthless amoral greed and homicidal intent. A menacing enemy, one who threatens the group with extinction, is truly needed in order to gain total solidarity; and if such an enemy does not exist, then one can be fabricated. A 1940 poster advertised the ultimate

FIGURE 6.9 Hitler Youth SS wartime recruiting poster

anti-Semitic film, *The Eternal Jew*. Five caricature 'Jewish' faces are framed by the Star of David and the lettering is a pseudo-Hebraic script.[209] These figures evince no relationship to anyone who could conceivably have ever existed: they are monsters from a children's story of long ago, ancestral terrors. Their eyes stare in a kind of murderous fear. They are designed to look as alien as possible with huge beards, big amounts of hair and strange spectacles to create an impression of devious and anarchic intelligence. And in 1941 the Nazis promulgated a poster/postcard/text inscribed with Hitler's death sentence on the Jewish race delivered before the Reichstag on 30 January 1939: 'should the international Jewish financiers succeed once again in plunging the nations into a world war, the result will be

FIGURE 6.10 Winter Aid poster (1)

not the victory of Jews but the annihilation of the Jewish race in Europe – Adolf Hitler.'[210] It is the prologue, and the invocation, to genocide.

The Nazis were mass-murderers, secretively so but with an important qualification. They believed in the power of 'mass suggestion' and the posters do hint at the enormity of their crimes. The aim was to prepare the ground, to enable the unthinkable to happen by creative interrogation, weakening the foundations of the ancient extant morality. For example, a poster from the 1930s promoted the Nazi monthly *New People*, the organ of the party's racial office.[211] The text reads 'this genetically ill person will cost People's Community 60,000 marks over his

FIGURE 6.11 Winter Aid poster (2)

lifetime. Citizens this is your money. Read *New People*, the monthly of the racial policy office of the NSDAP.'[212] This is a subtle invitation to euthanasia. What else can it really mean? We notice the quantification in monetary terms of physical incapacity, and its attribution as a personal loss to the reader; and also the contrast between the disabled man with the twisted limbs, contorted face, and his white-coated attendant, square-jawed, Aryan, virile. This then reveals the Nazis' talent for implication, not avowing the cruel authenticities of their intent but leading people on via loaded imagery and selective facts.

Good posters resonate. In Schwartz's resonance theory the viewer is the workforce and the messenger seeks to 'surface' what is already latent in the viewer's awareness,

FIGURE 6.12 Coal Thief wartime poster

articulating a mass of vaguely felt discontents.[213] Resonant images fester in our consciousness. And posters elicit a high recognition factor; the familiar local landscape is suddenly challenged by upstart intrusion. The vividness of poster is picked out against the urban greys, lending an effect that both heightens salience while also emphasising incongruity, the two critical elements in attention-getting.[214] The role of a poster is also to provide usable, simple arguments, both to facilitate self-persuasion (internal dialogue) and other-persuasion (external dialogue). The formula was to keep a message sparse and stereotypical, but frequently repeated to reinforce conviction;[215] its underlying premise being the power of the repeated exposure effect.

FIGURE 6.13 Blacksmith: home and front wartime poster

Klemperer had a poor opinion of the posters:

> in general Nazi posters all looked alike. One was invariably confronted with the same breed of brutal and doggedly erect warrior, with a flag or a rifle or a sword, in SA, SS or military uniform, or alternatively naked: they always displayed physical strength and fanatical Will; muscles, toughness and a complete absence of introspection were the characteristics of these advertisements for sport and war and obedience to the Will of the Führer.[216]

FIGURE 6.14 Nazi workman pre-1933 poster

Klemperer believed that 'all these pathetically heroic posters transposed the most monotonous bits of the monotonous LTI (Lingua Tertia Imperia – the Language of the Third Reich) into pictorial equivalents without enriching them visually in any way'. They had such slogans as 'Führer Command, and We Will Follow' or 'Flags Pledge Victory!' but these 'impressed themselves on the mind simply as banners'. Captions such as 'The Enemy is Listening Too' were hackneyed, that is to say image and slogan did not in his view reinforce each other because of the

FIGURE 6.15 Anti-Semite pre-1933 election poster

failure to connect the two in any conceptual way: 'I don't know any instance where one word and an image belong together sufficiently for the one to evoke the other.'[217]

Other methods

The Nazis were quick to codify their marketing advice and to spread it via brochure and training. Thus during the 'era of struggle' Stark, in *Modern Political Propaganda* (1930), promulgated what had now become the received NSDAP wisdom

FIGURE 6.16 Anti-Semite wartime poster

on the opportunistic exploitation of channels major and minor.[218] Other brochures elaborate these same lessons, and expand the repertoire, they overlap (i.e. 'how-to' books on propaganda reinforced the same core methodologies via cross-fertilisation).

Stark's advice can be tabulated thus Local press: the Party emphasise the local press, which is willing to print material in some cases and has a wide readership: so make announcements in the community calendar, send the newspaper a brief meeting report. But we again note that sense of a suspicious bourgeois: 'advertisements in

FIGURE 6.17 *The Eternal Jew* 1940 poster

the middle class press are usually very expensive and only support the enemy. They should be used only when absolutely necessary. Favourable treatment of the meeting should be made a condition of buying an advertisement.'[219] Postcards: postcards should be used as often as possible – 'they may even have an impact on Republican letter carriers', an interesting aspiration, they aimed for universal appeal. General: they also mention banners with short slogans, railway track advertising, roof top advertising, slide shows and film. The article notes the party's first films have already been produced: 'we too should use the most modern

FIGURE 6.18 The 'Genetically Ill' poster

advertising methods to serve our movement' (i.e. they explicitly articulate a marketing-derivative commercial methodology).[220] Verbal: next, they discuss propaganda through the spoken word in all its various forms – from talking with the individual, to choruses: 'the two forms of propaganda are inseparable' (i.e. written and spoken). Personal encounter: they promote discussion with the individual – 'this form is still the most effective, since the contact is established';[221] person-to-person selling (i.e. a personalised text) will always be best for creating conviction.

Stark offers, in addition to this, and yet more reminders that the party do not have much money, suggestions about:

Mail: they stress sending items by mail rather than handing them to people, because they are then more likely to be read. Casualisation: leave literature in railway carriages, restaurants, offices and doctors' surgeries and so forth (this echoes advice elsewhere).[222] Bulletin Boards: the emphasis is also on setting up bulletin boards and display cases where material can be exhibited such as the Illustrated IB (Illustrierter Beobachter), photographs and so on. Slide shows and films: Stark also commends slide shows and films, for example slide shows by Captain von Muck on the voyages of the Emden (arrange this with him a few months in advance). Also slide shows from SS headquarters in Munich on the events between 1919 and 1923, and films on 'racial science, sports, the S.A'.[223]

High media – art

The Nazis deployed de-politicised mediums for political purposes and thus gave cultural mediums a political accent. They politicised all channels of communication: an anonymised, malign intelligence was forever probing and seeking new ways of spitting out its message. Thus art was simply another mass medium and its connection with other propaganda forms and channels lay in its reproducibility. For the painterly image was endlessly recycled via postcards, public exhibitions, colour prints for the home, lush journals like Rosenberg's *Art in the Third Reich*, via also newspapers and especially (Germany's favourite), the illustrated weeklies, as well as the newsreels. The mass media had a watching brief to promote national art, which became a kind of parasitic discourse on other channels so that viewing some new aesthetic piece of super-nationalist rapture was easy. Art was important because it was a cipher for spirituality; Hitler remarked at the 1935 Nuremberg Rally 'no people lives longer than the evidence of its culture'.[224] Art lacked the emphemeral nature of the other marketing channels and gave the regime an ostensibly cultured face. All this was part of the idea, and the same can be said for the plastic arts; sculpture, like painting, could be seen, but it could also be reproduced. It was of course a key component of Hitler's self-construction as the self-conscious 'artist', who had sacrificed that career for the glory of the state. And it was part of Germany's assertion of cultural superiority to a barbarous world, its status as culture nation.

Art was thus a way of promoting the regime and its values differently, of softening the message; assertions that would look crass or incredible when said in speech or print can feel very different when expressed imagistically. Art elevates, it dignifies, and for a message as crude as the Nazis' these things were important – they had to seduce as well as bully in order to control public opinion. Moreover, Nazism went deeper than a particular set of policy prescriptions; these were not in fact the essence of the regime and some other policy could be always proclaimed that would thereby become equally Nazi. But Nazism was a mood, a gut feeling, an interior murmuring, interrupted by flashes of true rage; art could convey this well. Art was a tool of Nazi evangelism.

So much art is the literal art of the nineteenth century, there is no element at all of impression or abstraction. Thus *The Führer Speaks* (a famous Third Reich painting by Paul Mathias Padua, 1939) features a large German People's Radio on the windowsill and a small poster of Hitler stuck on the wall; a peasant home.[225]

The schemata is ideological – the men brooding and hirsute, the blonde young woman nursing a large little girl; intimations then of fertility and the reproduction of the race, for she is another of these big mothers that appear all over the place in Nazi art. She is also dressed in elements of traditional costume, and the only twentieth-century symbol these people possess is the radio; otherwise, they have emerged straight from some folkloric world. The values of the regime can be projected or rather quietly suggested with even greater indirection: thus a 1935 portrait by Fritz Pfuhle of a severe-looking young German woman in a black dress without makeup or jewellery, with face austere, hair very short and eyes that gaze straight at the viewer.[226] The effect is clinical, one would have thought that she was the representative of some fundamentalist religious sect in the backwoods of nineteenth-century America.

Nazi art generally offered little for interpretation, there was no 'loose change'. It can be characterised as superficial, for we may admire the technical virtuosity but no permanent deposit is left on the consciousness, and much depends on how we 'buy' a hyper-reality that observes seemingly every thread in the cloth. The symbol system, these naked males with cloaks at their feet, these statues such as Arno Breker's *The Warrior's Departure* (1942) that are almost Schwarzenegger-like in their musculature, is very explicit, even to the most witless of viewers. Thus a male wreathed in a cloak soars high into the air in forward thrust, and before him a great eagle. The obvious lineage is neoclassical, as with Adolf Wamper's *Genius of Sieges* (1940) but nevertheless there is the interposition of a later consciousness, vengeful, insecure, even hysterical. Even though the aesthetic is pastiche classic, the action orientation is not. Such images are more than idealised – they are governed by a knowledge of anatomy unavailable to the ancients, we literally see beneath the skin: this is a technician's perspective, particularly in the observation of musculature. So they are a synthetic of ancient and modern – hair, for example, close-cropped in the military style of the twentieth century rather than rebellious locks of classical antiquity. Other artists in the Nazi milieu took a different focus, trying to evoke Germany's artistic history by imitating Dürer, for instance, and drawing figures so as to suggest a woodcut.

Abstraction The more interesting paintings are not literalist but stylised within an ideological schemata. This makes them a more sophisticated take on the routine aesthetic ideal, transgressive of the reactionary dogma without formally sabotaging the genre. Thus a conservative and moribund idiom can be transcended, such as with *The Harvest* (the Great German Art Exhibition 1938), an example of how a subversive, even sinister note can be injected.[227] There are normative features – the child is blonde, the woman pregnant and touching her stomach, but these formulaic elements are challenged. For what is the symbolism of that cadaverous old man, face skull-like, body emaciated, set against a great sky? Art cannot always be dismissed because it took place in the context of the Third Reich. The technical quality of the works can be substantial. For example, *The Sower* (1937) by Oskar Martin-Amorbach offers a bucolic vista wherein perspective is deliberately distorted, the landscape a fantasy one where a glorious rainbow soars into deep blue skies and the muddy brown fields roll away to infinity; there is exaggerated attention to visual detail where every vein, every crease, every wrinkle of many wrinkles is minutely observed.[228] The aim again is to create effects which are more real than real, a hyper-literalness which becomes in fact a form of abstraction.

Thus certain tentative levels of stylisation are possible even within an ideology which constantly invoked realism. *The Tenth of May 1940* (Paul Mathias Padua), a painting about the forging of a river in dinghies, also shows how the genre can actually attain, in its pursuit of verisimilitude, a certain level of abstraction. Seen in rear-view, the soldiers are a tangle of bodies and helmets as they paddle the waters, yet composing a picture largely out of steel helmets gives the image a powerful symbolic charge. Another composition, of Hitler with combat troops (*Hitler at the Front*, Emil Scheibe 1942), presents simply a dense mass of faces backed up behind Hitler and set against a bright sky.[229] So the dark figures are set into relief, sharply etched. It is clearly more than poster work or commercial art because of the sheer amount of detail, the lines on the faces: the furrowed brows register the weight of labour which has gone into the creation of this picture. It is a celebration of the work of work and the work of war. Art was of course about excision as well as commission, but, typical of the Reich, there was originally no settled policy on modernity in art and the Nazi avant-garde (there was one) flirted with modernism. There was some praise for the Bauhaus, and early on Goebbels sought to encourage a 'National Socialist expressionism' with the complicity of the National Socialist Students' Union; regressive folkish art favoured by Rosenberg was attacked by Goebbels and even by Hitler.[230] But the anathema on futurism, cubism, expressionism, surrealism and abstraction was swift in coming: the new aesthetic criminalised even the nineteenth century, banned was Picasso but even Cezanne and Van Gogh, and 13,000 paintings were confiscated from the galleries.[231] The Degenerate Art Exhibition helpfully captioned these visual internees: 'thus the sick minds view human nature!' or 'German peasants in the Jewish manner'.[232]

The cutting-edge modernism of the poster contrasts with the regressive reaction of the painting, and yet both were public arts, public mediums and propaganda channels. The difference between these channels in their operational implementation says, however, a great deal about how the regime conceived propaganda; it drew a distinction between art and propaganda, the one was a spiritual essence of the regime and a vindication, the other a medium of persuasion. But this was a pretend distinction, for in practice they amount to the same thing. The aesthetic of the posters is often contemporary and sometimes verges on abstraction; the painting adopts a literalism or a craven imitation of the painterly style of past centuries. However, some of the paintings and most of the posters borrow from a commercial aesthetic, connecting through the world of consumer advertising in all its brash modernity.

Low media: schools

Education was a seminary of Nazi propaganda and its most efficient managed outlet, given the captive nature of the audience. The classroom experience was organised in ways that optimised propaganda value. Propaganda came with the authority of the pedagogue and the veneer of science: nostrums and arguments and lies are more difficult to discard when absorbed early, and children are ill-equipped to distinguish truth from falsehood or recognise the haemorrhage of bias into their curricula. Nazis also reduced school authority by offering an alternative seminary, the Hitler Youth, which undermined education because it undermined the educator.

Nazism's self-conception was also as a youth movement: youth is a *tabula rasa*, for the young have the special merit of no private or historical memory and their minds can be filled with the ideological rubble of the regime. Much propaganda activity preaches only to the already persuaded (i.e. a psychology of reinforcement but not conversion). People cannot simply be forced to believe, and attendance at rallies, reading magazines or listening to radio broadcasts remained an optional activity even in Nazi Germany. But in schools Nazis could colonise the mind. There were no choices and, therefore, no possibility of passive resistance. And the child would soon become an adult, carrying ideology into the adult world since they had never been exposed to alternative perspectives. Everywhere in the Nazi imperium much absorption of the propaganda was naïve. In the world outside the classroom, the ideology seeped into consciousness via the sugared blandishments of the entertainment industry; within, in the school world, it came disguised as education. Entertainment and education, two great spheres of cognitive activity and the mediums through which individuals come to understand their world, were both thoroughly acculturated to the Nazi worldview and the principal agents of its propagation.

The training of young Germans was celebrated as a kind of admixture of Corinthian ideal with robustly pragmatic technical education whose end had only one object in mind, the making of the war machine. There was no need to mount surveillance of lessons as the teaching profession was politically reliable. Nevertheless, a particularly important point (with relevance for today) was the shrinkage in the social status of teaching over the Third Reich, the diminution of which was attributable to its anti-intellectual climate ('we think with our blood'). But, despite the Nazi Teachers' Association praise for the onward march of folk community, the army despaired: 'many of the candidates applying for commissions display a simply inconceivable lack of elementary knowledge'.[233] So the schools became seminaries of propaganda – school essays, for example, became reductive, a 'regurgitation of propaganda handouts'.[234] The entire syllabus was colonised, nationalised and racialised. Weimar textbooks were pulped and booklets like 'History in Sub-Headings' replaced them.[235] Propaganda substituted for education: biology with its racial theoretics, history's era of struggle, battles of Tannenberg and so forth, German literature with its Nordic sagas and so on. Even the teaching of mathematics could be subverted:

> Nazi ideologists adroitly seized on the opportunity for subliminal conditioning presented by the wording of problems, so that a head for figures was now

developed by questions about artillery trajectories, fighter-bomber reaches and budget deficits accruing from the democratic pampering of hereditary diseased families.[236]

The teaching of religion atrophied, by official fiat; school assemblies were now party rallies.[237] Then there were the boorish, hearty, philistine graduates of the elite 'Adolf Hitler Schools', destined for the 'Castles of the Order', a self-conscious programme designed to create a new ruling class for the Nazi imperium over Europe. Its invented symbolism, which typified the Reich, was that of an elite patrician order whose door had been opened to the children of the Volk. Such were the nonentities produced by these eyries of gothicised mediocrity that many failed to get even an army commission.[238]

Ancient media: live oratory

Nazism grasped better than any other movement in history the power and centrality of the spoken word. Bracher argues that 'the most effective tool was the elaborate rite of the mass meeting',[239] and that leaflet and poster propaganda were less effective and their purpose anyway was to advertise the meetings process. The spoken word was both Nazism's liturgy and its sacrament, but what they had in mind was not eloquence as classically understood: there was to be no Nazi Gettysburg Address or Dunkirk Speech, no Third Reich version of Pericles's Funeral Oration. Words were political tools to be used economically and not wasted in speculative encomiums to future generations of the human race, so Nazi language was simple and standardised, it was repetitive, and it was violent. In this harsh rhetorical universe there was no philosophic abstraction or benevolent hopes addressed to mankind in general. Here was a contraction, not expansion, of the uses of rhetoric. But rhetoric did not exist in isolation for the Nazis: it was part of a larger physical performance, enhanced by context and the totalities of show – the music, formulaic ornateness and the resonance of symbol structures. This was a consumption experience of a live theatre, not one performer's art but an entire evening's play: 'that is the technique of National Socialism – to make the action of an authoritarian apparatus appear as the spontaneous activity of the masses'.[240] As Delia explains, the mass meeting, particularly where Hitler spoke, was the great ritual of Nazi propaganda;[241] its eucharist, but also the fulcrum of its propaganda ideology, instrumental, self-increasing, a climactic emotional experience that would exhilarate and exhaust.

The other media, newsreels, print, magazines, were in so many ways mere amplifiers of the auditorium that lay at the heart of the Nazi communication concept. But then they turned an entire nation into that auditorium: the word, now, could be heard as well as read as well as watched and this was the first age in which such a thing was possible, to project incendiary language to so many so quickly. Speech was no longer to be heard by some, to be heard about by some more. It became instead a national consummation, a blazing torch to light up the face of the remotest villager. Spoken rhetoric assumed a mystical quality partly because of the newly acquired universality of its domain, a global arena enabled by miraculous technology which had first appeared in rudimentary form only thirty years before; even banal sentiments when articulated through such a megaphone could amaze and thrill.[242] The effect was of an evangelist's revival meeting: Neumann quotes from Hitler in *Mein Kampf*, that the mass meeting impresses the isolated individual because he 'receives for the first time the picture of a greater community'. He steps out of his world and 'into the mass meeting and is now surrounded by thousands and thousands of people with the same conviction ... He himself succumbs to the magic influence of what we call mass suggestion.'[243] Goebbels describes how the individual can go from being 'a little worm into part of a large dragon'.[244] Hitler's ability to convert crowds and individuals included future Nazi leaders; ambitious people heard and were disorientated by the power of the vision, and many found themselves persuaded.

The speech was the sacerdotal moment between leader and led, an affirmation for the already converted and an epiphany for the new truth-seekers. The Nazis did not orate because they were good at it; it was a consciously chosen methodology, influenced by Le Bon but also by Hitler's understanding of the pivotal role of the revolutionary demagogue in European history, and in particular that history's latest and most tragic chapter, the Russian Revolution. Hitler 'was convinced that historical change resulted not from social forces or philosophical writings but from the work of "agitators led by demagogues in the grand style"'.[245] It was Lenin not Marx who ignited the Russian Revolution. Hitler attributed Lenin's achievement to the effect not of his political pamphlets but of his 'fomenting oratorical activity'. Hitler said 'the great religious and political avalanches in history' arise from 'the magic power of the spoken word', indeed, from 'the torch of the spoken word hurled into the masses'.[246] This was not, as in the mode of modern politics, experienced through the interlocutorship of the small screen. It was a collective participation in group affirmation. You helped create the noise, swell the throng, and therefore the effectiveness as proselytisation was enhanced through direct physical participation. It combined, moreover, a panoply of pleasures, the refreshment of ancient wounds and bigotries, the banishment of self-doubt, the obliteration of selfhood in all its inadequacies and the surrender to some mighty collective whole; therefore sharing its power, both subordinate and partner.

Neumann argued that 'magic [became] the major concern of National Socialist culture'.[247] The base for this was undoubtedly evidentiary: the mass rallies worked as persuasion devices, particularly when Hitler was himself present, and they did not just create new converts but ministered to the faith needs of the already converted. They were means to an end, but an end in and of themselves. The mass rally was the undiluted essence of Nazi propaganda. Thus according to von Wilucki 'the most effective propaganda method was undoubtedly the Hitler mass meeting. The fact that the Führer placed all his energy in the service of propaganda, and the way in which he did it, had an effect on the masses of voters.'[248] As for the annual party rally: 'attending it must be the sacrificial longing of each individual party comrade. The necessary funds should be saved by economy and by giving up on alcohol and tobacco over the course of the year' (NSDAP 1927).[249] What we have here is the austerity of a religious cult.

Hitler was the greatest of the rhetorical stars; but adjacent, on the podium, stands Goebbels:

> his voice, a powerful and so skilfully modulated baritone, could be anything from a scream to a caress. It was an extraordinary thing to emerge from so puny a frame, 'as if Niagara came pouring from an eye-dropper'. Goebbels's gestures were equally dynamic, the erect right arm which added to his stature, the eyebrows raised in sublime anger, the eyeballs rolling with mockery and scorn. Glib, resourceful, sarcastic, mordant, he deployed both sophisticated argument and crude invective. From his great gash of a mouth flowed warped and tainted versions of the truth as well as venomous exhalations of pure fanaticism. A virulent anti-Semite and a consummate actor, Goebbels practised his speeches in front of a mirror and played on the emotions of his audiences with cynical ease. His technique was different from that of Hitler, who seemed to reach out for the souls of his hearers: Goebbels whipped their bodies into wilder and wilder frenzies of enthusiasm and hatred, a witches' cauldron of excitement.[250]

The speaker was more than a public orator: he was the bearer of the party's message to German humanity, a public poet, rhapsodist of the party's glories, the symbol of the party itself and also the personification of the artistic value the party prized above all else, that of public eloquence. The mass meetings were effective from the beginning, for example 6,500 people attended a meeting in February 1921 to listen to Hitler.[251] The Reich Speakers' School educated cadet speakers in rhetorical method. They were the oratorical aristocracy, with a lucrative job, and constituted a minor branch of celebrity culture: the best received the grandly embossed Party Speaker's Certificate.[252] There were regional speakers and specialist speakers on particular themes such as Jews or Communism, or the British plutocracy, and speakers for brief, pithy campaigns.[253] But some themes such as anti-Catholicism were later ditched.[254]

Nuremberg

Nuremberg was a temple to the spoken word, but only in the sense of a bastardised homage to classic eloquence. Hitler would make as many as twenty speeches at Nuremberg.[255]

There were six rallies prior to the Second World War; Nuremberg was a stage set and Speer was its principal designer from 1933, creating a (100-foot wingspan) presiding eagle, majestic though temporary.[256] Building work continued throughout these years: adding concrete review stands, two smaller but more permanent eagles, paving, cladding, flak towers, spotlights, metal bowls for burning flames, plus the planting of 40,000 trees.[257] It was going to become a large town in fact consisting entirely of monuments, state symbols and reviewing stands such as the Zeppelin Field stadium, aiming to cover over ten square miles.[258] Nuremberg was, *inter alia*, a triumph of management, a flailing of the human senses achieved through micro-planning and the neglect of cost. The effects, this assault on human consciousness with visual stimuli, were neither random nor fortuitous; it is no accident that this imagistic manufactory of the Third Reich, Nuremberg, was also the focus of its most masterful organisation. The power of the imagery, its potency, freighted with foreboding, owes less to creativity than meticulous planning. Nuremberg can be understood as an organised mass hallucination, on industrial lines and as industrial process.

It represented then a formidable triumph of organisation and technology. Indeed, those were themselves a part of the propaganda, an articulation of the sheer efficiency of the regime. For this was a stage set of many thousands and the operational details of implementing it so that it worked, so that a fluent, fluid public form was achieved, this in itself was a triumph. Not merely the housing and drilling of vast numbers of human beings, the building of these stage sets or the apparently flawless orchestration, but beyond this the special technologies: the lighting effects, the media access, the amplification and sound systems, and all the other detailed considerations such as the personal security of the leader. And all this had to hang together and needed an underlying design not a fragmented impressionism. The events happened, moreover, over a period of seven days so the intense pace, the riot of symbols, had to be maintained, and maintained moreover before not just an enchanted Germany, which could hear the events on radio, but also an astonished world. Everything had to go like clockwork and such events were lavishly expensive. Nuremberg remains a masterpiece of theatrical production which was moreover the end of a process and an evolution. Nuremberg never began pitch perfect, coherent, enthralling; on the contrary, in Leni Riefenstahl's first film, *Victory of Faith*, about the 1933 Congress where Major Röhm presides alongside Hitler almost as the John the Baptist figure, the process and imagery seem visibly ragged at the edges. The polish is still missing.

Hitler was far more than the conceptualiser of Nuremberg, or even its highpriest: he was also its general manager. He supervised 'each aspect of the design, spatial arrangements and building materials of the complex'.[259] Hitler arranged 'every feature – schedules, marching troops, speakers, choreography, music, seating: surviving sketches were in his own hand. The impression was that the Third Reich was rooted in the First Reich of the Middle Ages.'[260] But Hitler often appeared more absorbed in the theatrics of the extravaganza than its ideological intent, obsessed with the architectural design of the ceremonies – props, sightlines, the focus on the leader.[261] The iconics – the forest of flags, the huge eagle, the 'leader corridor' – had an aim: to 'pummel the participants senseless' and heighten the impact of the Führer.[262]

The planning of Nuremberg Nuremberg was a theatre of symbols, the glory of its functions elevated by expensive materials such as limestone and granite. This stage set developed over time. The logistics were those of a very large army, which indeed it was, battalions of extras and theatrical performers for the biggest sound set ever conceived. They were transported by 500 special trains; the campsites held a quarter of a million people and restaurants would open around the clock: 'each province of the country had its own dining hall, offering local specialities at low prices'.[263] In 1938 there were 1,000 doctors, and thirty big events.[264] Thus the Nuremberg rally was epic in scale, for example the march past of 100,000 storm troopers and bearers of 30,000 flags and banners.[265] The preparation, drilling and planning lasted for the entire year. The British ambassador remarked that 'as a display of aggregate strength it was ominous; as a triumph of mass organisation combined with beauty it was superb'.[266] Then there was the all-important technical side, the ultra-powerful loudspeakers, and the 'Greek pillars of the enormous grandstand lit by 1200 spotlights'.[267] Hitler spoke at night, and 'as the sky darkened, the bulbs of 130 spotlights placed at intervals ... began throwing their beams straight upwards'.[268]

The mass meeting

Every rally was a memory of Nuremberg; and every Nuremberg injected the remembrance of its being into every rally. And, as with Nuremberg, no detail was left to chance, the supercharged emotionalism, the travelogue of human feelings from rage to euphoria, were achieved via precise organisation. Nazism, in other words, was among other things a methodology of evangelism, a rhetorical governance. On one point Nazi authorities are specific: the mass meeting must never be a didactic sermon, it was an epiphany, an invocation to a new existence. Pedagogy can never overcome the sluggishness of emotion: 'only an appeal to these mysterious powers themselves can be effective; and the writer can hardly ever accomplish this, almost exclusively the orator'.[269] And hence:

> the end is ... public meetings to fill the German people with its political will. Therefore, the meeting, in which the speaker uses his entire personality to transmit the will of the Führer, is the main weapon of National Socialist propaganda. To keep this weapon always sharp and powerful is the most important task of party leaders and propagandists.[270]

The meeting is the fulcrum: 'the public mass meeting is the place where an authoritative speaker proclaims the aims of our movement and the nature of our worldview', and, interestingly, 'meetings should be held regardless of the attendance'.[271] The meeting and the rhetorician are the core of that act, and there is an underlying philosophy: 'the public will always judge the Party by the way it conducts its meetings'.[272] Only a few highly competent speakers were permitted national exposure: over 200 speakers were listed in Stark's 1930 brochure yet only sixty of them were authorised to speak anywhere in Germany, the rest were limited to their Gau. Confirmation of their speaking ability had to be via the Gauleiter himself.[273]

The public speaker was a very important man in Nazi Germany so he had to be paid, well, and properly looked after. Instructions stress this. The speaker was the conduit of the party's meaning, the medium through which man and message could be united. In its official directions the party was didactic: find a heated room for speakers to sleep in, do everything to make them comfortable, inform the speakers about local conditions such as the number serving in the military or contributing to Winter Relief; provide the information in advance; be punctual.[274] The party guidelines for meetings were constantly improved and embodied in courses for speakers and directives, and no detail was left to chance.[275] But this was a voluntary movement and therefore many of these rules were aimed at giving a professional gloss to what was still largely an amateur organisation. Party booklets and articles were dense with instructions on how to conduct a public meeting. This attention to operational exactitude arose from the perception that the public meeting was the core of their propaganda activity, of course, but also the party's essential sacrament: the locus of its ritual enactments, its public church, the site of its hymn singing and the communal expression of its identity. Such a meeting had to be a symphony with no messy threads; nothing dishevelled or stumbling. The party managed to create such effects through an entirely standardised approach – there was no room for ambiguity, and each meeting had to look and feel like the other. In this way the consistency and integrity of the party's brand could be maintained.

Directions given to speakers were pragmatic; speakers on population policy could not be bachelors.[276] Alcohol was banned. But these were not in fact manuals of polemic, they included the injunction, for example, not to play for applause, speak with your hands at your side, avoid trite phrases, use tactful humour.[277] Everything was the opposite of Hitlerian style, and this was not accidental. So speakers had to be subtle. But the party was worried by the mechanistic nature of much of its public oratory – they advise speakers to speak with 'heart and blood'.[278] They sought an elusive *via media* between operatic hysteria, and robot apparatchiks who regurgitated pasteurised official sentiments to captive audiences. And there was, of course, a feedback loop – the collection of reports and questionnaires filed by speakers and other propagandists, what one might even call the marketisation of Reich oratory. Moreover, the ideas system of Nazism, fragmented, irrational, lacking intellectual and evidentiary basis, generated a need for constant affirmation. Live contact could actually enable people to believe that their objections had been answered, that is to say, the audience's ability to develop counter-arguments was sabotaged by the very euphoria generated by the rhetorical appeal.

The obsession with detail focused also on methods of heating and ventilation. No item was too petty and there was a recognition of just how physical discomfort could destroy the rhetorical and imagistic effects the party is trying to create. Hitler himself would check the acoustics of all the important meeting halls in Munich to determine whether one, say, called for a louder voice than another.[279] He noted the atmosphere, the ventilation and the tactical arrangements of the rooms; the official guidelines mentioned that a hall should always be too small and that at least a third of the audience should consist of the party's own followers.[280] The journals and books are a harvest of dicta for the conduct of meetings: equipment had to be pre-tested, the speaker had to talk for no more than twenty minutes before the slides and the speaker had to speak extemporaneously rather than reading from notes. The aesthetics, efficiency and effectiveness of meetings were a surrogate indicator of the party's prestige, with speeches being intended to give citizens 'a clear picture of the inner strength and unity of the party'.[281] Each meeting was to be closed by the chairman with a hail to National Socialism and to 'Führer Adolf Hitler'.[282] Activists were exhorted to manage expectations. The old habits of a rough contrarian movement had to be jettisoned now the party was powerful (e.g. not serving beverages and food once the meeting began, with smoking banned): 'we have to completely break the old habit some have of seeing an NSDAP meeting as a kind of entertainment during which a comfortable citizen can be instructed by the speaker about political events while enjoying a glass of beer'.[283] The writings hint at the early difficulties the party was encountering – 'the arbitrary selection of a well-meaning but unsuited party comrade as debate speaker is to be avoided under all circumstances'.[284] Appearances were of the essence and the image had to be of competence:

> singing a song at the conclusion of the meeting makes sense only if this can be done well. The meeting chairman should give directions. It is to be done standing up, not by singing one stanza as people are leaving. Scattered voices by several party members make a bad impression, particularly when the opponent begins to sing his battle song ....[285]

They demanded brevity – the chairman's introduction and conclusion should be at the most between three and five minutes, and party members were ordered to resist giving the impression that they knew what the speaker was going to say.[286] They condemn the 'frequent failure of political leaders in the front rows to applaud'. We are also reminded that 'the Führer still considers a well-run meeting to be the most important and valuable work the party does. ...!'.[287] Meetings can fail 'if even the smallest detail is not done well'. The chairman must not give the speech, but rather the assigned speaker, and the chairman was ordered to be precise: 'the chairman may not be the personification of the opposite of the attitude we demand'. Nazi propaganda authorities stress the importance of a good flag entrance and the necessary music: the old propagandists must applaud ('remember that the speaker is not trying to reach you, but everyone else. You, however, as cheering section, you are the examples. Success depends on you').[288] And propagandists must propagandise, actively selling the meetings (the reader of *A Propaganda Primer* is then edified by fourteen pages of detail on how public meetings should be decorated).[289]

Conclusion

The Nazis conducted their rhetorical blitzkrieg on German consciousness by mixing the newest media with the oldest, but always incorporating the advances in communications technology. They did not specialise in anything but specialised in everything, an incontinent media excess. Nazi propaganda exists on many levels both crude and subtle. At one level it is appalling, the pyrotechnics of bigotry, but in other ways it represents the art that conceals art, intelligently manipulative and smart and evasive. For example, a two-hour compilation of the news reports of the war period reveals just one anti-Semitic aside, the mention that the young commissar of a captured Russian army unit is Jewish.[290] And that is all; and this is surely deliberate. Consciousness was not merely assaulted, it was also seduced and charmed, sometimes as much by the absence of an idea or a form of persuasion as by its presence. Propaganda was a highway to absolutist control but that necessitated the conquest of mind and heart, which could only be achieved via persuasion not policemen.

Notes

1. Ross, *Media*.
2. Ibid.
3. Bracher, *German Dictatorship*.
4. Ross, *Media*.
5. Brendon, *Dark Valley*.
6. Ross, *Media*.
7. Evans, *Third Reich*.
8. Brendon, *Dark Valley*.
9. Ibid.
10. Ibid.
11. Ibid.
12. Anthony Rhodes, *Propaganda: The Art of Persuasion: World War II*, New York: Chelsea House Publishers, 1976.
13. Rutherford, *Hitler's Propaganda*.
14. Ross, *Media*.
15. Ibid.
16. Evans, *Third Reich*.
17. Ross, *Media*.
18. Evans, *Third Reich*.
19. Bullock, *Hitler and Stalin*.
20. Hale, *Captive Press*.
21. Ibid.
22. Hoffmann, *Triumph*.
23. Ibid.
24. Ibid.
25. Ibid.
26. Ibid.
27. Ibid.
28. Ibid.
29. Ibid.
30. Ibid.

31　William Shirer, *The Rise And Fall of the Third Reich*, London: Pan Books, 1981.
32　Wistrich, *Weekend*.
33　Kallis, *Nazi Propaganda*.
34　Rutherford, *Hitler's Propaganda*.
35　Ibid.
36　Ibid.
37　Kallis, *Nazi Propaganda*.
38　Thomson, *Easily Led*.
39　Ibid.
40　Burleigh, *Third Reich*.
41　Thomson, *Easily Led*.
42　Ibid.
43　Burleigh, *Third Reich*.
44　Bytwerk, *Bending Spines*.
45　Ibid.
46　Rutherford, *Hitler's Propaganda*.
47　Burleigh, *Third Reich*.
48　Bullock, *Hitler and Stalin*.
49　Jowett and O'Donnell, *Propaganda and Persuasion*.
50　Elizabeth Wiskemann, *Europe of the Dictators 1919–1945*, London: Fontana, 1975.
51　West, *Truth Betrayed*.
52　Ibid.
53　Herf, *Arab World*.
54　Neill Lochery, *Lisbon, War in the Shadows of the City of Light, 1939–45*, New York: Public Affairs Books, 2011.
55　Herzstein, *War*.
56　Shirer, *Rise And Fall*.
57　Farndale, *Tragedy*.
58　Herf, *Arab World*.
59　Angus Calder, *The Myth of the Blitz*, London: Jonathan Cape, 1991.
60　West, *Truth Betrayed*.
61　Farndale, *Tragedy*.
62　Herf, *Arab World*.
63　Ibid.
64　Romain Hayes, *Subhas Chandra Bose In Nazi Germany*, London: C. Hurst and Co., 2011.
65　Ibid.
66　Ibid.
67　Ibid.
68　Ibid.
69　Welch, *Propaganda*.
70　Ibid.
71　Herzstein, *War*.
72　Ross, *Media*.
73　Hoffmann, *Triumph*.
74　Ibid.
75　Ibid.
76　Ibid.
77　Ibid.
78　Gitlis, *Cinema*.
79　Hoffmann, *Triumph*.
80　Ibid.
81　Ibid.
82　Ibid.
83　Ibid.

84 Ibid.
85 Gitlis, *Cinema*.
86 von Wilucki, 'Tested Methods'.
87 Greg Mitchell, *The Campaign of the Century*, New York: Random House, 1993.
88 von Wilucki, 'Tested Methods'.
89 Ibid.
90 Herzstein, *War*.
91 Bytwerk, *Bending Spines*.
92 Manvell, *Films*.
93 Ibid.
94 Hoffmann, *Triumph*.
95 Herzstein, *War*.
96 Thomson, *Easily Led*.
97 Herzstein, *War*.
98 Manvell, *Films*.
99 Ibid.
100 Rentschler, *Ministry*.
101 Ibid.
102 Hoffmann, *Triumph*.
103 Thomson, *Easily Led*.
104 Hoffmann, *Triumph*.
105 Rentschler, *Ministry*.
106 Gitlis, *Cinema*.
107 Rentschler, *Ministry*.
108 Hoffmann, *Triumph*.
109 Rentschler, *Ministry*.
110 Ibid.
111 Hoffmann, *Triumph*.
112 Ross, *Media*.
113 Ibid.
114 Hoffmann, *Triumph*.
115 Bormann, *Hitler's Table Talk*, 25–26 September 1941.
116 Ibid.
117 Herzstein, *War*.
118 Ibid.
119 Hoffmann, *Triumph*.
120 Herzstein, *War*.
121 Ibid.
122 Ibid.
123 Hoffmann, *Triumph*.
124 Ibid.
125 Bracher, *German Dictatorship*.
126 Wistrich, *Weekend*.
127 Hoffmann, *Triumph*.
128 Ben Child, 'Nazi 3D films from 1936 discovered', *Guardian*, 16 February 2011.
129 Herzstein, *War*.
130 Welch, 'Charismatic'.
131 Herf, *Jewish Enemy*.
132 Bytwerk, *Bending Spines*.
133 Bruce Norman, *Here's Looking At You: The Story of British Television 1908–39*, London: British Broadcasting Corporation/ Royal Television Society, 1984.
134 Ibid.
135 Ibid.
136 Bytwerk, *Bending Spines*.

137 'Television Under The Swastika', Spiegel TV/Carlton Entertainment, International Historic Films, Chicago.
138 Friedman, 'V1 Rocket'.
139 Ibid.
140 Ibid.
141 Patter Batty, *Paper War: Nazi Propaganda in One Battle, On a Single Day – Cassino, Italy, May 11, 1944*, West New York: Mark Batty Publisher, 2005.
142 Friedman, 'V1 Rocket'.
143 Ibid.
144 Ibid.
145 Ibid.
146 Ibid.
147 Ibid.
148 Ibid.
149 Herzstein, *War*.
150 Ibid.
151 West, *Truth Betrayed*.
152 Herzstein, *War*.
153 Stark, *Political Propaganda*.
154 Ross, *Media*.
155 Rutherford, *Hitler's Propaganda*.
156 Ibid.
157 Ibid.
158 Stark, *Political Propaganda*.
159 Rutherford, *Hitler's Propaganda*.
160 Hale, *Captive Press*.
161 Ibid.
162 Ibid.
163 Ibid.
164 Ibid.
165 Ross, *Media*.
166 Ibid.
167 Ibid.
168 Kallis, *Nazi Propaganda*.
169 Hale, *Captive Press*.
170 Henderson, *Failure*.
171 Herf, *Arab World*.
172 Ibid.
173 Bytwerk, *Bending Spines*.
174 Kallis, *Nazi Propaganda*.
175 Hale, *Captive Press*.
176 Ibid.
177 Kallis, *Nazi Propaganda*.
178 Ross, *Media*.
179 Shirer, *Rise and Fall*.
180 Rutherford, *Hitler's Propaganda*.
181 Henderson, *Failure*.
182 Ross, *Media*.
183 Stark, *Political Propaganda*.
184 Herf, *Arab World*.
185 Ibid.
186 Kallis, *Nazi Propaganda*.
187 Newcourt-Nowodworski, *Black Propaganda*.
188 Neumann, *Structure and Practice*.
189 Calvin College, German Propaganda Archive, Posters 1939–45, no. 23.

190 Calvin College, German Propaganda Archive, Posters pre-1933, no. 24.
191 Ibid., no. 9.
192 Calvin College, German Propaganda Archive, Posters 1933–39, no. 4.
193 Ibid., no. 5.
194 Stark, *Political Propaganda*.
195 Ibid.
196 Rutherford, *Hitler's Propaganda*.
197 Ibid.
198 Ibid.
199 Ibid.
200 Ibid.
201 Stark, *Political Propaganda*.
202 Calvin College, German Propaganda Archive, Posters 1933–39, no. 24.
203 Rutherford, *Hitler's Propaganda*.
204 Calvin College, German Propaganda Archive, Posters 1933–39, no. 32.
205 Calvin College, German Propaganda Archive, Posters 1939–45, no. 10.
206 Klemperer, *Language*.
207 Ibid.
208 Calvin College, German Propaganda Archive, Posters 1939–45, no. 5.
209 Ibid., no. 3.
210 Rutherford, *Hitler's Propaganda*.
211 Calvin College, German Propaganda Archive, Posters 1930–39, no. 65: explanatory text by Randall L. Bytwerk.
212 Ibid, no. 65.
213 Tony Schwartz, *The Responsive Chord*, New York: Basic Books, 1973.
214 Gianluigi Guido, *The Salience Of Marketing Stimuli: An Incongruity-Salience Hypothesis On Consumer Awareness*, Norwell, Massachusetts: Kluwer Academic Publishing, 2001.
215 Rutherford, *Hitler's Propaganda*.
216 Klemperer, *Language*.
217 Ibid.
218 Stark, *Political Propaganda*.
219 Ibid.
220 Ibid.
221 Ibid.
222 Ibid.
223 Ibid.
224 Bytwerk, *Bending Spines*.
225 These images are visible in Adam, *Arts*.
226 Ibid.
227 Ibid.
228 Ibid.
229 Ibid.
230 Wistrich, *Weekend*.
231 Ibid.
232 Ibid.
233 Grunberger, *Social*.
234 Ibid.
235 Ibid.
236 Ibid.
237 Ibid.
238 Ibid.
239 Bracher, *German Dictatorship*.
240 Neumann, *Structure and Practice*.
241 Jesse G. Delia, 'Rhetoric in the Nazi Mind: Hitler's Theory of Persuasion', Southern Speech Communication Journal 37 (2) 1971.

242 Spotts, *Hitler and the Power*.
243 Neumann, *Structure and Practice*.
244 Welch, *Propaganda*.
245 Spotts, *Hitler and the Power*.
246 Ibid.
247 Neumann, *Structure and Practice*.
248 von Wilucki, 'Tested Methods'.
249 Anon, 'Propaganda', Munich: Reichs-Parteileitung der NSDAP, 1927, Calvin College German Propaganda Archive.
250 Brendon, *Dark Valley*.
251 Bracher, *German Dictatorship*.
252 Rutherford, *Hitler's Propaganda*.
253 Ibid.
254 Ibid.
255 Spotts, *Hitler and the Power*.
256 Rutherford, *Hitler's Propaganda*.
257 Ibid.
258 Ibid.
259 Spotts, *Hitler and the Power*.
260 Ibid.
261 Ibid.
262 Ibid.
263 Rutherford, *Hitler's Propaganda*.
264 Spotts, *Hitler and the Power*.
265 Ibid.
266 Henderson, *Failure*.
267 Rutherford, *Hitler's Propaganda*.
268 Ibid.
269 von Wilucki, 'Tested Methods'.
270 Ibid.
271 Stark, *Political Propaganda*.
272 Ibid.
273 Stark, *Political Propaganda*.
274 von Wilucki, 'Tested Methods'.
275 Fest, *Hitler*.
276 Herzstein, *War*.
277 Ibid.
278 Ibid.
279 Fest, *Hitler*.
280 Ibid.
281 von Wilucki, 'Tested Methods'.
282 Stark, *Political Propaganda*.
283 Huber, *Propaganda Primer*.
284 Stark, *Political Propaganda*.
285 Ibid.
286 Ibid.
287 von Wilucki, 'Tested Methods'.
288 Ibid.
289 Ibid.
290 German Wartime Newsreels Pt 1, International Historic Films, Chicago, 1985.

PART III
Legacy
The implications of the Nazi brand

7

HITLER OUR CONTEMPORARY

Brand heritage: the Reich as a power brand

The cult of Hitler today is framed by an understanding of the scale of the atrocity. But for the genocide of the Jews, he might have evolved into a super-Napoleon, the toast of cultists everywhere and nostalgia fetishists. Yet the iconography of the concentration camps, the pathetic debris of personal items, shoes and spectacles, the long silent lines of the doomed and the deceived queuing up for certain extinction – these are the interpretants. They trigger, in normal people, a visceral response: the Holocaust, like the Western Front, has become part of the landscape of modern memory. The imagery of both has acquired perpetual residence in the imagination, a past that is forever present.

But the impact of Nazi propaganda did not remain completely buried in the rubble of Berlin. They have bequeathed to us their image and their brand, the dull footage edited out. And this is a triumph they would have valued. Burleigh discusses the sensationalism, the debased forms in which the media celebrate the Third Reich: 'the Nazis cynically manipulated posterity as they had manipulated their contemporaries; by way of continuity, they are cynically manipulated in their turn by a "Hitler industry" for which there seems to be an insatiable market'.[1] And he adds 'a regime which had lived by image perished by it, in a final triumph of style over substance, as the greatest stage villains of all departed what they called the stage of history, leaving a lingering trail of evil beyond the curtains'. Today, therefore, Nazi Germany is part of a popular cultural industry, one that has communicated insights about that regime in symbolic ways, from Darth Vader to *Dr No*. But, while the representation of Nazism in science fiction sometimes gets closer to the truths than more cerebral studies, it also de-historicises them, makes them no longer real but part of a twilight fantasy world. These fictions are tenuously based on something that once existed; the archaeologists of the SS, for example, really did hunt down ancient relics for the enchantment of the Reich as they do in *Raiders of the Lost Ark*.[2]

Nazism's function as a brand is one reason why it has an imagistic perpetuity quite unlike any other regime that existed in history. Its branded quality does not alone explain this but it is nevertheless part of the explanation. But to the brand meanings understood by German contemporaries, the original targets, must be added later ones, for the brand became a cipher for boundless evil and nihilistic violence and egomania; a reminder of what we as human beings are capable of doing, that Nazism is a territory of the human mind. Such imagistic perpetuity is not fully explained by the historical significance of what the Nazis actually did and their responsibility for the Second World War. Rather is it a tribute to the dexterity of their image creation and the coherence of their image structure. The imagistic properties of the Nazi brand echoed in many unlikely places. Spotts, for example, claims that Mick Jagger and David Bowie watched *Triumph of the Will* together fifteen times and cites Bowie: 'he (Hitler) made an entire country the stage show – he was ahead of his time'.[3] The pop industry mines the surfaces of civilisations for outrageous imagery and finds refreshment in Nazi symbolism. Thus in Lady Gaga's 'Alejandro' (Steven Klein, 2009) de-individuated males pay homage to a female dominatrix in an eroticised militarist balletic. Another pop connection – during the 1980s Andy Warhol commissioned Hitler's court statuarist Arno Breker to sculpt actor-model Jo d'Allesandro (Breker was at Hitler's side in the famous photo before the Eiffel Tower; Warhol died before this commission could be executed).[4]

We have all lived through the Nazi era. Films and documentaries imaginatively reconstruct this period as no other. There is a life, and also an afterlife, to the Nazi brand; we retrieve their world not as it was but as they wanted it to be. Garth Jowett argues that 'since 1945 we have concentrated on the loss of the war by the Nazis, ignoring their incredible propaganda victories in Germany and elsewhere'.[5] Citing R.M. Waugh, he speaks of the 'populist image of the well tailored Nazi officer', and 'that the historical persistence of these images is testament to the strength of Nazi propaganda'. The films are of course a way of talking about the history of the Third Reich and often they attain a kind of metaphoric truth, penetrating some core essence of the regime via their melodramatic excess. *Night of the Generals* (Columbia Pictures 1967), for example, features a fanatical Nazi general (Peter O'Toole) who ravages a large sector of urban Warsaw, and also murders prostitutes as a private sideline: he is pursued by a 'good' officer-detective, played by Omar Sharif. The irony, of course, is that he is targeted for these individual murders and not the colossal war crimes; legalism and process continue to function beneath a macro-structure of criminality.

The Nazi was a staple of the post-war Hollywood movie industry; he was a way of affirming the meaning of being American and celebrating the American native virtues of guts, courage and dynamism: by showing America's antithesis, what it was not, it helped to define what in fact America was. And the post-Second World War US war movie is often another of the Hollywood genre studies about the damaged American male and how extreme conditions allow him to self-repair and attain validation even through death (*Von Ryan's Express* for instance, Twentieth

Century Fox 1965). And yet, in relation to the true horrors committed by Nazism, the post-Second World War Hollywood film is curiously forgiving, not least in its frequent distinction between the psychotic Nazi and the ordinary decent German officer and soldier. A film such as *Bridge at Remagen* (United Artists 1969) is firmly in this tradition. The German officers represent in the end those great qualities of loyalty, duty and courage, it is simply that they have to perform them in the context of a deranged regime which ultimately betrays them by its utter fanaticism. There is also the distinction between the German army and the SS perpetuated in Second World War and post-war movies, which project and sustain the myth that the army itself was not implicated in the atrocities. In the Cold War era, Germany was of course an important movie market, but beyond this there was a new adversary: Germans were part of the Western alliance, and from the mid-1950s part of NATO. Their past could not simply be written off as all evil and thus there surfaces a dual structure in the later twentieth-century chronicling of the Nazi era. In the new, Cold War, the truths of the old, hot war were conveniently forgotten. It was not until the film *Schindler's List* (Universal Pictures 1993) that moviegoers were really exposed to the actual savagery of Nazism. The after-life of Nazi propaganda has evolved as the direct personal memory of the regime has diminished. In this afterlife, Nazi imagery does not remain in some kind of refrigerated state. On the contrary, it is actively developed or applied thinly disguised to science-fiction. It has thus become a representative symbol system for the reductivist drive to hyper-chauvinism and abject homage to a supreme leader, the dulling of our humanity by the surrender of its ownership to the diktat of meta-organisations. And Hitler is a huge phenomenon. As an example of this, his rant (Bruno Ganz) to the assembled generals in the film *Downfall* (Constantin Film 2004) has long been one of the most popular of YouTube virals (to which banal English subtitles are continuously added, turning Hitler into everything from a hyperventilating corporate executive to a hysterical football club manager). Erik Rentschler quotes from a modern novel about Hitler on television: 'he's always on, we couldn't have television without him'. He adds:

> set designers for *Batman Returns* drew generously on the work of Albert Speer and Arno Breker. George Lucas restaged the closing scene from *Triumph of the Will* in the finale of *Star Wars*; a recent rock video by Michael Jackson likewise unabashedly recycles Riefenstahl's images of soldier males paying deference to their master. American artists pilfer the Nazi legacy with relish. The beautiful divers, dancers, and discus throwers of *Olympia* serve as prototypes for television commercials, magazine ads, and photo spreads.[6]

Is Nazism, then, symbolic of certain things that are latent within human nature, not about them, but us?:

> indeed, the incessant recycling of Nazi sights and sounds surely represents a crucial measure of today's postmodernism. A direct line leads from the Nazis'

vanguard deployment of pyrotechnic histrionics and audiovisual excesses to the profuse present-day investment in constant simulations and hyperreal events. In many respects, these images from the past are very close to us, closer than we might imagine, closer than some people might like.[7]

Others speak of 'the insidious posthumous infiltration of the Nazis into the modern consciousness through the most modern medium available. It was doubly insidious since most of the surviving footage was made at their behest, and not surprisingly depicts them at what they regarded as their best.'[8] For the Nazi 'has long ceased to be a real historical being. He now inhabits the daemonic twilight of the entertainment world: the mass-produced collective subconscious within which the Zulu warriors coexist with invaders from outer space and the Waffen SS.'[9] Yet the measure of their public impact may be gauged from a celebrity photo book, Piotr Uklanski's *Nazis* (1999), which features around 150 of the most famous actors of the twentieth century – even unlikely ones such as Ronald Reagan and Errol Flynn – playing German soldiers, officers or members of the SS.[10] It is difficult in fact to think of a famous actor who did not, at some point, play a German soldier, such a staple of the entertainment industry have Nazis become. One of Nazi propaganda's biggest cultural legacies is in the realm of science fiction; it has had a definitive impact on popular cultural products, everything from *Captain America* to James Bond's adversaries Goldfinger and Blofeld, and there is even a 'Third Reich' episode of *Star Trek*. This again raises the question of the relationship between Nazis and modernism, how far they represented a reaction to aspects of the modern condition and how far they anticipated some of the later developments. This sci-fi aura arises from the conception of the Hitler state as a technopolis, a world which worshipped technology and constricted the definition of what it is to be human in homage to some sort of scientifically baptised prototype, pursuing the technical edge in everything (e.g. television with its relaying of the 1936 Berlin Olympics). In a sense the Nazi has ceased to be an actual or even a historical figure and has entered the mythological realm, wherein science fiction is the legatee. He is no longer really real.

Were even the Nazis in on the act, recognising, at a certain level, the sci-fi aura of their regime? Early in the Second World War Marvel comics published an episode in which Superman demolished part of the German West Wall in occupied France. But news of this found its way into the weekly newspaper of the SS.[11] The SS response refers to Jerry Siegel, the co-creator of Superman:

> an intellectually and physically circumcised chap who has his headquarters in New York, is the inventor of a colourful figure with an impressive appearance, a powerful body, and a red swimsuit who enjoys the ability to fly through ether. The inventive Israelite named this pleasant guy with an overdeveloped body and an underdeveloped mind 'Superman'. He advertised widely Superman's sense of justice, well-suited for imitation by the American youth.

Siegel wanted 'to import the idea of manly virtue and spread them among young Americans' after seeing Germany and Italy's revival:

> we see Superman, lacking all strategic sense and tactical ability, storming the West Wall in shorts. We see several German soldiers in a bunker, who in order to receive the American guest have borrowed old uniforms from a military museum ... His true strength only shows itself in flight, however. He leaps into the air to tear the propeller from a passing German airplane. As we can see from the next frame, however, Superman has apparently made a mistake, since he seems to have encountered a Yid pilot. No German would say what the pilot says: 'Himmel! Vos is dat?'

The article claims of Superman 'instead of using the chance to encourage really useful virtues, he sows hate, suspicion, evil, laziness, and criminality in their young hearts'. They conclude that this author 'stinks'; from the SS then, the language of the school playground.[12]

The broader popular culture is also replete with Nazi reference. Even before the United States entered the war Charlie Chaplin was *The Great Dictator* (United Artists October 1940), but since that time James Bond villains, Austin Powers's adversary Dr Evil (who does indeed have a German sidekick) and so forth seek total dominion within some new global order: Hitler is the paradigm and the ultimate science fiction villain. Even the Daleks of *Doctor Who* were surely Fascists ('annihilate, obliterate, exterminate!'), similarly with *Chitty Chitty Bang Bang*'s child-persecuting Baron Bomburst, while Dr Strangelove's arm could never forget its previous allegiance no matter how hard he strove to control it. Hitler's surrogates are recurrent in the mass media, all of them mere shadows of the mad lunatic who tried to take over the world. And the indirect as distinct from the direct references are even more visible. Wistrich has observed:

> there is an enormous suggestive power inherent in Nazi mythology, a seductiveness in the emotions, images and fantasies which it released, that should not be underestimated. The alacrity with which the mass entertainment industry since the 1970s has marketed this aspect of Nazism in sumptuous movie and TV treatments is a signal warning.

And moreover:

> For it was already apparent 40 years after Hitler's death that in the popular culture of the West Nazism was often no more than a source of light-headed amusement, of distraction, perverse fascination and even sadomasochistic pornography ... It can be observed all around us in the way the Nazi insignia and emblems, the signs and symbols of the Third Reich from swastikas to black leather boots, have become part of pop iconography. Stormtroopers or SS uniforms, Hitler T-shirts and the skinhead or neo-Nazi rock music glorifying

violence still attract a part of the youth culture of both East and West ... this impact probably has as much to do with the power of kitsch, of images and of modern myths as with the sadism and criminality of the Nazis which culminated in the mass murder of European Jewry. It is often difficult to avoid contamination by this debased aesthetic, but the effort must be made to deconstruct and neutralise its appeal.[13]

The Nazi of the post-war D-movie is alpha male and wielder of ultimate violence, the preening possessor of a private seraglio, magnetically attractive to women towards whom in fact he is indifferent, and latently violent. But it is the menacing aspects of Nazism and the wish to affiliate with raw brute power which attracted many of its recruits in the first place: the science fiction/neo-pornographic entertainment industry does unwittingly surface and illuminate some basic truths. Hence in one French poster an SS man, leather coat over his shoulders, cigarette in a holder, is admired by seven pouting women in underwear;[14] and in another a monocle-wearing German officer, glove in hand, places his booted foot on a naked woman.[15] From rake to rape. But what does all this mean, this synthesis of Nazis with pornography, this Nazi as ultimate male? Given of course the actual things the SS did, such playful fantasies go beyond the worst possible taste, as they suggest some of the emotions which originally precipitated and sustained Nazism. Films such as *Gestapo's Last Orgy* 'are so preoccupied with immediate profit that they have no comprehension of, or concern with, possible "costs" to culture, memory, or for that matter, anything at all'.[16]

Interestingly, this tradition begins in the war itself with the RKO Radio Pictures film *Hitler's Children* (1943),[17] where the poster features an SS man whipping a girl against a backdrop of uniformed girls of the Bund Deutscher Mädel (BDM). But it is not enough to dismiss this as merely juvenile or sick: it testifies to the endurance of the imagery carefully created by the Nazis themselves that has penetrated the collective subconscious, a part of our culture in fact, a reservoir of expressive material for any theatrical exposition that plays with the dark side of human nature. Every one appeared to join in and in the 1970s it was the turn of the black community: a 'blaxploitation' film poster features a black SS man armed with Luger and women in revealing costumes.[18] Alongside the sexualised Nazi there is the nihilism, Nazism as explosions. Hence posters for *The Train* (United Artists 1964) feature Paul Scofield as a senior German officer standing haughtily against a blazing incineration of trains and railway lines, German soldiers and fleeing people.[19] Other publicity materials, for example, the film *Hell in Normandy* (1967) or *Achtung! The Desert Tigers* (1976) or *Tobruk* (1967) similarly emphasise above all Nazism as raging inferno, the symbol it has more than any other bequeathed to history.[20] Many films are of course both – a pleasing amalgam of sex and violence so that all human perversity is catered for. Images for *The Night of the Fox* (1990), for example, partake of both traditions: a woman wrapped in fur coat (and naught else), pistol firmly in the stockings of her exposed leg, poses smilingly against a background of explosions.[21]

There is a historic past but, with Hitler, a media present that is melodramatic but even, on occasion, comedic (such as *Look Who's Back*, a comedy about an inept Hitler returning to Germany and struggling with modern technology and conditions, 2015; and in *Iron Sky*, 2012, Nazis fled to the moon after 1945 where they build a space fleet to re-conquer earth in 2018). Nor does mass media really scrutinise the propaganda world of the Reich, it merely hands down the propaganda-conceived image. One rare exception is *Inglourious Basterds* (2009, Quentin Tarantino), one of the very few films to have surfaced the role of propaganda in the Nazi dystopia. A German sniper who killed two hundred and fifty of the enemy is the star of a new propaganda film called *A Nation's Pride* and the climax (a fantasy of revenge where Jewish soldiers kill top Nazis including Hitler and Goebbels) is structured round a cinema showing of this film before the Nazi elite.

The Third Reich lasted little more than twelve years, yet such has been the protracted media afterlife that it feels like a century. Hitler remains perhaps the only figure from history with whom all teenagers are intimately familiar, the one image and only memory that adolescence has managed to retrieve from all of the pasts of the human race. It is hardly surprising then that he resurrects as a force in adolescent depravity, everything from the Columbine High School massacre to the inspiration for Russian skinheads (the progeny of a people who lost vastly more than twenty million of their kin in the Second World War). The shadow of Hitler looms over the history syllabus of schools, not merely because of the significance of what he did in the global order but more than that, because of the vividness of the imagistic legacy: he is accessible to teach, to fire the minds of distracted youth. Hitler has transcended Hitler. He has become a concept, a point of reference, quite simply a structuring element in our global political and cultural consciousness. He lives as never before since 1945, and as the direct memory of the Second World War recedes the fascination with him has grown; why, for example, is there so much less public interest in Josef Stalin, so fewer books published, even though Stalin's infamy is (arguably) as extreme? But what we mean by 'Hitler' today lies principally in the domain of imagery, and his immortality is an achievement of his propaganda (typical *Daily Mail* headlines in any given week over the past decade might be: 'Hitler's secret flying saucer: did the Führer plan to attack London and New York in UFOs?', 18 November 2010, or 'The English debutante who staged Nazi orgies as a gift of love to Hitler', 11 October 2013, or 'The smiling face of Evil: Adolf Hitler grins as he poses with children ….', 31 March 2017).

There is an entire industry re-embodying the imagery of the Third Reich for a large global consumer market and retailing it through the internet. The aesthetic and symbol system have a power to insinuate into the regressive consciousness, their existence a synonym for mechanical discipline and warrior fanaticism. This afterlife, like the life, is deeply artefactual, and there is a stupendous trade in memorabilia. Books, daggers, websites, watches, clocks, T-shirts, posters, CDs, videos and iconography in all their various forms fester and propagate; and then there are those posters. The Nazis are forbidden, and therefore they are exciting, and the vividness, the inspired lunacy of their imagery continues to scandalise, its very insistence assuring replication through time and cyberspace.

One company (Your Third Reich HQ, PZG INC., Rapid City, South Dakota) fondly retails memorabilia such as photo books (*SS Division Horst Wessel, SS Hitler Youth Division, Knights' Cross Winners of the Waffen SS, Reichs Autobahn*). Or there is *Mein Kampf*; or a video of Goebbels's Total War speech; or a map which shows the huge tracts of 'stolen' German lands and the concentration of Germans in neighbouring countries. A reprint of the 1937 Stanley McClatchie book *Look to Germany, The Heart of Europe* is available, and a book on the Reich Chancellery, 'the most remarkable government structure ever built in Germany'. Then there are the busts 'imported from Europe', such as the *Adolf Hitler*, 'a brilliantly lifelike sculpture and made from genuine marble dust'; as well as the Barbie-type dolls. These include Rommel, while the Himmler figure 'includes: finest quality material and leather, leather hobnailed riding boots, authentic uniform ... cigar ...'. Certainly the commentary is partisan: 'Himmler was a truly gifted organiser and put his talent to good use for Adolf Hitler and the Third Reich. Hitler chose Himmler's elite SS to be the instrument to transform Germany's class conscious reactionary Wehrmacht into a National Socialist People's Army', and we are told that Germany's true form 'was not obtained until 1941 to 44'. Some idea of our world, indeed, as it might have looked had Germany won the war.

Hitler also reigns in cyberspace. And the production of Nazi propaganda is a contemporary process (kinesis), as well as a historic event (stasis). Parades, and speeches, songs and assorted imagery self-perpetuate in a virtual Reich whose legatees embellish its aesthetic for posterity. People actually 'produce' their very own Nazi propaganda in their own homes, piecing together the original pictures and songs to create a fresh synthetic of propaganda. For example, 'I Had a Comrade', the elegiac soldiers' lament popular in the Nazi period as a funeral march, occurs in many guises on the internet alongside retrieved imagery of military comradeship and menace. These are miniature Nazi epics, and they are followed with comments like 'my grandfather was in a panzer regiment', and continuing on from this 'so was mine'. So Nazi propaganda has a past and a present; film propaganda now available for free online includes *Triumph of the Will, Hitler Youth Quex, SA Mann Brand* and other complete films. Then there are the computer games. *Killzone 3*, a game published by Sony, commences with a Nuremberg-style rally where a fanatical dictator harangues his imperial cohorts. And Facebook pages like 'Prussia Reborn', while explicitly rejecting Nazi ideology, do heroise and sentimentalise the Wehrmacht via the heritage of its propagandist imagery. Some such social media sites (e.g. 'Very Wehrmacht', with its mysterious 'Der Kommandant'), arose not to regurgitate Nazi beliefs but to perpetuate an idea of the German Army of World War Two. They may be evanescent and even organised by college and high school students or, as was the case of 'Tiger Commander', are related to the playing of WW2-based computer games. Other sites such as 'This Was Germany' nostalgically retail Nazi pictography, or conscript neo-Fascist imagery in the service of illiberalism or indeed, as in the example of 'Trumpenreich', a crudely racialist agenda.

Notes

1 Burleigh, *Third Reich*.
2 Arnold, 'Past'.
3 Spotts, *Hitler and the Power*.
4 Marco Bodenstein, 'Andy Warhol, Arno Breker, Joe d'Allesandro'; Prometheus, *Internet Bulletin for Art, Politics and Science*, No. 80 Autumn (2001).
5 Jowett and O'Donnell, *Propaganda and Persuasion*.
6 Rentschler, *Ministry of Illusion*.
7 Ibid.
8 Burleigh, *Third Reich*.
9 A.P. Foulkes, *Literature and Propaganda*, London: Methuen, 1985.
10 Pyotyr Uklanski, *The Nazis*, Zurich: Editions Patrick Frey, 1999.
11 'Jerry Siegel Attacks!', *Das Schwarze Korps*, 25 April 1940, Calvin College German Propaganda Archive.
12 Ibid.
13 Wistrich, *Weekend*.
14 *SS Girls*, dir. Jordan B. Mathews, 1976; Uklanski, *Nazis*.
15 'S.S.Camp 5. – Women's Hell', directed by Sergio Garrone; Uklanski 1999.
16 Graeme Krautheim, 'Desecration Repackaged: Holocaust Exploitation and the Marketing of Novelty' *Cinephile* 5 (2) Spring 2009.
17 Uklanski, *Nazis*.
18 Ibid.
19 Ibid.
20 Ibid.
21 Ibid.

8

WAS ADOLF HITLER AHEAD OF HIS TIME?[1]

A review of comparative self-presentation

> *The perfect dictatorship would have the appearance of democracy, but would basically be a prison without walls in which the prisoner would not even dream of escaping. It would essentially be a system of slavery where, through consumption and entertainment, the slaves would love their servitude*
> – Aldous Huxley, 1931

> *Naturally, the common people don't want war ... but after all it is the leaders of a country who determine the policy, and it is always a simple matter to drag the people along, whether it is a democracy, or a fascist dictatorship, or a parliament, or a communist dictatorship. Voice or no voice, the people can always be brought to the bidding of the leaders. That is easy. All you have to do is tell them they are being attacked, and denounce the pacifists for lack of patriotism and exposing the country to danger. It works the same in every country.*
> – Hermann Göring, The Nuremberg Trials

Propaganda and the paternity of pseudo-democracy

Today we recognise the methods of Nazi proselytisation more clearly than we would have done half a century ago. In an era of political chicanery and the ubiquity of 'spin', of such phenomena as the perpetual political campaign, we need to take a fresh, and refreshed, look at what the Nazis actually did to package public opinion. There are commonalities between their world, then, and our world, now: and the essence of this is the notion that public opinion does not exist in some primordial sense but can be actively constructed. People may not necessarily 'know' what to think, the engineering of consent tells them. Hence, the now remote world of Nazi Germany is neither entirely alien nor entirely unfamiliar:

> in place of the dry, rational language of function and interest, they introduced a new vocabulary of iconography and rituals designed to enthral their

supporters, mock their enemies, and generally attract attention. Through the deliberate use of reductive stereotypes and visual metaphors, they represented the political equivalent of a sensationalist tabloid. This was, in short, political propaganda designed for a mass public that had been accustomed to the attention grabbing techniques of modern media spectacle.[2]

Communication ceases to be a mere instrument of government, one among many, but becomes instead the medium through which government governs. And in all such regimes, the leader is the brand. The leader is the party as well as the face of the party, and the party's success does not exist independently of the leader. This was true of Hitler, and of latter-day evangelical regimes. There are other common properties such as the constant blizzard of riposte and exculpatory rhetoric; the serial creation of external threats; the stress on imagery and public visuality, indeed, visibility; the debased use of statistics, and so forth. Thus, Robert Wistrich has observed:

> there is an important contemporary resonance in all of this. We live in a culture which turns more than ever on the power of images to transform our view of objective reality. Politics itself has long since become part of the brave new world of image making ... There seem to be no more great ideas or visions in politics, only the image and perception of the candidate and the way that he or she is sold to the public. In this art of selling, the distinction between reality and fantasy is gradually being lost; politics becomes a branch of advertising and media marketing. Form triumphs resoundingly over content ... in many respects the modern image makers are the children of Hitler and Goebbels, without even realising it and without in any way sharing their political ideology or moral outlook. For the Nazis were masters of presentation, packaging, public relations and visual propaganda.[3]

Indeed, Fascism, Communism and democracy may even be seen as possessed of a common ancestry, and Bracher suggested that we are dealing with a shared phenomenon precipitated by the French Revolution, maturing in the twentieth century.[4] The features of such a new civic order invoke majority rule and mass mobilisation through elections, ideological propaganda, militant nationalism and People's Armies – phenomena that possess both democratic and totalitarian possibilities: 'this development might be called the assertion of the rule of the autonomous individual within the state yet at the same time a manifestation of the threat posed to him by this modern, all-encompassing state'.[5] This would make Fascism not an antithesis of democracy but, disturbingly, merely an alternative political route triggered by a similar set of preconditions: 'according to this view, the totalitarian movements are the children of the age of democracy, having grown out of and being part of the problems and distortions of popular democracy'.[6] Fascism thus is pseudo-democracy:

> it lays claim to the will and the sovereignty of the people as the basis for political rule; it proclaims itself the executor of history, of historical necessity;

it stresses the higher legitimacy of its rule in pseudo-legal garb; it hides and intensifies dictatorial rule behind the screen of pseudo-democratically, pseudo-plebiscitarian controlled elections and mass meetings, of acclamation and propaganda; it poses as the true, total democracy which will, if necessary, force happiness on its citizens.[7]

An illicit comparison?

Since we may view propaganda neutrally – 'as a universal factor in political legitimation regardless of regime features' – comparisons between the selling of totalitarian regimes and democratic ones are not unreasonable;[8] but it is a correspondence of technique, not ethics. There are methodological parallels between modern governments' obsessive generation of imagery and the Nazis' shameless pursuit of a thoroughly manipulated and depraved public consciousness. But to what extent is this a permissible observation? Was it really the case that Hitler was ahead of his time, anticipating the modern in his extraordinary understanding of the power of rhetoric, the creation of public super-mythologies and the reliance to a great extent on government by symbolism? This author has argued: first, one has to be very explicit about where comparisons cease. Hitler's was a regime which bequeathed a mountain-range of corpses: ultimately, it was addicted to mass murder in the pursuit of European and Euro-Asian hegemony within an empyrean of the racially pure. To even attempt to compare this to more contemporary regimes would appear risible. They have not been in the business of transporting millions of innocent people, in cattle trucks, to industrial slaughter. And while Berlusconi might assert that 'we are the Falange' it is no more than a post-Fascist exercise in rhetorical nostalgia.[9] Nor is there any basis of connection in the content, the ideology of the regime; the facile theatrics of modern governments can scarcely be compared to genocidal ambition and the lust for world, or at least Eurasian, imperium.[10] It was actually the coalescence of propaganda with extreme ideology that was so nihilistic in its consequences; for example Imperial Japan's fabulous cruelty has limited relationship with the culture of bushido and Japanese heritage. Japan's two previous wars against Europeans, in 1905 and 1914–18, surfaced no allegations of atrocities, the propriety of Japanese troops was not in doubt. The cause is not tradition but fabricated tradition in the service of ethno-nationalism (in Japan's case a revived, or re-imagined, hegemonic Shintoism). And yet regimes set apart historically by era and by ideology sensed intuitively that public opinion was something that could be commodified, that (in Chomsky's sense) they could both be called engineers, and expert engineers, in the 'manufacture of consent'.

Public imagery All of them of course specialise in the creation of public imagery, that is to say the careful construction of theatrical scenes laden with symbol-rich content. A famous example of the latter is the George W. Bush USS *Abraham Lincoln* tableau, with its great 'Mission Accomplished' banner. These were symbolic governments. Appearances do not just matter, they are the main business. The Nazis' government by symbolism merely anticipated much later developments.

Thus, as we have seen, Hoffmann's Anschluss photo-journal, *Hitler in his Homeland* offers a scenic tour with the big armoured Mercedes cars conveying an idea of benevolent menace.[11] And we witness the personal touch, Hitler placing flowers on his mother's grave, a human, and humane, Hitler. The classic buildings permit 'heritage' shots, by association, Hitler becomes the fulfilment of that heritage, and nature is similarly visually eloquent in the form of the snow-capped Alps in the background. Then there is the power of a collective image that it is univocal, the creation of this facade of Austrian unanimity and the symbols of Austrian assent such as the cheerful border guards letting through the invaders; but there is also the implicit merging/drowning of an Austrian identity into a Teutonic one. A messianic progress then, a trajectory and a consummation in Vienna itself. And it is without cost.

Crowds of course are part of this stage set, and Goebbels had a well-oiled machinery for the production of instantaneous throngs. But he is not alone in this. The parties today attempt to control signification rather than let it occur spontaneously, they are cautious to excess; packaging is political corporatism and represents a failure in civic culture that makes the candidate a mere pantomime presence ('to no one's surprise, the five hand picked householders all turned out to be Labour supporters' etc.).[12]

Permanent campaign Another shared commonality is the phenomenon that Blumenthal evoked in *The Permanent Campaign* (an early analysis of the communications methodology of the Reagan era): that is, the tools used to gain democratic office were now used to run it, a radical departure.[13] Without question, this was also one feature of Nazi government, for example, the five 'referenda' which Hitler ran after his ascent to power in 1933. In theory, these referenda were pseudo-election campaigns, but in practice they were nothing of the sort. The Reich, of course, went much further in its espousal of this concept of the permanent campaign: more extreme, more shameless, infinitely more fraudulent. But its methodology was drawn from the same conceptual domain with, at its centre, the dramaturgy of one actor. The core of Hitler's act was serial role-playing, whether First World War veteran, ascetic, stormtrooper, brooding statesman: his appeal is incomprehensible without drawing attention to this facility (similarly today with Putin. The journalist Anna Politkovskaya drew attention to Putin's facility for mimicry, he was a thespian acting out multiple roles: 'on Cattle Breeder's day [Putin] is our most illustrious cattle breeder; on Builder's day he is our foremost brickie ... Today, as luck would have it, is International Human Rights Day, so Putin summoned our foremost champions of human rights ...).[14]

Rhetorical government

Rhetoric allows politicians to be evasive, to avoid a direct responsibility for the consequences of action by covering everything with a skein of vagueness. The rhetoric of Adolf Hitler was often quite anodyne, yet the banality of Nazi rhetoric is more than matched by the in-house products of presidents and prime ministers.

But the point perhaps is not so much the rhetorical styles as the permanence of rhetoric as a feature of their governments. The leader is first narrator, he creates a dramatic, pleasurable and coherent narrative to explain the past and elucidate the present; this is what in fact, rhetorically, Hitler spent much of his time doing. A latter-day example of this is one of the great pieces of populist twentieth-century rhetoric, Ronald Reagan's speech on the occasion of the *Challenger* disaster, where crucially he eluded public responsibility for incompetent planning and other political and managerial factors by clothing the event in a sheen of rhetorical uplift and neo-religiosity.[15]

Disaster and the rhetorical vision But spellbinding new-order rhetoric is so much easier than punctilious attention to facts, and political debacles and, indeed, military disasters are the consequence of a particular governing style, one which elevates the verbal (rhetoric) above the operational (application). Hitler's government morphed from its challenge to the verdict of Versailles into the true insanity of invading the USSR and declaring war on the United States, more or less simultaneously. Thus, in the rhetorical vision, words cease to be distinguished from action but become indeed the principal form of action. Hence, during the George W. Bush era one adviser informed a journalist that he was now a member of an anachronism, the obsolete 'reality-based community', since 'we're an empire now, and when we act, we create our own reality'.[16]

Slogans Rhetorical governance is structured around slogans. Goebbels of course created the slogan of the week, and indeed the slogan of the day, these were ways of telegraphing the purposes of the regime and building design and focus into its work. Under Reagan, the Republicans not only had a rhetoric committee but similarly sought out a thematic projection of government, with a theme for every month.[17] Tony Blair, with his unerring instinct for the nerve of modern culture, was a distinguished practitioner, his sloganeering ('People's Princess' etc.) being textbook illustrations of the resonance of the cynical soubriquet; these were sloganeering governments. Clearly the ideology serviced by these slogans, and by the ingratiating blandishments and perambulatory verbalisations of Tony Blair, was not even remotely comparable to the Third Reich. But it is projected by the same communications concept, the recognition that all regimes need a kind of debased public poetry, which is probably an accurate description of what we are really enacting in slogans and sound bites (*Volksgemeinschaft* for example would fit the rhetorical repertoire of David Cameron – his 'Big Society' etc.). The Iraq war indeed was calibrated via its sloganeering: 'This was a conflict which proceeded surrounded by a miasma of words, a penumbra of slogans, a verbal fog of coalitions of the willing, shock and awe, collateral damage, operation Iraqi Freedom, regime change, effects-based warfare ...'; and, of course, Weapons of Mass Destruction.[18]

Fraud and fabrication The Nazis in effect constructed a Potemkin village on a national scale and a mighty facsimile of a civilised Western democracy. One example of this was their changes to the entire public face of Germany for the 1936 Olympics, ordering trim gardens, houses painted, rubbish cleared; beggars were secreted away, prostitutes hidden, prisoners prevented from working near main roads. Nazi and Olympic flags fluttered compulsorily on buildings in principal thoroughfares, while 'in Berlin, the streets were patrolled every morning to ensure that the flags and decorations have not been damaged by the weather or vandalism'.[19] Embarrassments were concealed; the cosmetic brush swept nearly 600 gypsies into a new-build concentration camp. But, on orders from the sensitive Reichsführer Himmler, foreign homosexuals were ignored, and Hitler agreed to remove anti-Semitic signs for the duration. And then there was 'butter propaganda', limitless butter for visitors, lard and margarine for Berliners, their 'Hitler butter'.[20] By comparison, the more recent regimes of political lying seem tame, yet in a more trivial way fraud and fabrication have been a significant part of their act. For example, subterfuge was preface to the first Gulf War: as in the 'Kuwaiti babies' story, which headlined the claim that invading Iraqi soldiers had disconnected the incubators of premature babies. It was a complete fiction, invented by public relations firm Hill and Knowlton and retailed to the American media by the daughter of the Kuwaiti ambassador to Washington, who was posing as a refugee.[21]

Certainly, the regimes then and now recognised that the pictography of violence had to be sterilised, and that war imagery could not be permitted to grow naturally like weeds. Hence the US Army's Combat Camera teams; which were (as we have seen) paralleled in the Third Reich by the Propaganda Companies, or PK units, groups of journalists, film men, cameramen and crews. PK units were similarly under formal military discipline, and risked everything in the entrepreneurial search for the right image. Another common feature was the mass production of favourable news stories via the embedded journalist, again an idea familiar to Goebbels who recognised that, whatever his power over the German media, the international media had to be persuaded. As, indeed, he tried during the fall of France, soliciting the global press at every point.

Statistical propaganda These regimes operated in a scientific age, and therefore the questions of evidence and proof could never be resolved purely by assertion and robust phraseology. There had to be something more tangible in an empiricist culture and they did of course find it: the answer lay in the synthesis of data, Britain's 'New' Labour being accused of seeking to create a 'social statistical utopia'. Nazi propaganda, the posters for example, was awash with statistics – on car production, on export growth, and so forth. Constantly, images of data pyramids and mighty bar charts danced before the German public and it seemed at times as if the Volk lived in a veritable nirvana of numbers and pictograms. The trouble, as the Nazis found, is that there is a perceptible performance gap, a tension between the statistical assertion and the lived experience. No government can continuously deny experiential witness.

Illusion If we do not have enemies we can create them, and war would be unthinkable without what really amounted to a domestic industry of myth creation. The Nazi myth machine asserted that Poland had in fact actually attacked Germany, while in 1941, naturally, Germany had invaded the USSR in order to forestall an imminent Soviet attack. These myths, like the serial mythologies of the

Iraq war, were accepted because people experience an intense need for belief and therefore fail, or refuse to notice, the blemishes on the canvas. In the end illusion and reality become indistinguishable. Today we think of ourselves as educated out of credulity and yet our self-deceit becomes apparent in retrospect: for example, during the British General Election of 1997 a Labour Party broadcast actually featured an angel. In this madcap fiction, a couple and their children are leaving hospital and a kindly, helpful taxi driver picks them up *gratis* on a rainy night. He turns away to go, revealing a pair of fluffy wings. And yet, in 1997, in Britain, a social mood antagonistic to chronic individualism legitimated this fantasy (that, and the continued status of the NHS as something approaching a national religion).

It is facile, rhetorical bombast to compare our contemporary governments to the Nazis. Nevertheless, the (Republican) Willie Horton's commercial of 1988, which used the image of a black rapist-murderer; or the Swiss People's Party poster depicting a space covered in minarets; or the Northern League's image of an American Indian reservation as the fate of future Italians in a land of immigrants – all demonstrate the kind of toxic negativity of which we are today still capable. Such inflammatory texts create a social climate, but is there any basis of comparison with Nazi campaigning methodology? The answer is very tentative: and with the qualification that, again, the political causes which these techniques sustain are not comparable.

Some years ago this author suggested:

> Britain's 'New' Labour Government embodies a phenomenon for which the word 'spin' is descriptively inadequate. New Labour actually represents something much more radical and important than this – an entire regime whose core competence has lain in the generation of imagery. Its directors recognise that, in a sense, words speak louder than actions, and that the production of the correct imagery is politically more significant than the creation and execution of policy, the old concept of governing. Notoriously a functionary (Jo Moore) declared, as the Twin Towers were collapsing, that it would be a 'good day to bury bad news'.[22]

Are such tactics mandatory if governments are to get elected and re-elected? Are they pre-requisite for the exercise of power in modern and postmodern conditions?

Pseudo-democracy and the new order?

Pseudo-democracy This poses a further unsettling question: Was Hitler's regime less a historical accident than a prototype: an invention of modernity and a reaction to the conditions catalysed by modernity? We seem to be heading not so much for a democratic world but rather a propaganda augmented neo-democracy: surely this is descriptive of what Russia now is and what China will surely become? One comparator is Mussolini's Italy, i.e. the facsimile of democracy surrounded by a nimbus of nationalistic propaganda. But another is Nazi Germany:

the triumph of the ballot box is not foreordained, universal brotherhood is a difficult product to sell. For example one cannot assume that Russia and China will evolve into Jeffersonian democracies ... The common feature is, and will be, the use of propaganda as lubricant, augmented by the rituals of pseudo-democracy.'[23]

The pseudo-democratic states take the rituals of democracy very seriously. This is even true of China, which although it has historically invested in the notion of the party as the monopolist of competence also suffers a vociferous nationalist right-wing which it can neither control nor direct. There is a facsimile of consultation. It is more accurately described as populism, or more specifically a plebiscitory autocracy based on opinion management. Mussolini observed 'the fascist state organises the nation, but leaves a sufficient margin of liberty to the individual'. The Russian regime began to speak of 'sovereign democracy', and thus 'They are taking Russia to task for failing to implement the Western model of democracy: but the point of sovereign democracy is to deny the relevance of that model.'[24]

This new political entity offers an alternative to those who proclaim themselves anti-Western or who loathe Western civilisation and the models of development it offers: that is to say Western political cultures, which are both culturally liberal and politically and economically neo-liberal, while at the same time exhibiting the same traits: the concentration of all power into the hands of the few. This was, of course, pre-eminently true of The Reich which saw the degenerate West as its rival and antithesis. America in all cases is the great anti-culture, a society toxified by criminality, plutocracy, poverty and race tension, which is how interestingly enough the Nazis also projected it in their propaganda. And while Russia today seeks to divide the West, China, at least via its propaganda, is also actively hostile to it, speaking of the West's 'devilish claws'.[25] One recent video was described as a 'seven and a half minute phantasmagoria of the Communist Party's nightmares of Western subversion'.[26]

Fear The signature of these earlier Fascist/Nazi regimes was a particular dynamic that mixed propaganda with coercion: the one unworkable without the other. Fear is most effectively induced by the creation of an existential threat as a source of legitimacy for illegitimate regimes. Hitler could mobilise the existential threat of the Jews and international plutocracy; and today Putin invokes the (internal/external) terror of Islam and the (external) threat of NATO, while simultaneously exploiting the West's, specifically Europe's, new-found sense of extreme vulnerability. Like Goebbels before him (*Festung Europa*) he poses as the defender of western civilisation- claiming for example that 'a society that can't defend its children has no tomorrow'.[27]

Disinformation Disinformation is organised lying. It was an established and well integrated part of Nazism's methodology of control and incitement: for example, claiming that Saar leader Max Braun had fled; that Kolberg had not fallen to the Russians; that the Jews were not being massacred; that living conditions for guest workers (i.e. slaves) were good; that the radio station at Gleiwicz had been attacked by Poles; that there was an Allied plan to sterilise all Germans (the 'Kaufman plan');

that (many times) the British aircraft carrier HMS *Ark Royal* had been sunk (eventually it was). Today Russian disinformation, or *dezinformatsiya*, is designed to sabotage the notion of objective truth and paralyse action. Fronts had of course been a favourite resource of the old USSR: but this time they tenanted cyberspace, specifically two that appeared in the summer of 2016, Guccifer 2.0 and DC leaks. The latter claimed to be 'launched by the American hacktivists who respect and appreciate freedom of speech' and lubricated the social media attacks on Hilary Clinton.[28] This is, in fact, war. General Valery V. Gerasimov, chief of the general staff of the Russian armed forces, published 'what became known as the Gerasimov doctrine. It posited that in the world today, the lines between war and peace are blurred and that covert tactics, such as working through proxies or otherwise in the shadows, would rise in importance. He called it "non-linear warfare". His critics call it "guerrilla geopolitics".'[29]

Pseudo-realities and perception management The Nazis were masters of the pseudo-real, fabricating events, dissolving the barrier between truth and fiction: thus the 'miracle' weapons would win the war for Germany; the Allies could not replace their huge shipping losses; Jews were a major component of the Soviet government; German Jews were fully participating in the German Olympic squad; Germany did not have further territorial ambitions; Germany was not seeking war and would not attack Russia. All of these regimes seek to manipulate:

> they offer in other words no unvarnished truth, and any notion of objectivity is missing. The purpose of government is to tell people that they live in a Panglossian best in the best of all possible worlds. So a great edifice of perception is constructed that is ultimately neither truly true nor fully false, but hangs somewhere in the no man's land between truth and falsehood.[30]

What matters is feeling not fact: patriotic emotions supersede empirical truths so that Russia for example has always denied that their sponsor militias shot down the Malaysian airline on 17 July 2014. All the evidence was there: but no, they did not shoot it down. Propaganda as we have said works because it does not commit the error of asking for belief. Thus, the youthful workers in Russian 'troll farms' invent fables that ridicule or damn America or the Ukraine.[31] One example of Russian disinformation is the claim that the US government caused Ebola, reflecting, of course, the earlier Soviet-sponsored rumour that the US had created AIDS. What we have is the serial creation of pseudo-realities such that a fictive world is created and sustained. Fakery is part of propaganda. The director of the Isvetsia publishing house suggested 'image is not reality, but, rather, its reflection, which can be made positive'.[32]

Politics as consumption The Nazis, and Goebbels specifically, were, however, much more insightful about the tedium of orthodox propaganda with its smug pieties and sanctimonious exhortations to loyalty and discipline; and they pioneered forms of entertainment, particularly film, that contrived to secrete the message within a packaging of story, romance and flamboyance. This new language of persuasion was popular culture itself. Today the Chinese, in particular, are discovering the limitations of didacticism and search for an alternative, recognising like Goebbels that propaganda must entertain if it is to instruct. Increasingly their propaganda speaks with modern accents, imagery is drawn unapologetically from the world of consumption: 'the video boasts the production values and soaring music of a multinational firm's big brand advertising campaign'.[33] Thus, a film articulating the Chinese case in a South China Sea conflict was showing 120 times a day in Times Square; it was a propaganda response to a judicial ruling (Hague Tribunal).[34] The promise of a consumption utopia and a political utopia are interdependent and the stylisation hints at this. Alongside this is the attempt to humanise President Xi, for example via the rap group CD Rev – 'its patriotic music videos mostly in English featuring songs about China's claims in the South China Sea and Mao's legacy'.[35]

Moreover, Goebbels's central tenet – that entertainment was the key – became pre-eminently true of ISIS whose propaganda output mimicked mainstream entertainment, a parasitic discourse targeted at a generation with a brevity of attention span. Similarly they recognised the tedium of overt propaganda of the kind, for example, that Al Qaeda engage in. Steve Rose speaks of:

> what seems to be the Al Hayat style. Virtually every frame has been treated. The color is so saturated, the combatants appear to glow with light. Explosions are lingered over in super slow motion. There are effects giving the feel of TV footage or old photographs. Transitions between clips are sheets of flame and blinding flames. Graphics fly across the screen. Sonorous, auto-tuned chanting and cacophonous gunfire reverberate on the soundtrack ...[36]

Thus, there is the influence of modern media stylisation, particularly stylistic forms derived from Hollywood and even specific films like *The Hurt Locker*. There is even the influence of computer games (for example the direct influence of *Grand Theft Auto*). Bizarrely, Goebbels himself (as we have seen) co-opted and deployed Hollywood effects and style – the slickness, and so forth – to project a 'contemporary' feel. Thus, ISIS propaganda works through emulating the forms and feel of Western media products.

Conclusion

Our Hitler Hitler was merely the most vivid in a, by now, long line of public image makers, and, when governments fail today, they fail for want of this craft. Obama, for example, was elected via consummate skill in image management, but his deficiency lay in attempting to govern rationally, a neglect of symbolic control. There is no comparison between delusion on the Nazis' scale and the tribulations of later regimes; the one had, as Hitler himself would have said, a world-historical significance, the others have ultimately finite consequences. Nor is it entirely clear that Fascism itself, a political form that appeared to be consigned to the garbage tip of history in 1945, is utterly extinguished. Modern regimes that chauvinistically assert themselves, that embrace the narcotic of consumerism and conceal their essentially authoritarian nature behind a facade of rhetoric and a corporate ritual of idealistic humbug – could this not be a description of our emergent global order? Is Hitler not just about our past, but our future? And yet today Germany presents a different vista, consistently electing a middle-aged and unfashionable woman with a PhD in chemistry to be its leader. Not for Germans the Anglo-spheric preference for virile men with a full head of hair as leader, or for wars; for in Germany now it is the politics of anti-charisma that work. This is the derived lesson of their history.

But the goal of propaganda today, as formerly, is not necessarily to persuade at all or, indeed, to create believers; the understated object is really passive acquiescence rather than active partisanship. Regimes ask not for belief but for the facsimile of belief, not internal commitment but external compliance. In contemporary China one popular poet has even argued that the party does not want people to be too sincere in their love for it.[37] The citizen is being exhorted not so much to deny as to selectively see. They must in other words not commit Orwellian 'thought crime' but focus, ignoring the peripheral vision. This needs a strategy of distraction. In the twenty-first century our challenges may seem different as the memories of the genocide recede. Yet democracy has seldom looked more vulnerable than now with the emergence of pseudo-democracies like Russia, authoritarian regimes which incorporate democratic appeals as a strategy of control and invoke populism as a methodology of public arousal; or even, like Turkey, authoritarian states which successfully exploit a democratic base.

Nazi propaganda constitutes a rabid prototype of today, and this applies not just to modern regimes but to revolutionaries and terrorists as well. Much, obviously, has changed in the form, style and content of propaganda and political marketing since the Nazi era; but now, as then, it is communications technology which defines the propaganda product. Modern propaganda traces the movement from collectivism to individualism in ways simply unimaginable in the time of the Third Reich. ISIS, for instance, have harnessed a Twitter army of tens of thousands of people to relay these messages around the world and exploited all the properties of existing and emerging social media. This is an entrepreneurial propaganda format which fits in with the narcissistic zeitgeist of our own time. Yet much remains of the Nazi archetype: for propaganda remains the passport for conspiracy theories and in many ways these still constitute its *raison d'être*. It is about the creation of threats and especially existential threats such as Al Qaeda's marketing of the notion of a world conspiracy against Muslims, which is the equivalent of the Nazis' international Jewish conspiracy against Aryans.

Anticipatory account Is Hitler, then, an archetype, an anticipatory account of what came to be? A political innovator and entrepreneur, plagiarised, perhaps even consciously, by various kinds of demagogue and aspirational autocrat? Nor are Russia or China his exclusive legatees. The idea of democracy is being used not to establish governing parties in power legitimately but to embed authoritarian regimes vested in some concept of a nationalist utopia. And they can be of the left as well as of the right. The Chavistas in Venezuela have manipulated the forms of democracy while sabotaging the reality via the creation of an internal enemy (profiteering businessmen) and an external threat (international plutocracy and the USA): thus displacing responsibility for the crisis. But there are other candidates as well; President Duterte of the Philippines has specifically invoked comparisons with Hitler and the Holocaust in his murderous war on drug dealers and addicts, vowing to liquidate three million of them.[38] A further example is Turkey under Erdogan, which similarly manifests some of these hubristic traits of national egocentricism and democratic posturing. Such governments may remain full dictatorships or evolve into something less, a managed pseudo-democracy: but their propaganda is never just a tool of governing, it is the way legitimacy is claimed, sustained and replenished.

This is not of course the world anticipated in that benevolent delusion of Francis Fukuyama's, *The End of History*.[39] Seen in this perspective Hitler's regime seems less a historic accident than a paradigm of what was to come, not least because it represents an early response to the same stock conditions of modernity which these later regimes also reflect:

> A society of rootless, atomised individuals, produced by the modern workplace's need for mobility of labour and micro-specification of task, is a fearful society, and out of that fear emerges the need for solidarity. The 'modern' era of mass electorates was vulnerable to vividly dramatized messages that evoke a binary world of good and evil, and the corruption of political discourse by 'terrible simplifiers'...[40]

And yet one should also be realistic as to where the comparison stops: they are not seeking the genocide of the most culturally advanced elements within the society, as Hitler did, nor do they represent a lunatic thrust for Eurasian domination under the spell of a messianic leader. They are more rational than this.

Notes

1 This chapter borrows elements from two of my published articles. They are: 'Bush, Blair – and Hitler? A Review of Comparative Self-Presentation'. *Journal of Public Affairs*, 8 (4), November 2008, 293–303. And: 'Putin, Xi And Hitler? Propaganda and the Paternity of Pseudo-democracy', *Defence Strategic Communication: The Official Journal of the NATO Strategic Communications Centre for Excellence*, 2 (2017).
2 Ross, *Media*.
3 Wistrich, *Weekend*.
4 Bracher, *German Dictatorship*.
5 Ibid.
6 Ibid.
7 Ibid.
8 Kallis, *Nazi Propaganda*.
9 Martin Jacques, 'The Rise of the Right', *The Guardian*, 30 April 2008.
10 Nicholas O'Shaughnessy, *Politics and Propaganda: Weapons of Mass Seduction*, Manchester: University of Manchester Press, 2004; Ann Arbor: University of Michigan Press, Ann Arbor 2004.

11 Hoffmann, *Hitler*.
12 *The Times*, 3 May 2010.
13 Sidney Blumenthal, *The Permanent Campaign*, Massachusetts: Beacon Press, 1980.
14 Robert Cottrell, 'Death Under The Tsar', *New York Review of Books*, 14 June 2007.
15 Nicholas J. O'Shaughnessy, 'The Rhetoric of Rhetoric: Political Rhetoric as Function and Dysfunction', in J. Atkins, A. Finlayson, J.R. Martin, N. Turnbull (eds.), *Rhetoric in British Politics and Society*, Basingstoke: Palgrave Macmillan, 2014.
16 Ron Suskind, 'Without a Doubt: Faith, Certainty and the Presidency of George W. Bush', *New York Times Magazine*, 17 October 2004.
17 Nicholas J. O'Shaughnessy, *The Phenomenon of Political Marketing*, London: Macmillan, 1990.
18 O'Shaughnessy, *Mass Seduction*.
19 Walters, *Berlin Games*.
20 Ibid.
21 O'Shaughnessy, *Mass Seduction*.
22 Ibid.
23 Nicholas J. O'Shaughnessy, 'Putin, Xi And Hitler?'.
24 Cottrell, 'Death Under The Tsar'.
25 Javier Hernandez, 'Propaganda With a Millennial Twist Pops Up in China', *New York Times*, 1 January 2017.
26 Chris Buckley, 'Chinese Propaganda Video Warns of West's "Devilish Claws"', *New York Times*, 23 December 2016.
27 *Daily Mail*, 3 November 2016.
28 Max Fischer, 'Prizing Speed and Scoops, Media Became Ready Bullhorns For Russian Hackers', *New York Times*, 9 January 2017.
29 Andrew E. Kramer, 'How The Kremlin Recruited An Army Of Specialists To Wage Its Cyber War', *New York Times*, 30 December 2016.
30 O'Shaughnessy, 'Putin, Xi And Hitler?'.
31 Timothy Snyder, 'Fascism, Russia, and the Ukraine', *New York Review of Books*, 20 March 2014.
32 'The Propaganda of the Putin Era: Part Two: The Kremlin's Tentacles', *Institute of Modern Russia*, (5) 5 December 2012.
33 Angela Doland, 'Watch the Chinese Propaganda Ad Playing 120 Times A Day In Time Square', *Advertising Age*, 25 August 2016.
34 Ibid.
35 Hernandez, 'Propaganda'.
36 Steve Rose, 'The Isis Propaganda War, A High-Tech Media Jihad', *The Guardian*, 7 October 2014.
37 Perry Link, 'China: Capitulate or Things Will Get Worse', *New York Review of Books*, 24 October 2013.
38 *The Guardian*, 1 October 2016.
39 Francis Fukuyama, *The End of History and the Last Man*, New York: The Free Press, 1992.
40 O'Shaughnessy, 'Putin, Xi And Hitler?'.

EPILOGUE: THE FÜHRER AND THE DONALD

The ghost of a resemblance?[1]

Much has been made recently of alleged parallels between the authoritarian taint of current political events in the USA and the rise of European Fascism in the inter-war period. One Oxford researcher, Dr Kevin Dutton, has even declared that Donald Trump exhibits 'more psychopathic' traits than Hitler.[2] Is Fascism arising from its mausoleum? Does the polarisation in US society, and the recourse to demagoguery in the service of the retrieval of a better past, equate even superficially with the disintegration of the civic state in Europe in the twenties and thirties?

The first thing to say is that this is not all about Donald Trump. He represents merely the apex of a cultural trend and before he appeared there were movements and events that presaged his arrival. If Trump did not exist someone would have invented him. Secondly he is not a Fascist even though there are some significant comparisons with the language of Fascism – for example his notorious 'snake' anecdote (Muslims) parallels the Nazi-era *Der Stürmer* children's story of the snake (Jews).

However there definitely are similarities in communications method between the US today and the Fascist era in Europe, and all draw from the same polemical-evangelical script. This does not make the American right Fascist, or Trump a Nazi. It does however point to the recrudescence of persuasion techniques associated with these things and long thought extinct. Now, today, it is the Obama campaign of 2008 with its idealism, its focus on the future, its co-opted hordes of youth and digital and social media projection, that lies in the past. The old has become new for those who don't remember, with malign consequences.

This candidate and the hold he has on millions of Americans did not emerge from nowhere. Trumpery is not self-created but the consequence of the polemicisation of our political discourse arising out of the polarisation of our political culture. And the paladins of this culture – Fox News, Sarah Palin, Anne Coulter, the T-Party – inspire a great army of followers who decant their frustrations into cyberspace. The blogosphere shakes with their rage. In this it does indeed parallel Weimar Gemany. The Third Reich was also a culture war. It was not that a majority of Germans wanted Nazism, but that they didn't want democracy and there was no real political centre left in Germany, just Communist, Socialist and Fascist. Trumpery flourished in part because of Obama's failure to sell a counter-narrative and his drily intellectual approach to leadership – and similarly with Hitler's Weimar predecessor Chancellor Heinrich Brüning, who rejected exhortations to use the media and give Germans a powerful story.

And in terms of evangelical method there is an obvious parallel between Hitler's use of the living theatre of politics – the rhetorical assault before a live audience – and Trump's dramaturgy. For Trump has revived the mass rally, eschewing until late in the day established methods of political marketing such as advertising, direct mail and so forth. He knows that the media will relay his polemical performances, heavy in denunciation, into every home. As did Hitler, who ensured that Germans were able to buy a very cheap state produced radio (Volksempfaenger VE 301) that could only be tuned into the regime programmes. For both men, the theatre of politics was just as important as the instrumentality. In the view of one respected academic, a Hitler rally in the early 30s was 'well worth it' for the entertainment value. Crowds thrill to Trump's bullying bellicose manner; his playing to the gallery and demonisation of opponents, his egocentric fictions; his huge lies which go so far beyond anything seen before in American politics – what he says is largely imaginary. Missing however in the conventional analysis of Trump is the element of self-parody, he is a pantomime villain exhaling bluster, a wizard of Oz. That is part of the show, part of the entertainment.

The key similarity is the emotional strategy and, specifically, the way in which both maestros of rhetoric exploited the primal emotions of Pride, Fear and Anger.

Emotion: Pride Firstly there is the manufacture of a benevolent, proud past which the current order has violated as expressed in the phrase 'Make America Great Again'. In fact, the Nazis called their regime the Third Reich to commemorate its earlier incarnations – the first Reich, i.e. Charlemagne and the so-called Holy Roman Empire, and the second Reich, the Germany that was united under Bismarck and terminated in 1918.

The slogan 'Make America Great Again' is both the core rhetorical idea of the Trump campaign and also evokes the loss of the American dream. And, as with the Nazis, there is a truth buried amid the boundless morass of lies. The Versailles treaty was indeed a disgrace, as the Nazis consistently claimed; and it is also objectively the case that the material substance of the American idea is now elusive for many Americans.

Emotion: Fear Richard Hofstadter entitled his famous Harper's Magazine essay 'The Paranoid Style in American Politics' (November 1964). But paranoia is energised by the notion of an existential threat, and this idea, this nightmare, is what Trump offers the American people – the notion of an American way that is threatened, that may face extinction, subverted from within by treacherous elites and alien cultural saboteurs and from without by foreign states stealing American jobs and markets. Indeed the kind of rhetorical intensity promoted by Trump simply would not be possible if the issues were pedestrian. A crisis has to be created: no man, said Goebbels, is willing to die for the eight-hour day. There has to be a great cause, the cause of national survival itself. For the Nazis of course that crisis was the manufactured existential threat from the 'international' Jews – the notion that the German people were facing cultural and perhaps racial extinction. They promulgated this idea so vigorously that in the end they were projecting World War Two itself as primarily a war against the Jews who allegedly controlled the US, British and Soviet governments (in fact the Soviet Politburo had only one Jewish member).

Emotion: Anger And alongside the retrieval of past glory was the rhetorical sabotage of the existing regime – in the Nazis' case, Weimar, and for right-wing Republicans the Obama presidency. In both cases the status quo was essentially portrayed as illegitimate – the Nazis with their *dolchstosslegende*, or legend of the stab in the back, the 'betrayal' of the 1918 armistice and the Versailles treaty by liberals and social democrats; in Obama's case the onslaughts of the 'birthers', the claim that he was actually a Muslim and was educated in a 'madrassa' and so forth.

Above all both of them mobilised a politics of grievance and recognised that grievance does not have to actually exist objectively – it can be talked into people. I have described Hitlerite rhetoric as a protracted, brattish whine. Grievances are imaginary as well as real. Thus 'If I'm elected we're all going to be saying Merry Christmas again' is a typically resonant piece of Trump oratory, but who is actually saying that we should no longer say 'Merry Christmas'? It is a vigorous attack – against a straw man.

Then there is the cruelty, deliberate norm violation in fact, unfortunately a feature of the Trump campaign and also a key method of Nazi electioneering as with Goebbels's attacks on deputy Berlin police chief Bernard 'Isidore' Weiss, a fine public servant insulted among other ways by the device of photomontage to make him appear degenerate. And listen to Trump: on Carly Fiorina's appearance, on Megan Kelly. The climax of this ad hominem vitriol was to insult Khizr and Ghazala Khan, the parents of a dead Muslim soldier; jeer at Senator McCain for being taken prisoner in Vietnam; denigrate Judge Curiel's Mexican parentage; and to grotesquely mimic the mannerisms of *New York Times* reporter Serge Kovaleski who has chronic joint disease. Alongside this serial creation of objects of hate is the legitimation of violent solutions – to terrorism (torture them) and even to Hilary (Trump's threatening reference to 'the second amendment people').

The second similarity lies in the manipulative tactics which both employed – the manoeuvres, the panaceas, the frauds.

Tactic: Manoeuvre And another feature of both is their essential politicality. As a political party the Nazis were prepared to compromise and dissemble, for instance supporting the transport workers in the 1932 Berlin strike (losing much middle-class support in the process) and refusing to join the 'Watch on the Rhine' (the only party that did). In the early days they tried to be all things to all men and have even been called a 'catch-all party', actually issuing instructions that the swastika was not to be shown very much in highly middle-class areas. The Nazis were, in fact, supremely cynical political salesmen on the march to power: 'we don't want high bread prices, we don't want low bread prices, we don't want bread prices to stay the same, we want National Socialist bread prices'. As for the anti-Semitism, that was not stressed in areas with no anti-Semitic tradition and in those cases other groups would be targeted, Poles and Danes for example.

Trump similarly is definitely a politician and quite prepared to dump ideological baggage when it suits his political convenience – for example he modified his stance on the repatriation of migrants in the late August of 2016 as he pursued the more moderate Republican vote. He has been prepared to ditch policies that were getting in the way. Moreover although his support coalition includes 'Theocons' – evangelical Christians – he is nothing if not bohemian, silent on the sexual revolution, or tentative, in everything from abortion to gay marriage to transgender rights.

Tactic: Panacea The offer is of a fix – in Hitler's case, primarily to retrieve German pride and get revenge on those who had destroyed it, and conquer unemployment. The offer is of bold, simple solutions: Trump says build a wall, repatriate eleven million illegals, have a moratorium on Muslim immigration. And these resonate with many people. The offer, therefore, is a panacea. But it is framed by a nuance-free perspective that is coherent and easily comprehended: thirty-seven per cent of probable voters across the political spectrum support the moratorium.[3]

Tactic: Fabrication And then there is the fabrication and the fiction. In a sense, lying to all of them was just a deeper form of truth. Trump merely invents: 'Mexico must pay for the wall' or 'the concept of global warming was created by and for the Chinese in order to make US manufacturing non-competitive' are a co-creation of speaker and audience. Trump's evangelical methodology, like that of the Nazis, does not make the mistake of asking for belief. Like them Trump is inviting his listeners to share a fantasy. They are neither stupid, credulous nor vulnerable – rather what we see is a joint production. And these fictions really become frauds, since the worldview offered is ludicrously bleak and falsifies reality – five per cent unemployment is not an economic disaster yet Republican rhetoric persists in portraying it as such.

But Donald is not Adolf.

In fact, there are many parallels between Trump and Hitler which would explain their shared talent for outraging public opinion while simultaneously manipulating it. Thus Trump's demagoguery is legitimated by a colossal fame in the USA that long predates his candidacy. His popular media profile via *The Apprentice* is huge and it is easy for the *bien pensant* class to forget this or underplay the critical role of familiarity. Like Hitler (who did not found the NSDAP but joined it and rapidly became its propaganda director) he had a long exposure to media and therefore a training in it. And like Hitler he had never held political office before running for the highest one.

And both men, curiously, also theorised extensively about persuasion and its psychology – Hitler for the whole of chapter five in *Mein Kampf*, and Trump in the *Art of the Deal*: 'The final key to the way I promote is bravado. I play to people's fantasies. People may not always think big themselves, but they can still get very excited by those who do. That's why a little hyperbole never hurts. People want to believe that something is the biggest and the greatest and the most spectacular'. And then again 'I call it truthful hyperbole. It's an innocent form of exaggeration – and a very effective form of promotion.'

But Trump is not Hitler. Rather he stands in a specifically American tradition of populism. In fact the historical roots are deep. The further origins of the populist right and Trumpery lie way back in American history and he represents merely the continuity, with modern accents, of these ancient conflicts. There are many ancestors – Father Charles Coughlin in the thirties, Governor Huey Long's 'Every Man a King' campaign, George Wallace and others stretching back to the 'Know-nothings' of the mid-nineteenth century. Then there is Senator McCarthy with whom Trump directly connects via his New York lawyer (the late) Roy Cohn, who was McCarthy's assistant in the Army–McCarthy hearings and can be seen at his side in the old newsreels.

Nothing Trump does or says remotely justifies a serious comparison with the author of the Third Reich. The Nazi plans were always monstrous, and epic in scale – lebensraum in the East, necessitating the conquest of Russia, and secondly a *judenrein* Europe – originally conceived as deporting Jews to Madagascar and, when war frustrated this option, genocide. Violence underpinned everything the Nazis did and the propaganda state was merely the partner of the coercive state.

And even the comparison with Mussolini, though appealing, is inappropriate – Trump does not propose to imprison his political opponents or invade Ethiopia. There is no commonality of aims or ideology or ethics with the Fascism that seemed at one point to usher in a new dark age made, in Winston Churchill's words 'more sinister, and perhaps more protracted, by the lights of perverted science'. The radicalisation of Nazi rhetoric in the late 1930s becomes truly murderous:

> Look, there is the world's enemy, the destroyer of civilisations, the parasite among the peoples, the son of Chaos, the incarnation of evil, the ferment of decomposition, the daemon who brings about the degeneration of mankind.[4]

Ultimately this is not Donald Trump and should not be represented as such. It is an invocation to genocide and it is, quite literally, diabolical.

Notes

[1] This epilogue first appeared on History News Network, 2 October 2016 and Raw Story, 12 October 2016.
[2] *Independent*, 23 August 2016.
[3] The Conversation, 25 August 2016.
[4] Josef Goebbels, Nuremberg, 1937.

INDEX

Abel, Gustav 160
abstract art 236–7
Adler (magazine) 145, 149
Adolf Hitler Schools 239
Adorno, Theodor 205
advertising 5, 151–5, 167–71, 194, 217
aesthetics and the aestheticisation of politics 149–52, 177–8
Allen, Sheridan 70
d'Allesandro, Jo 256
All Quiet on the Western Front 39
Al Qaeda 273–4
Amann, Max 29, 148
anglophobia 85
Der Angriff 37, 143, 155, 213–14
Anschluss, the 185, 200–1
anti-Semitism 6, 9–10, 69–76, 80–7, 106, 146, 167, 224–5, 231–2, 241, 246, 269, 280
apologists for Nazism 91
architecture 138–42
Arent, Benno von 119
Ark Royal, sinking of 271–2
Arnold, Bettina 17
art and art criticism 30, 48, 149–51, 235–7
Art in the Third Reich (magazine) 16, 32, 235
Ascheid, Antje 7
atrocities 32, 41, 80, 84
'Attack on Cologne' (article, 1942) 173–4
avant-garde art 237

Bacharach, Susan 7
Baillet-Latour, Count 80
Bairnsfather, Bruce 91
Baker, F.O. 82
Balbo, Marshal 148
Baptism of Fire (film) 206
Baranowski, Shelley 8
Batman Returns (film) 257
battlefield images 211–12
Battleship Potemkin (film) 83, 159
Bauhaus, the 237
Beethoven, Ludwig van 182
Beevor, Anthony 49
Behrenbeck, S. 5
Benjamin, Walter 177
Beresford, Jack 16
Berkeley, Busby 61, 157–8
Berlin 138, 141, 269
The Berliner Illustrated 73–4, 109, 140, 148
Berliner Illustrirte Zeitung 121–2, 148, 184
Berliner Morgenpost 81, 182
Berlusconi, Silvio 266
Birchan, Professor 160
Birley, Robin 90–1
Bismarck, Otto von 108, 120, 126, 141, 278
Bismarck, sinking of 41, 91–2
The Black Corps (journal) 162
Blair, Tony 268
Blumenthal, Sidney 167
Bolshevism 26, 61, 78, 88, 112, 125, 149, 151, 159
bombing 130
boring nature of politics for the general public 51
Bormann, Martin 30, 34, 36–7, 42

Bose, Subhas Chandra 203
Bouhler, Philip 29, 68
Bowie, David 256
Bracher, Karl Dietrich 124, 194, 239, 265
brand imagery 22–4
brand management 19–22
branding of Nazism x, 5–6, 15–20, 24, 108, 126, 256, 265
Braun, Eva 119
Braun, Max 271
Breker, Arno 149, 236, 256–7
Bridge at Remagen (film) 257
British battledress 18
British Broadcasting Corporation (BBC) 42–3, 80, 92–3, 97, 200–2, 211
British Empire 148, 203
British Legion 90
British Union of Fascists 91
Browning, Christopher 9
Bruegel, Pieter 149
Brundage, Avery 79
Brüning, Heinrich 278
Bryant, Arthur 131
buildings 138–42, 147
bulletin boards 235
Bullock, Alan (Lord) 26–7, 106–8, 196, 200
Bürckel, Gauleiter 182
Burleigh, Michael 164, 255
Bush, George W. 266, 268
Bussche, Axel von dem 119
Bytwerk, Randall 7

Caesarism 175, 186, 208
Calvin College German Propaganda Archive 7–8
Cameron, David 268
Campaign in Poland (film) 206
Capra, Frank 97
Carter, Erica 7
cartoons 146, 157, 162, 203
Casablanca (film) 150
Catholicism and the Catholic Church 70, 84
celebrities 148–9
censorship 29, 39, 43, 48–9, 215
Cezanne, Paul 237
Chakotin, Serge 22
Challenger disaster 268
Chaplin, Charlie 259
charismatic leadership 105–8, 113–14, 120, 125–6, 132, 136, 205
Charlemagne 278
Chavistas 275
Chevalier, Maurice 146
China 270–4
China Seas (film) 162

Chomsky, N. 266
Christian Peace Movement 92
Churchill, Winston 32–4, 42–3, 116, 119, 130, 281
Ciano, Count 148
cinemas 205–6
city branding 18
civic organisations 62
class envy 46
Clausewitz, Karl Marie von 85
Clinton, Hillary 279, 272
Coca-Cola 166
Cohn, Roy 281
colonialism 203
Combat Camera teams (US Army) 209, 269
communication, new forms of 59–60, 65
Communist Party 76, 78, 88–9, 128, 168, 178, 195, 216, 265
computer games 262, 273
concentration camps 79, 83, 87–9, 183, 187, 269
conspiracy theories 8
consumerism 151–2, 157, 166–75; war seen as 171–5
Coughlin, Charles 60, 281
Coulter, Ann 277
counter-propaganda against Germany 91–2, 95–7
Cox, Sir Geoffrey 111
creative freedom 47–8
'Crystal Night' 96
Culbert, David 40
Cull, Nicholas 44
Curiel, Judge 279

Dachau concentration camp 183
Daily Express 98
Daily Mail 261
Davidson, J.C. 90
Davis, Brian Leigh 138
Davis, Elmer 94–5
Dawn Patrol (film) 162–3
death camps 90
Delia, Jesse G. 239
Delmer, Sefton 216
democratic regimes 265–6; vulnerability of 274; *see also* pseudo-democracy
desert war 173
Deutsche Allgemeine Zeitung 215
Deutsche Wochenschau 209
dictators: art approved by 123–4; belief in their own propaganda 126
Dietl, General 148
Dietrich, Marlene 159
Dietrich, Otto 29, 33–5, 37, 121, 148, 216

284 Index

Diewerge, Wolfgang 83
direct mail 60
disinformation 271–2
The Dismissal (film) 41–2
Disney cartoons 157, 162
documentaries 176, 206–8
Domizlaff, Hans 5, 15, 17
Donegal, Lord 98
Dönitz, Admiral 206
Doob, Leonard 79
Downfall (film) 257
Dresden 116
Durante, Jimmy 80
Dürer, Albrecht 149, 236
Duterte, President 275
Dutton, Kevin 277

Einstein, Albert 195
Eisenstein, Sergei 83
emotions, mobilisation of 3
entertainment, propaganda as 161–2, 238, 272–3
The Eternal Jew (film) 162–3, 224–5, 233
European Volunteer Movement 152
euthanasia 84–5, 97, 227
Evans, Richard 69–70
'evil genius' concept 107
exotic images 147–9

Facebook 262
Fascism 1, 9, 60, 105, 108, 132, 136–7, 161, 175, 177, 180, 186, 265–6, 271–4, 277, 281
Faulhaber, Cardinal 120
Federal Bureau of Investigation (FBI) 89
Fest, Joachim 27, 112–13, 170, 177–8
films 38–42, 46–9, 68, 86–7, 97–8, 136, 151, 155–65, 206–7, 256–61; control of 216; importance to the Nazis 159, 164; as an instrument of Nazi propaganda 159–63, 204–5; screenings of 65, 72, 205; sound in 198, 205
Fiorina, Carly 279
First World War 5, 9–10, 19, 42, 44, 85, 95, 125, 204
Flynn, Errol 258
Folkestone 80
Foreign Correspondent (film) 96
Foreign Office, German 48
Forster, Albert 30–1
Fortune, Major General 18
Fox News 277
Franco, Francisco 171
François-Poncet, André 110
Frankfurt 214

Frankfurt School 161
Frankfurter Zeitung 196, 215
frauds practised by the Nazis 78–80
Frederick the Great 108, 118, 126
Free India (journal) 203
Freiburg 80
Friedman, Herbert W. 212–13
frivolity in the Reich 146–7
Front Im Himmel (film) 206
Fry, Michael 132
Führer, use of the word 19–20
Führer myth 175
Führer principle 6, 105, 121
Fukuyama, Francis 275
funerals and funeral orations 36, 181–2
Funkhaus radio station, Berlin 201

Galen, Cardinal 84, 97
Ganz, Bruno 257
Garbo, Greta 35
Garrison Dora (film) 171
Gebühr, Otto 41
Gellately, Robert 68, 88–9
genocide 87, 187, 226, 281
Gerasimov, Valery V. (and 'Gerasimov doctrine') 272
German invasion of the Soviet Union 269
German soldiers, celebration of 209
Germanisation 31, 145
Germany today 274
Gestapo, the 88–9
Gestapo's Last Orgy (film) 260
Gitlis, Baruch 205
Gleiwitz rado station attack 10, 80, 271
Goebbels, Joseph 2, 6–10, 26–50, 66–8, 72, 77–86, 91–7, 108, 111–16, 120–1, 124, 136–7, 149–66, 171, 175, 184, 195–205, 209–15, 237, 240–1, 262, 265–73, 279; fight with the British media 42–5
Goldhagen, Daniel 9
Göring, Hermann 32, 46, 79, 121, 180–1, 184, 206, 264
Graf Spee, sinking of 45
Grainger, Stuart 163
Graves, Charles 98
The Great Dictator (film) 109, 259
The Great King (film) 40–1, 126
Greiser, Arthur 30–1
grievances: manipulation of 131; *real and manufactured* 4, 130–1, 279
Gropius, Walter 141–2
Grosse Liebe (film) 161
Grunberger, Richard 117
Gulf War 269
Gulliver's Travels 1

Habanera (film) 157
Hale, Oren 29
Halifax, Lord 114, 147
Hamburg 97
Hamilton, Sir Ian 131
Harlan, Veit 164
Harris, Sir Arthur 79
Hastings 80
Haw-Haw, Lord 43, 92–8, 202
Headlam, A.C. 91
Henderson, Sir Nevile 79, 106, 110, 112, 125, 177–8, 214–15, 243
Herf, Jeffrey 66
Herzstein, Robert 7
Hess, Rudolf 32, 34, 43, 71
Hierl, Constantine 148
Hill and Knowlton (PR firm) 269
Himmler, Heinrich 30–1, 36–7, 89–90, 125, 137, 262, 269
Hindenburg, Paul 107–8, 119–20, 180–1, 195, 204, 217, 223
The Hindenburg (airship) 183
historical discourse's role in advancing an argument 7
Hitler, Adolf x, 2, 5–7, 18–24, 26–37, 40–1, 50–1, 63–70, 77–9, 82, 91; appeal to intellectuals 117; appeal to women 115–16; appointment as Chancellor 78–9; as an advertising man 170; as the 'People's Chancellor' 121; as a producer and a consumer of media 160, 208; as a propagandist 27, 177, 240, 242; assassination plots against 33, 118; charm of 109–10, 114–15; comparisons with Donald Trump 278–81; democratic elections fought by 217; exceptionality of 5, 7, 105; fiftieth birthday celebrations 185–6; images of 20, 65, 70, 106, 119–31, 138, 147–9, 175–6, 185, 210, 217, 219–23, 237, 242; loyalty to and faith in 117–18, 124; the man 105–10, 121, 267; 'marketing' of 51, 108, 131, 217, 265; media interest in 6; personal role of 27–37, 40–1, 50; popularity of 110, 125; quotations from 15, 17, 31, 73, 138, 141, 149, 160, 170, 208, 215, 235, 239; rhetoric of 7, 111–16, 125, 130, 241, 267, 279; shadow cast by 261–2; skills of 23–4, 107–9, 177; speeches made by 107–15, 136–7, 178, 241; *see also Mein Kampf*
'Hitler industry' 255
Hitler movement 68, 121
Hitler myth 120, 128
Hitler Youth 39, 45, 64, 72, 126, 138, 143, 158, 179, 181, 225, 238, 262

Hitler's Children (film) 260
Hoffmann, H. 20, 109, 114, 162, 164, 185, 204, 267
Hofstadter, Richard 278
Hohlwein, Ludwig 221
Hollywood movies 157–62, 256–7, 273
Holocaust, the 3, 87–8, 255
homosexuality 163, 269
Hore-Belisha, Leslie 43, 93
Horne, Alistair 17
Horton, Willie 270
'house style' of Nazi propaganda 9, 16, 217
Hoyer, Hermann Otto 124–5
Huber, Franz J. 63
Hühnlein, Adolf 181
humour in the Reich 48–9
Huxley, Aldous 136, 166, 264
hyper-reality 149–50, 236–7

I Accuse (film) 84–5
ideology: absence of 6, 120, 178; components of 115, 322; in films 162; incoherence of 77, 203; *versus* marketing 203–4
Illustrierter Beobachter 120–1, 138, 143, 148–9, 171, 213
India 203
Inglorious Basterds (film) 261
International Olympics Committee (IOC) 79, 183
Internet resources 262
In the Name of the People (film) 47
Iraq War 268–70
ISIS 273–4
Islam 271
It Happened One Night (film) 157, 162
Italy 6

Jackson, Michael 257
Jagger, Mick 256
Jansen, Harald 81
Japan 266
Jesus Christ 125
Jew Süss (film) 87, 163
Jews, demonisation of 3
journalism: blacklisting in 66; on the front line 201; involved in propaganda 80; Nazi-inspired 157; professionalism of 216
Jowett, Garth 256
Joyce, William 43, 92, 98; *see also* Haw-Haw, Lord
Jugendlager, the 90

Kallis, Aristotle 7–8
Kaufman, Theodore 82–3

Keitel, Field Marshal 41
Kelly, Megan 279
Kershaw, Ian 28, 108, 117, 126–7
Khan, Khizr and Ghazala 279
Kiel 45
Killzone 3 (computer game) 262
kitsch 19, 143, 147–51, 260
Kleist, Ewald von 31
Klemperer, Victor 5, 16, 64, 87–8, 112, 116–17, 170, 187, 224, 229–31
Kohl, Helmut 68
Kolberg: the celluloid victory (film) 163–5
Kolberg and the Great King (film) 39–41, 67, 73–4
Kovaleski, Serge 279
Kracauer, Siegfried 137, 174, 210

Labour Front 29
Labour Party, British 270
Lady Gaga 256
Lanzinger, Hubert 107–8
Lawrence, T.E. 131
Le Bon, Gustave 9, 15, 106, 113, 125–6, 240
leadership image 121
leaflet propaganda 212–13
Lee, Ivy 20, 94
Lenin, V.I. 9, 61, 125, 240
Lewis, Joe 43
Life Goes On (film) 42
Life magazine 92, 94
lighting, use of 178, 243
Lisbon 201
Lives of Begal Lancer (film) 157
Lloyd George, David 43, 93, 131
Long, Huey 281
Look Who's Back (film) 261
Lorre, Peter 159
Lothian, Lord 45, 91
Low, Sir David 177–8
Lucas, George 257
Luckert, Steven 7
Lucky Kids (film) 157, 161–2
Ludendorff, Erich 204
Lueger, Karl 9
Luftwaffe, the 130
Lunn, Arnold 183
Lutyens, Edwin 141
Lutze, Victor 147

McCain, Senator 279
McCarthy, Senator 281
McClatchie, Stanley 83, 262
Mackensen, Field Marshal 180–1
Macpherson, Sandy 93

magazines 144–52, 171
managerialism 21
The Manchester Guardian 80, 82
Mann, Thomas 35, 109–10
Manvell, Roger 165, 174–5
market research 59, 67–9
marketing ix–x, 1–5; output of 64–7; techniques of 59–76, 194; unacceptability as a term in historical discourse 4–5; *versus* ideology 203–4; *see also* political marketing
marketisation of oratory 244
Marseille, Lieutenant 149
Martin-Amorbach, Oskar 236–7
Marx, Karl 240
Marxism 76, 171
Mason, James 163
May Day celebrations 66
Mein Kampf 9, 113–14, 132, 142, 204, 240, 262, 281
Memminger, Gustav 158
memorabilia of Nazism 261–2
Mickey Mouse films 157
middle-class support for Nazism 70–1, 279–80
military backwardness 186–7
Miller, Max 98
Ministry of Information, British 91–2
Ministry of Propaganda, German 34–8, 48, 66, 88, 163, 184
Mitcham, S.W. 31
'Mjölnir' 219–20
mobility, *geographic* and *social* 168
modernism 150–1
Molotov, V.M. 77
monarchy, loss of 119–20
Moore, Jo 270
morale 38, 45–9, 83, 95, 117, 125, 160, 203
'Morgenthau Plan' 82–3
Morrison, Herbert 43
Mother's Day 73
motor-cars, Nazis' use of 210
motor racing 151
Mrs Miniver (film) 42
Muhammad the Prophet 125, 203
Munch, Edvard 30
Munich 18
Munsterberg, Hugo 5
Munzenberg, Willi 194–5
Murdoch, Rupert 211
Murphy, James 132
Murrow, Ed 96
music 150–1
Mussolini, Benito 6, 16, 26, 112, 147–8, 270–1, 281
myth-making 269–70

National Health Service, British 270
national symbols 20–1
A Nation's Pride (film) 261
Nazi Party (NSDAP) 18, 60–2, 65, 68–71, 120–1, 174, 227, 231–2, 241, 245, 280; events organised by 16, 21; membership of 64
negativity in politics 195, 270
Neumann, Franz 27, 60, 76–7, 240
neutral nations 43–4, 79, 206
New British Broadcasting Station (NBBS) 92–3
New Delhi 141
New Statesman 183
newspapers: advocacy function of 216; alleged autonomy of 215; in Britain 98; control of 29–30, 33–6, 48–50, 196–7; importance of 213; leaked stories from 37; Nazi-controlled 61–3, 69, 78, 213–15
newsreels 174–5, 204–10; control of 28, 33, 39, 41, 47; involved in propaganda 81; length of 65; produced by the Allies 209; as a symbolic device 209–10
Nicolson, Sir Harold x, 59, 91–2
Niedermayer, Professor 31
The Night of the Fox (film) 260
Night of the Generals (film) 256
'Night of the Long Knives' 80
Noelle-Neumann, Elisabeth 68
Nolde, Emil 30, 149
normalcy, illusion of 157
North Atlantic Treaty Organisation (NATO) 271
Northeim 64–7, 70
Norway 34, 44, 78, 206
Nuremberg rallies 18, 175–80, 184, 207, 241–3

Obama, Barack 273, 277–9
obedience to authority 9
Oberkommando der Wehrmacht (OKW) 30, 50; *see also* Wehrmacht, the
obituaries 149
Oerter, Fritz 76
Ohm Krüger (film) 83
Olympiad (film) 184
Olympic Games 79–80, 98, 182–4, 211, 268–9
Opel Cars 167
opera 175, 178
opinion research 45–6, 67
opportunism, political 76–8, 113
organisation, Nazi emphasis on 26–7

O'Shaughnessy, Mary 90
O'Shaughnessy, Nicholas (author) ix, 270; *Selling Hitler: Propaganda and the Nazi Brand* 2, 8–10
O'Toole, Peter 256
Oven, Wilfred von 209
Owens, Jesse 184

'packaging', theory of 142–6, 177, 187, 264
Padua, Paul Mathias 235, 237
Palin, Sarah 277
Paris 145
Paris Match 152
Pathé News 97, 209
Patton, George 86
Paulus, Field Marshal 50
Paxton, Robert O. 1, 186
The People 98
People's Receiver 65, 198–9
persuasion, political 2; years of (1933–39) 6
Petain, Philippe 145
Pfuhle, Fritz 236
'phoney war' period 85
photographs as propaganda media 145
photo-journalism and photo opportunities 107–9
photomontage 195, 279
Picasso, Pablo 237
pictography 177, 269
Picture Post 96
Pius XII, Pope 96
Plenge, Johan 5, 17, 22
The Poisonous Serpent (children's book) 87
Poland 6, 30–2, 44, 78–80, 89, 97, 208, 216
policing 89
political intelligence 67
'political laboratories' 28
political marketing x, 2–5, 217, 274
Political Science Association, UK 2
Politkovskaya, Anna 267
popular culture 6, 137, 259, 272–3
populism 271, 274, 281
Porsche, Ferdinand 27
postage stamps 210
postcards 233
posters 152–6, 168–9, 202, 216–31, 237
'post-truth' society x
Potsdam 180–1
power structures in Nazi Germany 27–8
press, the *see* newspapers; magazines
propaganda ix–x, 1–10, 16, 21, 23, 26–32, 39–48, 51, 60–88, 94, 98, 108, 120–1, 130–2, 137, 159, 177, 184, 187, 195–8; accompanying conquest 65–6; aims of 10, 265, 274–5; centralisation of 66–7;

concealment of 146, 149, 152; contested leadership of 28–30; culture of 68; directed by Germany at other countries 94, 131, 201–4, 211, 269; as distinct from art 237; as distinct from news reports 216; distribution of 62–3; effectiveness of 116–18, 175, 210, 256; face-to-face 70; falsity of 98; in films, newsreels and documentaries 204–9; genres of 64; limitations of 96; as a major wartime industry 65; at mass meetings 240–1, 244–5; methods used for 84, 151, 210, 232; personnel involved in 61–6; poor quality of some types of 32, 47–8; in posters and paintings 217, 237; on radio 198–204; as a route to absolutist control 246; running the enemy's polemics against them 81–5; in schools 237–9; as a substitute for ideology 178; targeting of 69–76; and violence 4; as a weapon of war 85–6; *written* and *spoken* 234; *see also* counter-propaganda

Propaganda Company (PK) units 36, 48, 209, 269
A Propaganda Primer 245
The Propagandist (magazine) 210
'Protocols of the Elders of Zion' 79
Pruller, Wilhelm 213
Prussianism 138
Prynne, William 92
pseudo-democracy 270–1, 275
psychological warfare 4
public opinion 45–6, 67, 264, 266; manipulation of 175; personified in the leader 119
public relations (PR) 1, 3, 88–9
public speaking 243–5
purges 6
Putin, Vladimir 267, 271

racism 81
radio broadcasts 116, 166, 197–204, 216
Radio Caledonia 92
Radio Cymru 92
radio sets 65, 169, 171, 197–200, 278
rallies 175–80, 184, 188, 207, 239–45, 278
The Ramparts We Watch (film) 97
rational choice theory 106
Reagan, Ronald 258, 268
referenda held in Nazi Germany 267
Das Reich (newspaper) 64, 147, 157, 215
Reich Chamber of Culture (RKK) 38
Reich Chambers 28
Reich Speakers' School 241
Reichsleiter status 29

Rendulic, General 85–6
Rentschler, Eric 8, 136, 161, 166, 206–7, 257
reparations 126
Reserve Police Battalion *101* 9
resonance theory 227–8
restaurants, closing of 46
revolutionary movements, methods used by 60
rhetoric 21, 239–41, 244–6, 206–7, 267–8; *see also under* Hitler
Ribbentrop, Joachim von 29, 151
Riefenstahl, Leni 124, 184, 207, 242, 257
role-playing 121, 127
Rome 141
Rommel, General 18, 66, 182, 262
Röntgen, Wilhelm 84
Roosevelt, Franklin D. 33, 82–3, 92, 119
Rose, Steve 273
Rosenberg, Alfred 29–30, 41–2, 182, 235, 237
Ross, Corey 8, 17, 22
The Rothschilds Shares in Waterloo (film) 163
Royal Oak, sinking of 46–7
RPL (*Reichspropaganda-Leitung*), the Central Party Propaganda Office 45, 65, 66, 67
Rumbold, Sir Horace 106, 110
rumour as a tactic 89, 91
Runstedt, Field Marshal 182
Rural Post (journal) 71
Russell, Lord 90
Russia 270–4; *see also* Soviet Union
Russian Revolution 240
Rutherford, Ward 23, 112–14, 153, 159

SA Mann Brand (film) 152, 262
Sansom, Odette 90
Scheibe, Emil 125, 237
Schindler's List (film) 257
Schmeling, Max 43
schools 237–9
Schroeder, Christa 114
Schutz-Staffel (SS) 27, 32, 36, 67, 72, 87–8, 117, 137, 143, 162, 167, 235, 255–60
Schwartz, Tony 227–8
science fiction 258–9
Scofield, Paul 260
sculpture 149–50
Security Service (SD) 46, 49, 67
Sedan 146
'seduction' 177, 235, 246
segmentation of 'markets' 3, 60, 69, 71, 74
Sharif, Omar 256
Shaw, George Bernard 34
Shelley, P.B. 119

Shirer, William 111, 184, 197–8
Shovell, Sir Cloudsley 147
Siegel, Jerry 258–9
Signal (magazine) 77, 81, 95, 139–40, 145, 152, 157, 168, 173, 212
Simplicissimus (periodical) 49
Sinclair, Upton 205
slogans and sloganeering 268, 278
Snow White and the Seven Dwarfs (film) 157
social Darwinisn 28
Social Democrats 194–5, 216
social media 262, 272, 274
Society for Consumer Research 5
Soldiers of Tomorrow (film) 163
Sontag, Susan 207
Soviet Union (USSR) 5, 47, 77–8, 83, 86, 208, 268–9, 272
spectacle 175–80
speeches, editing of 34
Speer, Albert 16–17, 30–4, 37, 46, 68, 111, 114, 118–19, 124, 138, 142, 176–9, 241, 257
spin and *spin doctors* 43, 77, 264, 270
spoken word communication, power of 239–45
Spotts, Frederic 107, 178, 256
Stalin, Josef 5–6, 27, 116, 125, 177, 261
Stalingrad, battle of (1942) 5–6, 10, 49–51, 108, 113
Stalinism 10
Star Trek 258
Stark, G. 5, 62–3, 159, 217, 221, 231–5, 243
statistical propaganda 269
sterilisation 82–3, 271
stickers, use of 61, 212
Streicher, Julius 74
Strength Through Joy organisation 157, 168, 171
Stukas (film) 206
Der Stürmer 74, 79–80, 87
superman image 125–6, 259
swastika symbol 5, 15–20, 23–4, 63, 69, 116, 143, 148, 151–3, 179–82, 217, 221, 224, 259, 280
Swift, Jonathan 1
Swing, R.G. 80
symbols 16–24, 118–20, 137–42, 209–10, 266–7; choice of 22–3; power of 17; war of 22–4; *see also* swastika symbol

Tannenberg Memorial ceremonies 138, 180–1
Tarrantino, Quentin 261
Taylor, A.J.P. 7
teaching profession, social status of 238
television 176, 211
Tempo (newspaper) 155
terror, culture of 96
terrorism 131
theatricalisation of public life 177–8
Theresienstadt 187
'This Was Germany' (website) 262
Those Responsible for the War (film) 204
Tibetan expedition 151
The Times 33
Titanic (film, 1943) 39
'Toadstool' series of cartoon books 74–5
totalitarianism 9–10, 19, 47, 158, 198, 206, 209, 218–19, 265–6
The Train (film) 260
Trevor-Roper, Hugh 26
Triumph of the Will (film) 97–8, 125, 159, 184, 206–8, 256–7, 262
Troost, Paul Ludwig 138, 142
Troost, Frau 150
Trump, Donald 277–80
Turkey 274–5
Turner, Pierre 138

U-Boats Westward (film) 206
Ucicky, Gustav 22
Uklanski, Piotr 258
Ullrich, Volker 7
unemployment 76
uniforms 18, 138
United States: cinematic competition from 161; Germany declaring war on 268; media in 94–5; polarisation of society in 277; public opinion in 44–5, 97

V1 flying bombs 212
Van Gogh, Vincent 237
Vansittart, Sir Robert 43
Versailles Treaty 278–9
Vershofen, Wilhelm 5
VFA radio station 203
victimhood, politics of 130
Victory (magazine) 94–5
Victory of Faith (film) 207, 242
Vienna 185, 267
Viguerie, Richard 60
'Voice of Peace' (in France) 92
Volkische Beobachter 86–7, 213
Volkswagen (VW) 'Beetle' 27, 157, 168–9
Von Ryan's Express (film) 256–7

Wagner, Richard 176, 183
'wall newspapers' 210–11
Wallace, George 281

Wamper, Adolf 236
war crimes tribunals 90
warfare: as process 145; seen as a branch of persuasion 85
Warhol, Andy 256
Warsaw Ghetto 89
Waugh, R.M. 256
We're Dancing around the World (film) 207
Weber, Max 126
Wehrmacht, the 30, 50, 97, 187, 262
Weiss, 'Isidore' 195, 279
Welch, David 7, 86
Wells, H.G. 82
Wells, Josef 194
Wenck, General 81
Went the Day Well (film) 97
Wessel, Horst 181, 183
West, W.J. 92
Western films 157
Weston Brothers 98
White, Sir Dick 45
Wiesen, S. Jonathan 8
Will and Way (journal) 64

William, Crown Prince 181
William the First 108
Williamson, Henry 131
Wilson, Sir Arnold 179
Wilucki, Helmut von 69, 205, 240
Windsor, Duke of 92
Winkelnkemper, Toni 81–2, 130, 173
Wistrich, Robert 110, 149, 198, 259, 265
Witte, Karsten 207
Die Woche 148, 151, 171
Wodehouse, P.G. 98
women, Nazis' appeal to 72–5, 115–16
Workers' Challenge 92

Xi, President 273

Your Third Reich HQ 262
youth culture 259–60
youth recruitment to the Nazi Party 71–2

Zeesen radio station 98
Zeppelin Field stadium 179, 242
Ziegler, Philip 96

For Product Safety Concerns and Information please contact our EU representative GPSR@taylorandfrancis.com Taylor & Francis Verlag GmbH, Kaufingerstraße 24, 80331 München, Germany

Printed and bound by CPI Group (UK) Ltd, Croydon, CR0 4YY
13/12/2024
01805924-0024